Sin, Salvation, and the Spirit

SIN, SALVATION, AND THE SPIRIT

Commemorating the Fiftieth Year
of The Liturgical Press

General Editor: Daniel Durken, O.S.B.

THE LITURGICAL PRESS
Collegeville, Minnesota

Nihil obstat: Joseph C. Kremer, S.T.L., *Censor deputatus. Imprimatur:* ✠ George H. Speltz, D.D., Bishop of St. Cloud. July 17, 1979.

Printed by The North Central Publishing Company, St. Paul, Minnesota, U.S.A.
ISBN 0-8146-1078-1 (cloth)   ISBN 0-8146-1079-X (paper)
Library of Congress Catalog Card Number: 79-20371

*Dedicated to
the people of The Press*

Preface

This volume of essays is intended to commemorate the fiftieth anniversary of The Liturgical Press, which began in 1926. But this is 1979, three years into our second half-century of service, and the reader may wonder why the delay. The simplest answer to this question is just to say, "We've been busy."

Would that the next problem connected with this dedication page could be solved with another three-word answer. This problem concerns the adequate identification of all those men and women who comprise "the people of The Press." A list might have been made that would have surpassed the genealogies of Matthew and Luke. But the quantity of names would do little justice to the quality of the people who have contributed to the growth and the success of this apostolate.

The only name that dare not be omitted is that of our founder, FATHER VIRGIL MICHEL, O.S.B. This dynamic and imaginative monk, priest, professor, writer, and liturgist saw his dream of an American liturgical movement take shape and come true with the establishment of a liturgical press and the publication of a monthly liturgical review, *Orate Fratres*. The durability of both his dreams is a tribute to Fr. Virgil's insight and foresight. He and his work will not be forgotten.

For the rest, let it suffice to say that as surely as "Salvation Is a Family Affair" (so goes the title of Bruce Vawter's article in this volume), so is The Liturgical Press a family affair. The directorship of the Press has come from the Benedictine family of St. John's Abbey. But that directing would have been unproductive without the consistent labor and loyalty of so many.

Just as at a family reunion it is not always the patriarchal great-grandparents who get the most attention but the young nephew who arrives with a pretty new girl friend or the second cousin who hits a home run in the late afternoon ball game, so also does this dedication want to give special credit to family folks like the shipping-room wrapper who takes pride in a securely boxed order of books, the invoice clerk who double-checks her items, the address file clerks and key punch operators who decipher the scrawled name and address on an order form, the display room secretary who helps a browser find an eighty-cent pamphlet, and the hawk-eyed proofreader who pounces on an inverted *ie*. In the meantime, business, office, advertising, convention, and warehouse managers, copy editors, artists, and printers will continue to be taken for granted, but with renewed gratitude.

These fifty years and more have indeed been all in the family. Our golden jubilee was a quiet, almost unnoticed family affair. Happy anniversary, family!

Acknowledgements

The title and content of this memorial volume — *Sin, Salvation, and the Spirit* — are derived from these words of Jesus:

Then he said to them, "These are my words which I spoke to you, while I was still with you, that everything written about me in the law of Moses and the prophets and the psalms must be fulfilled." Then he opened their minds to understand the scriptures, and said to them, "Thus it is written, that the Christ should suffer and on the third day rise from the dead, and that repentance and forgiveness of sins should be preached in his name to all nations, beginning from Jerusalem. You are witnesses of these things. And behold, I send the promise of my Father upon you; but stay in the city, until you are clothed with power from on high" (Lk 24:44-49).

The aim and goal of the liturgy is to continue and fulfill the works and words of Jesus Christ by providing forgiveness and healing for our sin, by making salvation available and tangible for all who believe in his holy name, and by offering to us the experience of the power and the presence of the Spirit. Twenty-seven American Scripture scholars, men and women, Catholic and Protestant, have generously responded to the invitation to comment in a pastoral and popular vein on this threefold dynamic so basic to both liturgy and Bible.

For the special help they gave me at the initial stage of this project by defining and refining the volume's focus and by suggesting possible contributors I am indebted to these confreres and colleagues: Kilian McDonnell, O.S.B., Ivan Havener, O.S.B., Richard J. Dillon, and Joseph I. Hunt. The layout design was prepared by John Dwyer. Copyediting was done by John Schneider, proofreading by Dolores Schuh, C.H.M. Placid Stuckenschneider, O.S.B., designed the cover. Irv Kreidberg and his talented staff at the North Central Publishing Company have brought the book to its completion.

Daniel Durken, O.S.B.
General Editor

Collegeville, Minnesota
July 26, 1979

Foreword

The University of Aberdeen exegete I. Howard Marshall has recently suggested that "A sufficiently bewildering set of exegetical possibilities has now been produced to raise some doubts regarding the good Reformed doctrine of the perspicuity of Holy Scripture."[1] He writes this in the preface to a collection of essays he edits which "raise the questions that must be faced by defenders of this doctrine, so that in the end their acceptance of it may rest on a more solid base than a mere formal assent."[2]

The present collection by theologians of the Catholic and Reformed traditions has no such confessional intent. Yet all of its contributors share with their largely British evangelical colleagues the conviction that the Bible is the book of the Church, useful for teaching, for reproof, for correction, and for instruction in holy living. It is above all the treasure of the ordinary Christian. A few contributors at the outset attack the sensitive but largely unexplored question, at least by exegetes of the last two centuries, of the proper use of Scripture once modern criticism has revealed the meaning of the writings in their time. One essay examines the cultural transpositions required if we are not to be led astray by God's word in the matter of sexism. Another does the same with the oppressors and the oppressed in the realms of economics and politics. Most, however, confine their exercise of the hermeneutical task to the various periods of Bible composition. In doing so they greatly assist the preachers and teachers whose task it is to help others know what is perspicuous and what is not in the books of the Church's heritage.

A number of communities come together in the pages of this volume, none of them mutually exclusive: the pastoral and the prayerful, the scientific and the learned. Some monks of St. Benedict are here who teach the Bible in various abbeys, colleges, and universities of this country. There are the editors of *The Bible Today*, a publication of The Liturgical Press, and certain long-term contributors; likewise, those who in-

---

1. I. H. Marshall, ed. *New Testament Interpretation. Essays on Principles and Methods* (Exeter: The Paternoster Press, 1977), in "Introduction," 15.
2. *Ibid.*

struct in the Bible on the faculty of St. John's University, Collegeville, and in its vigorous summer sessions are represented. In all, a collection of scholars is assembled here who regularly pray the Bible as they plumb and expound its meaning. This does not validate all their positions, but it provides a special reason to trust them beyond their erudition. They know that the Bible is not a collection of documents of ancient history but a book of faith and praise.

The volume is primarily a work of Lucan theology, with some important background on sin, salvation, and God as Spirit supplied from the Jewish scriptures. This places it among the growing library of titles in the scholarship of Luke-Acts, a trend inaugurated earlier in this century by Harnack and Cadbury, and declared to have become "suddenly a burning issue" by Käsemann in 1960. But if the world of criticism came upon Luke late, this was not the case of Christians generally. If, in a familiar generalization, Peter (through Matthew) is the great one of the Roman Church, John of the Orthodox, and Paul of the Reformed, the author of Luke-Acts in an important sense constructs a bridge joining the three. His are "the times and seasons," for it is he who has given the churches the Annunciation, the Visitation, the Nativity of John the Baptist, the Presentation (or Candlemas), Christmas, Pentecost, and the Ascension. He is the great storyteller of Christendom; without his tales of the forgiving father, the traveler left for dead on the Jericho road, the rich man and the beggar, and the wily manager we would be much the poorer. But he is above all the interpreter to the Church of the new age it found itself thrust into, a theologian as creatively powerful in his constructs as Paul is in his. No one can read the essays deriving from Luke 24:44-49 that follow without conceiving new respect for the Lucan achievement and new gratitude to the Spirit of God that impelled it.

The new insights I gained from this reading are too numerous to catalogue. The list will differ, in any case, for each reader, whatever a person's previous acquaintanceship, enthusiasm, or lack of it for the third evangelist may have been. And there are challenges. Regarding John Alsup's Munich dissertation on the Gospel appearance stories — but I forbear. I content myself with thanks to The Liturgical Press and its editors, past and present, for the opportunity to be associated with them in marking the Press' fiftieth anniversary by this characteristic piece of prayer and scholarship.

Gerard S. Sloyan

Temple University
Philadelphia, Pennsylvania

Contents

The Contributors

CLAUDE PEIFER, O.S.B., is novice master at St. Bede Abbey in Peru, Illinois, and an associate editor of *The Bible Today*.

ELISABETH SCHÜSSLER FIORENZA is associate professor of theology at the University of Notre Dame, Notre Dame, Indiana, and the author of numerous articles on questions of New Testament interpretation and of feminist theology.

EUGENE H. MALY is professor of Sacred Scripture at Mt. St. Mary's Seminary, Norwood, Ohio, and chairman of the editorial staff of *The Bible Today*.

AUGUSTINE STOCK, O.S.B., is professor of Sacred Scripture at Conception Abbey, Conception, Missouri, and the author of *The Way in the Wilderness* and *Counting the Cost*.

BRUCE VAWTER, C.M., is chairman of the religious studies department of DePaul University in Chicago, professor of biblical literature, and the author of a number of books on the Bible.

BERNHARD W. ANDERSON is professor of Old Testament theology at Princeton Theological Seminary, Princeton, New Jersey, and the author of *Understanding the Old Testament*.

ALBERIC CULHANE, O.S.B., is associate professor of theology at St. John's University, Collegeville, Minnesota, and field supervisor since 1975 of the excavations at Bab edh-Dhra'.

AELRED CODY, O.S.B., is master of novices and junior monks at St. Meinrad Archabbey, St. Meinrad, Indiana.

WALTER HARRELSON is professor of Old Testament in the Divinity School of Vanderbilt University, Nashville, Tennessee, and has served as rector of the Ecumenical Institute for Advanced Theological Studies in Jerusalem.

JOSEPH JENSEN, O.S.B., is associate professor of theology at The Catholic University of America, Washington, D.C., executive secretary of the Catholic Biblical Association, and the author of *God's Word to Israel*.

CARROLL STUHLMUELLER, C.P., is professor of Sacred Scripture at the Catholic Theological Union in Chicago, and Old Testament book review editor of *The Bible Today*.

A. JOSEPH EVERSON is pastor of Hope Lutheran Church in St. Paul, Minnesota.

ROLAND E. MURPHY, O. CARM., is professor of Old Testament at Duke University Divinity School, Durham, North Carolina, co-editor of the *Jerome Biblical Commentary* and one of the translators of the *New American Bible*.

MONIKA E. HELLWIG is professor of theology at Georgetown University, Washington, D.C.

JACK DEAN KINGSBURY is associate professor of New Testament at Union Theological Seminary in Virginia at Richmond, and the author of *Matthew: Structure, Christology, Kingdom*.

NEAL M. FLANAGAN, O.S.M., is professor of New Testament studies at the Graduate Theological Union in Berkeley, California, and the author of *Mark, Matthew, and Luke: A Guide to the Gospel Parallels*.

REGINALD H. FULLER is professor of New Testament at the Protestant Episcopal Theology Seminary in Virginia at Alexandria and the author of *Preaching the New Lectionary*.

JEROME KODELL, O.S.B., is director of formation at New Subiaco Abbey, Subiaco, Arkansas, and a teacher in the Academy of the abbey.

DEMETRIUS R. DUMM, O.S.B., teaches Sacred Scripture and serves as rector of St. Vincent Seminary, Latrobe, Pennsylvania.

RICHARD J. DILLON is professor of New Testament at St. Joseph's Seminary, Dunwoodie, New York, and adjunct associate professor of New Testament at Fordham University, Bronx, New York.

JOHN H. SIEBER teaches Sacred Scripture at Luther College in Decorah, Iowa.

DAVID STANLEY, S.J., is professor of New Testament studies at Regis College, Toronto, Ontario, Canada, and the author of *The Prayer of Jesus in Gethsemane*.

J. MASSYNGBERDE FORD is associate professor of theology at the University of Notre Dame, Notre Dame, Indiana.

JOHN KOENIG is professor of New Testament at the General Theological Seminary in New York City and author of *Charismata: God's Gifts for God's People*.

PETER F. ELLIS is associate professor in the Graduate School of Religion and Religious Education at Fordham University, Bronx, New York.

IVAN HAVENER, O.S.B., is assistant professor of theology at St. John's University, Collegeville, Minnesota.

JEROME D. QUINN is professor of Old and New Testament and of Hebrew at the St. Paul Seminary, St. Paul, Minnesota, a member of the Pontifical Biblical Commission, and currently CBA Visiting Professor at the Pontifical Biblical Institute and Scholar-in-Residence at the North American College in Rome.

Abbreviations

ADAJ	Annual of the Department of Antiquities of Jordan
BA	*Biblical Archaeologist*
BASOR	*Bulletin of the American Schools of Oriental Research*
BDF	F. Blass, A. Debrunner, and R. W. Funk, *A Greek Grammar of the New Testament*
BZ	*Biblische Zeitschrift*
CBQ	*Catholic Biblical Quarterly*
DBS	*Dictionnaire de la Bible, Supplément*
FRLANT	Forschungen zur Religion und Literatur des Alten und Neuen Testaments
IDB	G. A. Buttrick (ed.), *Interpreter's Dictionary of the Bible*
JAAR	*Journal of the American Academy of Religion*
JBC	R. E. Brown, J. A. Fitzmyer, R. E. Murphy (eds.), *The Jerome Biblical Commentary*
JBL	*Journal of Biblical Literature*
LPGL	G. W. H. Lampe, *Patristic Greek Lexicon*
LSJ	Liddell-Scott-Jones, *Greek-English Lexicon*
NPNF	Nicene and Post-Nicene Fathers
NTA	*New Testament Abstracts*
NTS	*New Testament Studies*
SBFLA	*Studii biblici franciscani liber annuus*
SBT	Studies in Biblical Theology
TDNT	G. Kittel and G. Friedrich (eds.), *Theological Dictionary of the New Testament*
ZNTW	*Zeitschrift für die neutestamentliche Wissenschaft*

PART ONE

Perspectives from Biblical Studies

Claude Peifer, O.S.B.

THE EXPERIENCE OF SIN, SALVATION, AND THE SPIRIT AS A PREREQUISITE FOR THE UNDERSTANDING OF THE SCRIPTURES

The popular biblical movement appears to have reached a certain point of crisis. On the one hand, after the temporary dominance of a "secular city" mentality which followed Vatican II, there now seems to be an unprecedented interest in the Bible among ordinary Christians as the source and center of their spirituality. On the other hand, this interest, in many cases, appears to be of a different quality than the leaders of the biblical movement had intended: if not outright fundamentalist, it at least often tends to give short shrift to serious study of the Bible in favor of hastening on to immediate practical application. Who could have predicted, even ten years ago, that the 1970's would witness the curious spectacle of Catholics joining fundamentalist churches and Bible-thumping revivalist prayer groups in order to find the personal contact with Christ through the Scriptures of which they claim to have been deprived in the Church of their baptism?[1]

This phenomenon raises, in a contemporary form, the perennial problem of the understanding of the Scriptures. Indeed, there can be no question that the Bible has been given to us for the *life* of the Church: the Holy Spirit did not intend it to be solely an object of erudition, but primarily a source of nourishment for the Christian people. The problem, however, is how we come to understand the meaning of this Word of God which is conveyed to us in very human words. What is the role of human effort in this understanding and what is the gift of grace? Who has the better understanding of a biblical text: the trained scholar who spends years in the exhaustive study of a single verse and produces an erudite dissertation with all the apparatus of scholarship; or the born-again Christian who, in a flash of illumination, is moved by that same

3

verse of the Bible to a total conversion of life? Are these approaches to Scripture mutually exclusive?

Conditioned as we are by our own time and culture, we may easily lose sight of a wider perspective. I should like, therefore, to compare our own attitudes toward this problem with those of the early Church to see whether the Fathers may shed some light on the question. At first sight it may seem that their view (or rather that of the limited segment of patristic tradition which I shall examine) is incompatible with the convictions of modern exegesis. I hope that it may be possible to show not only that the two are reconcilable, but that they mutually complete and enrich one another.

Modern Biblical Criticism

The contemporary scientific approach to the Bible began about two centuries ago. Indeed, its remoter origins can be traced back to the Renaissance and to figures such as Erasmus in the sixteenth century and Richard Simon in the seventeenth, who already anticipate it in some respects. But it was only the eighteenth century and especially the nineteenth that witnessed the full development of scientific criticism. The auxiliary sciences of text criticism, philology, comparative linguistics, ancient history, geography, and archeology contributed to the perfecting of a methodology for the study of documents from the past. But it was primarily philosophical developments which changed people's attitude toward the Bible and allowed it to be approached purely as a historical document. The Enlightenment made reason the sole arbiter of truth, whereupon rational criticism claimed the entire sphere of human thought and life, including religion, as its rightful domain. In the nineteenth century there was added a new awareness of the importance of evolutionary development in all human affairs, and consequently of the time-conditioned character of the biblical literature. Therefore the way to understand the meaning of the biblical writers was to apply to their work the same scientific methods which illuminated any document from antiquity.

While the convictions and attitudes represented by this view are clearly unacceptable to faith, the methodology itself is quite neutral. This insight, however obvious it may appear to us now, was acquired only gradually and at the cost of extreme anguish. During the nineteenth century Catholics generally looked upon scientific biblical criticism as an insidious threat to faith because they could see it only in the rationalist context in which it had appeared in the concrete. Just as it was beginning to find some acceptance in the Church, the Modernist crisis erupted, and the reaction put it out of bounds again for several more decades. Raymond Brown has observed that our own century can be divided into three periods with respect to Catholic attitudes toward biblical studies:

a period of opposition to scientific criticism up to about 1940; then of gradual acceptance of it up to about 1970; and finally, of assimilation of its implications during this final third of the century.[2]

The official notice of its acceptance by the Church was the 1943 encyclical of Pope Pius XII, *Divino Afflante Spiritu*. The encyclical emphasizes the importance of approaching the Scriptures in their original languages, of using a critical text, of profiting from the deeper knowledge of antiquity available today to revise earlier interpretations, and of making use of auxiliary sciences to recreate the culture of the ancient Near East in order to understand the literary forms then in common use. More recent ecclesiastical documents have increasingly taken the position that modern scientific methods are useful if not, indeed, indispensable for biblical studies, notably the Constitution on Divine Revelation of Vatican II and the Biblical Commission's 1964 instruction *On the Historical Truth of the Gospels*. These declarations make it clear that the Catholic Church has repudiated fundamentalism with its claim that the correct understanding of Scripture is spontaneously and immediately available to any Christian who simply opens the Bible.

The Church's recent espousal of the methods of modern criticism seems to be an irreversible step. In the wake of *Divino Afflante Spiritu* there came about a veritable revolution in the place of the Bible in the Church. From those years dates the beginning of the Catholic popular biblical movement.[3] Its expressed purpose was to spread knowledge of and love for the Bible among the faithful. Its method was to translate the discoveries of scientific criticism into a language which the educated non-specialist could understand, to offer him or her the fruits of erudition without its complexity and technical features. The ordinary Christian was assured that one did not have to be a biblical scholar to understand the Bible, but that a certain amount of knowledge was necessary. Inevitably, there appeared a lunatic fringe whose principal objective was to exploit the shock value of certain critical positions. By and large, however, the popular movement proceeded with prudence and patience in its attempt to educate the faithful in the meaning of the Bible and to replace the false ideas which were held over from an era in which an interest in the Scriptures was thought to mark a person as "Protestant."

In any case, there grew a more or less widespread consensus as to what is necessary for the understanding of Scripture: it requires an increase of knowledge, to be obtained by the human effort of study, and made available, ultimately, by the application of scientific methodology to the Bible. While this may range all the way from the research scholar working on the original text to the schoolchild becoming acquainted with the most elementary features of biblical history, the difference is only one of degree. In every case it is supposed that our understanding of Scripture is dependent upon the use, to some degree, of biblical criticism, that is, upon the use of our reason to arrive at the author's meaning. Indeed, as we shall see later, no competent scholar would express it in such a simplistic fashion and without important qualifications. But this has been the general attitude, the peculiar mind-set, so to speak, which is characteristic of the past few decades amid the enthusiasm engendered by the Catholic discovery of the value of scientific biblical studies and the richness of their contribution to the understanding and life of the Church.

The Ancient Monastic Tradition

With this attitude which has, at least until recently, been dominant in the contemporary Church, I should like to contrast the views of some of the Fathers, especially those who represent the monastic tradition in the early Church. Far from agreeing with the modern contention that the application of human intellectual powers constitutes the key which opens up the understanding of the Scriptures, they are often extremely suspicious of the intrusion of reason into this domain, and warn that "vain erudition" is powerless to reveal the meaning of the Word of God. The understanding of the Scriptures is purely and simply a gift of the Holy Spirit. One can dispose oneself to receive this gift only by advancing towards moral perfection through conversion and purification. Indeed, the acquisition of learning may even make matters worse by inducing pride, which is the very opposite and negation of the requisite qualities. Therefore the understanding of Scripture is in no sense achieved by intellectual effort, but rather by moral and ascetical striving.

This thesis is set forth most fully and completely by John Cassian, that indefatigable encyclopedist of monastic theory, who collected, systematized, and communicated to the West the tradition that he had learned in Palestine and Egypt. He treats of the understanding of the Scriptures several different times. The earliest mention of the subject occurs in Book 5 of the *Institutes*, where Cassian tells of the heroic virtue of Abba Theodore:

> As some of the brothers were admiring the splendid light of his knowledge and asking him to explain certain passages of Scripture, he told them, "The monk who wants to acquire an understanding of the Scriptures should under no circumstances waste his efforts on the books of commentators; rather he should apply all the exertion of his mind and energy of his heart to purifying himself of the vices of the flesh. As soon as these have been driven out and the blindfold of the passions removed, at once the eyes of the heart will naturally perceive the mysteries of the Scriptures (*sacramenta scripturarum*). For they have not been revealed to us by the grace of the Holy Spirit so that they may remain unknown or obscure; rather they become obscure through our own fault when the blindfold of our sins covers the eyes of our heart.

"But when those eyes are restored to their normal condition, then the reading (*lectio*) of the Sacred Scriptures is of itself more than sufficient for them to contemplate genuine knowledge, and they do not need the assistance of commentators, just as our bodily eyes do not need anyone to teach them to see, provided they are not afflicted with cataracts or the total darkness of blindness. The reason that such disagreements and errors have risen among them is that many of them rush into the work of exegesis without making any effort to purify the inner man; hence, in proportion to the grossness and impurity of their hearts, they put forth opinions contrary to the faith and to one another, and they are unable to embrace the light of truth."[4]

For Cassian, Theodore himself is an excellent example of this gift of the understanding of Scripture:

I knew the Abba Theodore, a man endowed with great holiness and knowledge, not only in the ascetical life, but also in the understanding of the Scriptures. This he had acquired not so much from the effort of reading and from secular literature as solely from purity of heart, for he could barely speak or understand more than a few words of Greek. Once when he was searching out the explanation of some very difficult question, he persevered in prayer unflinchingly for seven days and seven nights, until a revelation from the Lord provided him with a solution to the problem.[5]

According to Cassian, therefore, God's Word has been revealed to us for our benefit, and he intends that we should be able to understand and assimilate it. The fact that we cannot penetrate its "obscurity" is not due to God's intention but to our sinfulness. Contrary to God's plan, sin has entered upon the scene and blinded us so that we cannot perceive his message. The only way this obstacle can be overcome, then, is by conquering sin so that it no longer obstructs our vision of the true meaning of the word. Our ascetical efforts, however much they may be the result of grace (Cassian was preoccupied with this problem in the wake of the Pelagian controversy and has been somewhat misleadingly labeled a "semipelagian"), require of us an attitude of openness to conversion. This is the prerequisite that is really indispensable for acquiring a right knowledge of Sacred Scripture.

If Cassian has little regard for the authors of commentaries on Scripture, it is not because he is a Philistine who scorns intellectual accomplishment: elsewhere he speaks approvingly of the great learning of Jerome, even though they took opposite sides in the controversy over Origenism.[6] He does seem put off by the numerous contradictory opinions expressed by the exegetes: a sentiment which would certainly meet with sympathy from many people today, including, I dare say, some biblical scholars. But his fundamental objection is that their work is premature; they are not yet ready to understand the Word of God because they have skipped the preliminaries. He does not say that study is totally useless, but he surely holds that it is useless if not preceded and accompanied by ascetical purification. He enlarges upon this theme again in his *Conference on Spiritual Knowledge:*

> It is impossible for an impure person to obtain spiritual knowledge, regardless of how much sweat he may have expended upon reading. Nobody would pour a rich ointment or good honey or a valuable liquid into a container that is filthy and foul-smelling. A container that has been contaminated with some reeking corruption will ruin even the most sweet-smelling myrrh more easily than it will take on its qualities of beauty and attractiveness, for clean things are dirtied much more easily than dirty things can be cleansed. It is the same with that container which is our heart: until it has been cleansed of all putrid corruption of vices, it will not deserve to receive that blessed ointment of which the prophet says, "like the ointment on the head, which dripped on Aaron's beard, which dripped down to the hem of his robe" (Ps 132:2). Nor will it preserve unsoiled that spiritual knowledge and the words of the Scriptures which are "sweeter than honey and the honeycomb" (Ps 18:11).[7]

The obvious objection to this thesis is that sanctity and knowledge do not belong to the same order of reality. Grace is not a substitute for natural gifts and abilities: hence an unlettered person, even though endowed with a high degree of sanctity, remains incapable of dealing with technical exegetical problems. Cassian has foreseen the objection, and he states it clearly through the mouth of his protagonist Germain:

> How does it happen that many Jews and heretics, as well as Catholics who are ensnared by various sinful habits, have acquired a perfect knowledge of the Scriptures and can rejoice in the excellence of their spiritual teaching; whereas, on the other hand, an enormous number of holy men whose heart is cleansed from any stain of sin are satisfied with the devotion of simple faith and know nothing of the mysteries of a deeper knowledge? So how can that opinion of yours be correct which makes spiritual knowledge depend solely upon purity of heart?[8]

The Abba Nesteros, to whom Cassian attributes this Conference, replies at length, with abundant Scriptural documentation to support his assertions. The substance of his answer is as follows:

> One who does not carefully consider every word of a statement cannot adequately grasp the force of the argument. Indeed, I have already said that people of this kind possess only the skill of logical reasoning and the gift of speaking convincingly, but that they cannot penetrate to the deeper meaning of the Scriptures and the mysteries of its spiritual senses. . . . Since Scripture says that "all the treasures of wisdom and knowledge are hidden" (Col. 2:3) in Christ, how can a person who has scornfully refused to find Christ or, when he has found him, sacrilegiously blasphemes him or at least corrupts the Catholic faith by his sinful

actions, be thought to possess authentic knowledge? . . . . The people you have mentioned do not have that knowledge, which the impure cannot possess, but only a *pseudonymon*, i.e., a pseudo-knowledge, of which the blessed Apostle says, "Timothy, keep safe what has been entrusted to you. Avoid worldly, empty talk and the contradictions of what is wrongly called 'knowledge'" (1 Tim 6:20) . . . . Those who seem to have acquired what looks like knowledge, or who really devote themselves to the reading of the sacred books and to memorization of Scripture, but still cling to their carnal vices, are marvelously described in Proverbs: "Like a gold ring in the snout of a pig is beauty in a woman of evil life" (Prov 11:22 LXX).[9]

What are the sources from which Cassian derived this doctrine? We may suspect a priori that they are no different on this particular point than for his spiritual teaching as a whole. On the one hand, he has absorbed the wisdom of the desert, that unsophisticated, practical, biblically inspired Christianity practiced without pretense by the Coptic peasants to whom Egyptian monasticism owed its origin. On the other hand, a man well educated in the culture of late antiquity and equally at home in Greek and in Latin, he became a disciple of Evagrius of Pontus, the brilliant associate of the Cappadocian Fathers and admirer of Origen, who, from his cell in the desert of Nitria, evolved a highly sophisticated system of spirituality and became the leader of the erudite, Greek-speaking party of monks. Subsequently Cassian was a friend and associate of men of the caliber of John Chrysostom, Honoratus of Lerins, and the future Pope Leo the Great.

The monasticism of Egypt, both eremitical and cenobitic, was rooted in biblical teaching and nourished by a day-to-day familiar contact with the Bible.[10] Monks quite routinely memorized the Psalter and other quite extensive sections of the Scripture which they used regularly, and some even managed to learn the whole Bible by heart. According to St. Athanasius, the great Anthony told his monks that "the Scriptures are really sufficient for our instruction."[11] Often the meaning of a passage of Scripture was the subject of an instruction or *collatio* given by an elder or of a discussion among monks; in the cenobitic monasteries of Pachomius the superior frequently gave biblical catecheses to all the brothers. Thus Cassian's eighth *Conference* is entirely devoted to an exposition of the meaning of the "principalities and powers" mentioned in Eph 6:12 and Rom 8:38. The *Sayings of the Fathers*, which were collected later but take us back through oral tradition to the origins of monasticism, also speak of biblical discussions among the semi-anchorities.[12]

In the desert literature, however, together with great reverence for the Scriptures, we also find a pronounced fear that they may be misused. The monks found it supremely incongruous that one's apparent zeal for the Bible should lead him to do precisely what the Bible forbids.

Thus to be attached to the possession of a codex is contrary to the evangelical command to rid oneself of every obstacle to the Kingdom. To be more zealous about copying the Scriptures, or studying them, than about putting them into practice, is a dangerous trap for a monk. Still worse is the subtle deception of pride in the knowledge one has gained about the Bible.

Consequently, intellectual speculation was regarded with suspicion: it drew attention to the person, exalted the human achievement, instead of focusing all attention upon God and his message. Thus it could be fatal to compunction, that inner disposition of the heart that is the indispensable prerequisite for hearing God's Word. Human reason is not indispensable and may even be an obstacle. To reduce the Scriptures to an object of study, discussion, and speculation, to think that our human efforts are capable of penetrating to the depths of its meaning — this is unspeakable arrogance and profanation of the Holy. It is better to wait in humble silence for enlightenment from the Lord. If the ancient monks, therefore, hesitated to apply rational methods to the study of the Bible, it was only because they reverenced it so highly as something divine.[13] In this respect Cassian's teaching is the faithful echo of the solitaries of Nitria and Scetis.

By the time he arrived in Egypt, however, the teaching of the elders was being intellectualized and systematized by Evagrius and his associates. Though he never mentions his name, Cassian was certainly a disciple of Evagrius, for his whole system is borrowed from the brilliant monk of Pontus, who in turn leaned heavily upon Origen.[14] Indeed, the use of Origen was the bone of contention that aroused fiery passions in the controversies which began in the late fourth century and continued off and on until the anathematizing of "Origenism" at the fifth ecumenical council in 553.[15] Origen was the most influential thinker in the Church, at least up to Augustine. His influence is lurking in the background of Cassian's teaching about the meaning of the Scriptures.

Origen's views on this problem derive from his whole vision of the Bible.[16] For him, the task of the interpreter is to discover the spiritual sense. In opposition to both the Gnostics who rejected the Old Testament and the Jews who still awaited literal fulfillment of it, Origen defended what had already become a traditional Christian view, that it is a preparation for and figure of the New Testament. While the exegete should first explain the literal sense, i.e., the meaning of the words which the sacred writers used, he must go on to the spiritual sense, i.e., what God wishes to say to us through this text that is obsolete as far as literal fulfillment is concerned. This typological approach was not new with Origen, but he applied it in a uniquely brilliant way. Sometimes, it is true, he let himself be carried away into arbitrary theories. Far from being opposed to using human reason to elucidate the literal meaning of the text, he was the most advanced scholar of his time in his scientific work on the Bible, especially in textual criticism. But when it comes to the spiritual sense, this cannot be determined by any mere human effort. It demands faith and, beyond that, enlightenment by the Holy Spirit: this is not his personal opinion, but the belief of the whole Church:

> The Scriptures were written by the Spirit of God, and, besides that meaning which is immediately apparent, they have another one which most people are not aware of. For the things that are written in the Scriptures are signs of certain mysteries and images of divine things. In this respect the entire Church holds the same view: the whole Law is indeed spiritual, but the spiritual meaning which it contains is not known to everyone, but only to those whom the grace of the Holy Spirit has endowed with the word of wisdom and knowledge (1 Cor 12:8). [17]

In his homilies and commentaries on Scripture, Origen is often at pains to show that it is not his own ability which enables him to interpret the Scriptures, but divine enlightenment. Gnosis, the spiritual knowledge of the meaning of God's Word, is a charismatic gift. Of the Fourth Gospel he says, "No one can understand this Gospel unless he has leaned against the breast of Jesus and taken Mary as his mother." [18] And in commenting upon a parable, he observes:

> I believe that the exposition and interpretation of such things lie beyond human ability: only the Spirit of Christ who spoke these things can enable us to understand them as Christ meant them. "What person knows a man's thoughts except the spirit of the man which is in him? So also no one knows the thoughts of God except the Spirit of God" (1 Cor 2:11). Likewise, apart from God, no one knows the things spoken by Christ in proverbs and parables except Christ's Spirit. And only the one who shares the life of Christ not only insofar as he is Spirit but also insofar as he is Wisdom and Word can look upon the truths which are revealed in this passage. [19]

Since it is Christ's Spirit who enlightens the mind of the interpreter, the latter must live the life of the Spirit. Receptivity to the charism of gnosis, then, requires moral perfection. Origen is the first to have worked out a systematic presentation of growth in the spiritual life. Evagrius took over his ideas and developed them into a precise system of monastic ascetical and mystical doctrine. Fundamental to the system, which reappears in a somewhat simplified form in Cassian, is the distinction between the "active" life (*praktike*) and the higher life of contemplation and intimate knowledge of God (*gnostike, theoretike*). The passions must be subdued and the heart purified before a person can receive the gnosis which includes understanding of the spiritual meaning of Scripture. It is clear from this why Cassian insists that one who wishes to understand Scripture should exert himself not in study but in acquiring purity of heart. Chadwick expresses it as follows:

> This direct knowledge of God, or *gnosis*, is given by God. A man must prepare himself for it, but, when it comes, it comes from above. It is made possible because man is made in the image of God, and is therefore akin to God, and longs for fellowship with God. A man prepares himself by purifying himself. When his eyes are ready to see, the light shines down, and there is *gnosis*. It is like a revelation of God, unfolding the secrets of heaven to men of faith, dazzling the eye of spirit and lifting the mind to higher wisdom, filling the soul with an ecstasy which words cannot express, and making him one with the divine. There is nothing common between this *gnosis* and the half-knowledge which comes from rational inquiry or philosophical speculation.[20]

The Understanding of the Scriptures as a Contemporary Problem

What is a modern scholar to think of this approach to exegesis? M. F. Wiles, after sketching Origen's thesis that the Holy Spirit, since he is the real author of Scripture, is also the indispensable source of an understanding of its meaning, replies:

> Such an answer is the delight of the pious and the despair of the critical scholar. What is one to say of it if one wishes to be both at once? The suspicion with which the scholar is inclined to greet such an insistence is due to a fear that it may be used as a short-cut in a way designed to obviate the need for hard thinking, a fear that it may be thought to justify an appeal to intuition which will evade the drudgery of serious study and research.[21]

In short, the modern scholar is afraid of fundamentalism and illuminism. He may agree with Wiles that such concern is groundless in the case of Origen,[22] and yet fear what it can become in the hands of less responsible enthusiasts: indeed, there is no need to speculate, for the evidence is readily at hand.

On the other hand, what might the Fathers have thought of modern critical scholarship? Would Cassian, for instance, have written off the whole project as a blatant display of human pride, an intrusion of natural reason into the sphere of the divine that has nothing to contribute to the understanding of what God has to tell us through the Scriptures? Would the "books of commentators" which he disdains include the last two centuries' output of exegetical literature? I rather think not. The numerous discussions in his works about the interpretation of various biblical passages show a familiarity with the exegetical questions and methods of his time that is far from fundamentalist. In the Origenist controversy of 399 Cassian was on the side of the scholars against the Coptic fundamentalists, and left Egypt definitively in the company of the exiled Greek-speaking intellectuals. He was a follower of

Origen, and the latter would no doubt be delighted with the technical possibilities of modern criticism. Imagine what the architect of the Hexapla might do with a computer!

The concerns of the ancients and of contemporary biblical scholars, therefore, are not mutually exclusive. It is rather a question of different emphases. The Fathers were primarily concerned with the divine character of Scripture: while not entirely excluding the import of the human element, they minimized it in their zeal to perceive what God is saying to the Church. Their approach gave preference to the pastoral over the purely scientific and critical, which they were generally less well equipped to investigate. Modern biblical scholars, on the other hand, have become aware of the culturally conditioned character of every human enterprise and have accordingly emphasized the human factors in the Bible, which modern techniques have enabled them to explore more thoroughly. The same tendency is apparent in the contemporary approach to other incarnational realities: the person of Christ, the Church, the liturgy. This pervasive concern runs the risk of neglecting the transcendent element, just as the Fathers sometimes undervalued the contingent. Both elements must be kept in perspective, and it has never been easy to maintain the balance.

Serious biblical scholars today are not unaware of the limitations of critical exegesis: they do not pretend that of itself it gives all the answers. Father Roderick MacKenzie has dealt sensitively with this question in an article entitled, "The Self-Understanding of the Exegete."[23] He argues that the work of a believing biblical scholar is different from the purely critical exegesis of an ancient text in two respects. The first is that the existence of the canon is prior to any critical work and cannot be judged by it. This fact confers upon biblical literature a "plus-value" that remains beyond the reach of critical methods, since it can be attained only by faith:

> His work of exegesis must be extended and continued, to include the discovery and exposition of this plus-value. More concretely: because he believes the work to contain not only words of men but also the word of God, he will endeavor to "hear" this word in the text, to understand it and to interpret it to others. If he stops short of that, his exegesis remains inadequate and incomplete. For brevity's sake, I shall refer to this last stage of the exegete's task as "theological exegesis," since it is explicitly based on faith in the Church's affirmation of the divine authority of Scripture. This plus-value, as here described, does not take anything away from the other values — and problems — inherent in the book as words of men.[24]

The second difference is that the biblical interpreter is dealing with what he believes to be the word of God. Whereas other scholars may exercise their critical judgment upon the content of the works they study, the believing exegete must listen and submit to an authoritative Word which judges him:

> When all allowances have been made for the normal human limitations of hagiographers and evangelists, there remains the towering fact that through them God is speaking. To him, men — including critics and exegetes — must listen in total humility and submission. Men's words are conditioned and limited by their culture, period, language, etc. But God's word is free and everlasting, unconditioned and absolute. . . . When God speaks, man must listen and obey. This obligation is timeless; perhaps better, it is perpetual, of all times. God's word is as binding on us as on Moses' contemporaries. Hence the existential thrust, the here-and-now validity, of the theological interpretation which the exegete must provide, when he penetrates below the time-conditioned words of men to the timeless and unconditioned word of God. Unlike his colleagues, the Platonists and Thomists, he is conveying a message which is intrinsically imperative for each of his readers. [25]

This "plus-value" or surplus of meaning was, of course, taken for granted in ancient times, and was explained by typology and allegorical exegesis. These methods evolved into the theory of the four senses, which held sway through the Middle Ages [26] and was not abandoned completely until recent times, when Catholics embraced critical studies and with them the dominance of the literal sense. There remains, however, a consciousness that this surplus of meaning is present (the liturgy's use of Scripture constantly supposes it), but we no longer have a universally accepted explanation for it. Hence in recent decades the *sensus plenior* has been proposed as a means of integrating this insight into an overall theory of the senses of Scripture. [27] There has been little agreement, however, about how best to define and formulate it, and not all exegetes have been receptive to the idea. There does seem to be need for an acceptable theory of a more-than-literal sense that would do justice to the legitimate claims of scientific exegesis and at the same time leave room for that surplus of meaning whose existence has always been recognized in the Church. [28]

This problem has recently been analyzed in a perceptive article by Sister Sandra Schneiders, [29] who suggests that the solution lies in a redefinition of the literal sense to include that "excess of meaning" that is communicated by the text to one who recognizes it in faith as the Word of God. She is anxious to avoid a formulation that would suggest that God has put a meaning into the text that somehow bypasses the human authors, or that would restrict the understanding of Scripture to professional exegetes. She proposes that the way to a solution lies in the adoption of a philosophical hermeneutic like those of Paul Ricoeur or Hans-Georg Gadamer: a classical text should be seen not as something that contains meaning, but that mediates it. Meaning is actualized when the consciousness of the interpreter is challenged by the text; hence the meaning always exceeds the author's conscious intention, though it does not violate it. Such an application of contemporary language theory to the problem seems at least to offer a promising approach to a more satisfactory formulation.

If some biblical scholars have been skeptical about the *sensus plenior* or similar theories, it is primarily because they are afraid of endangering the role of critical exegesis, which was finally accepted in the Church only after such bitter struggles and anguish. But in the past few years the domination of scientific criticism has begun to be attacked from a number of different angles: its position had barely been established when the challenges began to appear. By far the most serious threat is the uncritical acceptance of a fundamentalist outlook by ordinary Catholics who are anxious to obtain spiritual nourishment from the Scriptures. Luis Alonso-Schökel has represented their viewpoint as follows:

> Can this complexity (of today's biblical science) really be imposed by the biblical text (they might ask), or does it come largely from the type of problems that exegetes set themselves? Both the layman and the initiate can be surprised to find themselves suspecting, at the back of their minds, that all the problems that professional exegetes set themselves are not really of any relevance or importance for the understanding of Scripture, but are rather the initiation rites for a very exclusive club. Are they not all really insoluble problems whose continued airing serves merely to give a semblance of activity to a number of really idle people? . . . . Then exegetes have developed their own particular language. . . . Does such a terminological barricade help to actualize the Bible, to make it accessible to Christians all over the world today? Or is it just a defensive wall around the privileged city of the specialists? . . . . So the gravamen of this critical look seems to be negative. Biblical science today is more of a hindrance than a help to an understanding of the Scriptures. If one draws this conclusion, one can easily be led into the familiar demand for a return to the simple life, to the freshness of personal and immediate understanding, rooted in the experience of life itself.[30]

It is not only the non-professionals, however, who are challenging the position of the exegetes. François Refoulé has provided a survey and a critique of the growing protest movement, especially in France, but he notes that it is perhaps even more radical in the Anglo-Saxon world.[31] He points to the increasing rebellion against the "authority" of the exegetes, which is seen as simply another form of clericalism, against their elitist pretensions to dictate what others must accept, against their attempt to fix in advance what can only be discovered by experience. Among scholars themselves, moreover, he notes the objection that the historicism of exegesis has widened the gulf between the text and the reader: hence the demand of the new hermeneutical theories and the structuralists for a plurality of meanings and interpretations, for which they provide a theoretical justification. One frequently hears that there can be no such thing as "objective" exegesis.

While some of these contentions are excessive, we would be ill-advised to ignore the preoccupations that have given rise to them and the legitimate desires of this "anti-exegesis." If Raymond Brown is correct in judging that the remainder of this century will see the Church's assimilation of the results of biblical criticism, the agenda must not be restricted to her acceptance of critical discoveries with their implications, but must include the restoration of the Bible to the faith and life of ordinary believers as the principal source of their spiritual nourishment. It is at this point, it seems to me, that we may situate the relevance of the insights of the ancient monastic tradition.

This tradition asserts unequivocally that the understanding of Scripture is a charism, a gift of the Holy Spirit, which is granted in proportion as one advances through ascetical purification to a state of charity. It is not, therefore, a purely intellectual attainment: while faith includes an intellectual component, it is not restricted to the intellect, but involves the surrender of the whole person. If there is a sense in which knowledge comes first and then love, it is equally true that by loving we come to know: love leads to enlightenment. The lover wants to please the beloved: the one who loves Christ keeps his commandments out of love. And it is by so doing, by living the Christian life in its fullness — and this means living it in the context of a believing community, with its worship and charity — that one comes to understand more and more the mind of God and hence the word of God. As we conform our lives progressively to his demands, we gain a deeper insight into the meaning of his revelation.

This knowledge is intuitive, derived from experience, and self-authenticating. It is "to know God" in the biblical sense of that phrase. The early Church called John the Evangelist "the Theologian" not because he had developed an intellectual system philosophically grounded, but because he had come to "know God" through intimate union with his Son. "We saw it, and testify to it, and proclaim to you the eternal life which was with the Father and was made manifest to us" (1 Jn 1:2). It is in this sense that Origen can affirm that no one can understand the Gospel unless he has rested against the breast of Jesus.

The Bible is not merely a record of past events; it is a mirror in which we see ourselves reflected. There we see what God is like and how he deals with us. A communication is established that operates in both directions: we learn from the Word of God how to live, but the experience of living the Christian life itself contributes to our understanding of the Word. We are not bystanders looking in from the outside: we ourselves enter into the dynamic of sacred history.

We learn about sin from the sin of Israel, but we do not really know the meaning of sin until we have experience of it in ourselves and come to know our wretchedness and emptiness; and in knowing this, we come really to understand what the Bible tells us of sin. We learn of salvation in reading of the exodus, but we do not know the full meaning of it until God's saving power reaches into our own lives: then we understand his word more satisfactorily. We do not *know* the Spirit — in the full, personal sense of the biblical term — until we become consciously aware of his presence and activity in our hearts, and cry out with him, "Abba, Father!" (Gal 4:6; Rom 8:15). What happens in the Bible happens in our life, and each of these diptychs reflects light upon the other: the Word of God is actualized in us, and the experience of it deepens our understanding of the word which is proclaimed. St. Bernard of Clairvaux perceived this clearly when he said, "Everyone among you who feels this experience within himself understands what the Spirit is saying, for his word and his activity cannot be in disagreement. This is why a person understands what is said: what he hears from without he experiences within." [32]

Cassian likewise shows his awareness of this dynamic when he says that the monk who sings the psalms becomes, so to speak, the psalmist himself: the words, when actualized, are not simply those of an Old Testament prophet, but become the expression of the monk's own sentiments:

> Penetrating into all the sentiments of the psalms, he will begin to sing them in such a way that he pours them forth with the deepest compunction of heart, not as words composed by the psalmist, but as if he had written them himself as his own prayer. At least he feels that they were meant directly for him and knows that what they express was not only fulfilled in the psalmist, but finds its fulfillment every day in his own life. . . . Penetrating into the same state of mind in which each psalm was sung or written, we become its author, so to speak, and rather than following its meaning, we anticipate it, so that we perceive the significance of what it says even before we understand the letter.
>
> We find all our own sentiments expressed in the psalms. Seeing all the things that occur in them as if in a clean mirror, we gain a deeper understanding of them. Instructed by our own reaction to them, we perceive these things not merely as something we have heard, but things we have actually seen. They are not merely something we have memorized, but we give birth to them from the depths of our heart as something arising from our own nature, so that we penetrate their meaning not from the act of reading but by our own former experience. [33]

It is remarkable how closely this passage echoes the contemporary desire "to overcome the imprisonment of the biblical message in the past,"[34] to return "to the freshness of personal and immediate understanding, rooted in the experience of life itself."[35] In a similar vein, a contemporary theologian writes, "According to John's Gospel (3:21), it is the one who *does* the truth who comes to the light. . . , not the one who has the light who can then act in truth. Or take this passage of John's first epistle (3:18-19): how do we know that we are of the truth? Not by loving words or languages, but in action, in reality. . . . It is those who seek the face of God who come to know what his face is, and not those who know who God is who can accordingly know where to find him."[36]

This does not dispense us from the hard intellectual work of biblical criticism: it merely defines its role more precisely. The contingent aspect of the Scriptures is amenable to rational criticism, and this criticism remains indispensable. It has, therefore, an important service to provide for the Magisterium and for the entire Christian community. It cannot, however, confer that fullness of understanding of the Word of God in which the Church and the individual Christian come into intimate confrontation with him. On this level, it is the Holy Spirit who "will teach you all things, and bring to your remembrance all that I have said to you" (Jn 14:26). He opens our understanding to the deep things of God when we open our hearts to him.

NOTES

1. A recent example is the gentleman who has opened a Bible shop called "Storehouse of Love" in the heart of Pittsburgh's pornography district, and who harangues the area's patrons with fervent threats of hellfire and appeals to repentance. He is reported to be a converted Roman Catholic. See G. S. Miller, "Born-Again Crusader Invades Pittsburgh's Pornography District," *The Wall Street Journal*, Feb. 8, 1979, 1.

2. R. Brown, *The Virginal Conception and Bodily Resurrection of Jesus* (New York: Paulist Press, 1973) 3–15.

3. *The Bible Today*, "a periodical promoting popular appreciation of the Word of God," began publication in 1962. Father Celestin Charlier had begun to publish *Bible et Vie Chrétienne* in Belgium already in 1953.

4. *Institutes* 5:34. This and the following patristic texts are cited according to my own translation.

5. *Ibid.*, 5:33.

6. *Institutes*, Preface; *On the Incarnation*, 7:26.

7. *Conferences*, 14:14.

8. *Ibid.*, 14:15.

9. *Ibid.*, 14:16.

10. See my article, "The Biblical Foundations of Monasticism," *Cistercian Studies* 1 (1966) 7–31, and the literature cited therein.

11. *Life of Anthony*, 16.

12. See B. Ward, *The Sayings of the Desert Fathers: the Alphabetical Collection* (Kalamazoo: Cistercian Publications, 1975) 4 (Anthony, 19); 140 (Poemen, 8); 155 (Poemen, 119); 181 (Sisoes, 17).

13. See the texts cited by J.-C. Guy, "Écriture Sainte et vie spirituelle," *Dictionnaire de la Spiritualité* 4 (Paris: Beauchesne, 1960), col. 162.

14. See S. Marsili, *Giovanni Cassiano ed Evagrio Pontico: dottrina sulla carità e contemplazione* (Rome: Herder, 1936); O. Chadwick, *John Cassian* (Cambridge: The University Press, 1968²) 82–92.

15. See A. Guillaumont, *Les "Kephalaia Gnostica" d'Évagre le Pontique et l'histoire de l'Origénisme chez les grecs et chez les syriens* (Paris: Éditions du Seuil, 1962).

16. On Origen's interpretation of Scripture, see H. de Lubac, *Histoire et ésprit* (Paris: Aubier, 1950); J. Daniélou, *Origen* (New York: Sheed and Ward, 1955) 131–199; M. F. Wiles, "Origen as Biblical Scholar," *The Cambridge History of the Bible*, I (Cambridge: The University Press, 1970) 454–489.

17. *On First Principles*, 1, preface, 8. For the traditional character of this doctrine, compare Justin Martyr, *Dialogue with Trypho*, 92: "Unless a man, through the great favor of God, receives the power to understand what has been said and done by the prophets, the appearance of ability to respect the words or events will be of no advantage to him." See also Origen, *Homilies on Exodus*, 4:5; Gregory of Nyssa, *Against Eunomius*, 3:1, 42; *Life of Moses*, 2:173.

18. *Commentary on John*, 1:4.

19. *Commentary on Matthew*, 14:6.

20. O. Chadwick, *op. cit.*, 85.

21. M. F. Wiles, *art. cit.*, 486.

22. "In the case of Origen such fears are without foundation. His conviction of the inescapable necessity of the Holy Spirit's guidance for the work of scriptural interpretation goes hand in hand with a readiness to pursue the most detailed textual or lexicographical research in the interests of a more precise exegesis. Just as in the inspiration of scripture the Holy Spirit does not bypass the human mind but enhances its capacities, so with its interpretation it is the divine Logos making his abode within the human mind who imparts to that mind the spiritual insight which it needs" (*ibid.*).

23. *Concilium* 70 (1971) 11–19.

24. *Ibid.*, 12–13.

25. *Ibid.*, 15–16.

26. See H. de Lubac, *Exégèse Médiévale: les quatre sens de l'Écriture*, 4 vols. (Paris: Aubier, 1959–64). The theory of the four senses is already propounded by Cassian in *Conferences*, 14:8.

27. The question of the *sensus plenior* has been thoroughly examined by Raymond Brown, "The History and Development of the Theory of a *Sensus Plenior*," *CBQ*, 15 (1953) 141–162; *The Sensus Plenior of Sacred Scripture* (Baltimore: St. Mary's Seminary, 1955); "The *Sensus Plenior* in the Last Ten Years," *CBQ*, 25 (1963) 262–285; "The Problems of the *Sensus Plenior*," *Ephemerides Theologicae Lovanienses*, 43 (1967) 460–469.

28. In his article, "Hermeneutics," *JBC* 605–623, R. Brown discusses the "more-than-literal" senses, 610–619.

29. "Faith, Hermeneutics, and the Literal Sense of Scripture," *Theological Studies*, 39 (1978) 719–736. Similar concerns are expressed by D. McCarthy, "Exod 3:14: History, Philology and Theology," *CBQ*, 40 (1978) 311–322; G. Montague, "Hermeneutics and the Teaching of Scripture," *ibid.*, 41 (1979) 1–17.

30. "Is Exegesis Necessary?", *Concilium* 70 (1971) 30–38; the citation is on 32–33.

31. "L'exégèse en question," *Le Supplément*, 111 (1974) 391–423. See also J. Barr, *The Bible in the Modern World* (New York: Harper and Row, 1973) 35–52.

32. *Sermons on the Canticle*, 37:3.

33. *Conferences*, 10:11.

34. S. Schneiders, *art cit.*, 728.

35. L. Alonso-Schökel, *art cit.*, 33.

36. J.-M. Pohier, "L'interrogation de la psychanalyse," *Le Supplément*, 105 (1973) 148–172; the citation is on 166–167.

Elisabeth Schüssler Fiorenza

"FOR THE SAKE OF OUR SALVATION. . . ."

BIBLICAL INTERPRETATION AS

THEOLOGICAL TASK

The relationship and interaction of the community of faith and of biblical interpretation has become problematical and difficult. On the one hand, the Christian community claims the Bible to be canonical Holy Scripture for today; on the other hand, biblical scholarship has cast it more and more into the distant past and made it into a book fraught with complexities unintelligible to the ordinary believer.[1] This problematic relationship between the Christian community and the Bible is thus characterized by the tension between the search for meaning in the contemporary situation and the historical particularity of the biblical texts.

The community of faith is generally concerned with contemporary questions of Christian faith and life-style, and turns to the Bible in its search for answers and meaning. The historical-critical approach of biblical scholarship, however, underlines the specific historical character of biblical texts. Because it brings out the historically and culturally conditioned, and therefore limited, character of biblical statements, it emphasizes how remote and estranged the Scriptures are from the contemporary problems of the Christian community. This dilemma raises the fundamental theological question as to how historically and culturally determined writings can have any theological significance and authority for contemporary persons and communities without losing their historical character and being transformed into a-historical universal principles and timeless norms.

This deep cleft between the interests of the community of faith and of historical biblical scholarship indicates a shift in theological

This is a revised form of a paper presented in February, 1978, at the Wooster Clergy Academy of Religion. I am grateful to Professor Glenn Bucher for insisting on the topic.

paradigms. The category of paradigm evolved in the methodological debates of the natural sciences. According to Thomas S. Kuhn,[2] a paradigm represents a coherent research tradition and creates a scientific community. Since paradigms determine the ways in which scientists see the world, a shift in paradigm means a transformation of the scientific imagination and demands a basic "conversion" of the community of scientists. For instance, a shift from Aristotelian to Newtonian physics or from Newtonian physics to relativity means a scientific revolution in which old data are seen in a completely new perspective. For a period of time different paradigms may be competing for the allegiance of the scientific community, until one paradigm replaces the other or gives way to a third.

The usefulness of this theory for theology and the community of faith is obvious. It shows the historical "conditionedness" of all scientific investigation. It also maintains that no neutral observation language is possible but that all scientific investigation demands commitment and a community of persons dedicated to such a perspective. Moreover, it helps us understand that theological approaches, like all other scientific theories, are not falsified but are often replaced, not because we find new "data," but because we find a new way of looking at old data.

It is obvious that the tensions and problems in the relationship of the community of faith to the Bible are today occasioned by such a shift in theological paradigms. Whereas traditionally the Bible was understood in terms of divine revelation and canonical authority for the Church, since the Enlightenment it is studied as a collection of historical writings.[3] Because this new historical-value-neutral paradigm was developed over against a doctrinal-orthodox understanding of the Bible, it did not completely win the allegiance of the Christian community, which often continues to adhere to the doctrinal paradigm. Since pastors are educated to study the Bible in terms of the historicist paradigm but are committed to the service of the Church, which understands the Bible not as a historical work but as proclaiming the word of God for today, they are especially caught in this paradigm shift. The hermeneutical discussion and the sociology of knowledge school in turn have questioned the historicist paradigm, so that a new theological paradigm has emerged. However, this new theological paradigm has not yet replaced the other two because its pastoral-theological implications are not yet sufficiently recognized by theologians and pastors alike. Since all three paradigms presently compete for the allegiance of the community of faith, it is necessary to analyze them further.

I. The Dogmatic Paradigm: The Bible — A Direct Word of God

This paradigm is concerned with the truth-claims, authority, and meaning of the biblical text for the Church and Christian faith. It con-

ceives of the authority and truth-claim of the Bible in a-historical, dogmatic terms. In its most consistent form, it insists on the verbal inspiration and literal inerrancy of the biblical books.[4] All the words of the Bible
are inspired — those that pertain to faith and Christian living as well as
those that speak to matters of history or to issues of the natural and
social sciences. In this understanding the Bible not only communicates
the Word of God but *is* the Word of God. The theological presupposition
of this paradigm is expressed in the liturgy, when it is announced after
reading a biblical text, not that "This is the Word of the Lord in the words
of Paul" or "in the words of the Fourth Gospel," but "This is the Word of
the Lord." The Bible is not simply a record of revelation but revelation itself. Therefore it is directly binding and has absolute authority: the Bible
becomes a miraculous divine book.

First: On a popular level the Bible functions as a divine oracle. We
are all familiar with the spiritual gesture in which one opens the Bible
after praying, points with closed eyes to a verse, and sees it as God's
directive for the particular situation for which guidance is asked. This
biblicist understanding of Scripture as a divine oracle promotes a certain
consumer mentality. As we can have instant coffee without grinding the
beans and filtering it, so we can have instant inspiration and understanding of the biblical text without bothering with the paraphernalia
of historical investigation. The Bible becomes for many Christians a security blanket that provides ready-made answers to difficult existential
and theological problem. This popular approach to the Bible understands the minister and preacher to be the "mouthpiece" of God. In
turn, he/she is in danger of preaching as "the Word of God" what is only
his/her own word or prejudice.

In controversial theological questions, the Bible functions as proof-
text or first principle. As such it often takes the place of arguments for
one's own position. The standing formula is: "Scripture says,
therefore. . . ." Or "The Bible teaches, therefore we have to. . . ."
Such an argument presupposes that the Bible reveals eternal truth and
timeless principles. The biblical books are a source for proof-texts that
are often taken out of context in order to legitimate predetermined dog-
mas, principles, or institutions of the Church. On this level, the Bible
often functions as ideological justification of the moral, doctrinal, or
institutional interests of the Church. This approach can include historical exegesis in its argument, in order to provide a more sophisticated
proof-text argument.

A crass example of such a misuse of an exegetical argument is the
recent Vatican statement[5] against the ordination of women. The document accepts the insight of New Testament scholarship that Jesus did
not always follow the accepted norms of his culture; therefore, it argues,
Jesus could have ordained women if he had wanted to. That he did not

do so is a clear indication that Scripture is against the ordination of women. The argument appears completely logical. Yet it forgets to mention that New Testament scholarship seriously questions whether Jesus could have been thinking of ordaining anyone to the priesthood as we understand ordination today.[6]

Second: A variation of the proof-text approach is the illustrative or theme approach, in which the biblical text is used to say something else. This allegorical mode of interpretation is one of the most traditional approaches to the Bible. Augustine's interpretation of the parable of the Good Samaritan illustrates this (*Quaest. Ev.* II, 19): A man (Adam) went from Jerusalem (state of original happiness) to Jericho (state of mortality). The robbers are the devil and his angels, the Samaritan is Christ, the inn is the Church, the innkeeper is not Peter but Paul; oil represents the comfort of hope, and wine the exhortation of faith. Such an allegorical approach, which uses the text to say something else, is often found today in modified form in systematic and practical theological reflection.[7]

The psychoanalytical approach understands the biblical text to symbolize or illustrate a psychological state. Although such an approach recognizes the validity of historical analysis, such an analysis is not brought to bear on the third stage of reflection, where the distance between the subject and the object collapses into the fundamental question: How does the text resonate in us? The story of the healing of the paralytic (Mk 2:1-12) elicits questions as the following: Who is the "paralytic" in you? With what aspect of ourselves does this character resonate? Who is the "scribe" in you and what is the relationship of the "paralytic" and the "scribe" in you? "Now who are these four helpers? What resources are available to bring us to the healing value? What would it be like to marshal your paralytic and helpers to move to the healing source? That, after all, is what the story's about, isn't it?"[8] Here the historical text becomes a *chiffre* or illustration for an intra-psychological state and problem.

Such an illustrative approach is also found in the liturgical approach to Scripture. In the liturgy, however, the text does not stand as a *chiffre* for a psychological state but serves as an illustration for a theological theme or statement. Insofar as the lectionary does not use only one reading but combines three quite disparate texts, it uses the Bible as a source-book for appropriate texts to reinforce a liturgical motif. The community of faith, whose only contacts with the Bible are often the Sunday Scripture readings, thus never receives a comprehensive understanding of a biblical writing in its historical context or encounters a biblical book in its totality, but experiences the Bible mainly as a proof or illustration for a theological theme or principle.

The preacher, on the other hand, is torn between the task of liturgical preaching and the approach of contemporary biblical scholarship which insists that a text has to be understood in its wider context. The growing number of commentaries on the lectionary attempt to overcome this dilemma by providing scholarly-popular exegesis and pastoral suggestions, but are not able to do so because the present structure of the liturgical readings does not allow the interpretation of a biblical text on its own grounds. This dilemma is aptly expressed in the following conversation between two preachers. "When I have found a text," says the first, "I always begin by studying the context in order to make sure of its original setting and meaning." "When I have found a text," replies his colleague, "I never look up the context for fear it will spoil the sermon."[9]

In short, this doctrinal paradigm understands Scripture as verbally inspired to be the direct revelation of God. As such it reveals not only theological truth but also scientific truth. It provides us with infallible answers to our questions, with timeless principles for our actions, and with dogmatic guidelines for our theological reflection. Since, however, Church authority is aware that people have found and will find different justifications for their own beliefs, it appropriates biblical interpretation for its own authority. The hierarchy and theologians as the representatives of the institutionalized Church guard scriptural revelation and protect it from error. In this doctrinal paradigm Scripture is in danger of becoming an ideological justification for Church doctrine and practice on the one hand, or personal edification and legitimization on the other. It is true that the Reformation attempted to recapture the critical potential of Scripture vis-à-vis the Church and personal piety. Yet in Protestant orthodoxy, biblical exegesis became again completely absorbed by dogmatics, insofar as it was used for providing proof-texts for the doctrinal system.[10]

II. The Historical Paradigm: The Bible, a Book of Past Times

Historical criticism of the Bible was developed in confrontation with the dogmatic understanding of Scripture and the doctrinal authority of the Church. This historical approach linked its attack on the dogmatic understanding of Scripture with an understanding of history that was objectivist, value-neutral, and rationalist. Such an understanding of exegesis was modeled after the natural sciences and attempted to create a purely objective reconstruction of the facts. As objectivist scientific historiography, it intended to unearth the historical data and therefore defined history as "what actually took place or happened." In this paradigm, theological meaning and truth become identified with historical facticity. If one is not able to establish a historical event as fact with objective accuracy, it cannot be true. For example, if the Bible says that the world was created within a week, but natural science speaks of the evolution of the world and of humans in thousands of years, then the Bible is proven wrong and therefore not true.

First: In reaction to the historicist criticism of the Bible, Christian apologetics asserts and attempts to show that the Bible is a record of historical facts and scientific insights and therefore true. Christian apologetics does not question the presuppositions of historicist criticism, but attempts to defend the Bible on the same grounds. While radically rejecting historical criticism as dangerous for the faith, it nevertheless shares the historicist contention that religious truth is identical with historical-factual truth.

Moreover, fundamentalist apologetics has linked the theological concept of inerrancy to the historicist understanding of truth.[11] Roman Catholicism shares in this fundamentalist biblicism insofar as it was very reluctant to accept biblical criticism and to free itself from pre-critical doctrinal positions.[12] This is probably one of the main reasons why serious historical-critical scholarship is still not widespread in American Catholicism. Raymond Brown has pointed out that there is not one outstanding "first-class American Catholic graduate Biblical school," and there is a general reluctance to investigate sensitive theological areas in the light of biblical criticism.[13]

Although the hermeneutical discussion has challenged the basic presuppositions of the historicist paradigm as inadequate for the interpretation of the Bible, ecclesiastical circles still operate under it. Although biblical historical scholarship is officially acknowledged by the Church, religious educators and preachers are hesitant to hand it over to the community of faith, for fear that it would destroy the faith of the laity. When I asked my seminary students what they thought about the question we are discussing here, they confessed that they would be very hesitant to share exegetical insights and methods with the community of faith. Historical-critical insights can be digested by the clergy, but they do not belong in preaching and meditation. It is obvious that these students feel threatened by the scholarly interpretative approach to the Bible, because they were themselves reared under the historicist apologetic paradigm. "Lay" people, on the other hand, resent the fact that the clergy attempt to keep them uneducated in matters of biblical scholarship. For instance, when college students encounter the synoptic problem for the first time, their reaction is not so much to condemn the Bible as to condemn their parochial religious education for never mentioning this problem.

Second: This reluctance to communicate historical-critical scholarship to the community of faith is not caused just by fundamentalist clericalism, which considers the minister as the sole Scripture "expert," but it is also engendered by the self-understanding of exegetical scholarship. Although academic historical criticism has become suspicious of the objectivist-factual understanding of history, it still adheres to the dogma of a value-neutral, uninvolved historiography.[14] It studies the biblical texts, not as canonical texts of guiding importance for the community of faith, but as historico-religious documents of Judaism and Christianity in antiquity or as Jewish and Christian literature of the Greco-Roman world. Since such a history-of-religions approach refuses to reconstruct the faith claims of the biblical texts and to ask the question of their significance and authority today, it makes the canonical claims of Scripture obsolete. The historical-critical scholarship promoted in the academy reconstructs as objectively as possible the historical meaning of the text, but on methodological grounds refuses to discuss the significance of the biblical text for the community of faith today. The biblical interpreter becomes a historian of antiquity who is accountable to the academy but not the community of faith. For fear of destroying the historical integrity of the Bible by making it relevant for today, scholars often make it so irrelevant that it loses all interest for anyone but the student of antiquity. Bible study is of the same order as the study of Homer or Virgil.

In this historical paradigm, exegetes understand themselves as historians of religion but not as theologians. The task of exegesis is, then, to provide the historical "data" for the theological reflections of systematic or moral theologians.[15] The task of biblical exegesis is to study the biblical text as historical source that is a part of ancient history, or to study it as literature and to discover the literary interest that shaped the text and what it meant to its original audience. The task of exegesis, however, is not to ask what the biblical text means for Christian and ecclesial self-understanding today; therefore biblical interpretation is limited to historical and literary inquiry, but, strictly speaking, is not a theological endeavor.

Third: Since most American graduate departments which train future theologians and teachers operate under this paradigm that understands Scripture as a source of ancient history or literature, seminary teachers approach the Bible with the same perspective. They usually leave it to their ministerial students to bridge the gap between the exegetical-historical and the ministerial task. The minister is supposed to become the mediator between value-neutral, historical exegesis and the Church's commitment to the Bible as Scripture, between what the Bible meant and what it means today. Future ministers of the Word sense this disparity between their ministerial task and their exegetical training, but are often not able to pinpoint the problem accurately. They either attempt to extend the university model of historical criticism into their pastoral work or they forget what they have studied in seminary and graduate school and fall back into the doctrinal-fideist paradigm. Since they were taught a methodological procedure that consisted of a value-neutral historical exegesis as a first step, and theological or pastoral application as the second, not integrally related step, the temptation is great to relinquish laborious historical inquiry for the sake of ready-made piety or dogmatic interests.

This failure of biblical scholarship not only to ask for the meaning of the text in its historical context but also to search for the significance of the text for us today is, in my opinion, one of the main reasons why historical-critical scholarship has such slight impact on the Church community today. I recently attended a biblical conference where scholars bemoaned how little influence biblical scholarship has today on Church policies and teachings. The next day, when a paper on women in early Christianity was read, the same scholars insisted that it does not make any difference whether or not Jesus preached a sexist gospel. As soon as historical-critical questions were raised in the context of a contemporary debate, the questions lost their scholarly interest, because they were inspired by a contemporary discussion within the Church.

III. The Pastoral-Theological Paradigm [16]

If the Bible as a historical *and* canonical book is to gain more influence in the life of the contemporary Church, then it is necessary to chart a new paradigm of biblical interpretation that would integrate the two competing paradigms that determine biblical interpretation today. This new paradigm has to take seriously the methodological insights of historical-critical scholarship, but must also radically question the presupposition that value-free, neutral, and uncommitted exegetical research is possible. Biblical interpretation cannot limit itself to working out what the author and the text *meant*, but it also must critically elaborate what the theological significance of the text is for today. This new paradigm could be called pastoral-theological insofar as it holds the pastoral situation and the theological response to it, the historical and the theological aspects, the past and the present, in creative tension. It understands the Bible, not as a conglomeration of doctrinal propositions or proofs, not as historical-factual transcripts, but as the root-model of Christian faith and life.

Such a new paradigm was prepared by two developments in biblical scholarship. The methods of form- and redaction-criticism [17] have demonstrated how much the biblical writings are theological responses to pastoral-practical situations, while the hermeneutical discussion [18] has made obsolete a value-free, objectivist study of historical texts. At the same time, critical theology has maintained that it is not sufficient to understand the historical meaning of biblical texts. What is also necessary is a critical evaluation of their ideological function within an ecclesial or societal context. [19] Not only perceptive understanding but also critical judgment is necessary in order to set free the liberating traditions of the Bible and their significance for the community of faith today.

Content and Context

Form- and redaction-criticism have demonstrated that the biblical tradition is not a doctrinal or exegetical tradition, but a living tradition of the community of faith. In order to understand biblical texts, it is important not just to analyze and understand the *context of a given text* but also to know and determine the situation and community to which this text is addressed. This is obvious when we study the Pauline letters. Whereas the Pauline literature was long seen as a compendium of the theological teaching and principles of Paul, scholars today understand them as letters and not as dogmatic handbooks. The letter of Paul to the Galatians could not have been written to the Corinthians and vice versa. Similarly, the Gospels were written for concrete communities with specific problems and theological understandings. It is therefore necessary not only to study the content of the biblical writings but also to determine the situation and type of community to which they were written.[20]

Form- and source-criticism have shown that the material that the biblical writers transmit was collected and selected and formulated in such a way that it could speak to the needs and situation of the community of faith. The materials and traditions about Jesus, for instance, were selected and reformulated so that they would have meaning for the Christian community that transmitted them. It can be seen that the early Christians were free in their usage of the Jesus-traditions. They changed or reformulated them and reinterpreted them by bringing them into a different context and framework. Not only does Matthew change the form of Mark's text on the great commandment[21] from a scholarly dialogue to a controversy dialogue, but he also reformulates the question. Whereas in Mark the lawyer asks which commandment is the chief or first commandment, Matthew changes the question into one for the "key" to the Law, in order to adapt the question to the Jewish discussion, where it was most important to know how one could do justice to the 613 commandments. Luke, on the other hand, connects the controversy dialogue with the story of the Good Samaritan and shifts the emphasis from knowing the commandments to doing them. Thus the Gospel writers were not content to repeat formulas and stories just because they belonged to the tradition, but they reformulated them in order to respond to the needs of the Christians of their own day.

However, form- and redaction-critical studies can be criticized for focusing too narrowly on the community and for conceptualizing the situation of the early Christian communities too much in terms of a confessional struggle between different theologies and church groups.

Such a reconstruction often reads like the history of the European Reformation in the sixteenth century or a description of a small town in America where five or six churches of different Christian groups are built within walking distance of one another. We must, therefore, recognize that the early Christian writers responded not only to inner-theological or inner-church problems, but that the early Christian communities were missionary communities[22] deeply embedded in their own culture or critically distancing themselves from it. The biblical writers transmit their faith response to the cultural and religious problems of their own time. They indicate that Christian faith can be acculturated or countercultural.

The studies of the social world of early Christianity underline that Christian faith and revelation is always intertwined with its cultural, political, and societal contexts,[23] so that we no longer are able to neatly separate biblical revelation from its cultural expression. It does not suffice to understand texts just as religious-theological texts. What is necessary also is to analyze their societal-political contexts and expression. While, for instance, the historicist approach to the miracles of the New Testament discusses whether or not they actually could have happened or whether they happened as they are told, the historical-theological approach debates whether miracle-faith is a genuine Christian expression of faith or whether it shares too much in the magic beliefs of the times when it understands Jesus in analogy to the miracle-workers of antiquity.

While the historical-theological understanding emphasizes a "heretical" Christian group as the proponent of such crude miracle-faith, the societal interpretation of miracle points out that miracle-faith was widespread in lower classes who were uneducated and did not have money for medical treatment. The miracle stories, therefore, strengthen the hope of those who were exploited and oppressed. For instance, the demon in Mk 5:1-13 is called Legion, with the same name as the Roman soldiers who occupied Palestine. The story presents an irony of the Roman exploitation when it has the demon expelled into a herd of pigs, animals that were, for Jewish sensitivities, the paradigm of ritual impurity. Miracle-faith is here protest against bodily and political suffering. It gives courage to resist all life-destroying power of one's society.

In sum: In reinterpreting their traditions, the biblical writers do not follow the doctrinal or historicist paradigm but the paradigm of pastoral or practical theology, insofar as the concrete pastoral situation of the community is determinative for the selection, transmission, and creation of the biblical traditions. The New Testament authors rewrote their traditions in the form of letters, gospels, or apocalypses, because they felt theologically compelled to illuminate or to censure the beliefs and praxis of their communities. The biblical books are thus written with the intention of serving the needs of the community of faith and not of revealing timeless principles or transmitting historically accurate records. They therefore do not locate revelation just in the past but also in their own present, thereby revealing a dialectical understanding between present and past. The past, on the one hand, is significant because revelation happened decisively in Jesus of Nazareth. On the other hand, the writers of the New Testament can exercise freedom with respect to the Jesus traditions because they believe that the Jesus who spoke speaks now to his followers through the Holy Spirit.[24]

The relevance of this understanding of tradition is obvious for the Scriptures. We have to learn that not all texts speak to all situations and to everyone. It is therefore necessary for the minister to learn how to determine the situation and needs of his or her congregation with the same sophistication with which he/she studies the biblical texts. Moreover he/she has to be aware of the sociological, psychological, cultural, and political influences that shape the world and self-understanding of the community of faith. A repetition of biblical texts does not suffice. For example, if a minister preached about the theology of grace expressed in Rom 9–11 during the time of the Nazis but did not say something about the gas chambers of Auschwitz and the annihilation of the Jewish people, he did not preach the gospel but perverted the biblical message. The pastoral-theological paradigm does not permit a mere repetition or application of biblical texts, but demands a translation of their meaning and context into our own situation.[25]

The Bible as Root-Model of the Christian Church

Historical-critical studies therefore teach us that there is not one single way of formulating Christian proclamation and theology or of building Christian communities and living as a Christian. The pastoral-theological paradigm therefore demands a redefinition of what canon means.[26] The canon should not be viewed, as in the doctrinal paradigm, in an exclusive fashion as a negative judgment on all the other early Christian writings that were not included by the Church among the books of the New or Old Testament. Instead, the canon should be understood in an inclusive fashion as creating a pluriform model of Christian Church and Christian life. The canon includes not only the New Testament but also the Jewish Scriptures, not only one Gospel but four, not only the Pauline letters but also James or Hebrews, not only Acts but also the Apocalypse. It includes writings that were written not only in Palestine but also in Asia Minor or Greece, not only to Jews but also to Gentiles. It encompasses not only Matthean but also Johannine theology, not only apocalyptic but also realized eschatology.

This concept of canon, however, also has implications for our pastoral-theological practice today, insofar as it demands that we distinguish more carefully between preaching or proclamation and teaching or catechesis. If the canon presents the root-model of Christian community and faith, then we are bound to explore all dimensions of this model. Whereas the task of preaching is to select those biblical texts that speak to the situation and questions of the contemporary faith-community, the task of teaching is to preserve the multiplicity and pluriformity of the early Christian traditions and communities. The task of teaching is to transmit *all* the biblical traditions, whether they are meaningful and relevant in a specific Christian community-situation or not. There are situations where it would be wrong to proclaim certain biblical traditions, and times when one is not able to do more than to keep the tradition of biblical faith. We cannot preach them because we do not really understand them or they do not come alive for us. Yet we have to keep and preserve them because we are aware of the danger of destroying the pluriform root-model of the biblical canon.

The interrelation between teaching and preaching, however, should not be understood in such a way as though the teacher has to preserve objective biblical historical data and the preacher or theologian has to apply these data to a contemporary situation or problem. It should also not be understood in the sense that the teacher approaches the Bible in a value-neutral scientific attitude, whereas the preacher has to be committed to the Christian community and its interests. Such an objectivist and value-neutral stance of the teacher would go against the very intentionality of the New Testament books themselves, which were written for the community of faith.

Moreover, the hermeneutical discussion has pointed out that an objectivist, value-neutral historiography and exegesis are not possible, since the interpreter[27] always approaches the text with specific questions or in a specific way of raising questions, and thus with a certain understanding of the issues with which the text is concerned. The interpreter's mind is not a *tabula rasa*, but before we attempt to understand how an author deals with a given subject matter and before we can get interested in a text, we have to have a certain common interest, understanding, or life-relation to the issues of which the text speaks. Just as we have to have an appreciation of music in order to understand a textbook on musicology, so must the biblical interpreter have a certain relationship to the community of faith and to the religious questions raised by it if he/she wants to grasp the intentionality and subject matter of these texts.

In other words, understanding takes place in a circular movement: interpretation and answer are to some extent determined by the question, which in turn is confirmed, extended, or corrected by the text. A new question then grows out of this understanding, so that the hermeneutical circle continues to develop in a never-ending spiral.[28]

Therefore, understanding of a text depends as much on the questions and presuppositions [29] of the interpreter as on material explanation. The interpreter who is really interested in understanding the text is prepared to have his/her presuppositions corrected if necessary. However, illegitimate prejudice refuses to alter its preconceived judgment when new insights are derived from the text and thus reduces the hermeneutical spiral to a vicious circle. Such presuppositions and prejudices of the interpreter or of a theological school, however, are not only psychologically but also societally and culturally determined.

These insights of the hermeneutical discussion have far-reaching consequences for the study and interpretation of the Bible within the community of faith. Students of the Bible should be trained not only to correctly analyze historical texts and literary forms but also to reflect methodologically on their own presuppositions or prejudices as well as on those of scholarly interpretations. It is obvious in this context how damaging it is that almost all biblical scholars are middle-class, white males who are highly educated and belong to the clergy. Therefore it is essential to break down the monopoly of this class on biblical interpretation if the Bible is to truly become again Scripture for the community of faith. It is absolutely mandatory that very different people with different life-styles, different social backgrounds, and different personal experiences should become involved in the interpretation of Scripture. [30] Such an involvement of people with different experiences and perceptions will generate new questions not raised previously in biblical interpretation.

It is therefore necessary that biblical scholars not only discuss the questions raised by the historical scholarship of their colleagues but also pay attention to the questions and discoveries of the community of faith. [31] The task of biblical scholarship is therefore not only the historical scientific research but also the scholarly validation or rejection of the discoveries and questions raised by the communities of faith that respond to the historical biblical text always on the basis of their own Christian experience. Biblical interpretation and preaching are not possible without listening to such experiences of very different people. Just as no preacher can any longer afford to prepare a sermon on a biblical text in the seclusion of the study without having discussed it with a group of people beforehand, [32] so must biblical scholarship address the questions of the community of faith if it is to be of service to the Christian community.

Revelation "for the Sake of Our Salvation"

If we take seriously that the biblical writings are pastoral-theological responses to the situations and problems of their own times and communities, then we have to expect that not all writings are of theological significance for us today. A "hermeneutic of consent" to the historical-theological meaning of the biblical texts does not suffice.[33] We not only have to understand these texts but also to evaluate them theologically. For instance, in the face of the all-destructive powers of modern warfare, the question must be raised whether we still can pray the curses of the Old Testament psalms against the enemies of Israel. Feminist theology queries whether we can repeat the patriarchal biblical language for God today, and political theology doubts that biblical texts which speak of God as an absolute monarch are still adequate. What is necessary, therefore, for theological interpretation today is not only an understanding of their historical-theological meaning but also a critical-theological evaluation of their theological function in the history of the Church and in the contemporary Church.

Such a need for a critical evaluation of the various biblical texts and traditions was always recognized within the Christian Church. While the doctrinal paradigm selected those passages of Scripture that supported ecclesial doctrine, the historical paradigm evaluated the theological truth of biblical texts according to their historicity. The pastoral-theological paradigm of contemporary biblical criticism has not only established the canon as the inclusive pluriform root-model of Christian Church but also has highlighted that the canon includes various, often contradictory theological responses to the historical situations of the early Christian communities.[34] Since not all these New Testament responses are of equal theological quality and can equally express Christian revelation, New Testament scholarship attempts to find theological criteria or "a canon within the canon"[35] in order to evaluate the various early Christian traditions. The doctrinal paradigm formulated such a "canon" after the model of revelatory essence and historical expression, timeless truth and culturally conditioned language, or constant tradition and changing traditions. When the "canon within the canon" is formulated along the lines of the historical paradigm, scholars juxtapose Jesus and Paul, Pauline theology and Early Catholicism, the historical Jesus and the early Church. Divine revelation and truth is, in this perspective, identified with the earliest historically verifiable traditions.[36]

The pastoral-theological paradigm has to formulate its own criterion, which cannot be derived from the biblical texts but from the Christian communities to which these texts speak today. Such a criterion does not judge the theological validity of biblical texts with relationship to their own communities, but evaluates these texts with respect to the theological insights and questions of the Christian community today. The Constitution on Divine Revelation of Vatican II acknowledges that Scripture "*contains* revelation, namely, in the form of a written record; but that not all of Scripture *is* revelation."[37] It follows Augustine and Thomas in formulating a criterion that limits revealed truth and inerrancy to matters pertaining to the salvation of the Christian and human community. "Therefore, since everything asserted by the inspired authors or sacred writers must be held to be asserted by the Holy Spirit, it follows that the books of Scripture must be acknowledged as teaching firmly, faithfully, and without error that truth which God wanted put into the sacred writings *for the sake of our salvation*."[38]

"Salvation" here should not be understood just as salvation of the soul, but in the biblical sense of total human salvation and wholeness. It cannot be limited to the liberation from sin, but must be understood to mean also liberation from social and political oppression. Conversely, oppressive and destructive biblical traditions cannot be acknowledged as divine revelation. For example, feminist theology has pointed out that women are oppressed and exploited by patriarchal and sexist structures and institutions. Therefore, according to this criterion, biblical revelation and truth can today be found only in those texts and traditions that transcend and criticize the patriarchal culture and religion of their times. A pastoral-theological interpretation of the Bible concerned with the truth and meaning of Scripture in a post-patriarchal culture and society has to maintain that solely the non-sexist traditions of the Bible present divine revelation if the Bible is not to become a tool for the further oppression of women.

Such a critical scrutiny and evaluation of biblical texts according to whether or not they contribute to the salvation, well-being, and freedom of women should not be understood in terms of the doctrinal essence-historical relativity model as though we were able to separate culturally conditioned patriarchal expression from a timeless non-sexist essence of revelation. It likewise should not be understood in terms of the pristine beginnings-deterioration model as though non-patriarchal traditions are limited to the earliest traditions of the New Testament. Such a critical criterion of evaluation has to be applied to *all* biblical texts, in order to determine how much they contribute to the "salvation" or oppression of women.[39]

I have proposed here that the difficulties of the community of faith with the Bible are engendered by the rivalry of three different paradigms of interpretation. While ecclesial pronouncements and popular fundamentalism often cling to the doctrinal paradigm, the study of the Bible in the academy is determined by the historical paradigm. At the same time, a third paradigm has emerged in biblical scholarship that I have here characterized as pastoral-theological. T. S. Kuhn has pointed out that a new scientific paradigm must also create a new scientific community with common interests, journals and channels of communication if it is to replace the preceding one. Whereas the reference community of the doctrinal paradigm is the teaching authority of the Church, and that of the historical paradigm is the academy, the emerging pastoral-theological paradigm has not yet engendered its own scientific reference community. At present its institutional basis is the seminary or academic departments of religion, where the seminary educates future ministers of the faith-community, and the academy educates future scholars and teachers of religion in antiquity.

As long as the pastoral-theological paradigm of biblical interpretation does not engender its own American institutional basis, we will not be able to escape the present dilemma of biblical interpretation. Such an institutional basis could be centers of pastoral-theological interpretation that would gather together a scientific community and facilitate the cooperation of biblical scholars, of priests and ministers, and of the active members of the community of faith in studying the Bible. Such centers would have to explore scientifically not only the historical meaning of biblical texts but also the doctrinal interests of the institutionalized churches, the presuppositions of academic historiography, and, last but not least, the needs and situations of the contemporary community of faith in its societal-political contexts. Involved in such pastoral-theological biblical centers should be persons from different churches and communities, from different races, classes, sexes, ages, and cultures, from different professions and educational backgrounds.

Such centers would have to fruitfully integrate historical-theological scholarship and the contemporary theological needs and insights of the community of faith in order to say God's word in a new language, so that the Bible will contribute to the "salvation" of contemporary people. Their task would not be inspirational popularization and pious application of the biblical text to our own situation but rigorous intellectual theological scholarship committed to the needs of the community of faith. The beginnings of such a new scientific reference community of the pastoral-theological paradigm are already found all over the country in task forces and study groups dedicated to such pastoral-theological interpretation of the Bible.

NOTES

1. For the literature on the scholarly discussion of this problem, see especially P. Stuhlmacher, *Historical Criticism and Theological Interpretation of Scripture: Toward a Hermeneutics of Consent* (Philadelphia: Fortress Press, 1977); E. Krentz, *The Historical-Critical Method* (Philadelphia: Fortress Press, 1975) especially 55–58; D. H. Kelsey, *The Uses of Scripture in Recent Theology* (Philadelphia: Fortress Press, 1975); W. Wink, *The Bible in Human Transformation: Toward a New Paradigm for Biblical Study* (Philadelphia: Fortress Press, 1973).

2. Thomas S. Kuhn, *The Structure of Scientific Revolutions* (Chicago: University of Chicago Press, 1962); I. G. Barbour, *Myth, Models, and Paradigms* (New York: Harper & Row, 1974).

3. See R. Grant, *The Bible in the Church: A Short History of Interpretation* (New York: Macmillan, 1960); H. J. Kraus, *Geschichte der historisch-kritischen Erforschung des Alten Testaments* (Neukirchen: Neukirchener Verlag, 1969); R. E. Clements, *One Hundred Years of Old Testament Interpretation* (Philadelphia: The Westminster Press, 1976); W. G. Kümmel, *The New Testament: The History of the Investigation of Its Problems* (Nashville: Abingdon, 1972).

4. See the excellent analysis of J. Barr, *Fundamentalism* (Philadelphia: Westminster Press, 1978).

5. See text and analysis in L. and A. Swidler (eds.), *Women Priests: A Catholic Commentary on the Vatican Declaration* (New York: Paulist Press, 1977) and C. Stuhlmueller (ed.), *Women and Priesthood: Future Directions* (Collegeville: The Liturgical Press, 1978). For the strained relationship between exegesis and dogmatics, see J. L. Houlden, *Patterns of Faith: A Study in the Relationship between the New Testament and Christian Doctrine* (Philadelphia: Fortress Press, 1977).

6. See my book *Priester für Gott. Studien zum Herrschafts und Priesterbegriff in der Apokalypse*, Neutestamentliche Abhandlungen 7 (Münster: Aschendorff Verlag, 1972) and my article "Cultic Language in Qumran and in the New Testament," *CBQ* 38 (1976) 159–177 for the literature.

7. See the articles of A. Smitmans and H. Harsch, in H. Harsch and G. Voss (eds.), *Versuche mehrdimensionaler Schriftauslegung* (Stuttgart: Verlag Katholisches Bibelwerk, 1972).

8. W. Wink, *op. cit.*, 56f.

9. See C. K. Barrett, *Biblical Problems and Biblical Preaching*, Biblical Series 6 (Philadelphia: Fortress Press, 1964) 37.

10. See P. Stuhlmacher, *op. cit.*, 36.

11. See J. Barr, *op. cit.*, 312: "This is one of the main features in the fundamentalist mind: the fact that a man says he believes in Christ does not seem objective to them, you can't trust that or rely on it, but if he believes in the Bible as infallible and inerrant then that seems to lend objectivity. Objectivity thus comes to mean that the truth is not in people."

12. T. A. Collins and R. E. Brown, "Church Pronouncements," *JBC* II, 624–632.

13. "Difficulties in Using the New Testament in American Catholic Discussion," *Louvain Studies* 6 (1976) 144–158.

14. See K. Stendahl, "Biblical Theology, Contemporary," *IDB* 1:418–432, and F. Hahn, "Probleme historischer Kritik," *ZNTW* 63 (1972) 1–17.

15. B. Lonergan's eight functional specialties in theology are often understood in such a way. See his *Method in Theology* (New York: Herder & Herder, 1972).

16. I understand "pastoral" here not in the sense of a theology for pastors or ministers but of a theology pertaining to the community of faith. Most discussions on biblical preaching see the problem too narrowly as that of pastors or preachers.

17. See N. Perrin, *What Is Redaction Criticism?* (Philadelphia: Fortress Press, 1969); J. Rohde, *Rediscovering the Teachings of the Evangelists* (Philadelphia: Westminster Press, 1969);

J. Reumann, "Methods in Studying the Biblical Text Today," *Concordia Theological Monthly* 40 (1969) 655–681; W. G. Kümmel, *Das Neue Testament im 20. Jahrhundert*, Stuttgarter Bibelstudien 50 (Stuttgart: Verlag Katholisches Bibelwerk, 1970).

18. For a review of the hermeneutical discussion, see R. E. Brown, "Hermeneutics," *JBC* II, 605–623, and J. A. Sanders, "Hermeneutics," *IDB* (suppl. vol.) 402–407.

19. See J. Habermas, "Der Universalitätsanspruch der Hermeneutik," in *Kultur und Kritik* (Frankfurt, 1973) 264–301, and the theological work of Francis S. Fiorenza; see also my article "Feminist Theology as a Critical Theology of Liberation," in W. Burkhardt (ed.), *Woman: New Dimensions* (New York: Paulist Press, 1977) 36f.

20. See L. E. Keck, *The New Testament Experience of Faith*, and his article "On the Ethos of Early Christians," *JAAR* 42 (1974) 435–452.

21. See V. Furnish, *The Love Command in the New Testament* (Nashville: Abingdon, 1972).

22. See *Aspects of Religious Propaganda in Judaism and Early Christianity* (Notre Dame: Notre Dame University Press, 1976), which I have edited.

23. See J. C. Gager, *Kingdom and Community* (Englewood Cliffs: Prentice-Hall, 1975); N. K. Gottwald and F. S. Frick, "The Social World of Ancient Israel," in *The Bible and Liberation* (Berkeley: Radical Religion Reader, 1976) 110–119; G. Theissen, *Sociology of Early Palestinian Christianity* (Philadelphia: Fortress Press, 1978); W. A. Meeks, "The Social World of Early Christianity," *CSR Bulletin* 6 (1975) 1, 4f.

24. See N. Perrin, *What Is Redaction Criticism?*, 76f.

25. J. A. Sanders, "Hermeneutics," *op. cit.*, 406f., advocates the rule of "dynamic analogy" for such a translation and distinguishes the constitutive and prophetic mode of interpretation.

26. For a discussion of the problem see J. Charlot, *New Testament Disunity: Its Significance for Christianity Today* (New York: E. P. Dutton, 1970), and E. Krentz, "A Survey of Trends and Problems in Biblical Interpretation," *Concordia Theological Monthly* 40 (1969) 276–293.

27. See R. MacKenzie, "The Self-Understanding of the Exegete," in R. Murphy (ed.), *Theology, Exegesis and Proclamation*, Concilium Series 70 (New York: Herder and Herder, 1971) 11–19; R. L. Rohrbaugh, *The Biblical Interpreter* (Philadelphia: Fortress Press, 1978).

28. See E. Schillebeeckx, *The Understanding of Faith* (New York: Seabury, 1974).

29. See T. Peters, "The Nature and Role of Presupposition: An Inquiry into Contemporary Hermeneutics," *International Philosophical Quarterly* 14 (1974) 209–222.

30. See F. Herzog, "Liberation Hermeneutic as Ideology Critique," *Interpretation* 27 (1974) 387–403.

31. This is especially emphasized by liberation theology. See the article of L. Cormie, "The Hermeneutical Privilege of the Oppressed," and the review article by J. A. Kirk, "The Bible in Latin American Liberation Theology," in *The Bible and Liberation* (Berkeley: A Radical Religion Reader, 1976) 157–165.

32. See the very interesting report of J. Rothermund, "Laien als Partner in der Predigtarbeit," *Wissenschaft und Praxis in Kirche und Gesellschaft* 67 (1978) 187–201; and especially the two volumes edited by E. Cardenal, *The Gospel in Solentiname* (Maryknoll, N.Y.: Orbis Books, 1976).

33. P. Stuhlmacher, *op. cit.*, 83ff., has coined this expression. In a "hermeneutics of consent" we must not only ask how we relate to the text. "But in addition we must again learn to ask what claim or truth about man, his world, and transcendence we hear from these texts" (85).

34. See E. Käsemann, "The Canon of the New Testament and the Unity of the Church," in *Essays on New Testament Themes* (London: SCM Press, 1964); and J. Charlot, *op. cit.*, 39–94.

35. See J. C. Turro and R. E. Brown, "Canonicity," in *JBC* II, 514–534, especially 532ff.

36. For such a proposal see S. M. Ogden, "The Authority of Scripture for Theology," *Interpretation* 30 (1976) 242–261, who follows W. Marxsen.

37. W. Abbott and J. Gallagher (eds.), *The Documents of Vatican II* (New York: America Press, 1966) 108.

38. *Ibid.*, 119 (emphasis added).

39. See also my articles "Understanding God's Revealed Word," in *Catholic Charismatic* 1 (1977) 4–10, and "Interpreting Patriarchal Traditions of the Bible," in L. Russell (ed.), *The Liberating Word* (Philadelphia: Westminster Press, 1976) 39–61.

Eugene H. Maly

SIN AND FORGIVENESS

IN THE SCRIPTURES

One of the more fascinating and significant aspects of the Hebrew language is the wide range of meanings that the various terms can have. The terms can be said to embrace totalities rather than parts. By this is meant that a particular word can refer to the whole of a reality, only a part of which would be indicated by the word in our languages.

Probably the most commonly recognized illustration of this totality approach is had in the terms used to express the human person. In Hebrew there is no word for "person," which is perhaps as close as we can come to expressing the total human reality. The Hebrew terms are understood as totality expressions with a special orientation. This carries over into the New Testament also, where the corresponding Greek words have the same totality meaning. Thus, "soul" (*psychē*) is the human person as endowed with an inner life oriented to all kinds of activities. "What does it profit a man if he gains the whole world but suffers the loss of his soul?" (Mt 16:26). Traditionally, in accord with our understanding of the word, we have thought that the "soul" here refers to the spiritual principle inside each of us and which is distinct from the "body." To the Semitic mind, however, it meant the human person. That is why the NAB translates the word in this case as "himself."

Similarly, when an individual "knows" something, that knowledge is not just an intellectual perception of the object, but a total appropriation of the object insofar as that is possible. The whole or totality of the "knower" is involved, including mind, will, emotions, even at times the body, as when a man "knows" his wife. This totality range allows for all the descendants of a patriarch to be included in a reference to him. Israel, Jacob's new name (Gen 32:29), refers also to the nation descended from him. Melchizedek, the priest-king, had blessed Abraham (Gen 14:18-20). Christ, therefore, is a high priest according to the order of Melchizedek, not of Levi, because Levi was already in Abraham's loins when the patriarch was blessed by the greater one, and so he (Christ) must belong to the greater order (see Heb 7:1-17).

This totality range can also include at times the antecedents and consequences of an action. A case of the former is had in the word "obey." For us the word means compliance with an order or request and is generally understood as applying to the action itself. Hebrew has no word for "obey" in this sense. The concept is expressed in this form: "to listen to the voice of," or simply, "to listen to." In this understanding of the word, it is important not only that an action be performed in accord with a command but also that the word of command be received into the "soul" of the person being addressed. In fact, there seems to be a greater emphasis on the reception of the word, implying that if the word is good for the one receiving it, it will almost automatically be carried out and have good consequences. If a bad word is "listened to," it will have bad consequences.

In the garden scene in Genesis, God tells Adam, "Because you listened to the voice of your wife . . ." (3:17). As a matter of fact, he both listened and acted. The Hebrew word contains both concepts as one continuous action. The verse could just as well be translated, "Because you obeyed your wife. . . ." In another passage Abraham is told of blessings to come because "you obeyed my command" (Gen 22:18). Literally the form is the very same as in 3:17, that is, "you listened to my voice."

We might note also that even the consequences of the listening to and acting are implicitly contained in the Hebrew word. In the case of Adam, the voice or word that he listened to and allowed to enter into his "soul" was not a good word, and because of that the consequences are necessarily evil. They flow from the very act of receiving the evil word that produces the evil act. In the case of Abraham, it was a good word that he had listened to and received; this was the "voice" of God. The consequences, then, of the ensuing action are bound to be blessings.

J. Pedersen was the first to make a thorough examination of this aspect of the Hebrew language.[1] Several statements emphasize the point we have been making. The Israelite "directs his soul towards the principal matter, that which determines the totality, and receives it into his soul, the soul thus being immediately stirred and led in a certain direction."[2] Knowledge "is not an abstract recognition or a perception of details, but an appropriation of the totality and, first and foremost, of its main features. . . . In accordance with this the ideas of the Israelite are neither abstractions nor details pieced together, but totalities."[3]

Pedersen sees this totality approach manifested not only in individual words but also in sentences and in paragraphs. Thus, in the first sentence of an argument there is already contained in some way what will be contained in the following statements and even in the final one.

There is an association between the totality statements that each succeeding statement serves to make more clear. In Western logic each
statement in the argument makes a completely new contribution, and
the conclusion then follows from a bringing together of what is new in
each statement. "The Israelite does not argue by means of conclusions
and logical progress. His argumentation consists in showing that one
statement associates itself with another, as belonging to its totality."[4]

It should be noted that Pedersen's analysis has been severely criticized in more recent studies, in particular by James Barr.[5] One of the
major criticisms has been of Pedersen's contention that through a study
of the structure of the language we get an understanding of the Semitic
mentality. Thus, because a single word, as we have seen, can include
the notion of hearing a command and carrying it out, it does not mean
that Hebrew thought did not recognize the difference between the two
acts. But this criticism does not vitiate the whole of Pedersen's contribution, especially his emphasis on the wide range of meaning in the Hebrew words and the associative nature of the Hebrew approach to literary expression, exemplified in a special way in its predilection for parallelism.

Sin

All this helps to serve as a necessary background to an understanding of the biblical concept of sin. We are already made aware of this
when we realize the comparatively large number of words for "sin" in the
Hebrew Bible. Just like the words for the human person, these words do
not express parts of the reality of sin; rather, all of them are "totality"
words referring to the whole of the reality but with a distinct orientation.
The Greek translation does not always allow for this richness of the
concept, since it reduces the number of words to only a few. But when
analyzing the concept, it is necessary to take account of this great variety
of ways of expressing the totality in the original text. ". . . the relatively
rich linguistic differentiation in the Hebrew may be very largely discerned of itself by reason of the fact that only with the strongest reservations, if at all, can we count on a uniform and self-contained concept of
sin in the authors of the OT; the problem of sin is complicated by a series
of detailed questions of linguistic history."[6]

We do not intend to examine the whole vocabulary for "sin" in this
article. Rather, we want to provide sufficient evidence for understanding the reality as found in the Scriptures. We can use the word *pesha'* as
an illustration. In its secular usage it means "to rebel," generally against
another party that is related in some way to the one rebelling. For example, in 1 Kg 12:19 we read that "Israel went into rebellion against David's
house to this day." There was a disruption of the unity that had existed

before. Also, there is implied a deliberate act of the will on the part of the one rebelling.

When this is transferred to the religious arena, we can expect to find these same elements present. Thus, in Is 1:2 we read, "Hear, O heavens, and listen, O earth, for the Lord speaks: Sons have I raised and reared, but they have (*pesha'*) against me." The word could be translated simply as "sinned." But most modern versions, showing an awareness of its special orientation, have translated *peshá* as "rebelled." That word brings out the deliberateness of the action, the fact that Judah had consciously revolted against the Lord. But it does not include the note of a close relationship that had existed between Judah and God that now was disrupted, a relationship that is implied in the word and which the reference to "sons" makes clear. Therefore, the NAB prefers the translation "have disowned me." This would suggest that the breaking off of the relationship is theologically more significant than the decision of the human will. No single word can capture the full meaning of the Hebrew term.

But more important is the range of action included in the Hebrew notion of sin. For us "sin" suggests a concrete action done here and now. A good illustration of the Semitic understanding of sin is provided by the Letter of James: "Rather the tug and lure of his own passion tempt every man. Once passion has conceived, it gives birth to sin, and when sin reaches maturity it begets death" (1:14-15). Sin, therefore, has a story that begins within the "soul" of the person and continues with the external action that leads to final dissolution or death.

Various Hebrew words show at least part of this range of meaning. Perhaps the more popular example given is the verb to "covet," used for one of the Ten Commandments (Ex 20:17). A traditional explanation is given by Martin Noth in his commentary: "But it describes not merely the emotion of coveting but also includes the attempt to attach something to oneself illegally."[7] More recently there has been some debate about the legitimacy of this position, but there is at least fairly common agreement that Hebrew verbs of desiring do have some relationship to the subsequent action, at times implied in the word itself.

There is clearer evidence that the concept of sin includes also the consequences of the act. Pedersen waxes eloquent in his treatment of this aspect of sin. He sees sin as a dissolution of the soul which "must spread dissolution round it."[8] This is evident in the frequency with which the Israelites saw some evil end as being the necessary consequence of an evil act performed earlier. When Abimelech died in a violent form, the biblical author writes, "Thus did God requite the evil Abimelech had done to his father in killing his seventy brothers" (Jg 9:56). His blood-guilt followed him until it found its proper conclusion.

Gerhard von Rad has argued forcefully for this manner of understanding sin in the Scriptures. He finds nothing there to justify the separation that we assume between sin and its punishment. "The evil deed was only one side of the matter, for through it an evil had been set in motion which sooner or later would inevitably turn against the sinner or the community to which he belonged. On this view, the 'recompense' which catches up with evil is certainly no subsequent forensic event which the sin evokes in a completely different sphere — that is, with God. It is the radiation of the evil which now continues on: only so does the evil which the sin called out reach equilibrium." [9]

Von Rad finds a linguistic confirmation of this in the way in which the same Hebrew word is used for both the sinful deed and for its consequences. In Num 32:23 Moses tells the people, "But if you do not do so, behold you have sinned against the Lord, and be sure your sin will find you out." The second instance of the word "sin" clearly does refer to the penalty or the consequences of sin, as the NAB translation indicates more clearly: ". . . you can be sure that you will not escape the consequences of your sin." Von Rad sees the same kind of identification of sin and penalty in Cain's plea to the Lord, "My sin is too great to bear" (Gen 4:13). But this is said immediately after the Lord had told him what would happen to him as a result of his deed. Consequently, most modern versions translate the word as "punishment." [10]

Is not the same manner of thinking behind the Johannine statement that makes the act of judgment or condemnation of the unbelievers coterminous with the sin itself? ". . . he who does not believe is condemned already . . ." (Jn 3:18). It is true that the strong sense of realized eschatology in John has much to do with statements such as these. But involved also is the intimate association of the sin with judgment, of the act and its consequence. " 'Judgment' has taken place *ipso facto* by the act of unbelief." [11] John Marsh puts it even more forcefully: "It is not a sentence inflicted by a judge after the commission of a crime, but *an inherent part of the choice* that some men make when faced by the divine gift." [12]

What we have, then, in this study of the notion of sin in the Scriptures is a movement that is begun with the conception of evil in the heart, which then moves forward to the actual doing of the deed, and then, because of the quasi-simultaneity of the sin and its consequences, ends inevitably in ruin. It might be said that the movement is almost irreversible, at least from act to consequence, on the part of the sinner. It should be noted, of course, that we are dealing here with what is commonly called "mortal" sin today, a radical breaking off of one's relationship to God. It would appear that it is this irreversibility of the movement of sin that lies behind the statement in Heb 6:4-6: "For when men have once been enlightened and have tasted the heavenly gift and become sharers in the Holy Spirit, when they have tasted the good word of

God and the powers of the age to come, and then have fallen away, it is impossible to make them repent again, since they are crucifying the Son of God for themselves and holding him up to contempt."

Forgiveness of Sin

It is only against this background of the conception of sin that the biblical doctrine of the forgiveness of sin can be properly appreciated. For now it is understood why God alone can be seen as having such power in himself. The astonished reaction of the scribes to Jesus' assurance to the paralyzed man that his sins were forgiven is perfectly intelligible: "Why does the man talk in that way? He commits blasphemy! Who can forgive sins except God alone?" (Mk 2:5-6).

There are a number of passages in the Scriptures where the necessity of God's initiative in the forgiveness of sins is so clearly stated as to leave no doubt about its character as a firm biblical conviction. In those few occasions where there is mention of one human person forgiving another's sins, the context generally indicates that it is a question of simply forgetting about them for the sake of a restoration of relationship, or that the sinning person, not the sin itself, is forgiven by the one offended. Thus, in Gen 50:17 Joseph's brothers repeat their father's plea that Joseph forgive them their wrongdoing. This is to be understood, however, not as a radical reversal of their sinful condition before God, but as a refusal by Joseph to seek vengeance on them, as the context makes evident (see v. 15). In the case of Jn 20:22-23, the risen Lord confers a special power on the disciples, which only confirms the conviction that such is not a power enjoyed by all.

A striking instance of the divine exclusiveness of this forgiving power is found in Lam 5:21. The NAB translation has it in this form: "Lead us back to you, O Lord, that we may be restored." As a matter of fact, the two verbs are of the same root and can be translated in the same way: "Make us come back to you, O Lord, and we shall come back," or, "Convert us and we shall be converted." The repetition of the same verb in both cases makes it quite clear that the action on the part of Israel is impossible without the prior and enabling action of God. God alone can convert a sinner, and then only by forgiving the sin and reversing the movement of estrangement from himself.

Another interesting text is found in Hos 2:25b: "I will say to Lo-ammi, 'You are my people,' and he shall say, 'My God!'" The "Lo-ammi" (meaning literally "not my people") is presented as the name that Israel was given because of her apostasy. So completely had the covenant relationship between Israel and God been destroyed that Israel's nature as God's people had been totally reversed, as the new name indicates. It required an act of creation on the part of God to restore the relationship. St. Paul was keenly aware of the innovative character of God's work in this passage, which he quotes in Rom 9:25. What is interesting is that he uses it to indicate the conversion of the Gentiles. Some scholars have seen this as a poor choice of a text by Paul, as though he was not aware that the prophet was referring to Israel. Rather, Paul knew that Israel's sins had actually made her similar to any pagan nation. (Amos says this openly in 9:7.) The conversion of the Gentiles is no more difficult than was that of sinful Israel. Divine forgiveness is an act of creation.

It is Paul, again, who actually refers to this initiative of God in bringing sinners to himself as an act of creation. In the context of the reconciliation of sinners, he writes, "This means that if anyone is in Christ, he is a new creation" (2 Cor 5:17). In the same context he goes on to speak about God reconciling sinners to himself. He comes to a climax in his injunction to the Corinthians when he exhorts them to "be reconciled to God!" (v. 20). The anomaly of a passive imperative brings out the fact that sinners are simply unable to reconcile themselves to God; they can only allow the reconciling grace of a forgiving God to work in them.

In still another passage, Paul goes out of his way to stress the divine operation of grace which is completely independent of any human initiative. In Rom 5:8-10 he mentions twice that God's reconciling love was at work "while we were still sinners." The simultaneity of the human condition and the divine action is so forcefully argued that one might conclude that they are even reconciled to God as sinners, that is, without any effect on the sinful condition. But Paul would recognize the contradiction in such a conclusion, since it would destroy any real meaning that the word "reconciliation" might have. We must say, then, that he is willing to risk that misunderstanding only because he is so insistent on the absolute necessity of a prior divine action.

There are two other passages in the Gospels that can be used to illustrate this principle of divine forgiveness. The first is, in a way, crucial to all that we have seen thus far. It concerns the proper reading of the Greek text. It is the story of the penitent woman as told by Luke (7:36-50). When Simon, the Pharisee, complained to Jesus about the "sort of woman" who had anointed his feet, Jesus told a brief parable and then spoke to Simon concerning her. She had performed the acts of hospitality that Simon had failed to provide. The verse that follows this (v. 47) is the critical one and is differently translated. In the NAB we read: "I tell you, that is why her many sins are forgiven — because of her great love. Little is forgiven the one whose love is small." In this version it is clear that (divine) forgiveness is dependent on the human love. The amount of forgiveness is in accord with the amount of love. If this is the correct translation, we must conclude that Luke is presenting another principle of forgiveness that, at least on the surface, seems to contradict what has been argued thus far.

The RSV, which is generally considered a translation that hews close to the original text, has this rendering of the verse: "Therefore I tell you, her sins, which are many, are forgiven, for she loved much; but he who is forgiven little, loves little." The first statement, about the woman's sins, seems to be in agreement with the NAB translation. But the "for" here can be understood, like the Greek *hoti* that it translates, in a consecutive rather than in the ordinary causal sense. And that, in fact, is the meaning indicated by a note in the Annotated Edition: "her great love proves that her many sins have been forgiven."

Finally, this meaning is made abundantly clear in the JB, which has: "For this reason I tell you that her sins, her many sins, must have been forgiven her, or she would not have shown such great love. It is the man who is forgiven little who shows little love." Both parts of the verse are saying the same thing — that divine forgiveness precedes and makes possible human love — and both are in agreement with the other passages we have seen. That this is the meaning of the verse is also confirmed by the parable which precedes this passage, and in which the principle was stated by Jesus that the one to whom the larger sum is remitted is the more grateful. Since the parable was told as an illustration of the penitent woman's action, we would hardly expect Jesus, or Luke, to reverse the principle in the application.

A final, though less striking, instance of a possible misunderstanding of our principle is had in the story of Zacchaeus (Lk 19:1-10). Three points come through quite clearly: Zacchaeus is considered a sinner who undergoes a conversion, he exhibits evidences of conversion, and Jesus is the medium of salvation. The question revolves around the precise relationship of the first two points to the third. A surface reading would suggest that Zacchaeus first welcomes Jesus "rejoicing"; then, when the crowd denounces him as a sinner, he mentions good deeds apparently as a sign of conversion. Only then does Jesus make the statement about salvation coming to the man's house.

It would be difficult, however, to think that Luke intended here any contradiction of the principle of divine initiative in forgiveness, since he is most keenly aware of that principle, enunciated, among other places, in the parable of the two debtors that we just considered above. Rather, Luke would almost certainly have seen the divine initiative at work in a forgiving way when Jesus looks up at Zacchaeus in the tree and says, "Zacchaeus, hurry down. I mean to stay at your house today" (19:5). That gesture alone was more than enough to change the heart of a sinner and to make him proclaim his new way of life publicly. And that it is seen as a new way of life, not a long-pursued practice that might have "merited" Jesus' words, is brought out by the translations of JB and TEV especially, where the verbs "to give" and "give back" are in the future.[13]

Conclusion

We need but to conclude this paper with a brief summary of our argument. In the Scriptures sin is seen as having a wide range of meanings. But especially in the rich variety of terms in the Hebrew Bible do we recognize the reality of sin as a movement that begins in the inner "soul" of the human person, makes its way into the external world through an action or omission of some kind, and then continues its inevitable course in the dire consequences that are painted so vividly throughout the Bible. Thus sin, once conceived and acted out, tracks an almost inexorable course that the sinner is unable to stem or reverse.

It is because of that human hopelessness in the face of sin and because of their experience of true, radical conversion to the Lord that the Scriptures must see the forgiveness of sins as the result of a prior act of divine grace. That act, of course, must have its human response, as the case of the penitent woman and of Zacchaeus make clear. But they are consequences of, not conditions for, the divine forgiveness. And that proceeds from pure unmotivated love.

NOTES

1. J. Pedersen, *Israel: Its Life and Culture* I–II (London: Oxford University Press, 1926).
2. *Ibid.*, 108.
3. *Ibid.*, 109.
4. *Ibid.*, 115.
5. James Barr, *The Semantics of Biblical Language* (London: Oxford University Press, 1961).
6. G. Quell, "hamartanō," in *TDNT* 1:270.
7. Martin Noth, *Exodus: A Commentary*, trans. J. S. Bowden (Philadelphia: Westminster Press, 1962) 166.
8. Pedersen, 419.
9. Gerhard von Rad, *Old Testament Theology*, trans. D. M. G. Stalker, 2 vols. (New York: Harper & Row, 1962) 1:265.
10. *Ibid.*, 1:266.
11. R. Schnackenburg, *The Gospel According to St. John*, trans. Kevin Smyth (New York: Herder & Herder, 1968).
12. John Marsh, *The Gospel of Saint John*, Pelican Gospel Commentaries (Baltimore: Penguin Books, 1968) 184; italics added.
13. See F. Blass and A. Debrunner, *A Greek Grammar of the New Testament*, ed. R. W. Funk (Chicago: Chicago University Press, 1961) #323.

Augustine Stock, O.S.B.

THE DEVELOPMENT OF THE CONCEPT

OF REDEMPTION

Redemption, an important concept in its own right, is interesting for another reason. It exemplifies how legal concepts may be turned into religious concepts, and these in turn both give rise to further social legislation and serve as the model for an even higher form of the same concept.

Basically redemption is "taking back what belongs to a family." The ancestors of the Israelites had redemption laws. When it happened, the Exodus was interpreted as a proper act of redemption. Then the Exodus became the basis for further legislation: Israel should care for the downtrodden and the defenseless, remembering what the Lord had done for them in the Exodus, when they were downtrodden and defenseless. One particular model of redemption was levirate marriage, but its career was limited. Redemption in its most archaic form, that of the "taking back of blood," survived as the principal basis for the most advanced of all metaphorical references to redemption, for the metaphor of the spiritual redemption by God.

Redemption in attested law pertains to the responsibility for recovering or retaining family property (Lev 25:25; 27:9-33); buying release of a kinsman from voluntary servitude entered into because of poverty (Lev 25:47-55); receiving restitution (Num 5:8); and acting the part of "the redeemer of the blood," the kinsman who avenges a murder (Num 35:9-28; Dt 19:6-13; Jos 20:2-9). Levirate marriage is the legal provision that if brothers live together and one of them dies leaving no son, the other brother shall marry the widow. The first son of this union shall take the name of the brother who died (Dt 25:5-10). These two forms of redemption were distinct to begin with; we find them joined in the Book of Ruth.

Most people nowadays subscribe to the view that law was not always distinguished from religion, that originally all precepts were deemed to be of a religious character. Supposedly a separation of law and religion was achieved at a more advanced stage of civilization. People think this way because, in the first place, this is what we find in the Bible: it was God who told us not to murder, and the like. In this connection we must remember that the Bible is a collection of literature arranged by priests and prophets, who were neither competent nor desirous to furnish an impartial exposition of Hebrew law. They subordinated law to religion; they represented legal rules as religious rules.

But there is a way around this. We can go to the portions of the Bible where the priestly editors were less active — to the non-legal portions (legends and annals) — and examine any legal ideas that may chance to occur there. It was with this in mind that Professor David Daube entitled the pertinent essay "Law in the Narratives."[1] The story of Joseph's coat (Gen 37:31ff.), for example, reveals a number of legal concepts: the shepherd's responsibility for the sheep under his care, his need to give evidence of loss, and so on. Jacob is asked to "discern" (hikir) whether it is his son's coat. And he discerned it (hikir). The term refers to a formal discovery of, and making a declaration about, a fact of legal relevance.

When Moses reached the vicinity of Mount Nebo, the Lord said to him: "Lift up your eyes westward and northward and southward and eastward, and behold the land with your eyes" (Dt 3:27). This seems to point to one form of transferring property. "There appears to have been an ancient rule concerning land and buildings, to the effect that, provided you took me to the spot and pointed out the property to me, this counted as *traditio*: I acquired control and the transfer was good."[2] This incident, moreover, is especially important for another reason. It is a case from which it may be seen how priests and prophets, with their theology, obscured the legal substance of history and legend, or even entirely transferred legal concepts into the religious sphere.

The priestly editors became concerned with the question: Why had Moses died before the promised land was reached? And they found an answer: because of a sin. This is a case where law came first and religion followed. "Originally the episode of Moses' seeing the land was introduced as of real importance, indeed, as fully explaining, since it explained away, that terrible fact in Hebrew history, his death before the final conquest. Later a more theological version appeared in which his end was related to the supreme principle of just reward, a principle so often to be met with as governing the Biblical presentation of events."[3] Moses' sin and punishment were superimposed on the original, "legal" vision of Moses' acquisition of the land.

Now it would seem that something very like this happened also in the case of the biblical concept of redemption. And again we must go to non-legal material to see the original law clearly, in this instance to the psalms. The number of verses involved is limited, but they are significant.

Hebrew has many words to denote the general, theologized concept of redemption: (*hosheʻa, hoṣil, gaʻal, padah*). To delineate the legal concept, we will be concerned primarily with the latter two, *gʼl* and *pdh*. They are close in meaning. But "whereas *gʼl* signifies the buying back of a man or thing that had once belonged to one or one's family but had got lost, *pdh* signifies the ransoming of a man or thing whose fate otherwise would be destruction, consecration or slavery."[4] *Gʼl* has also been characterized as a technical term of civil law, particularly family law, where the emphasis is not on the ransom paid, but on the blood relationship, while *pdh* is a term of commercial law, where the emphasis is on the object given. We might associate "to ransom" with *pdh* and "to buy back" with *gʼl*, but it is safer to translate the latter as "to take back," because as often as not he who recovers pays no ransom. *Gʼl* can also apply to an inanimate thing, while *pdh* cannot.

The metaphor "to ransom Israel" (*pdh*) may strike us as simpler and stronger, yet "to take back" (*gʼl*) is used predominantly where Israel's final deliverance is concerned. And this brings us to the heart of our thesis: *gʼl* in its metaphorical, religious application descended from *gʼl* as occurring in the social legislation of the Torah.

As often as not *gʼl* involved no payment, and in many, perhaps in the majority of passages where *gʼl* is used metaphorically, there is nothing to suggest the idea of payment. On the other hand, those legal cases in which *gʼlah* depends on payment were of particular importance in the eyes of the prophets. These cases formed the basis of most of the prophetic metaphors about Israel's redemption — even while the idea of payment dropped out.

Gʼl is an outstanding example of a legal notion being taken up and made into a religious notion by priests and prophets. Daube suggests what seems a plausible evolution. "Early Hebrew law had the institution of *gʼlh*, of redemption, in cases like enslavement of debtors or murder: the enslaved debtor or murdered man was to be 'redeemed,' was to be taken back into his old family. Gradually, the concept arose of God as redeemer of the nation, a development that received its main impetus from the fact that Israel's deliverance from Egypt by God was construed as an application, on a higher plane, of the ordinary laws regarding redemption. In the end, the notion of redemption was even more spiritualized, and God thought of as redeeming His people not only from physical slavery but also from the fetters of sin and death."[5]

There was a serious flaw in *gʼlh*. Once you were ruined to such an extent that you had to sell your land or your liberty, the chances of recovery on your own were slender. *Gʼlh* worked well if you belonged to a rich and powerful family; otherwise you were out of luck. It was at this point, it would seem, that the transformation of the concept of *g'lh* from a legal concept into a religious one started. At some point it was suggested that the state (king) should intervene in behalf of the otherwise defenseless. Psalm 72 would seem to give evidence of such a development.

Psalm 72 is one of the royal psalms and deals with a king who was a native Israelite monarch of the pre-exilic period. It also belongs to the group of messianic psalms. The divine conflict with evil leads up to a great climax in the messianic psalms. These psalms contain the idea that the intervention of God will take the form of the raising up of a ruler who will be equipped with the power and authority to deliver the people from their enemies.

The general theme of Psalm 72 is that God is concerned about the establishing and upholding of just rule and good government. The essential features of these are the judging of the poor, the saving of the children of the needy, the breaking of the oppressor, the spreading of the fear in God throughout all generations. Verses 12-14 dwell on the responsibility of this ideal king to protect and defend the weak and defenseless members of society. These are the verses with which we will be primarily concerned:

> 12 For he delivers (*hiṣil*) the needy when he calls,
>   the poor and him who has no helper.
> 13 He has pity (*ḥws*) on the weak and the needy,
>   and saves the lives (*nephes*) of the needy.
> 14 From oppression and violence he redeems (*g'l*) their life;
>   and precious is their blood (*dm*) in his sight.

As we saw earlier, Hebrew has a number of words to denote the general, theologized concept of redemption and two of these appear here: *hiṣil, ḥws*. But we also have the more specific term *g'l*, and significantly it appears in conjunction with blood, *dm*. The appearance of *ḥws* in conjunction with *nephes* may also reflect the original legal stratum.

G'lh worked well if one belonged to a rich and powerful family; otherwise the person had little chance. But the moral leaders of the Hebrew people were aware of the inadequacy and iniquity of the system. At some period, it appears, they demanded that where a man had no relatives who could protect him from oppression, the state (king) should intervene in his behalf. Psalm 72:14 describes an ideal king who undertakes to redeem one if relatives are unable to do it. The reference is at once to redemption of the poor who are enslaved, redemption of the property of the poor, and redemption of the blood of the poor who are murdered.

This is a cry for legal reform; the state ought to see to it that the laws concerning redemption be carried out. Unfortunately it remained largely wishful thinking. "No Hebrew government was high-minded and strong enough to put poor people with no connections in the position enjoyed by the members of wealthy clans. It is perhaps more than accidental that, as far as I can see, the Psalm just quoted is the only instance of the king being urged to exercise the function of a redeemer." [6]

A special kind of redemption was levirate marriage, attested in Gen 38, Dt 25:5-10, and the Book of Ruth. This too seems to be of ancient origin.

For a time it was accepted as practically self-evident that the Book of Ruth dated from the late post-exilic period. It was also believed that in the LXX tradition the book had been violently wrenched from its place in the Writings and inserted after the Book of Judges solely on the score that Ruth was an ancestress of David. But recent commentators on Ruth have changed their positions toward both these matters. The number of alleged Aramaisms, taken to be signs of late composition, has steadily declined. E. Campbell (Anchor Bible) maintains that the theological perspective fits well into the early monarchic period and concludes that the origins of Ruth lie in the Solomonic period and that it was fixed in writing in the ninth century.

Modern commentators are still agreed that the tradition which places Ruth among the Writings rather than after Judges must be original. Yet Ruth takes on striking meaning when viewed in the later context. The Book of Judges ends with the story of the Levite's concubine, how she was ravished by the men of Benjamin, and how the tribe was punished (19–21). There are verbal correspondences that suggest a relationship between this story and the Book of Ruth.

The two stories are completely contrastive. In Jg 19–21, everything is done wrongly. Old institutions are thoroughly misapplied. The Ruth story presents a striking contrast. Here things go as they should, people make the right decisions. Yet the style of life that exercises caring responsibility is not represented as a foregone conclusion for God's people. It is portrayed as attainable but elusive. Things could have gone wrong at many points. "The impact is that living out a righteous and responsible life is a matter of determination to do so." [7]

As the story goes, Elimelech from Bethlehem of Judah has become a sojourner (*ger*) in Moab. He dies leaving a widow, Naomi, and two sons. The sons marry Moabite women, Orpah and Ruth, but both sons die, leaving childless widows. Naomi decides to return to Bethlehem and urges her daughters-in-law to return to their "mothers' houses." At first they both declare that they will go with Naomi, but Orpah changes her resolve and returns to her people. Naomi then addresses Ruth again: "See, your sister-in-law has gone back to her people and to her gods; return after your sister-in-law" (1:15).

Already here the idea of levirate marriage is suggested. "Sister-in-law" (*y^ebimtek*) seems to mean something more than just sister-in-law. The other clear occurrences in the Old Testament of the root *ybm*, to which this noun is related, are in Dt 25 and Gen 38, and in both they constitute technical terminology having to do with levirate marriage. This usage is still current.[8] The noun that occurs here in Ruth is used in Dt 25:7, 9 to designate a widow in relation to her husband's brother; a corresponding masculine noun designates the brother in relation to her, while a denominative verb names the action of fulfilling levirate responsibility. In Ruth this language appears to be generic rather than legal, but the storyteller may have chosen his word to keep levirate custom in the minds of his audience, a hint of the resolution to come.

Naomi and Ruth arrive in Bethlehem at the beginning of the barley harvest. The next episode begins with the observation: "Now Naomi had a kinsman of her husband's, a man of wealth, of the family of Elimelech, whose name was Boaz" (2:1). "Kinsman" is from the root *yd*·, "to know." It has been argued that it should be vocalized *m^eyudda* and translated "covenant-brother." *M^eyudda* designates a close friend or intimate in the seven passages where it appears in the Old Testament. The meaning of the term lies very close to that of *go'el*. A hint of its original meaning comes from the recent demonstration that the verb *yd*· is an important part of treaty/covenant terminology in pre-Israelite Canaan and in Israelite theology. *Yd*· is a reciprocal action in a treaty relationship between overlord and vassal; each "knows" the other, that is, recognizes the other as partner in treaty. It would seem that "the story-teller confronts us here with an archaic term belonging to a societal structure that teaches beyond blood ties. It adds the dimension of covenant responsibility to that of family responsibility."[9]

For our purposes, the striking thing is the juxtaposition of the two terms *go'elim* and *m^eyudda'im* in Ruth. An interweaving is found in Ruth: the storyteller introduces Boaz at 2:1 as a *m^eyudda*·, "covenant-brother," then has Naomi refer to him as "one of our *go'elim* (redeemers)" in 2:20, only to have her refer to him as "of our kinship (*moda'at*)" at 3:2. Thereafter the term *go'el* takes over completely.

Ruth tells Naomi that she is going out to glean, and "luck brought her" to Boaz' field. He makes her acquaintance and is gracious to her. When Naomi is informed of this in the evening, she declares: "Blessed be he by the Lord whose kindness (*ḥesed*) has not forsaken the living or the dead!" Naomi also said to her: "The man is a relative of ours, one of our nearest kin [from *g'l*]" (2:20).

There then follows the mysterious encounter at the threshing floor. In many subtle ways the storyteller intimates the danger involved for both Ruth and Boaz. Things could have turned out differently if either had been less resolved that *ḥesed* should be observed. That Ruth should take the risk she did shows the strength of her conviction that Boaz was "a man of substance" (2:1).

When Naomi begins to lay forth her plan she says: "Now is not Boaz our kinsman" (*moda'tanu*, a unique feminine noun from *yd'*, "to know"). Campbell states, "It seems to me inescapable that we be guided by the terms *m^e yudda* in 2:1 and *mg'lnw*, 'one of our circle of redeemers,' in 2:20." [10] Accordingly he translates it "one of our covenant circle." They are the larger entity of which *m^e yudda'* designates a single member.

When Boaz has his midnight surprise, Ruth says to him: "Now spread your skirt ("wing" of cloak) over your maidservant, for you are next of kin [*g'l*]" (3:9). Ruth's request of Boaz is marriage.

In the codes of law, no connection is drawn between marriage and redemption. The Deuteronomic Code gives a discrete levirate marriage law in Dt 25:5-10, while the Holiness Code gives a discrete redemption law in Lev 25:25 and 27:9-23. It is in the Book of Ruth that we find them united. From this it can be argued that (1) The Ruth storyteller wove his tale after the time of the codes of law, bringing together what the law codes had as separate, perhaps even as a primary purpose. (2) Ruth and Gen 38 (Judah and Tamar) come from a time prior to the formulation of the Deuteronomic law, which limits the application of the law to a smaller and more intimate family circle and relaxes its stringency. (3) The most likely approach is that we are not to think of one common legal code covering the whole land. What was decided in a civil case in one town could differ from what was decided in another. As for the law codes in the Torah, "they constitute political attempts under specific historical circumstances to normalize practice, probably mostly at the capital cities, but they can hardly be thought of as simply overpowering and setting aside the age-old traditional practices in a given outlying town." [11]

After their escape from bondage, Moses and the people sang to the Lord: "Thou hast led in thy steadfast love the people whom thou has redeemed" (Song of Moses, Ex 15:13). When Jacob imparted his last blessing to his sons, he praised God's angel as the one who "redeemed me from all evil" (Gen 48:16). This language is old enough to have been used about God very early in Israel's history with the full implication it bears in later legal formulations. God shows familial concern and protects both people and property (Israel is both to him!). This establishes the pattern for all human redemption. "Redeemers are to function on behalf of persons and their property within the circle of the larger family; they are to take responsibility for the unfortunate and stand as their supporters and advocates. They are to embody the basic principle of caring responsibility for those who may not have justice done for them by the unscrupulous, or even by the persons who live by the letter of the law." [12]

Levirate practice operates on the basis of two fundamental principles: first, the wife of a dead man is to be supported and protected, and, second, family property is to remain within the family. The practice is not simply concerned with producing a male child, nor even with producing an heir to the dead man's property. It is concerned every bit as much with the care of the widow. Indeed, the care of widows is the main motive of Naomi's speculations in chapter 1 about the prospects of levirate marriage for herself.

Therefore the basic principles underlying the Israelite use of the levirate practice are very much the same principles as those pertaining to redemption practice in general, and are in turn among the basic ones undergirding all Israelite law and custom. The juxtaposition of redemption and levirate practices in Ruth is a natural one. The fact that we can find no legal code that puts the two together is probably irrelevant and due as much to the paucity of our sources as to any other cause. The social framework in which levirate marriage functioned probably included both blood and covenant ties, the latter reaching out beyond family interests to a circle in which ties were entered upon even more voluntarily and graciously than might be the case in a family.

But the career of levirate marriage was to be a limited one. Redemption in general was to have a great career in the New Testament, but not levirate marriage. "That custom gradually fell into disuse and, in the case of the widow of one's brother, was even directly prohibited."[13]

Release from the obligation of levirate marriage is made possible through the ceremony of *halitzah*, described in Dt 25:7-10. In the Talmudic period, many rabbis, fearing improper motives in the fulfillment of this commandment, gave preference to *halitzah*, although subsequently there have been differences of opinion on this question. Maimonides upholds the custom and is followed in this respect by Sephardic communities. Others gave preference to *halitzah*, and this became the accepted custom among Ashkenazi communities.

There was a flaw in ancient Israelite redemption. As we said earlier, it worked well only if you belonged to a rich and powerful family. At one point it was suggested that the king should intervene in favor of the defenseless (Ps 72:14). But this remained largely wishful thinking. This experience, it would seem, began the transformation of the concept of redemption from a legal concept into a religious one.

As a consequence of the failure of the law, the social reformers placed their faith in God. They now declared that a man whose relatives were incapable of redeeming him, his land, or his blood would be helped by God himself. Many passages in the Bible represent God as redeeming the poor. Prov 23:10 reads: "Do not remove an ancient landmark or enter the fields of the fatherless; for their Redeemer [*g'l*] is strong; he will plead their cause against you." Here we are no longer entirely in the province of law but in the province of religion. "But it should be observed how closely at this stage the religious concept corresponds to the original legal concept. God, the loyal relative of the poor, redeems for them their property which the unjust thinks he can withhold from them for ever, just as, under the ordinary rules, a rich man would redeem what a kinsman of his has been deprived of. Even the concluding threat, 'He shall plead their cause with thee,' is in keeping with this description of God as maintaining the rights, at law, of a patron relative." [14]

The Proverbs passage involves the laws concerning the redemption of a man's property. But there are also passages that speak of the persecuted pious which ought to be interpreted as implying that God will also enforce the laws concerning the redemption of a murdered man's blood. These passages are especially important for the future history of the concept of redemption. Ps 9:13 is such a passage.

Westermann characterizes Psalm 9 as a "lament in transition to declarative praise." [15] Though in the midst of suffering (v. 13), the psalmist gives praise to the Lord because he has shown himself to be a redeemer of the defenseless. "For he who avenges blood [*doresh damim*] is mindful of them; he does not forget the cry of the afflicted" (v. 12). And in Psalm 119 we read: "Look on my affliction and deliver me, for I do not forget thy law. Plead my cause [*riba ha-ribi*] and redeem me [*g'l*]; give me life according to thy promise." [16]

The Lord God will not only enforce the laws concerning the redemption of a man's property. The two passages above "about the similar case of the persecuted pious, ought perhaps to be interpreted as implying that He will also enforce the laws concerning the redemption of a murdered man's blood." [17] In 9:12 the term *g'l* itself does not occur. "But this is not decisive. Psalm 9:13 (12), in particular, speaks of God as 'claiming the blood,' *drsh dmim* of murdered men, a phrase that may well come from the sphere of blood feud in which 'redemption,' the 'taking back,' of the victim's blood plays a prominent part." [18]

At any rate, the idea of God as redeemer of the blood of Israel became common in the writings of the Old Testament. It was not only the poor whom God was supposed to save as redeemer; for Old Testament writers God was the owner and relative of the whole people. Therefore, whenever the nation had to submit to the yoke of a conqueror, God could assert his claim. In most cases it is not clear exactly on what basis God redeems Israel; we are not told precisely in what capacity God buys back his people, whether as owner or as relative.

Yet this notion still reflects the original legal provisions about redemption. When their ancestors had actually been slaves to the Egyptians, God had stepped in, thus assuming the place of relative and owner. He would again and again, they concluded, exercise his right as relative and owner and deliver them from their tyrants. The great deliverance from Egypt was construed as a proper act of redemption, on the model of the ordinary social laws regarding the deliverance of slaves.

When God first announced the Exodus to Moses, he promised him: "I will give this people favor in the sight of the Egyptians; and when you go, you shall not go empty" (Ex 3:21). The "despoiling of the Egyptians" has its origin in Dt 15:13, which provides: "When you let a Hebrew slave go free from you, you shall not let him go empty-handed; you shall furnish him liberally." Through the liberation from Egypt, the Hebrews became the people of God or the slaves of God. Under the legislation found in the Bible, property redeemed by a relative does not belong to the redeeming relative. But "it is quite possible that, in a legislation earlier than that which we find in Leviticus, when a relative redeemed property or a slave, that property or man, up to the final year of release at any rate, fell to the redeemer."[19] When Jeremiah redeemed his cousin's field, he kept it as his own (32:6ff.).

In many cases laws are said to have been laid down because of the deliverance from Egypt. The laws concerning redemption were the main element in the interpretation of the Exodus, and the Exodus, thus interpreted, in turn influenced social legislation. "There is the ancient Hebrew social legislation on redemption; there is its application to the case of Egypt; and there is the exploitation of this case, thus construed, to provide the basis for the social legislation."[20]

In the Old Testament, besides the passages in the Law where redemption is used in the strict sense (buying back, taking back), it is often used of deliverance simply, either of Israel or of the individual. God acts as a worthy kinsman would do for the honor of his kin.

An intriguing text is found in Job 19. In the midst of his tribulations Job cries out: "Oh that my words were written! Oh that they were inscribed in a book! Oh that with an iron pen and lead they were graven in the rock forever! For I know that my Redeemer lives, and at last he will stand upon the earth; and after my skin has been thus destroyed, then from my flesh I shall see God" (vv. 23-26). Job wishes that his words were written in a book, on a copper scroll, inscribed on a cliff, which will resist the ravages of time, so that he may be vindicated by posterity. In his utmost destitution, rejected by friends, deprived of heirs, attacked by God, uncertain of future fame, Job's faith leaps for a moment to the certainty that after death his most cherished wish will be fulfilled. But who is the *go'el*? Job has already called for a mediator between God and man (9:33-35) and for a witness who will defend man before God (16:19-21). The *go'el* may be this Vindicator through whom Job hopes to obtain an audience with God himself (v. 26).

But others think that the *go'el* is God himself. "In Job xix.25, God is invoked as redeemer clearly because those who would be the natural, ordinary redeemers, brothers, relatives and friends, have failed: 'He hath put my brethren far from me . . . my kinsfolk have failed, and my familiar friends have forgotten me; they that dwell in mine house, and my maids, count me for a stranger' (19:13ff.). Moreover, the phrase 'he shall stand' refers to the standing up as claimant and witness in a law-suit." [21] A similar idea is expressed in Lam 3:55: "I called on thy name, O Lord, from the depths of the pit; thou didst hear my plea, 'Do not close thine ear to my cry for help!' . . . Thou hast seen the wrong done to me, O Lord; judge thou my cause." In "thou hast taken up my cause" Daube again sees a term of legal procedure.

Both texts, therefore, connect the metaphor of redemption by God with its legal basis. "This is not a mere linguistic curiosity, though it is true that language frequently reflects an earlier stratum which is no longer present in the mind of him who speaks. In this case, a good deal of the legal setting of ordinary redemption was taken over and adapted by priests and prophets even when they worked out redemption of the purely religious kind. We have also to consider that, while priests and prophets evolved the religious notion of redemption, the social laws with the legal notion continued all the time. Thus there remained a constant opportunity of relating the religious notion to its secular ancestor and again and again rejuvenating it in this way." [22]

In visions of final salvation God acts more frequently as the re-deemer of the enslaved and wrongfully withheld than as the redeemer of blood. Yet, the concept of God the redeemer of blood is far from uncommon. When God takes back captive Israel, he does it, in nearly all prophecies, not in a mild, quiet manner, but at the same time destroying the cruel oppressors. This has important New Testament consequences.

Ultimately the priests and prophets moved even farther from the original legal starting-point. They maintained that God would redeem the faithful not only from physical misfortune but also from the clutches of error, evil, and death. And those texts that emphasize the spiritual side of salvation allude primarily to redemption of a murdered man's blood. In the case of spiritual salvation, salvation from sin, the destruc-tion of the opposing party, of sin, is even more requisite than in the case of salvation from human enemies. As death and grave are to be utterly destroyed, the parallel with the redemption of a murdered man's blood, carried out by killing the murderer, is particularly appropriate.

When God redeems man from sin, he redeems not so much his body or property as his *nephesh*. "Just so it is the soul which, in the case of murder, has to be redeemed by the *go'el ha-dam*, the redeemer of blood. It may be recalled that the old law of retaliation begins, *nephesh tahat nephesh*, soul for soul. . . . The redeemer of blood 'redeems,' 'takes back,' the blood; that is to say, according to early notions, he frees the blood from evil masters, from the fetters in which the murderer has bound it, and thereby enables the soul to find its proper resting-place." [23]

The prophet Hosea advanced the idea of the Lord's freeing the blood, the soul, the persons of his own from the power of evil masters, and St. Paul proclaimed the fulfillment of this desire. Hosea threatened Israel with destruction, declaring that by casting Yahweh aside she had cast aside her chance to live. At the thought of it, the Lord cries out: "Shall I ransom them from the power of Sheol? Shall I redeem them from Death? O Death, where are your plagues? O Sheol, where is your destruction?" (13:14). Writing to the Corinthians about Christ's resurrection, St. Paul ends with a hymn of triumph over death. "Death is swallowed up in victory." "O death, where is thy victory? O death, where is thy sting?" (1 Cor 15:54f.).

Freely accommodating Hosea's words, Paul suggests the destruction of the enslaving evil power. Death has a sting like a serpent. "Sin has been vanquished by Christ the Redeemer. Thus death, like a serpent deprived of its venomous sting, can no longer harm those who are in Christ. Paul suggests this is due to the abrogation of the Law that gave sin its power by giving a knowledge of God's commandments and threatening death to the sinner, without giving the poor man the strength to keep them." [24]

When redeeming the soul from sin, God in a higher sense does the same as the redeemer of blood. Spiritual redemption from sin was likened by the prophets to redemption of a murdered man's blood rather more readily than to redemption of slaves or property. Thus it came about that the form of redemption which strikes us as most archaic, that undertaken by the go'el ha-dam, survived as the principal basis for the most advanced of all metaphorical references to redemption, for the metaphor of the spiritual redemption by God.

Spiritual redemption is the noblest of redemption. It is a redemption not from material sufferings, loss of land, or liberty or blood, but from moral, religious sufferings, iniquity, wickedness, and despair. First proclaimed in the Old Testament, this form of redemption was worked out and given new significance in the Gospels. Jesus reclaimed the world, not from material sufferings, but from the worse dangers of moral evil. Some of his followers thought that his aims were secular, and when they found out that they were not, they left him.

Jesus reclaimed the world from moral evil, offering himself as a ransom by vicarious satisfaction. And here, "it may be remarked, the legal substratum is far stronger than one might be inclined to think. When considering the history of vicarious sacrifice, it is important not to forget ancient legal institutions like that of 'rb, 'surety,' or the Roman vindex and sponsor, and ancient legal customs like that of taking hostages. It has never been properly investigated how far they may have influenced the religious development. The result that I wish to stress is that the idea of God or Jesus redeeming mankind from sin and damnation, apparently a purely religious idea, derives from those ancient rules on insolvent debtors and victims of murder, on the preservation of the existing clans and the patrimony of clans." [25]

Mk 10:43-45, about the ambition of the sons of Zebedee, is the key synoptic passage. James and John come to Jesus and ask to sit at his right and left in his glory. Jesus replies that while the rulers of Gentiles lord it over them, it shall not be so among his followers. Anyone who wants to be great shall be a servant. "Whoever would be great among you must be your servant (*diakonos*), and whoever would be first among you must be slave (*doulos*) of all. For the Son of Man also came not to be served but to serve, and to give his life as a ransom (*lutron*) for many" (10:43-45).

In the New Testament, *lutron* is found only here and in the Matthew parallel. Outside the Bible the word is used of the ransom of a prisoner of war or a slave. In the LXX (almost always in the plural) it represents, with one exception, one of our redemption roots (*kpr, pdh, g'l*). It denotes the half-shekel poll tax (Ex 30:12); the money a man paid to redeem his life, which was forfeit because his ox had killed someone (Ex 31:30); the price paid for the redemption of the firstborn (Num 18:15); the money by which the next of kin ransomed an enslaved relative (Lev 25:51); or the payment for the redemption of a mortgaged property (Lev 25:26).

But while *kpr* (*g'l, pdh*) may underlie the thought of Mk 10:45, another Hebrew word, never represented by *lutron* in the LXX, probably contributed to the use of *lutron* here — "guilt-offering" (*'asam*). This word is used in Is 53:10 ("when he makes himself an *offering for sin*"), and it seems likely that Jesus had this passage in mind. The use of *diakonein* seems to point to a reference to the Servant, and "for many" looks like an echo of the repeated *rabbim* in Is 53. Jesus was "thinking of himself as the Servant who was to suffer vicariously for the sins of others. But the meaning of his vicarious suffering and his giving himself as a *lutron* to his Father cannot be read off from any Old Testament passages, but must be understood (insofar as it can be understood at all by us) from the actual history of his passion." [26]

Writing to the Corinthians, St. Paul urges them to shun immorality. Their bodies are members of Christ, and they must not make them members of a prostitute. "You are not your own; you were bought with a price" (1 Cor 6:20). John Ruef writes that "the reference is a rather crass one. Paul probably has in mind the price paid to the prostitute in return for her services. This would still be the case if one were to accept Hering's thesis of the temple prostitute. The price then would be worship of the temple deity. 'You are the one,' says Paul, 'who has been bought (by

God), therefore you owe your body to him and the service which he requires is his glorification.' This is not a very delicate way of putting it, but the Corinthians were probably not very delicate people." [27] H. Conzelmann also notes: "The metaphor is not developed. The point is merely that you belong to a new master. Beyond this the metaphor should not be pressed." [28] Yet he does not keep it separate from the idea of redemption. "The interpretation of redemption in the sense of ransom is presumably traditional; it is found again in 7:23 (cf. Gal 3:13; 4:5)." And Ruef notes: "Most commentators attempt to relate this 'purchase' motif to the 'ransom' motif used elsewhere by Paul (Rom 3:24) and the Gospel tradition (Mark 10:45), or the 'substitution' idea of Gal 3:13."

Arguing from Scripture that justification is by faith and not by works, St. Paul writes to the Galatians that "all who rely on works of the law are under a curse. . . . Christ redeemed us from the curse of the law, having become a curse for us — for it is written, 'Cursed be every one who hangs on a tree'" (3:10, 13).

For J. Fitzmyer, the effects of the salvation event are reconciliation, expiation, justification, and redemptive liberation. And another notion often linked with redemptive liberation is that of "acquisition, possession." Yahweh not only freed the Hebrews from Egyptian bondage but acquired a people for himself, especially through the covenant of Sinai. It was a deliverance that terminated in acquisition, and even in adoption.

> In Gal (3:13; 4:5) Paul uses *exagorazō* to describe the freedom from the Law that the Christ-event has brought about. . . . This rare word is never used in the LXX in a context of manumission, nor is it ever found in any extrabiblical texts referring to sacral manumission. It is a compound of *agorazō* and usually means to do more than 'to buy.' However, it is used by Diodorus Siculus (36:2) of the buying of a slave (as a possession) and again (15:7) of the setting free of an enslaved person by purchase. In the latter context, though there is no mention of *lytron*, it is obviously a case of ransoming someone enslaved. If then, the notion of ransom by purchase is applied to Paul's use of the word, one should avoid overstressing the juridical details, since his full notion of 'redemption' is colored by the OT idea of 'acquisition.' Paul never calls Christ *lytrōtēs* (redeemer-goel, this word is used only of Moses, Acts 7:35); nor does he ever speak of *lytron* (ransom) as such. He calls Christ Jesus 'our redemption' (*apolytrōsis*, 1 Cor 1:30) in a majestic phrase that identifies the person of Christ with his deliverance and sums up a Pauline view of Christ. But it is important to note that even though it is 'through the redemption which is in Christ Jesus' (Rom 3:24) that men obtain the remission of their sins (cf. Col 1:14; Eph 1:7), yet it is specifically 'a redemption of acquisition' (Eph 1:14). [30]

"Christ redeemed us from the curse of the law, having become a curse for us" (Gal 3:13).

Christ has bought us [Jewish Christians especially] from the curse of the Law. The Law with its manifold prescriptions enslaved man, and from this enslavement man has been delivered by Christ's "purchase" (1 Cor 6:20). Like Yahweh of the Old Testament who through his covenant "acquired" his people (Ex 19:5), so Christ by his covenant blood, shed on the cross, "bought" his people. This purchase, however, emancipated the new people of God from the Law and its curse; through faith in Christ Christians have become "free" (Gal 5:1). . . .

After the fashion of a rabbinical logic, Paul passes from one meaning of "curse" to another: from the curse on the man who does not observe all the Law's prescriptions to a specific curse uttered in the Law against a man hung on a tree (Dt 21:23). . . . The verse must be understood in connection with 2:19: Christ was crucified "through the Law." In dying as one on whom a curse of the Law fell, Paul sees Christ embodying the totality of the Law's curse "for us" (just how he does not say). But he died to the Law, and in his death we died vicariously; he put an end to the Law with its prescriptions (Eph 2:15), and became the "end of the Law" (Rom 10:4). So Mosaic observance and Christian living are henceforth incompatible."[31]

The author of First Peter recalls the significance of God's deeds in Christ (1:3-12), and on this basis he exhorts his readers to holiness. "You know that you were ransomed from the futile ways inherited from your fathers, not with perishable things such as silver or gold, but with the precious blood of Christ, like that of a lamb without blemish or spot" (1:18-19).

The Christian's redemption has been realized through the death of Jesus Christ. This has brought about a liberation from the religious futility that converts inherited from their fathers. In striking contrast to this existence lived in utter loss is set the invaluable price of their redemption, which so marvelously lends value to life in faith. "You know that you were ransomed from the futile ways inherited from your fathers . . . with the precious blood of Christ" (1 Pet 1:19).

NOTES

1. In *Studies in Biblical Law* (Cambridge: Cambridge University Press, 1947) 1–73.
2. *Ibid.*, 27.
3. *Ibid.*, 31.
4. *Ibid.*, 39.
5. *Ibid.*, 42.
6. *Ibid.*, 46.
7. E. Campbell, *Ruth*, The Anchor Bible (Garden City, N.Y.: Doubleday, 1975) 30.
8. See Z. Scharfstein, *Shilo Dictionary*, 127: *yabem*, "to marry deceased brother's wife"; *y^{e}bamah, y^{e}bemet*, "brother's wife, woman obliged to marry her deceased husband's brother."
9. Campbell, *op. cit.*, 90.
10. *Ibid.*, 117.
11. *Ibid.*, 134.
12. *Ibid.*, 136.
13. *Studies in Biblical Law, op. cit.*, 54.
14. *Ibid.*, 46f.
15. C. Westermann, *The Praise of God in the Psalms*, trans. Keith Crim (Richmond: John Knox Press, 1965) 79.
16. *Ibid.*, 153f.
17. *Studies in Biblical Law, op. cit.*, 47.
18. *Ibid.*
19. *Ibid.*, 51.
20. *Ibid.*, 53.
21. *Ibid.*, 57.
22. *Ibid.*
23. *Ibid.*, 58.
24. R. Kugelman, "The First Letter to the Corinthians," *JBC* II, 274.
25. *Studies in Biblical Law, op. cit.*, 59.
26. C. Cranfield, *The Gospel According to Saint Mark* (Cambridge: Cambridge University Press, 1959) 342.
27. J. Ruef, *Paul's First Letter to Corinth* (Baltimore: Penguin Books, 1971) 51.
28. H. Conzelmann, *1 Corinthians* (Philadelphia: Fortress Press, 1975) 113.
29. Ruef, *op. cit.*, 51.
30. J. Fitzmyer, "Pauline Theology," *JBC* II, 816–817.
31. J. Fitzmyer, "The Letter to the Galatians," *JBC* II, 242.

Bruce Vawter, C.M.

SALVATION IS A FAMILY AFFAIR

A difficulty for Christian piety which has also often been the occasion of unhappy distortions of Christian theology is that otherwise beautiful word in the vocabulary of salvation which we know as "redemption." "Redemption," of course, when we look it up in a dictionary, means "to buy back," to regain something or someone that has been held in bond against a price that has now been paid. "You are not your own," Paul told the Corinthians. "You have been purchased, and at a price" (1 Cor 6:19-20). And in the somewhat parallel 1 Pet 1:18-19 it is said that the purchase price of our redemption was neither silver nor gold but the far more precious blood of Christ.

To say that the concept of redemption has disturbed Christian piety and distorted Christian theology may sound very negative in the face of the demonstrated fact of how much it has also enriched and nourished them both: "I know that my Redeemer liveth!" One would certainly not want to belabor or to exaggerate the negative. Nevertheless, who has not at times been uneasy when praying to a merciful Father who — we were told — had relieved his creatures of the terrible burden of their sins only after he had exacted a satisfactory price which they were unable to pay and which had to be paid for them instead by the death of his only Son? The same Son, be it noted, who exhorted his followers to treat friends and enemies with equal love, to return good for evil, to forgive without counting the times or the merits of those who must be forgiven. Surely the Christian must sometimes have come to the conclusion that a rather higher degree of disinterested compassion was expected of him or her than had been demonstrated by the divine Being who is Author of the Christian existence.

What caused this malaise in popular piety and, as we have said, sometimes in serious theology as well was the fallacy that comes so easily to us — the fallacy of trying to turn metaphor and analogy into literal reality. A kindred example of the misunderstanding of metaphor that has led both piety and theology down ways that are now seen as unde-

65

sirable despite original good intentions is the masculine language habitually applied to Deity in the Bible and the religions derived from it. God as our Father, for instance, was certainly a figure of speech intended first and foremost to epitomize divine love in a way that could hardly be equivalently conveyed by expressing the relationship as one of Creator to creatures; and, in Christian theology at least, the figure of God the Father cannot be separated from that of Son and Spirit as manifesting an archetypal love that is exemplary for the Christian life. Yet we know, when we think about it carefully, that God is neither man as male nor man as human, that God is sexless, that God is not, therefore, a father as we know fathers in our human condition. But we do not always think carefully, and as a result we can ignore the presence of analogy and therefore confuse the analogy with the truth that it was only pointing to. That is what has happened too often when we thought about "redemption."

What does it really mean when we say that God or Christ has "redeemed" us? According to the New Testament, the redemption we have in Christ is the forgiveness of our sins (Col 1:14), a gift of God to us (Rom 3:24). It is an act of grace and mercy, not the result of a commercial transaction, and if, by metaphor, some price is mentioned, it has been only to insist, as our better theologians have always understood, that redemption was and is a serious business which therefore *cost much* (again an unavoidable metaphor).

The New Testament has had no source for its redemptive language, for the way in which it figures redemption and salvation, other than the Old Testament. Therefore it may prove to be instructive if we consider one of the more important of the Old Testament metaphors of salvation, that of *gā'al*, redeem, *gō'ēl*, redeemer, and *gě'ullâ*, redemption. Not only will this consideration help put the theological concept of redemption in proper perspective, it will soon become evident that there are dimensions to it as appear from its Old Testament roots that are all too often lost in its casual use in Christian language. It is not, be it noted, the only Old Testament term and concept employed in the language of redemptive salvation, but, as will immediately appear, it is certainly one of the most suggestive and theologically rewarding.

Gā'al, *gō'ēl*, and *gě'ullâ* are, we acknowledge at the outset, commercial language, and the metaphor they apply to salvation is a commercial metaphor; but it is commercial in a very special way, unlike, for example, other terms and concepts used with equal frequency, like *qānâ*, which merely means to buy or acquire, or *pādâ*, which means to free, that is, to free a slave, which was done customarily by purchase. This commercial metaphor with which we are dealing came out of no highly organized mercantile society such as was Israel in its imperial days or even in its less imperial days when it was nevertheless part of the ancient Near Eastern imperial system of Assyria or Babylonia or Persia. It came, rather, from the simpler days of Israelite society when the family, and the extended family in clan or tribe, were all that made up society. As far as we know, *gĕ'ullâ* was something peculiarly Israelite, and the term did not exist in the other Semitic languages cognate with Hebrew.

One of the best examples we have of *gĕ'ullâ* in action — here not directly in a theological sense — is in chapter 32 of the Book of Jeremiah. In this instance, while the city of Jerusalem was under siege by the Chaldeans who would eventually conquer it and lay it waste, a certain Hanamel, cousin to the prophet Jeremiah, came to him and said: "Please buy my field in Anathoth [the town near Jerusalem which was Jeremiah's ancestral home], in the district of Benjamin; as nearest relative, you have the first claim to possess it; make it yours"(Jer 32:8). Jeremiah, though he had prophesied a Chaldean triumph and, in fact, had been taken into custody for his pains by the Jerusalemite king who regarded him as a defeatist and a national liability, acceded to his cousin's request. He did so to testify that though now his people must suffer foreign domination in punishment of their sins against their God, the time of restoration would also come through the mercy of this same God. "Just as I brought upon this people all this great evil, so I will bring upon them all the good I promise them. Fields shall again be bought in this land, which you call a desert, without man or beast, handed over to the Chaldeans. Fields shall be bought with money, deeds written and sealed, and witnesses shall be used in the land of Benjamin, in the suburbs of Jerusalem, in the cities of Judah and of the hill country, in the cities of the foothills and of the Negeb, when I change their lot, says the LORD" (Jer 32:42-44).

What we are interested in here is the familial background of this transaction. The "nearest relative" of whom Hanamel spoke is our *gō'ēl*, literally, "redeemer" or "vindicator," or, as we shall see in a moment, even "avenger." In a society which predated centralized authority and depended for its stability on that of the family, maintenance of the family inheritance was a prime consideration. Society was threatened when family property was alienated, when the family unit of society was put in jeopardy by being deprived of the natural means of its independent subsistence and exposed to the sufferance of outsiders. So it was that the "nearest relative," like Jeremiah in this case, had the moral obligation to "redeem" the family property from the threat of alien hands. It is this same concern that motivates the property-redemption legislation in about twenty-five passages of Lev 25 and 27. Also the action of Boaz with regard to the inheritance of Naomi in a score of passages in Ruth 2-4 — a situation complicated in this instance by the concurrent issue of the marriage of Boaz with Naomi's daughter-in-law Ruth, something that probably originally had nothing to do with *gĕ'ullâ*.

The *gō'ēl*, however, did not play the merely passive role of stepping in to prevent by his prior claim a family embarrassment. His function could be also quite positive, employing force, if need be, to stave off alien encroachments (see Prov 23:11). And his obligation extended to the family honor as well as to its property, for the "name" which was the identity of the family consisted in more than the material things it possessed. Thus, in an age which pre-existed courts of law, judicial processes, and orderly punitive processes, the gō'ēl might be called upon to take the only measure that could guarantee some semblance of vindictive justice by becoming the "avenger" of a slain kinsman (see Jos 20:3, 5, 9 and 2 Sam 14:11). The mingling of property "vindication" with blood "vengeance" in the legislation of Num 35:12-27, Dt 19:6, 12, etc., indicates how closely associated and even identified these functions were in the thought of ancient Israel.

And so, with this background, we come to understand how the God of Israel could come to be regarded as Israel's gō'ēl, and how, centuries later, the New Testament could in the same spirit conceive of a redemption by this same God that would affect not the Hebrew people only but a people of God which, potentially at least, is the whole of the human race he created.

When did this metaphor first come to be applied theologically in relation to God's salvation of his people? First of all, it is very easy to say who was the first to make a great thing of it, to constitute it a cornerstone of his theological edifice. That person, beyond question, is the anonymous prophet of Israel's exile whom we customarily term the Second Isaiah, who is responsible directly for chapters 40–55 of the Book of Isaiah and also, directly and indirectly, for some passages in the so-called Trito–Isaiah sections of Is 56–66 or even such a "Proto-Isaianic" verse as Is 35:9. This prophet, who was also, as far as we know, the first thinker to conceive of God's creative action as a work of salvation — an idea that was taken up by the Priestly author of the "first" creation story in Gen 1:1–2:4a — likewise in about twenty-five instances figures the God of Israel as its gō'ēl in redeeming it from captivity. (It may be thought interesting that the Second Isaiah always uses in this connection forms of the verb gā'al but never the substantive gĕ'ullâ. The phenomenon would doubtless reward investigation. Neither does the Gospel of John, much concerned with faith, ever employ the substantive for this concept but always the verb "believe.")

Was the Second Isaiah (who must have flourished sometime between the years 587–535 B.C.) anticipated in this theology? The response to this question, unfortunately, must remain uncertain because the evidence is ambiguous. The concept appears in a number of Psalms (Pss 19:15; 69:19; 72:14; 74:2; 77:16; 106:10; 107:2; 119:154), most of which, if not all, are of postexilic composition and subject, therefore, to the influence of Second Isaiah. It appears in Jer 31:11, which could be authentically the work of Jeremiah, written out of a situation not unlike the Second Isaiah's but also, like Jer 50:34, could be a later addition to the Book of Jeremiah. It appears in Ex 15:13, as part of the "Song of the Sea," an ancient poem which, nevertheless, has undergone a great deal of later elaboration, and in Ex 6:6, a "Priestly" passage which, we have already noted, manifests a theology much dependent on the Second Isaiah. It appears in Lam 3:58, beyond question a postexilic passage that could hardly have escaped the influence of the great exilic prophet. But it also appears in Gen 48:16, and in Hos 13:14 and Mic 4:10, passages which nobody will lightly dismiss as obviously recent additions to the Old Testament documents and which instead may be very ancient indeed.

(We are leaving out of consideration possibly the most famous theological usage of *gō'ēl* in the Old Testament, that of Job 19:25. "I know that my Vindicator lives," reads the New American Bible, indicating by its capitalization that God is the *gō'ēl* that Job had in mind. But did he? The scholars cannot agree on the meaning of this enigmatic verse, and for this reason, if for no other, we are prepared to declare it out of bounds for our present discussion. Job may have had in mind a totally different theology, as unique to that book as the book itself is unique in the Old Testament.)

There is nothing repugnant in the view that it was, in fact, the Second Isaiah who first thought of Israel's God as its *gō'ēl* and, in doing so, reached back to authentic Israelite roots that were no less valid for having been neglected for several centuries. After all, it was the Second Isaiah alone of the prophets (except perhaps for his contemporary Ezekiel, one time) who has mentioned the patriarch Abraham. The patriarch Jacob, who gave his name Israel to a people, appears in the prophetic literature notably elsewhere only in Hos 12, and there in a posture that is hardly flattering. Outside the Book of Genesis the patriarchal history of Israel's remote beginnings hardly turns up in Hebrew literature until the time of Second Isaiah.

What we are saying is that in Second Isaiah's time, a time when Israel had lost the sureties of its earlier age that had been summarized in land and temple and kingship, other sureties had to take their place. Such new sureties could be, at first glance, fairly trivial: the Sabbath rest, for example, or circumcision, or other externals such as the dietary laws governing kosher food, all of which served to preserve and emphasize religious identity. The anthropologist Mary Douglas in her study of the "bog Irish" in England has shown how, in a kindred cultural context, such externals have exercised a stabilizing and unifying force that demonstrates them to be anything but trivial. It will be remembered that it is the Priestly creation story of Genesis that represents the Creator God as completing the ordered world in a work-week of six days and then resting on the seventh day, thus sanctifying the Sabbath for humanity by his example. And it is in the Priestly version of the story of the covenant God made with Abraham (Gen 17) that circumcision is featured as the sign and seal of this "everlasting covenant" between God and Abraham's descendants.

Traditional religious externals, a traditional remote patriarchal age to which it was profitable to recall a people's hearts and minds, and language that pictured a saving God acting the role of a traditional family redeemer, all these are parts of a single whole. It would be an exaggeration to pretend, in the last instance, that Second Isaiah represented God as *gō'ēl* only to make of salvation a "family" affair. As a matter of fact, the parallels in which *gā'al* is set in these prophetic writings show that in his theology the word has a far wider and richer significance than this.

For one thing, Second Isaiah's pairing off of the ideas of salvation and creation — another example he set for the Priestly theologian — is in the minds of many a far more suggestive and profound contribution to Old Testament soteriology than this one we have been discussing. Neither, however, should we minimize the importance of this one. When, as he often does (e.g., in Is 43:14), he identifies the *gō'ēl* as "the Holy One of Israel," his hearers could not have failed to be reminded that the God who had created and redeemed them was none other than the God of the patriarchs, the God who was known as the familiar of their fathers Abraham, Isaac, and Jacob (Israel). (Even as the Priestly theologian in Ex 3:15 is careful to have it made known to Moses that Yahweh, the name under which God would be known in the historical experience of the people of Israel, was indeed the patriarchal God of Abraham, Isaac, and Jacob.)

Also, if the late William F. Albright was correct in his interpretation of the divine title used in Gen 31:53 and 31:42, the exilic prophet could also have been evoking by this means a strikingly similar designation of the patriarchal God that had been made long ago. The title, *paḥad* of Isaac, is frequently translated "Fear of Isaac," but few have ever been really happy with this translation. On the basis of some comparative language evidence, Albright thought it should rather be translated "Kinsman of Isaac," and in this opinion he has been followed by numerous other scholars.

It is hoped that this brief exploration of a small bit of Old Testament salvational theology will have been of help to the reader in putting into proper perspective the ways in which the people of Israel thought of their redeeming God, ways which were not always of awe and dread but also of familiarity and family feeling.

Bernhard W. Anderson

SIN AND THE POWERS OF CHAOS

In the familiar story of the Garden of Eden, found in the first book of the Bible, the serpent is portrayed in a strangely ambiguous manner. This villain in the plot displays hostility toward God, seduces the woman and man with a clever theological argument, and in the end is punished with a heavy divine curse. Yet the text states explicitly that the serpent is only one of the wild creatures that Yahweh God has formed from the ground (Gen 3:1; cf. 2:19). The ambiguities in the portrayal probably reflect tensions between traditional elements used by the narrator and the present form of the story. The "Satanic" aspect of the serpent, which prompts William Heidt to say that "this was no ordinary garden snake" but the figurative representative of "an outside evil influence," [1] is undoubtedly a holdover from earlier mythical tradition in which the serpent (or dragon) was regarded as a divine being, at the head of the powers of evil and chaos, who was hostile to the creator god. In the present form of the story, however, the serpent has been radically demythologized, with the result that he is scarcely more than "a literary tool used to pose the issue of life and death" for human beings. [2] The narrator does not intend to exculpate the man and woman by suggesting that evil has its origin in some power external to the human will. Rather, the emphasis falls upon the freedom of human beings to rebel against the Creator's command and the tragic consequences of the misuse of their God-given freedom. This is a story about "sin," not about the wider dimensions of the evil that corrupts human history or the cosmos.

On the other hand, when we turn to the last book of the Christian Bible, the Apocalypse of John, we find that the serpent has regained his former mythical status. In the Christian Apocalypse the serpent is not a mere beast of the field, distinguished from other animals by his cunning (see Mt 10:16, "as wise as serpents"). Instead, the serpent symbolizes the power of evil, external to the sphere of human freedom, that is demonically at work in the course of history, namely, "that ancient serpent, who is called the Devil and Satan, the deceiver of the whole world" (Rev 12:9). In language reminiscent of the Canaanite myth of Baal's victory over Leviathan, the Primeval Serpent, this sinister force is portrayed as "a great red dragon, with seven heads" (Rev 12:3; see 27:1; Ps 74:12-19).[3] Here the Serpent is the archenemy of God, the leader of the hosts of chaos, who foments a rebellion that spreads through the whole creation. Given this larger understanding of the problem of evil, it follows that God's victory through his chosen agent, Jesus the Messiah, is more than deliverance from the bondage of sin. God's saving work also includes deliverance from the uncanny powers of chaos, manifest in oppressive institutions (the autocratic state) or imperial ambitions, that victimize the "meek" of the earth and plunge human history into suffering and catastrophe.

The purpose of this essay is to trace in broad outline the theological movement that leads from "the serpent in the Garden" to "the dragon in the Sea," with the intention of understanding more fully the Christian gospel of God's deliverance of his people from sin and the powers of chaos.

I

The Bible is the story of a people who dared to believe in the real presence of God in spite of all appearances and arguments to the contrary. For both Jew and Christian, the word *Immanuel*, meaning "God with us," is a central affirmation of faith. The God of the Bible is neither totally beyond history nor completely immanent within the process of human history; rather, to use the language of the prophet Hosea, Yahweh is "the Holy One in your midst" (Hos 11:9b). It is precisely this affirmation of faith, however, that prompts serious reflection and even questions about God's ways.[4] How can people of faith believe in God's real presence in the face of rampant injustice and terrible human suffering? The opening cry of a psalm of lament, which came to Jesus' lips on the cross, finds a poignant echo in the lives of many: "My God, my God, why hast thou forsaken me?" (Ps 22:1). The problem of "evil" is the final test for any religion or philosophy.

Many of the sufferings of the world can be explained by the concept of sin. This is the interpretation that is given in the opening part of the Bible (Gen 1–11). In the sketch of Primeval History, the flaw in God's creation is traced to human freedom. The first man and woman were fully responsible for their deed, and no "extenuating circumstance" exonerated them for their misuse of freedom. Moreover, actions had inescapable consequences. The rebellion in the garden set in motion a chain reaction of events that spread out from the family into the world and led to the sad state of affairs with which the flood story begins: God's creation was spoiled by violence (Gen 6:11-12).

This is a true story, not because it presents accurate ancient history, but because it portrays realistically the world in which we live: a world in which human beings are called to responsibility and in which their actions have inescapable consequences. In a profound sense, we are "in Adam," the type who represents humanity in its sin and failure. And yet one does not have to read very far beyond the Primeval History before this explanation of suffering and disaster proves to be insufficient. Those who in faith believed God's promise to go with his people on their journey into the future raised questions.

An illustration of "honest-to-God" questioning is found in a story concerning Abraham's dialogue with Yahweh on the eve of a holocaust: the total destruction of Sodom and Gomorrah (Gen 18:16-23). Well before Abraham's time, if we may believe reports concerning the contents of tablets found recently in the ruins of ancient Ebla (in Syria), these two thriving cities engaged in commercial relations with the kingdom of Ebla, which flourished some 2500 years before the Christian era. Located on a geological fault that runs through the Jordan Valley, Sodom and Gomorrah apparently were inundated during a seismic upheaval that changed the boundaries of the Dead Sea. The biblical narrator, however, does not suggest a "naturalistic" explanation of the disaster; for undoubtedly he would have asked rhetorically with Amos: "Does evil befall a city unless Yahweh has done it?" (Am 3:6b) Rather, the narrative expresses concern about a theological question: the question about the point where human responsibility and divine judgment meet.

The story opens with a soliloquy in which Yahweh says that he is going to take Abraham into his confidence. After all, Abraham is the bearer of the promise that will yield blessing for all nations; and he has been made responsible for teaching his descendants "to keep the way of Yahweh by doing righteousness and justice." He ought to know, then, that "because the outcry against Sodom and Gomorrah is great and their sin is grave," Yahweh is about to act (Gen 18:17-21). Abraham, however, is not satisfied with Yahweh's determination to destroy the cities and specifically protests the indiscriminate destruction of the righteous along with the wicked. Suppose there are fifty righteous persons in the city? Forty-five? Forty? With great courtesy and deference, he presses his question until the number is finally reduced to ten, each time gaining a concession that Yahweh would not destroy the whole city if a certain number of righteous persons were in it. The heart of Abraham's expostulation with God is the question: "Shall not the Judge (*Shopeṭ*) of all the earth do justice (*mishpaṭ*)?"

It would be easy to translate Abraham's question into modern experiences: the holocaust that consumed six million Jews, the atomic destruction of Hiroshima and Nagasaki, the terrible destruction of life and land in Vietnam, the crushing injustice that falls on people in urban ghettos, etc. It is inconceivable, so the children of Abraham maintain, that Yahweh, whose saving intention is manifest in the history of his people, would do anything else than obtain justice. Admittedly, Sodom and Gomorrah were sinful cities; but did the punishment fit the crime? Interestingly, the biblical narrator rounds off the story of the imminent destruction of the cities of the Jordan plain with the laconic remark: "Yahweh went his way" and "Abraham returned to his place." The question was left hanging in the air.

The story of Abraham's expostulation with God is akin to other literature of protest, including Jeremiah's confessions, psalms of lament, and above all the Book of Job. In literature of this kind there is no disposition to ignore the depth and pervasiveness of human sin and the need of divine forgiveness. The insistent question is whether the doctrine of sin provides a fully adequate explanation of the human predicament or of divine salvation.

II

To sense the sharp point of this question, which was felt sensitively in the period of the Exile and subsequently, let us consider two of Israel's theological perspectives that sought to articulate God's presence in the midst of his people. In the Old Testament the key term for expressing the relationship between God and people is *berith*, "covenant." The term expresses both the divine initiative in establishing the relationship and the obligation that devolves on the responding people. Salvation and obligation are interpreted with different theological nuances in two major covenant "theologies" of the Old Testament, namely, those associated with Moses and David.

The Mosaic covenant is set forth fundamentally in the Torah Story (Pentateuch). The materials found in this canonical unit of Israel's scriptures, known in Christian circles as "the Old Testament," are very complex and betray evidence of having undergone a long history of tradition before receiving their present form. At the heart of the tradition, however, is a story of liberation. When a band of slaves, helpless and hopeless pawns in the imperial politics of ancient Egypt, cried for release from oppression, Yahweh the God of their ancestors sensed their suffering, heard their cry, and opened a way out of a no-exit situation (Ex 3:7-8). Beholden to their liberating God, who gave them freedom, identity, and a future, the people were responsible to obey his covenant stipulations (the Decalogue and its casuistic elaboration). Good news of salvation (gospel) is the basis of liturgical and ethical obligation (law).

The classical exposition of the Mosaic covenant is presented in the Book of Deuteronomy, the perspective of which dominates the so-called Deuteronomistic History extending from Joshua through 2 Kings. In this theological view, the people of Israel, having been graciously liberated from bondage and oppression, are called to full responsibility before God under the sanctions of the blessing and the curse, of well-being and disaster. Yahweh chose to bind himself to the people and to involve himself in their history; but this divine-human relationship could be threatened, if not annulled, by the people's behavior. In this covenant theology the word "if" is very important: "If you will obey my voice and keep my covenant . . ." (Ex 19:5-6). This covenant conditional is emphasized in the proclamation of Deuteronomy, for instance, in a climactic passage which begins:

> See, I have set before you this day life and good, death and evil. If you obey the commandments of Yahweh your God which I command you this day. . . . then you shall live and multiply, and Yahweh your God will bless you in the land which you are entering to take possession of it (Dt 30:15-16).

The Mosaic preacher then turns to the ominous alternative: "But if your heart turns away, and you will not hear. . . ." (Dt 30:17-18). The upshot is a call to decision *today*:

> I call heaven and earth to witness against you this day, that I have set before you life and death, blessing and curse; therefore choose life, that you and your descendants may live, loving Yahweh your God, obeying his voice, and cleaving to him . . . (Dt 30:19-20).

In popular piety, then as now, this kind of covenant theology could easily degenerate into a simple doctrine of rewards and punishments: If you obey God, all will go well; if not, expect trouble. The great prophets who stood in the Mosaic covenant tradition, chiefly Hosea and Jeremiah, did not cater to this simplistic gospel. Jeremiah, for instance, stressed the conditional "if" of the Mosaic covenant (e.g., Jer 4:1-2). But his preaching for repentance was informed by a profound awareness of the deceitfulness of the "heart" (that is, mind and will), or as we might say, reason's power to rationalize (Jer 17:9); and his penetration into the human problem was matched by a new awareness of the power of divine grace, which, acting through catastrophe, frees the will from bondage and makes possible a new beginning, a new covenant.

It is noteworthy, however, that prophets who stood in the tradition of the Mosaic covenant did not allow any explanation of suffering and disaster that would exonerate God's people. Not once did they suggest that some sinister power of evil, external to Israel's life, seduced and victimized the people. They made no reference to Satan or to any demonic power at work in Israel's history. On the contrary, in their preaching the people were held to be fully responsible and therefore fully culpable. Hence, when Yahweh's judgment fell upon Israel in the form of a foe from the north, the people had no one to blame for the catastrophe but themselves. "Your ways and your doings have brought this upon you," Jeremiah proclaimed; "this is your doom [ra'ah: "evil, disaster"], and it is bitter; it has reached your very heart" (Jer 4:18).

Prophets of this theological persuasion preached for repentance — for a change of lifestyle that would demonstrate a turning away from false loyalties ("gods") and a return to Yahweh, the God of the covenant.[5] With amazing consistency, they interpreted Israel's sufferings in the political arena as *deserved punishment for sin*. But this covenant theology proved to be inadequate to face the terrible sufferings that Israel experienced in connection with the event of 587 B.C.: the fall of Jerusalem and the exile of much of the population into Babylonia. This situation is reflected in Psalm 44, a communal lament in which the people protest that God's punishment is not commensurate with their sin.

> Thou hast made us like sheep for slaughter,
>   and hast scattered us among the nations.
> Thou hast sold thy people for a trifle,
>   demanding no high price for them.
>
> . . . .
>
> All this has come upon us,
>   though we have not forgotten thee,
>   or been false to thy covenant.
> Our heart has not turned back,
>   nor have our steps departed from thy way. . . . (Ps 44:11-12, 17-18).

The lament concludes with a petition that includes the question of whether God was really present in their midst.

> Why dost thou hide thy face?
> Why dost thou forget our affliction and oppression? (Ps 44:24)

III

The troubles of history also made it difficult to understand the presence of God in the theological perspective of the Davidic covenant which is set forth classically in 2 Sam 7:4-17 (Nathan's oracle to David) and which dominates the Chronicler's History (1–2 Chronicles). According to the terms of this covenant, Yahweh bound himself unconditionally to the Davidic king in an "everlasting covenant" (*berit 'olam*) or covenant in perpetuity, thereby assuring Israel of dynastic continuity and social stability despite changes of administration or threats from foreign foes. Furthermore, Yahweh chose the temple of Zion to be the place where he was present in the midst of his worshiping people just as, correspondingly, he was enthroned in his heavenly temple (cf. Is 6:1-8). Thus God's presence in the midst of his people was connected with two salvific institutions, Davidic kingship and Zion temple, both of which Yahweh had "elected" (Ps 78:67-72). The eighth-century prophet Isaiah of Jerusalem was profoundly influenced by these twin convictions of royal covenant theology, as evidenced by his portrayal of the Anointed One who will bear the name Immanuel (Is 7:14-17; 8:5-8) and rule peacefully on the throne of David (9:2-7), and his concern for the inviolable security of Zion (31:4-5; 37:33-35).

According to this covenant theology, suffering is understood as Yahweh's discipline or correction. A conditional "if" qualifies Yahweh's everlasting covenant with king and, through the mediatorial king, with the people. If the king in his exercise of power were to commit iniquity, then Yahweh would "chasten him with the rod of men, with the stripes of the sons of men" (2 Sam 7:14b), but he would not remove his *hesed* or covenant loyalty from him (2 Sam 7:15a). A psalmist elaborates the themes of Nathan's oracle to David:

> If his children forsake my law,
>   and do not walk according to my ordinances,
> if they violate my statutes
>   and do not keep my commandments,
> then I will punish their transgression with the rod
>   and their iniquity with scourges;
> but I will not remove from him my steadfast love [*hesed*],
>   or be false to my faithfulness.
> I will not violate my covenant,
>   or alter the word that went forth from my lips (Ps 89:3-34).

In the spirit of royal covenant theology, Isaiah also set before the people the alternatives ("If you are willing and obedient . . . but if you refuse and rebel . . .", Is 1:19-20) and announced that Yahweh's judgment was for the sake of discipline and purification (Is 1:21-28).

In the Davidic covenant, as in the Mosaic covenant, people were called to responsibility before God and suffering was understood as the consequence of human failure. It was difficult, however, to square this view with the hard facts of life. In the Deuteronomistic History the kings of Israel and Judah are measured according to the standard of David, whose success resulted from his obedience to Yahweh's covenant law. Few kings measured up to David, Josiah being a notable exception: "Before him there was no king like him, who turned to Yahweh with all his heart and with all his soul and with all his might, according to all the law of Moses" (2 Kg 23:25). But good king Josiah, the king who was another David, was killed at Megiddo when interfering with Pharaoh Neco's military advance northward. It is significant that the Deuteronomistic historian passes over this tragic event briefly, without any theological comment (2 Kg 23:29-30).[6] Clearly, the notion that suffering was Yahweh's judgment for apostasy was weighed in the balance and found wanting. Morever, it is striking that at one point the Chronicler, in reviewing the history of the monarchy from David on, changed the record found in the Deuteronomistic History. David's taking of a census, an act of royal power that had disastrous consequences, he attributed to a sinister power: to Satan, the archenemy of God (1 Chr 21:1; see 2 Sam 24:1).

It is not surprising, then, that Davidic covenant theology also led to lament in which suppliants wondered whether God was really present with his people. Psalm 89, which begins with hymnic praise to Yahweh for his promises of grace to David, concludes with a lament in which the question is raised as to whether Yahweh has gone back on his word. The defeat of the king in battle and the humiliating conquest of the nation's strongholds provided the occasion for a cry out of the depths of distress:

> How long, O Yahweh? Wilt thou hide
>   thyself forever?
> How long will thy wrath burn like fire?
>
> . . . .
>
> Yahweh, where is thy steadfast love [*hesed*] of old,
>   which by thy faithfulness thou didst swear to David? (Ps 89:46, 49)

IV

Thus the question that was raised with greater and greater urgency was whether the sufferings of the present age can be accounted for adequately by a doctrine of sin. Whether standing in the Mosaic or the Davidic covenant tradition, the prophets displayed an amazing consensus in their interpretation of Israel's sufferings. They did not portray the people as hapless victims of demonic forces beyond their control or of an inexorable power of Fate. Instead, they took the people to task for their failure to exercise their God-given responsibility. The blame fell fully on the people — not on some external power or powers from an evil spirit-world. To cite the great prophetic summary of God's requirements of his people, they had failed to do justice, to practice *hesed* (loyalty), and to walk humbly with their God (Mic 6:8). Hence, the disasters that fell upon them were deserved punishment for sin, the legitimate consequence of covenant betrayal. This view, however, was too sweeping, too simplistic to do justice to the facts of life. In the experience of people who went through the valley of death's shadow when Jerusalem was destroyed and many were carried into Babylonian exile, Abraham's question — asked in connection with the destruction of Sodom and Gomorrah — must have been raised with deep anguish.

Such a question was raised by a prophet, Habakkuk, on the eve of the fall of Jerusalem, when Babylonian military might was sweeping like an irresistible avalanche over the ancient world. His expostulation with God occurs in two parts or cycles, each of which is composed of a "lament" and an "oracle of salvation." The first cycle (1:2-11) begins with the typical cry of a lament, "how long?"

> O Yahweh, how long shall I cry for help,
>   and thou wilt not hear?
> Or cry to thee "Violence!"
>   and thou wilt not save?
> Why dost thou make me see wrongs
>   and look upon trouble?
> Destruction and violence are before me;
>   strife and contention arise.
> So the law is slacked
>   and justice never goes forth.
> For the wicked surrounds the righteous,
>   so justice goes forth perverted (Hab 1:2-4).

Yahweh's response to the prophet's question only accentuates the dilemma. Believe it or not, so he is told, Yahweh himself is behind the violence of the Chaldeans — an aggressive nation that determines its own justice and deifies its own might.

Dissatisfied, the prophet renews his expostulation with God. The second cycle (1:12–2:5) begins with another lament, in which it is recognized that an unjust conqueror may be the agent of divine judgment (cf. Is 10:5-19, where Assyria is "the rod of Yahweh's wrath"). The people undoubtedly deserve divine discipline, but surely relative distinctions must be made between those who use power ruthlessly and those who are victims.

> Thou who art of purer eyes than to behold evil
>   and canst not look on wrong,
> why dost thou look on faithless men,
>   and art silent when the wicked swallows up
>   the man more righteous than he? (Hab 1:13).

Even granting that the people are sinful, the punishment does not fit the crime. One can almost hear the echo of Abraham's question: "Shall not the Judge of all the earth do justice?" The oracular response to the prophet's lament seems to be more satisfying this time. The enigmas of life, he is told, cannot be understood now. But wait! In God's own time the meaning will be made clear and in his own way the righteous will be vindicated. In the meantime, "the righteous shall live by faith," that is, by radical trust in God whose faithfulness is the ground of hope, in spite of all present evidences to the contrary.

Christians are apt to rush from this great text to the New Testament, where it is read in a new context of interpretation (Rom 1:17; Gal 3:11; Heb 10:38-39). It is important, however, to hear Habakkuk's cry of lament in the context of the political and social situation of the time, where people who were dislocated from their homeland and victimized by powerful oppressors found it difficult to believe in God's presence in the world. Second Isaiah spoke to such people in exile, who feared that their way was "hidden from Yahweh," their justice "disregarded by their God" (Is 40:27); and he consoled them by proclaiming that "those who wait for Yahweh shall renew their strength" (Is 40:31). To the anguished cry "how long?" came the answer "wait!" in the case of Habakkuk. If, however, God's saving presence has any meaning for this world in which people are suffering, waiting cannot be prolonged interminably.

Perhaps the cry "how long?" which was heard repeatedly during the late prophetic period, is an indication of the crisis of Israelite prophecy. This cry, familiar in Israel's laments and those of the ancient Near East, "was a crucial question during times of tribulation," as J. J. M. Roberts observes, "whether those tribulations affected a group or only a single individual. The failure to get a divine response to the question added to the sense of God-forsakenness and intensified the despair of the lamenting party."[7] In the period of the Exile and afterward, the laments of Israel demanded a clearer answer to the question of the time-limit of Yahweh's judgment on his people and a deeper perception of the nature of the evil that afflicted Israel and the nations. In this period prophecy found expression in a new idiom: apocalyptic.

One of the outstanding features of apocalyptic literature is the disclosure to a seer of the answer to the question "how long?" in terms of a definite divine time-table. For instance, there was an effort to understand anew Jeremiah's prophecy concerning the seventy years of exile (Jer 25:8-14), both in Zechariah (Zech 1:12, 7:5) and in the apocalypse of Daniel, where it is understood to mean seventy weeks of years (Dan 9:1-27). The message of apocalyptic is that God's people do not have to wait an interminably long time for deliverance. The kingdom of God is coming with power speedily. The day of salvation is measurably near.

In addition to calculations of the time-limit of God's wrath, apocalyptic provides a new understanding of the radical power of evil. This new understanding does not cancel out a contrite awareness of sin as found in prophetic preaching or in psalms like *Miserere* (Ps 51) or *De Profundis* (Ps 130). In the very situation where Daniel attempts to understand Jeremiah's enigmatic prophecy of seventy years, he offers a prayer of confession in which he acknowledges his own sin and the sin of the people Israel (Dan 9:4-19). "To the Lord our God belong mercy and forgiveness," he prays, "because we have rebelled against him and have not obeyed the voice of Yahweh our God by following his laws, which he set before us by his servants the prophets." He goes on to confess that, because "all Israel" has transgressed the divine law, "Yahweh has kept ready the calamity and has brought it upon us; for

Yahweh our God is righteous in all the works which he has done, and we have not obeyed his voice." And he concludes by casting himself solely on "amazing grace": "We do not present our supplications before thee on the ground of our righteousness, but on the ground of thy great mercy. O Lord, hear; O Lord, forgive; O Lord, give heed and act. . . ." However, appeals for repentance in the manner of classical prophecy are not characteristic of apocalyptic, which was concerned primarily to console and strengthen the faithful in times of trial. The shift in emphasis, from repentance to consolation, reflects a change in historical perception: the action-consequence syndrome of "sin" is part of a much larger historical evil that holds people as victims in the grip of massive, oppressive powers over which they have no control. People need divine deliverance not just from the bondage of sin but from the tyranny of evil powers at work in society and in the whole course of history.

The vision described in the seventh chapter of Daniel is crucial for this new historical understanding. Here the tyranny of evil is symbolized by four beasts that arise from the depths of the "sea," the mythical source of the powers of chaos. Each beast is more terrible than the previous one, suggesting that evil increases in magnitude or, as we would say, things go from bad to worse, until the drama reaches its catastrophic climax and the oppressive "beast" is burned in the all-consuming fire. Since the locus of evil is from "below," in the depths of the historical process itself, the victory must come from "above," transcendently, or in the symbolism of the vision, by "one like a son of man" (that is, one whose appearance is like a human being in contrast to the likeness of horrible beasts) who comes "with the clouds of heaven." According to this view, nothing can halt the inexorable movement toward the victory of God's kingdom over the empire of evil which seduces, victimizes, and oppresses people. In later apocalyptic formulations God's victory over the powers of evil and chaos was expressed in terms of the conflict between the kingdom of God and the kingdom of Satan.

V

In summary, Israel's historical experiences led to a profound apprehension of the power of evil which called for a correspondingly deep understanding of God's saving power. In the final analysis, the issue is not simply "sin" and deserved punishment but the disturbance brought about by evil that infects human society and corrupts the course of human history. To return to the story of the Garden of Eden, the serpent that deceives humankind is not just a beast of the field but, in a larger perspective, the mythical representation of the uncanny powers of chaos that the Divine Warrior must overcome in order to establish his kingdom. In a sentence from the "little apocalypse of Isaiah" (Is 24–27), we read that in the final time Yahweh, the Divine Warrior, will conquer the powers of evil.

> In that day Yahweh with his hard and great and strong sword will punish Leviathan the fleeing serpent, Leviathan the twisting serpent, and he will slay the dragon that is in the sea (Is 27:1).

It is not a far cry from this passage, which resounds with overtones of the Canaanite myth of Baal's conquest over his adversary, to the portrayal of the consummation found in the Revelation of John. In the vision of the Christian apocalypse, at the time of the great finale, when a Hallelujah Chorus will ring throughout God's whole creation, the Beast that rose from the Sea will be slain (Rev 13), "the dragon, that ancient serpent who is the Devil and Satan" will be bound (Rev 20:1-3), and the Sea — the source of chaotic evil — will be no more (Rev 21:1).

The early Christian community, whose life, thought, and worship are reflected in the writings of the New Testament, was the beneficiary of Israel's long struggle with the problem of sin and evil. Jesus' preaching, as reported by Mark, includes a call to repentance in the spirit of the prophets of Israel: "The Kingdom of God is at hand, repent . . ." (Mk 1:15). The same evangelist, however, portrays the Messiah waging a battle against the kingdom of Satan and announces, in the spirit of apocalyptic writers, the imminent triumph of the Son of Man. God's salvation is not only deliverance from the bondage of sin (as in the story of the healing of the paralytic, Mk 9:1-8; Lk 5:17-26); it is also deliverance from the demonic powers of the empire of Evil (Satan).

Both of these dimensions are needed today in any full exposition of the human predicament and of divine liberation. Some years ago a book appeared under the title *What Ever Happened to Sin?* by Karl Menninger, M.D. The doctrine of sin may not be as much on people's minds as it once was, but sin is still a reality that requires the healing of divine forgiveness. Seward Hiltner, a recognized leader in the field of pastoral theology and one who has been closely associated with the work of the Menninger Foundation, observes that sin and repentance belong to the processes of therapy; indeed, "there is a rough analogy between awareness of sin as diagnosis, concerned about what is wrong, and repentance of sin as either therapy or constructive change, concerned about righting whatever is wrong." Furthermore, he continues, in a larger sense society itself needs to repent; hence, unease about the sin manifest in social institutions, conditions of poverty, or oppression of the weak should not "paralyze action" but "stimulate it constructively."[8] These words are in keeping with the prophetic insights of the Old Testament and the New. But modern people are also aware of being caught in the grip of powerful social and historical forces that seem to be beyond their power to remedy. These forces sometimes are at work within an individual, as though possessed by a demon;[9] and on a world scale they sweep like an avalanche over human lives, afflicting tremendous suffering and moving with inexorable momentum toward disaster, perhaps nuclear catastrophe. The doctrine of sin (whether 'actual' or 'original') and deserved punishment is inadequate to explain the larger dimension of evil that victimizes people.

In the text of Lk 24:44-49, which provides the overarching theme for these essays, we read that "repentance and forgiveness of sins should be preached in his [Christ's] name to all nations." Clearly, this is part of the Good News that the Church proclaims and celebrates. If, however, we are to understand the full range of God's gracious salvation wrought through the life, death, and resurrection of Jesus Christ, Luke's statement needs to be supplemented by other New Testament witnesses, especially Paul, who was heavily influenced by apocalyptic thinking.[10] The Apostle displays a profound grasp of the power of sin and of God's gracious liberation from sin's bondage. For Paul, however, God's crucial victory manifest in the death and resurrection of Jesus Christ liberates people not only from the power of sin but from all powers of evil, darkness, and chaos, including — in apocalyptic terms — "the last enemy," Death, which will finally be destroyed (1 Cor 15:26). Hence, there is absolutely nothing, in the range of history or the cosmos, that can separate God's people from his presence and his care.

> What shall separate us from the love of Christ? Shall tribulation or distress, or persecution, or famine, or nakedness, or peril, or sword?
> . . .
> No, in all these things we are more than conquerors through him who loved us. For I am sure that neither death, nor life, nor angels, nor principalities, nor things present, nor things to come, nor powers, nor height, nor depth, nor anything else in all creation, will be able to separate us from the love of God in Christ Jesus our Lord (Rom 8:35, 37-39).

NOTES

1. William G. Heidt, O.S.B., *The Book of Genesis: Chapters 1–11,* Old Testament Reading Guide 9 (Collegeville, Minn.: The Liturgical Press, 1967) 26–32.

2. Phyllis Trible, *God and the Rhetoric of Sexuality* (Philadelphia: Fortress, 1978) 111. She remarks: "Certainly, he [the serpent] is the villain, but then the story itself is not about a villain. Nor is it about evil, cosmic or chthonic. Instead, it is about human obedience (life) and human disobedience (death) as defined by God."

3. See further my discussion in *Creation versus Chaos* (New York: Association Press, 1967) 134–135, 155–159.

4. See Emil Fackenheim, *God's Presence in History* (New York: Harper, 1979) who discusses this subject in the context of "Jewish Affirmations and Philosophical Reflections."

5. See further my study of prophetic preaching, *The Eighth Century Prophets* (Philadelphia: Fortress, 1978), ch. 3: "Turning Away and Turning Around."

6. Some scholars maintain that the original Deuteronomistic history ended at 2 Kg 23:25 on a note of praise for King Josiah and that a second version of the history presented events after his reign and expanded the work elsewhere. See Frank M. Cross, "The Themes of the Book of Kings and the Structure of the Deuteronomistic History," *Canaanite Myth and Hebrew Epic* (Cambridge, Mass.: Harvard University, 1973) 274–289. The debate over whether there was one or two versions, however, does not mitigate the difficulty that Deuteronomic theology had in coping with historical tragedy.

7. J.J.M. Roberts, "Of Signs, Prophets, and Time Limits: A Note on Ps. 74:9," CBQ 39 (1977), 478.

8. Seward Hiltner, *Theological Dynamics* (New York: Abingdon, 1972), ch. 4 on "Sin and Sickness," especially 81–86.

9. See Hiltner's tentative "Footnote on Demons," *ibid.,* 102–104.

10. See further my lectures, *The Living Word of the Bible* (Philadelphia: Westminster, 1979) 93–96.

PART TWO

Old Testament Studies

Alberic Culhane, O.S.B.

SODOM AND GOMORRAH:

PERCEPTION AND POSSIBILITY

It is rare, an early excavator at Bâb edh-Dhrâ' wrote of another esteemed archaeologist, when prestigious administrative obligations do not sound a death knell to continued "academic pursuits in American higher education."[1] Happily, Nelson Glueck proved to be an exception to the rule; similarly remarkable is my colleague, Rev. Dr. William G. Heidt, O.S.B. While Father Heidt was director of the flourishing Liturgical Press from the late forties until 1978, the translator of the Heinisch Old Testament trilogy and editor-contributor to the *Old* and *New Testament Reading Guides*,[2] he nonetheless did full-time teaching and significant pastoral work. He awakened interest in, and imparted an understanding of, the Bible and archaeology to many graduate students, as the present writer would like gratefully to witness.

Among the many helpful ruling principles Heidt made clear are two that find particular resonance in what follows: a personal observation, with introduction, on the 1975, 1977 Early Bronze Age excavations at Bab edh-Dhra',[3] near the Lisan (tongue) of the Dead Sea, Jordan — a site often associated with the biblical "sin cities" of Sodom and Gomorrah. The two Heidt dicta are (a) that one's *perception* of a truth may and, for many reasons, often does vary widely from the "truth" itself; and (b) that, in one's interpretation, there can be and often is a critical difference between the *possible*, the *probable* and, if attainable, the *certain*.

A non-taxative list of recent Bronze Age studies[4] appears, in retrospect, to underscore the crucial consequence of the Heidt "home truths," especially as those studies speak to artifact evidence, sociocultural conditions, and settlement patterns of the Early Bronze Age in the Near East. Nearly all excavations, notably including those currently in progress at Bab edh-Dhra', add various details to the chronological framework of Syro-Palestinian archaeology.[5] Conversely, as Wright's work illumines, the present state of archaeology, in critical self-appraisal, cannot be divorced from its past state.

Archaeology in the twentieth century, a discipline developed only in the last century from Western Europe, is, in essence, the conception of cultural differences in time. Willey and Sabloff may have put the matter for the "new archaeology" as well as any: "Archaeology is the study of the human cultural and social past whose goals are to narrate the sequent story of that past and to explain the event that composed it. The discipline attempts to achieve these goals by excavating and analyzing the remains and monuments of past cultures and the contexts in which they are found."[6]

Yet, given the vagaries, fortuities, and complexities that are present in any record of a mute past, restraint in reportage is always a becoming posture for an archaeologist's theoretical and methodological synthesis. Such prudent circumspection has not always been followed (as we may note below).[7] Fortunately, however, modern archaeology as a whole is much more aware that it has passed from strict historical schematization to reconstruction of prehistoric and historic life-ways within sites and cultural units — and in the working and functioning of cultures. It recognizes that the *perception* of the past itself varies in accordance with the ruling view of history resident in the inquirer.

The present conceptual models of archaeology (utilizing a set of techniques of digging, recording and manipulating data) have undergone vast changes in the last decade. Archaeology today, whether in its sub-groupings — for example, Palestinian, maritime, or biblical — or other "special interest" stances, is no longer a mere matter of chance digging inspired by the hope of great riches, of "proving" religious texts, or of any other narrowly parochial (e.g., geo-political) intent. This is not to suggest that, for instance, modern Syro-Palestinian archaeology does not have the potential for greater illumination of the Bible. With increasing precision in retrieving empirical data and because of developing sophistication in interpreting it, ancillary discoveries from modern Syro-Palestinian archaeological endeavors which persons of a biblical stance find compatible *do occur* — "spin-off" discoveries of value like the 1960's development of teflon coating within the burgeoning NASA exploration program. But the scope of the field work of modern Syro-Palestinian archaeology, to use the same instance, is much broader in its chronological, geographic, and cultural horizons.[8] Of course, it should be noted here that, dependent upon the archaeologist's general mental framework or "model" within which further observations and reasoning can take place, the "sense" made of the observed phenomena is able to be defended, to a degree. That is, more than one model can exist at the same time, and each can be "true" in its own way. Again, perception, possibility.

Furthermore, no longer can an individual, renaissance person singly perceive, structure, and then declaim the course of man and his history from the excavation of unique, however promising sites.[9] A core staff of specialists within the growing disciplines of faceted anthropologies to paleo-ethnobotanists and zoologists (each having authority to speak the disciplines' insights and values) utilize the developments in the field[10] and in the laboratories.[11] It is perceived at present that the latter multi-disciplinary approach *alone* makes it possible to reconstruct, in varying degrees of likelihood, the ways of life and death of anonymous people of remote antiquity. Thus, while the incipient achievements of recent archaeological work are again studied, and as more data are revealed through successive study of preserved materials and recorded matter from excavations, archaeologists may gain further insight into T. S. Eliot's statement of one of modern archaeology's "values" — that the past is prolog. Eliot wrote: "Time present and time past/Are both perhaps present in time future/And time future contained in time past" ("Burnt Norton," the first of the *Four Quartets*).

Serving as a prelude to an account of Bab edh-Dhra' and its *possible* recognition as the biblical "sin city" of Sodom, an example is at hand of the problems encountered by an archaeologist if he forgets that his *perception* of the past is directly conditioned by the means of approach he uses (e.g., literary, biblical, archaeological) and by the type of evidence he employs. The recent parade example is enmeshed in varied prognostications made lately about the portent, value, or meaning of Tell Mardikh, Syria.

Tell Mardikh was identified in 1968 by stratified inscription as Ebla, a formerly obscure city mentioned in scattered documents of the second and third millennia B.C.[12] By the 1974 season at Ebla, in the ruins of a palace destroyed by the Akkadians in the twenty-third century B.C., an archive was found to contain more than fifteen thousand tablets. Some of these tablets mention, according to the former epigraphist Dr. Giovanni Pettinato, the cities of Sodom and Gomorrah (*possible* Bab edh-Dhra' and Numeirah).[13] Also appearing on the tablets are more than five thousand geographic names and such personal names as Ab-ra-mu, E-sa-im, and king Ebrum (identified by Pettinato as Eber, the eponymous founder of the Hebrews, Gen 10:21). From one biblical perception, immediate reminiscence seems to coincide with the Gen 10, 14, 18, 19 accounts that list such names — and such apparent geographic locations as the "Five Cities of the Plain."[14] Clearly, a biblical literalist's temptation, not to say that of some recognized scholars in associated disciplines,[15] is to equate the names mentioned[16] in the Ebla tablets with the Genesis accounts to "prove" the historicity of the Bible and then to push back the age and possible location of the biblical patriarchs to about five hundred years before the prevailing view of biblical history — for, after all, Islamic scholars have often held that Abraham's epic journey occurred in 2300 B.C.[17]

In his perception, however, Paolo Matthiae, the Italian director of the excavations at Ebla from their beginnings, noted again lately that such claimed biblical associations (and the geo-political/religious uses to which they might be put) are not, in fact, based on real evidence found in this city-state of some 250,000, the megalopolis of some 35,000 inhabitants. "The Divine Name, Yahweh, does not appear at all in the Ebla tablets. This highly developed urban civilization of the third millennium Ebla cannot be soundly compared with the nomadic culture of the patriarchs" (see La Fay, *National Geographic*, 740).

Added historical problems include that of the prevailing view regarding King Sargon of Akkad (2340–2284 B.C.). While Sargon seems to have defeated the Eblaites around 2300 B.C.,[18] his grandson, Naram-Sin, less than a century later, constructed a basalt victory monument to himself detailing an "Ebla, never before subdued in history."[19] Matthiae writes that there are further questions deriving from the fact that cuneiform signs are capable of conveying many meanings — that the cuneiform citations currently understood by some as naming the last three Cities of the Plain could also properly indicate *merely* the names of three metals then in production. For, after all, Ebla was renowned for quality metals and metal-working, and Eblaite language and writing, born of trade, are a previously unknown northwest Semitic amalgam maintained by an academy of scribes who were the earliest known outside of the land of Sumer.[20] Again, perception and possibility . . . probability . . . certainty?

Since the above is, briefly, the current conundrum concerning Ebla, as one approaches the possibilities and questions posed by recent excavations at Bab edh-Dhra' — the received opinion, by local tradition and otherwise, *suggests* that these sites may be the storied Sodom and (Numeirah) Gomorrah[21] — the summary thoughts of Piggott correctly set a caution regarding perception and the possible:

> If we use purely archaeological evidence (that is to say, the surviving relics of the material culture of extinct communities, exclusive of any literary documents that may or may not exist), we will get one sort of a view of the past . . . if on the other hand we have written documents of some kind we can give an added dimension to our view of the past, by using the documentary evidence to obtain information on those activities which are not directly reflected in the material objects they made or used. . . . (*Indeed*) if we are to understand what the historian and prehistorian is getting at, we must remember that *we can perceive the past in varying ways and the sort of past we see is conditioned by this type of evidence on which it is based*[22] (emphasis added).

THE EXCAVATIONS

For 'tis not verse, and 'tis not prose
But earthenware alone
It is that ultimately shows
What men have thought and done!
(Godley, of Oxford, 1910?)

We awoke at 2:30 A.M. those days of May to July, 1977. That in itself was not decidedly different from the earlier excavations in 1975. To travel to the site near the Lisan of the Dead Sea from the Crusader town of Kerak meant a 4000-foot vertical descent, sloping and curving downward on the unfinished roadway to reach the extensive Bab edh-Dhra' (Gate of the Arm) site. In order to manage a "first breakfast" and to pick up the day's water before we left Kerak's Moab mountains, we retired the previous evening about 9 P.M.

Thus, we caravaned daily at 4 A.M. to the site, the lowest inhabited spot on earth. As the sun was appearing along the sides of the Great Rift in the southern Ghor (Plain) of the Dead Sea, the temperature would be a pleasant 65 degrees F. We were prepared for what would come — some hours of 130-plus heat as we worked to the last of our humid day, around noon.

Once at the site, we picked up our individual supplies of water, tools, sifters, and recording paraphernalia and broke into three groups to go off to our several locations at the Bab edh-Dhra' townsite[23] and cemetery, and to Numeirah, a second site of excavation some thirteen kilometers to the south. At each place we were joined by local workmen, the Ghorani, who are said to be descendants of slaves from the Horn of Africa during the Middle Ages. Although done by a somewhat larger staff (forty-five faculty members and students from North American institutions), the routine was the same as in the initial year (1975) of the planned fifteen-year project. Alternately overheated, frustrated, elated by finds, impatient for the "second breakfast" break at 9 A.M., we began to learn nearly as much about ourselves individually as we learned about the sites.

Bab edh-Dhra' Townsite

During the 1977 season,[24] we were able to make significant progress into the surprisingly rich remains of the ten-acre, walled townsite. We now know that this fortified city was inhabited continuously throughout most of a major period of Ancient Near Eastern History, the Early Bronze Age I, II, III (hereafter given as EB, with sub-phase designations such as EB IA), approximately 3200 to 2200 B.C.[25] Much of the townsite

91

shows heavy wind and water erosion; increasingly from the south defense wall moving north, vast erosional fissures have dumped great
patches of the city into the Wadi Kerak[26] over a 5000-year span. But as
the 1977 season ended, we had found, in many of the six major "fields"
chosen for excavation in this large, regional (we thought) city, a considerable depth of occupation debris — at surface EB III, then downward
EB II and EB I. In 1975, satellite encampments *outside* the city walls
revealed considerable EB IV occupation on the east, south, and southwest of the townsite, and EB IA (3150–3050 B.C.) to the west. Although
there were a few scattered EB IV (ca. 2300–2050 B.C.) evidences inside
the walls of the Bab edh-Dhraʻ townsite, we are presently convinced
that the "fortress city" life came to an abrupt end by destruction late in
EB III, perhaps by the EB IV peoples from the North or by Sixth Dynasty
Egyptians.

The Northeast Tower

The northeast tower (Field XI), first discovered in 1975, was
thoroughly opened in 1977. Still the highest preserved point in the north
of the city (although erosion has denuded its north face and sides), the
tower has several phases, the earliest phase almost entirely of mudbrick
construction, the later, intriguing phase of stone with mudbrick
superstructure evincing destruction in EB III. The full relationship of this
tower to the north city wall eludes us; such information may never be
available because of the severe erosion of the north wall and because,
about ten years ago, the military pulled out innumerable stones for other
purposes.

Sanctuary (?)

At the southwest end of the city, on the second highest spot of the
townsite (Field XII), two wide layers of stone that had been perceived in
1975 as a walkway were discerned in 1977 to be the 1.25 meter-wide
foundation walls of an EB III and earlier EB II rectangular building of
stone-and-mortar formation and mudbrick superstructure. The full dimensions and extent of this large, impressively treated building are not
yet fully known because the major "grid" balks (separating digging
squares) run through its center and end sides. Still standing five
fieldstone courses high, the inside walls appear to be plastered, the
plaster still showing finger and hand impressions in places. The broadroom structure entrance is, significantly, offset on the long western wall
facing the Dead Sea.[27]
On the inside we found pieces of ivory, a preserved section of
wooden pillar fifteen centimeters high resting on its flat stone pedestal,[28] a decorated beam with plastered dado-design,[29] two large stones

for possible support of wooden pillars of EB III phase, evidence of flagstone flooring of the same period, and matting impressions of floor or ceiling use.

Outside, the courtyard area to the west showed considerable mud-brick destruction debris on top of mudbrick paving and plaster that, leading westward, abuts a circular installation of near-cyclopean stones; it is about three meters in diameter. A further four meters west, before what appears to be a cobbled bordering wall of the courtyard, is a finely levigated pillar or tabun construction in association with a plastered flooring.

Such evidences as these in Field XII suggest a temenos (temple precinct) or sanctuary area, but present perceptions will not lead to conviction before further excavation and further study are made of EB temples and their accoutrements,[30] such as those at Ai, Ein Gedi, Jericho, Arad, and elsewhere. Again, perception, possibility.

Another very interesting fact is that the natural gravel, which is "bedrock" at the site and seems to be found everywhere, could have served as an efficient natural drainage function. Yet, in some places, such as in Field XII, we discovered that the surfaces of the EB III and EB II phases were separated by a gravel fill, showing that some of the gravels in the area were man-laid and not natural. As Rast notes, judging from the considerable burn on the floor of the earlier EB II structure, it appears that this earlier phase may have been destroyed by fire and that the later edifice was built to succeed it.

As often happens when we plan a season to end on a specific date, the last days of digging in Field XII in 1977 produced exciting evidence of a wall of white "huwar" mudbrick without the heavy temper used by the later EB II-III people. It appeared in several squares of Field XII and in Field XIII associated with EB IB pottery. In Field XII, this wall ran tantalizingly under and perpendicular to the EB III and II structures. An EB IB sanctuary also? Excavations in 1979 will help to clarify the matter.

The Western Wall (Gate?)

Against the exterior of the western defensive wall known from earlier excavations by Lapp in 1965, 1968,[31] a trench in Field XIII brought our attention to a white marl, artificial mound piled against the town wall after the manner of ancient defensive *glacis*[32] installations. Yet, a *glacis* usually runs up against the walls. In this instance the marl may have served some other function, and only continued excavation will shed light on our educated guess that the western entry gate to the city is not far from this place.

In any event, it is now clear that the latest city wall, constructed in a segmented clockwise fashion, was built on stone foundations and had a mudbrick facing and mounting. Additionally, a florit of square, well-fired bricks inscribed with markings identical to those found earlier in the cemetery charnel [33] houses were in tumble everywhere in the area. These suggest a formidable western defensive tower near the "gate." The succeeding seasons of excavation should illumine these finds.

Again typically, on the very last day of the season we found a substantial mudbrick wall about 3.50 meters below surface start, and bearing EB IB pottery; it was partially uncovered and then, necessarily, covered over again until summer 1979.

New Fields

We opened three new fields in 1977 in order to assess the now-suspected plethora of complicated settlement remains. From the 1975 work, we knew that Bab edh-Dhra' is not really a "tell" in the Petrie perspective; [34] rather, as in Field XII, three major periods of EB occupation are found within the city at a depth of a meter or less. However, in 1977, in a new Field XIV in the city center, we uncovered, against a southern slope, a well-preserved mudbrick retaining wall, the bottom of which we did not reach. The initial indications of deep settlement remains and buildings will be investigated further in 1979. [35]

Beginning work in new Field XVII was also auspicious. North of Field XIV, a limited trench resulted in one of our most interesting discoveries of the 1977 season. In erosional fissure number II at the desiccated northern area of the site, Field XVII is a massive slump of occupational layers and living surfaces, the presenting side of which is over *five* meters deep! Finding this concentration and depth of EB occupational debris may well provide us with a "ceramic clock" from top to bottom of stratified pottery, with installations also *in situ*. Our plan to dig a small trench quickly for a sample sequence had to be postponed; barely thirty-five centimeters down we uncovered a doorway and flooring of a fine mudbrick dwelling with curious small plastered holes in the living surface. Once more, the 1979 excavations in this field will have the priority of opening a much larger area for stratified digging of these signal settlement remains and architectural features.

Since the northern areas of the site are excessively eroded, we also decided in 1977 to place a trench in order to discover possible remnants of the town's EB III defensive wall system that is found on all the other sides. As a result of this sounding, we did uncover a hefty mudbrick wall that, possibly, may have served defensive purposes. Yet, above that wall was a later EB IV mudbrick structure, rarely found anywhere, not to mention *within* the Bab edh-Dhra' townsite itself. The phasing of these two constructions is complicated, and while we found two well-preserved spear/daggerhead weapons (both in broken-up brick debris), judgments about the phasing must await future excavation. At the lower level, possible EB III, we unearthed a ceramic upper tournette of a potter's wheel — a valuable discovery in view of the fact that it is during the EB horizon that wheels were introduced in the production of pottery.

When the 1977 season ended on July 2, it was clear to us that, different from the 1975 experience, the Bab edh-Dhra' townsite offers a notable depth of occupation debris, much of it *in situ*. That the site was occupied continuously from about 3100 to 2300 B.C., with peaceable transitions from EB I to EB II and not so peaceable between EB II and EB III,[36] when final townsite destruction occurred, appears to us as probable. Such factors are especially helpful in making beginning, although sound, correlations with the cemetery tomb indications from the various phases. The preserved city site is larger, extending farther north than we had earlier judged. In like manner, the beginning of urban life at Bab edh-Dhra' occurred earlier, in EB IB (Predynastic Egypt) rather than in EB II. Further excavation will make these present suppositions more conclusive, beyond the current probability,[37] but continuing excavation here will also certainly help to solve questions about EB peoples known to date almost exclusively from their tombs.

Bab edh-Dhra' Cemetery

Continuing work in the extensive, intensively used cemetery included, in 1977, a team of specialists from the Smithsonian Institution, Washington, D.C.[38] We opened a large number of shaft tombs[39] in order to retrieve mint skeletal material for study, say, of population types of the third millennium B.C. Much diagnostic skeletal material in these previously undisturbed burials was found, while, in the excavating, other outstanding discoveries were made as well in 1977. Among the more than nine hundred whole and undamaged ceramic pots and stone pieces was a juglet containing grape pits, one bowl with protein residue, a peach pit, and actual (not mere impressions of) reed matting still intact.[40]

All in all, sixteen shaft tombs with their associated thirty-eight chambers and two charnel houses with unusual features were excavated in 1977. Of the latter charnel houses, one, called G 1, was a round house of late EB IA (ca. 3100 B.C.), while Tomb A 56, also a round building, had pottery dating, by its Abydos jugs and other forms, to EB II (ca. 2850–2550 B.C.). This latter tomb thus provides an important example of a transitional tomb style, a transit from shaft to round constructions; it not only fills a gap in our knowledge of EB pottery but also offers convincing evidence of the development of tomb types at the site.

Further, in the perfectly sealed four chambers of Tomb A 100, three of the chambers contained the usual and expected disarticulated bone piles in the center with accompanying EB IA (ca. 3100 B.C.) pottery around the periphery. The fourth chamber, however, A 100 North, was especially significant for us. It held a fully laid-out (articulated) skeleton and EB IB (ca. 3000 B.C.) typical line-group painted ware.

In sum, the charnel houses at the site already contribute to our understanding insofar as they illuminate the socio-cultural dynamics of the EB age. The shifts from non-settled life to the formation of town life and its accompanying permanency of settlement, population growth, and encounters with the environment under its limitations — all these called for adaptations on the part of the inhabitants. On the cemetery's northern ridge we also found, very unexpectedly, some scattered mudbrick walls belonging to an early EB IA settlement with its (rarely ever found) domestic-use pottery. Heretofore no EB IA crudely made "cooking pot" ware had been found at Bab edh-Dhra'; we had, previously, only the very delicate, fine ware of the tomb-furnishings type in abundance.

Numeirah

A site of about two acres some thirteen kilometers south of Bab edh-Dhra', Numeirah is called by Schaub an archaeologist's "dream site," because the single-period, EB III, material is exceptionally undisturbed from the time of destruction. It was dramatically clear to us in the depth of destruction debris ranging two meters downward that the townsite was left just as it was from the EB III destruction until 1977.

We began a six-square trench through the center of the elongated, oval-shaped town. Digging north from the southern, outer face of the preserved defense wall, we came upon a series of rooms stretching nearly to the northern wall. The contents of the rooms appeared at this time to indicate an industrial sector. One room presented two stone-lined storage bins; another held a curious installation made of fired ceramic in five built-up sections — together standing 1.20 meters tall, about .75 meter in diameter.

The lowest part of this strange "soak pit" structure [41] is seated in the natural gravel core (bedrock at the site) and has holes at its base. Our ceramic technologist, Dr. Robert Johnston, took samples of the material to the Rochester Institute of Technology, but the results have not yet been published. Was this "thing" for levigating clay for pottery-making, for metallurgy, grain storage?

Because Numeirah was destroyed, apparently throughout, at one time and everything was left as it was at the time of its demise, some of the pottery could be reconstructed easily and some was found intact. Especially intriguing was the uncovering of some items of daily life such as a carbonized heap of grapes with even their skins preserved, a large hole-mouth jar, and quantities of barley and wheat. But the most engaging single object found at Numeirah in 1977 was a seal impression around the shoulder of a large store jar. The impression shows two animals — a crouching goat or ram seemingly eating a bush and, behind it, a lion perhaps ready to devour the goat. Impressions such as this one have been found at Jericho, Meggido, and Byblos, but its point of origin may be in Mesopotamia or even northern Syria.[42]

Regional Studies

In the initial 1975 and 1977 seasons, we also began the ongoing study of the region of the five "cities" — Bab edh-Dhra', Numeirah, es-Safi, Feifeh, and Khanazirah. Delimited by natural features, the zone is contained by the Dead Sea to the west, the Moab mountains to the north and east, and a circle of limestone cliffs to the south. Future aerial and land surveying, mapping and field excavation, along with continuing geological and environmental exploration, will tell us the use made of resources, more about the possible ways of daily life and death, and, surely, whether or not there are, as suspected, still more prehistoric and historic sites in the zone.[43]

Early accounts of some of these regional and environmental studies are already available in the preliminary excavation reports[44] of 1975, wherein are detailed the evidences of sophisticated cloth-making done at Bab edh-Dhra' from ca. 3100–2500 B.C., the variegated animal and human faunal remains, and an impressive list of ancient plants identified to date. We think that these environmental and regional studies are unique and will prove to be among the most important illuminating works of the seasons ahead.[45] It is a given that the environment affects man wherever he is and that man affects the environment wherever he is, and that both are traceable.

Summary

After these concerns with a description of primary archaeological documentation, there can be a selective consideration of the question: "Are Bab edh-Dhra' and Numeirah *probable* Sodom and Gomorrah?" Yet, as an introduction to the question, something more has to be said.

Often, it seems, publicists of any cause ground their projections, not on scholarship or valid archaeological evidence (see below), but on speculation, special pleadings, and a mystical belief in the righteousness of the cause. Recently a report of a survey of Stone Age sites in the Wadi Araba, Jordan, conveyed the following archaeologically visible note; it directly converges on the concern about perception and the possible.

> The very small size of many of the flints indicated either that they were used by very small people or that the hunting of small birds and hares, and drilling of small holes was done by children. From the shape and size

of even the larger flints it seems possible that their users were physically smaller than their predecessors and their successors in the area. From the scarcity of large scrapers it is a possibility that they did not wear many clothes, or if they did. . . .[46]

The present mysteries and simplistic viewpoints concerning the Wadi Araba or Ebla or Bab edh-Dhra'-Numeirah as being Sodom and Gomorrah are closely analogous in many ways. An individual's *idée fixe* not only blocks the path of rational statement and supporting archaeological evidence but also urges the asking of the "wrong" questions.

What is the evidence for Bab edh-Dhra' and Numeirah being labeled as the Sodom and Gomorrah of the biblical texts? Certainly the firmest evidence is literary and traditional. The Book of Genesis, along with persistent local tradition, suggests in geographical allusions and geological considerations that Lot's city of Sodom was located in the southern Dead Sea area of the Lisan or southward in the Ghor (Plain). As a conjecture in the 1920's, the renowned scholar W. F. Albright guardedly speculated that Sodom and Gomorrah and the Cities of the Plain were, perhaps, buried under the Dead Sea or in the bitumin/salt mass of land once covered by its waters at a higher level than in the recent past. In any case, he was the first to identify Bab edh-Dhra' as *an* Early Bronze Age site — the last phase of which, EB IV (dates and nomenclature are still disputed), was near to the traditional historical dating of the time of the biblical patriarchs.

Yet, even though the excavations at Bab edh-Dhra' are only beginning, it is clear that the townsite and cemetery existed throughout the major periods of Early Bronze I, II, and III, with the oblivion of destruction coming to the town only late in EB III (ca. 2300 b.c.). Some significant encampment occupation *outside* the destroyed city continued onward through EB IV. Such facts might seem to fit the time of destruction of the biblical Sodom and Gomorrah as indicated in the biblical accounts if one moves the traditional dates for the patriarchs some four centuries earlier.

However, *all* the presently excavated EB sites along the Jordan Rift and Valley (e.g., Ai, Ta'annek) also evince city-life destruction or abandonment in late EB III. To account for the destruction, Lapp suggested that there was possible wholesale internecine warfare between the "city-states" of late EB III;[47] Hennessy argues that the instrument of this widespread destruction was the Sixth Dynasty of Egypt.[48] Whatever is nearer the truth, since the destruction spoken of in Genesis is decribed as unique — an altogether discrete and *singular* destruction of Sodom and Gomorrah while the other cities lived on — the disagreements and ambiguities between Old Testament accounts and archaeological evidences are immediately apparent. It would be singular if Bab edh-Dhra' and Numeirah were *not* destroyed or abandoned in EB III. Thus, the textual evidence and the archaeological evidence do not mesh as some would like them to do.

The linguistic argument/identification of Bab edh-Dhra' and Numeirah as biblical Sodom and Gomorrah is weaker still, disconcerting. Such would necessitate a consonant change from the LXX's "GH" to N, Hebrew *'ain* to *nun*. The fact that each name contains an "m" and an "r" is probable coincidence, but in any case, no epigrapher would easily grant a consonant shift, unless perhaps there was an equivalent consonant or it was a standard shift. GH and N are not equivalent consonants, nor would the substitution of one for the other be a standard shift in writing system or sound (e.g., a simple inversion in the order of the letters). Thus, the suggested linguistic evidence for identification does not lead to conviction or even probability.[49]

Further problems arise as one attempts connections of Bab edh-Dhra' and Numeirah, both destroyed in EB III, with the other so-called Cities of the Plain. Es-Safi mortuary remains are primarily EB I evidences, as is the present weight of evidence at Feifeh and Khanazirah. If the archaeological evidence is taken seriously — and it should be — Feifeh, es-Safi, and Khanazirah were not in existence when Bab edh-Dhra' was destroyed six hundred years later. It is true that all these sites are situated on similar fingers of land with perennial water sources in association. But, once again, it must be said that arguments from analogy are always notoriously weak.

Frankly, in a superficial, simplistic perception, the archaeological evidence may look as if it agrees with the textual, biblical evidence. Yet, taking both sources of evidence seriously, there can be no such simplistic correlation made or maintained at present. It seems probable that future aerial and ground surveys of the entire southern Ghor and Wadi Araba could produce more EB sites — such as EB IB Ein Feidan, recently discovered.

Such surveys will also clarify some of the mysteries still adhering to the Bab edh-Dhra'-Numeirah excavations now in early seasons — so early that it can be said that there is a *possibility* that Bab edh-Dhra' and biblical Sodom are the same. But without some "library" tablet inscriptions (yet to be found, insh'allah) or boundary markers (yet to be found) saying: "This is Sodom; (Numeirah) Gomorrah is thirteen kilometers due south at the Wadi Numeirah," there is clearly no perception of *probability* or *certainty* in identification of these sites with biblical Sodom and Gomorrah.

In conclusion, it may be said that to ask and to try to answer the question, "Are Bab edh-Dhra' and Numeirah biblical Sodom and

Gomorrah?" is legitimate from the point of view of biblical interest. But at this stage of research, from the Syro-Palestinian archaeologist's stance, it is a "wrong" question to pose because it particularizes and diverts attention from the important, much wider values to be gained from the excavation of these sites — values among which are the following:

From these sites, much more knowledge will be garnered of a period of fundamental historical, cultural importance — the Early Bronze Age. EB settlement patterns and incipient urbanization, currently diffusely argued, will be given noteworthy clarification. The present debates about the ceramic and chronological transitions from EB I to EB II, and from EB III to EB IV/MB I, will have telling light shed on them, for even in the initial seasons of excavations at Bab edh-Dhra‘ and Numeirah, it appears almost certain that these sites will become "type-sites" for such studies in the next decade of Syro-Palestinian archaeology.

A great deal more, much of it heretofore unknown except from tomb remains, will be learned about EB town life, the environment and man mutually affecting each other — cultural changes and human adaptations that had to be made, even because of climactic variations. Again, the careful delineation of present, real ambiguities between Old Testament literature and archaeological evidence — adding depth to cultural views of ancient *and* modern man — will be aided or clarified. Furthermore, the regional and environmental studies now in progress promise important ethnographic and geological results, including data on climate and rainfall, the hydrology of the region, and cultivation possibilities.

Finally, as research always begets more research, by constant refining and correcting, excavation objectives can only be fully appreciated when the results from Bab edh-Dhra‘ and Numeirah are coordinated with those from other known (and perhaps yet to be discovered) Early Bronze Age sites of the southern Ghor and Araba.

Satellite photo (NASA) of Jordan River flowing southward into the Dead Sea. Bab edh-Dhra' site is on the land mass immediately east on the Lisan (tongue) that juts toward the Dead Sea's western shore at the bottom of the picture. (Photo courtesy National Aeronautics and Space Administration) • Map of the Lisan and southern Ghor (plain), showing four other major EB sites.

Aerial photo, looking northwest, shows Bab edh-Dhra' site between roadway and Wadi Kerak fissure. The Dead Sea and Lisan are in the background.

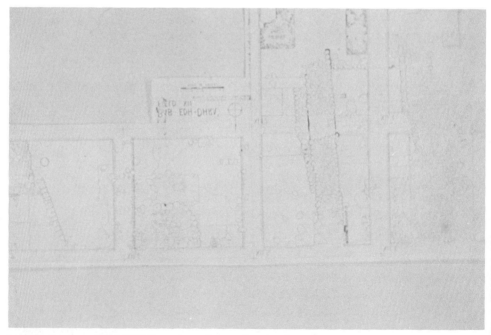

Architect's plan of Field XII "sanctuary" area showing broadroom, rectangular structure with doorway on west, and round installation and bordering wall further west.

102

A javelin blade at the angle it was embedded in the north defensive wall of the Bab edh-Dhra' townsite.

Photo of the Numeirah site's 1.80-meter ceramic installation, called the "thing" in 1977; it may have been used in pottery production.

Architectural drawing of the "thing," showing its placement in surroundings of gravel and into the bedrock at the Numeirah site. The Kerak campsite tents taken from a remaining rampart of the Crusader castle, the Bab edh-Dhra', where expedition members lived. In the left background can be seen the start of the Wadi Kerak as it begins its 4000-foot plunge southward, down to the Lisan of the Dead Sea.

Bab edh-Dhra' shaft tomb chamber 91E, an EB IA tomb, shows a burial worker's peach pit between the pottery to the east and the disarticulated bone pile to the west.

Bab edh-Dhra' cemetery's shaft tomb chamber 100 N. with its stone paved flooring, articulated skeletons, and pottery *in situ*. (Photo courtesy Kjell Sandved, Smithsonian Institution)

A typical EB III hole-mouth jar being excavated from the sometimes two-meter-deep destruction debris at Numeirah in 1977.

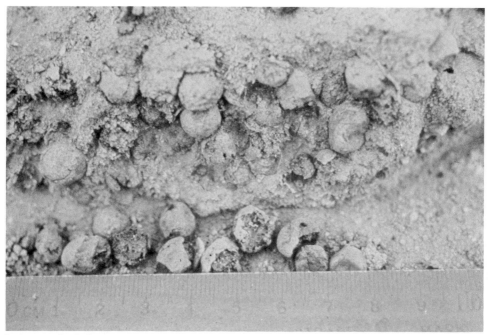

A cluster of whole grapes, carbonized with their skins intact, found *in situ* in the destruction debris of Numeirah in 1977.

Rectangular stone "temple" building, looking northeast, showing doorway and the main balks of squares 1, 2, 4 and 5 still running through the center of the building.

Inside the "temple" building, looking northeast, two phases of the building are clearly discernible; the upper phase, EB III, is represented by the upper stone resting on a flagstone. The lower, earlier phase, EB II, is seen with the stone base and its 15 centimeters of wooden pillar still resting on it.

An unbaked clay figurine, often found in the tomb remains at Bab edh-Dhra', has pierced ear holes and female and male characteristics.

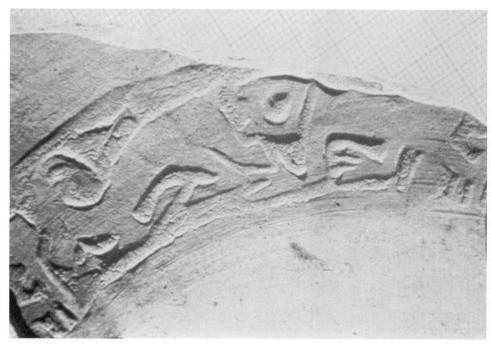

An intriguing seal impression on the shoulder of a jar found at Numeirah in 1977. The horned animal, chewing on a bush and ready to be devoured by a lion, suggests Mesopotamian contacts at the Numeirah site.

NOTES

1. Paul W. Lapp, "Palestine in the Early Bronze Age," in *Near Eastern Archaeology in the Twentieth Century: Essays in Honor of Nelson Glueck* (hereafter *NEATC*), J. A. Saunders, ed. (Garden City, N.Y.: Doubleday & Company, Inc., 1970) 101. Hereafter, the typonym reflecting the location of the ruins will be given simply as Bab edh-Dhra'.

2. During this time he was also instrumental in establishing the popular publication of contemporary, scholarly biblical research in the periodical *The Bible Today*.

3. The ongoing excavations are led by the co-directors, Dr. Walter E. Rast and Dr. R. Thomas Schaub, of Valparaiso University and Indiana University of Pennsylvania, respectively. They have attracted many other specialists and students from, for example, the Smithsonian Institution, the Rochester Institute of Technology, and from some fifteen other universities and colleges. The writer has served as Field Supervisor since 1975 and is indebted (except for possible errors) to the directors and others at the site, and to the just-published (1978) preliminary report for 1975 (Rast, Schaub, and others) in the *Annual of the American Schools of Oriental Research* 43 (1976) 1–60. Additional information and interpretation come from the interim report/lectures of Rast and Schaub at the SBL/AAR/ASOR meetings in San Francisco, December, 1977; conversations with various specialists in the field and, at A.C.O.R. in Amman, with Dr. James Abbott Sauer; and the writer's own field and post-season notes. Also see Donald J. Ortner, "Cultural Change in the Bronze Age," *Smithsonian* 9, no. 5 (August 1978) 82–86; David McCreery, "Preliminary Report of the A.P.C. Township Archaeological Survey," *Annual of the Department of Antiquities of Jordan* (*ADAJ*) 22 (1977–78) 150–162; and Michael Finnegan's article in *American Journal of Physical Anthropology* 49, no. 1 (July 1978) 39–46, which details an alternate measurement system for population studies of human remains found.

4. See, for example, summaries of earlier and present stances in such authors as G. E. Wright, "The Archaeology of Palestine," in *The Bible and the Ancient Near East: Essays in Honor of W. F. Albright* (London: Routledge and Kegen, 1961) 72–101, and the same author's *The Pottery of Palestine* (New Haven: ASOR, 1957). W. G. Dever, "The 'Middle Bronze I' Period in Syria and Palestine," in *NEATC* 132–150; "The People of Palestine in the Middle Bronze I Period," *Harvard Theological Review* 64 (1971) 197–226, and (with S. Richard) "A Reevaluation of Tell Beit Mirsim Stratum J," *BASOR* 226 (April 1977) 1–14. Paul W. Lapp, *The Dhahr Mirzbaneh Tombs* (New Haven: ASOR, 1966) and "Palestine in the Early Bronze Age," in *NEATC* 101–124. K. Kenyon, "Syria and Palestine, ca. 2160–1780 B.C.," *Cambridge Ancient History*², I, fasc. 29. Ruth Amiran, "Chronological Problems of the Early Bronze Age," *American Journal of Archaeology* 72 (1968) 316–318. Kay Prag, "The Intermediate Early Bronze Age: An Interpretation of the Evidence from Trans-Jordan, Syria and Lebanon," *Levant* 6 (1974) 69–116; besides offering a useful list of some EB IV/MB I sites, in note 148, Prag gives a succinct scheme of the leading ideas on chronology and terminology for the Early Bronze Age. Robert J. Braidwood and Gordon R. Willey, *Courses Toward Urban Life* (Edinburgh, 1962), especially the article by Jean Perrot, "Palestine, Syria, Cilicia," 147–164. Note particularly Thomas L. Thompson's "Observations on the Bronze Age in Jordan," *ADAJ* 19 (1974) 63–70, his *The Historicity of the Patriarchal Narratives: The Quest of the Historical Abraham* (Berlin: DeGruyter, 1974), and J. B. Hennessy, *The Foreign Relations of Palestine During the Early Bronze Age* (London: B. Quaritch, 1967). See also note 14 below.

5. For a thoughtful, summary consideration, see also G. E. Wright, "The Phenomenon of American Archaeology in the Near East," in *NEATC* 3–40.

6. Gordon Willey and Jeremy Sabloff, *A History of American Archaeology*, ed. Glyn Daniels (London: Thames and Huelson, 1974) 12.

7. For example, the history of interpretations of Tel Anafa, Jalame, Tell Mardikh, the multiple excavations at Tel Gezer, and so on. The objective now is usually not merely to

gain the history of a site but also to clarify the cultural process itself. See especially W. G. Dever, "Archaeology," *IDB* (suppl. vol.) 44–52.

8. It is, rather, the deliberate pursuit of ordered knowledge about man and his past in which excavation of a site takes place as a field technique for obtaining *all* the materials on which a working hypothesis can be based and from which defensible inferences can be drawn.

9. See below for the confusions related to the Ebla site, prevailing views of Near Eastern history, and so on.

10. Consult any of the general introduction books or periodical accounts that have appeared within the last decade detailing the history of field techniques, laboratory developments, or the "changing history of man." Especially recommended are W. G. Dever, H. D. Lance and others, *Gezer Excavation Manual* (1976), and Dever's article on "Archaeology," in *IDB* (suppl. vol.), along with C. L. Redman's *Research and Theory in Current Archaeology* (1973). A more popular approach could be found in Philip C. Hammond, *Archaeological Techniques for Amateurs* (1963).

11. A few of the more arcane, recent developments are to be found in such areas of study as paleoserology of human remains, potassium argon dating of geological samples, thermoluminescent dating of pottery, palynalysis of plant remains, and archaeo-magnetic analysis of ceramic remains.

12. Aspects of the tangled skein of things may be found in such disparate sources as Giovanni Pettinato, "The Royal Archive of Tell Mardikh-Ebla," *BA* 39, no. 2 (1976) 44–52; Paolo Matthiae, "Ebla in the Late Early Syrian Period: The Royal Palace and the State Archives," *BA* 39, no. 3 (1976) 94–112; and Richard F. Dempewolff, "Putting Biblical Pieces Together," *Popular Mechanics* 149, no. 5 (May 1978) 103–107, 278–283. Fuller explanations may be found in Matthiae's book on Ebla scheduled for publication in Spring 1979. [After these words were written, the writer came upon a book that summarizes well, journalistically, the multi-phase religious and political uses to which some of the Ebla material has been subject. See Chaim Bermant and Michael Weitzman, *Ebla: A Revelation in Archaeology* (New York: Times Books, 1979).]

13. Howard La Fay, "Ebla: The Splendor of an Unknown Empire," *National Geographic* 154, no. 6 (December 1978) 730–759.

14. That there is much disagreement about these Old Testament passages, and among the various (perceptions of) biblical interpreters, is well known. For example, consult and compare the classic writings of Bruce Vawter, *A Path Through Genesis* (1961) or E. A. Speiser, "Genesis," *Anchor Bible* (1964), as centrist interpreters with, say, Thomas L. Thompson's *The Historicity of the Patriarchal Narratives*, a work that deserves real attention, if not agreement; also cf. these with O. Eissfeldt's article on Genesis in *IDB*, (E-J) or with E. Maly's "Genesis" in *JBC* I, 7ff. alongside B. G. Wood, "Sodom and Gomorrah and Noah's Ark," *Bible and Spade* 3, no. 3 (Summer 1974) and "Sodom and Gomorrah Update," *Bible and Spade* 6, no. 1 (Winter 1977). The various perceptions are especially relevant when considering the personages, geography, and local traditions of Gen 14 and the "Cities of the Plain" notations. Note C. Westermann and R. Albertz, "Genesis," *IDB* (suppl. vol.), at 360.

15. A scholar of no less repute than D. N. Freedman, quoted in "A City Beneath the Sands," *Science Year* (1976), noted that the similarity of the city names and the duplication of the order in which they occur, in the Bible and in the Ebla tablets, "cannot be coincidence." Here it should be noted that Freedman has an article concerning these matters about Ebla in *BA* (December 1978). Unfortunately, the issue was not available in Amman, Jordan, by press deadline.

16. See Matthiae, *BA* (September 1976) 101.

17. And so on and on. Near Eastern history need not be rewritten; it simply has to be written. Also see Adnan Hadidi, "Archaeology and Politics," *ADAJ* 22 (1977–78) 6–12.

What has happened concerning Ebla is that publicists of various persuasions in the volatile political atmosphere of the Middle East have become aware of Matthiae's discoveries and are interpreting them to fit various preconceived theses. In the recent past, people have used such methods, often for their quasi-political convenience, to show that God is an astronaut or to show that nation states, particularly in the developing world, have, now, legitimacy given to their often dubious claims. "Now Ebla is the center of an academic dispute which is an extension of the wider Arab-Israeli conflict." See the perceptive article by Andrew Lycett and Maureen Abdallah, "Archaeology — Digging into the Political Past," *The Middle East*, no. 51 (January 1979) 98–104. See also P. Matthiae, "Tell Mardikh: The Archives and Palace," *Archaeology* 30, no. 4 (July 1977) 244–253.

18. There is a victory inscription of Sargon's conquest.

19. See Matthiae, *BA* (September 1976) 111.

20. In this context, it is interesting to consider the scholarly work of Denise Schmandt-Besserat, who argues against the current belief that writing first occurred about 3500 B.C. in present-day Iraq. Relying on her studies since 1969, Schmandt-Besserat recently projected a quite convincing four-stage evolution of early recording systems, stretching from 8500 to 3100 B.C. Her studies of the earliest uses of clay in the Middle East lead her to conclude that the origin of writing occurred much earlier than was previously assumed. See Denise Schmandt-Besserat, "On the Invention of Writing," *Syro-Mesopotamian Studies* 1, no. 1 (April 1977) and "The Earliest Uses of Clay in Syria," *Expedition* 19, no. 3 (1977) 28–42.

21. An intriguing set of items urges such a possibility. The strongest literary evidence is in the salient geographical allusions and geological considerations of the Book of Genesis, and with persistent local traditions; these suggest the southern Dead Sea basin as a likely site for Lot's city of Sodom. Other commonly cited linguistic and archaeological "evidence" convinces some persons of possible identification of the site with Sodom: (a) local tradition names the Dead Sea as the "Sea of Lot," one citation among many others; (b) present and past evidence of bitumen, salt, and sulphur are found in abundance in the area; (c) there are analogies at Bab edh-Dhra' to some finds at other, so-called patriarchal sites; (d) the writer's personal communication with a number of biblical literalists indicated their belief that Numeirah is a later version of the name Gomorrah; (e) initial Bab edh-Dhra' excavations of 1975, 1977 indicate the end-of-town-site-occupation "destruction" to be late EB III period; (f) the Rast-Schaub survey of 1973 produced five similar Early Bronze Age sites, on five similar outspurs of land with perennial water sources in association, and most of these sites appeared to have similar mortuary remains as well as tower and wall constructions; (g) after the rather intensive, although limited, survey of the pertinent area of the southern Ghor (plain), no other Early Bronze Age sites appeared to be located there.

Some of these sets of circumstances, along with beginning archaeological indications in the early 1970's, suggested to Rast and Schaub the conditional discreet statement that graces the conclusions of their 1973 survey report (emphasis added): "The sites *may* bear on the biblical tradition of the 'Cities of the Plain' (Gen. 14, 18, 19) long believed to be located in this area. . . . *If* the biblical traditions find roots going back as far as the Early Bronze Age, the sites reported here *may be* of some importance." See Walter E. Rast and R. Thomas Schaub, "Survey of the Southeastern Plain of the Dead Sea," *ADAJ* 19 (1974), at 19. These two authors' tentative statement has been enormously expanded on, but not with Rast's or Schaub's assent, in, for example, *Bible and Spade* (1974, 1977).

22. Stuart Piggott, "Introduction: The Man-Made World," *The Dawn of Civilization* (New York: McGraw-Hill, 1961) 12.

23. The walled townsite is about two times larger than the Jerusalem of King David's time.

24. The 1977 preliminary report is nearing completion and should be published in

1979. This fully detailed account will include technical data too complex to be treated here, along with reports from the paleo-botanists, geologists, the regional/environmental studies, and so on. See note 43 below.

25. The site will have important contributions to make to studies of settlement patterns, urbanization, and burgeoning city-state developments in the Near East during this period and earlier. The writer is fully aware of the need for caution, such as that given by Braidwood, when stating that there is *real* urbanization before there is evidence of proved centers with public structures and elements of civilization such as monumental architecture, long-distance trade, craft specialties, and so on. See, for example, Robert J. Braidwood and Gordon R. Willey, eds., *Courses Toward Urban Life* (Edinburgh, 1962) 351f.

26. The term "wadi" found in Arab place names can refer to anything from a small gulley to a rift of canyon proportions, any of which may contain rivers of episodic flow. See the interesting studies of such geologic factors in D. H. Kallner and R. Amiran, "Geomorphology of the Central Negev Highlands," *Israel Exploration Journal* 1, no. 4 (1951) 107–120; and Friedrich Bender, *Geology of the Arabian Peninsula: Jordan*, Geographical Survey Paper 560-I (Washington, D.C., 1975).

27. Certainly the extensive debate continues about what constitutes a temple or sanctuary area at such Early Bronze sites as Bab edh-Dhraʿ. The considerable literature includes G. Loud, *Megiddo II* (Chicago, 1948); Judith Marquet-Krause, *Les fouilles de'Ay (et-Tell), 1933–1935* (Paris, 1949); J. Garstang, *The Story of Jericho* (London, 1948); Ruth Amiran and Y. Aharoni, *Ancient Arad* (Israel Museum Guide, 1967); D. Ussishkin, *BA* 34 (1971) 23–39. These and other writings about EB temples concentrate on the architectural style, the stratigraphy and chronology, while noting that all examples are similar in plan: a large broadroom structure with the entrance always facing east and onto a courtyard containing bamah and basin; on the inside, two to four stone bases for wooden pillars fixed on a long axis, and, in most cases, benching along some of the sides. See architecture of Field XII, Bab edh-Dhraʿ, in the forthcoming preliminary report of 1977 and the article by A. Ben-Tor, "Plans of Dwellings and Temples in Early Bronze Age Palestine," *Eretz Israel II* (1973) 25, 92–98.

28. This base and pillar remnant were associated with EB II pottery; the wood is being dated by carbon 14 tests.

29. It may have functioned as a ceiling beam or as a shelf construction for the EB III structure. Its length, presently 1.20 meters, still cannot be determined because part of it is still hidden in the north balk of square 5.

30. Among the problems encountered here are those that bring to mind another Heidt "home truth": Similarity is not identity — that is, arguments from analogy are always recognized as among the weakest. Known similar "temples" have the entrance and courtyard to the east; Bab edh-Dhraʿ's is to the west. Many have benching around the walls; thus far, Bab edh-Dhraʿ shows no firm indications of such benching. However, Ein Gedi is a kind of prototype for EB temples and is judged to be a Chalcolithic-to-EB structure; Bab edh-Dhraʿ's "sanctuary" could also be transitional, or specifically arranged for a regional (one can see *to* Numeirah) purpose or need.

31. P. Lapp, "Bab edh-Dhraʿ," *Revue Biblique* 73 (1968) 556–561.

32. A *glacis* is a French term that indicates a defensive installation of the Bronze Age. It is a packed, steep slope of dense aggregate that neither animals nor men could scale or climb easily.

33. A name first used by Lapp of the Bab edh-Dhraʿ cemetery to describe the numerous round and rectangular funerary buildings. They often contain layers of many skeletons, pottery, cloth, axe heads and so on, but the burning does not appear to have been a practice of cremation. The mudbrick buildings were, in ancient times, built half-in/half-out of the ground surface and may have been used and reused over a several hundred-year period.

34. At the turn of the century, Sir W. Flinders Petrie had a rule of thumb that every meter or so of occupation debris indicated another phase or period of ancient history. Such neat delineation and even distribution of remains is rarely, if ever, at hand.

35. On a visit to the site several weeks after we had left it in 1977, the late, acclaimed British archaeologist Dame Kathleen M. Kenyon came to the same interpretation, independently.

36. At the 1977 SBL/AAR/ASOR meeting in San Francisco, Rast presented clear evidence of *changes* in mortuary practice at Bab edh-Dhra' in EB IA and IB, and for EB II and III. From city and cemetery evidence, using figures from Robert McC. Adams, *Land Behind Baghdad*, Chicago University Press (1965), Rast calculates conservatively a population of six hundred at the site at any given time, and over ten thousand during the centuries of EB II and III. See the preliminary report of 1977.

37. See Perrot article cited above. Perrot, in his balanced conclusion, cites incipient urbanization as being later in Palestine than it was in Mesopotamia. He writes that around 3000 BC., the *premiere installation urbaine* appeared and contained multi-roomed rectangular houses, sanctuaries, paved streets, sewers, and so on. These features are in process of being confirmed at Bab edh-Dhra'.

38. The team was led by Dr. Donald J. Ortner, physical anthropologist at the National Museum of Natural History, and included Dr. Michael Finnegan of Kansas State University. They were especially interested in discovering the average length of life; relative numbers of men, women, and children; and diseases that afflicted the population. But they also made studies of burial practices and what these tell about the social structure at Bab edh-Dhra'. Their results converge well with evidences from the townsite. (See note 25 above.) In a private communication, Finnegan noted that there were no "giants at the site" (one possible 6'4" skeleton was reputed, in the 1960's to be from Bab edh-Dhra'), but people averaged 5'3" to 5'6" and appear to have been longer-lived than their Mediterranean contemporaries.

39. The transition in tomb types follows roughly the EB period's major phases of EB I, EB II–III. Shaft tombs with, usually, four chambers approximately three feet high and six feet in diameter are EB I; transitional round, "beehive" charnel houses (mimicking the shaft tombs) and the later rectangular charnel houses are dated to EB II and III. Reproductions of several of these tombs, with their contents, are to be seen at the National Museum of Natural History, Washington, D.C.; one will be constructed soon at St. John's University, Collegeville, Minnesota. The loan of these materials was made possible through the courtesy of the Jordanian Department of Antiquities and its director, Dr. Adnan Hadidi.

40. With the wealth of ceramic wares both in the cemete y and townsite, Bab edh-Dhra' may well be the "type-site" for the Early Bronze Age, ai d of the transition to the Middle Bronze Age, currently a disputed transitional period. The site will almost certainly add important knowledge of the total history of the Near East, which is presently very uneven and incomplete. Yet, in any case, a highly developed social organization and settlement pattern are already evident.

41. The closest analogy the writer ever encountered is pictured in the *Dawn of Civilization* (see note 22 above), 241.

42. In *Archaeology* 30, no. 4 (note 17 above), P. Matthiae speaks of "lions-assaulting-goats" objects, which he understands as the conventions of Mesopotamia of the Early Dynastic Period (ca. 2900–2350 B.C.).

43. Staff specialists engaged in specific environmental and regional studies are Dr. Robert Johnston, on clay sources and radiography; Dr. James Richardson II, David McCreery, and Dr. Jack Harlan, on agronomy and non-vertebrate and flotation studies; Dr. Michael Finnegan, on human and animal faunal remains and taxonomic studies; Dr. Jack Donahue, on geological studies; Susan Short, on core samples and palynalysis. A complete list of participants and staff will be included in the Final Report.

44. See Rast, Schaub, and others, note 3 above.

45. For a useful, clear presentation of what environmental studies have to contribute to an archaeological perception, see John G. Evans, *Introduction to Environmental Archaeology* (Ithaca, N.Y.: Cornell University Press, 1978).

46. R. L. Raikes, "Notes on Some Stone Age Sites in Wadi Araba and the Dead Sea Valley" (unpublished manuscript, January 1979) 18.

47. See Lapp, in *NEATC*, 117f.

48. See *Foreign Relations* (note 4 above) 85–90.

49. Dr. James A. Sauer, director of the American Center for Oriental Research in Amman, Jordan, has spoken to this point both in lecture and in private conversation with the writer. He makes the point that if the present and longstanding name Numeirah meant nothing in Arabic (and there are Arabic site names that do not mean anything), or if Gomorrah could be shown to mean something itself, there might be a case for considering some relationship between these two names. But the name Numeirah does mean something, viz., the place of the "small, female tiger." And other so-called Cities of the Plain names also mean something — for example, Khanazirah, the place of the "female wild pig," and Bab edh-Dhra', "the gate of the arm." Ancient name traditions do carry through with spelling changes, but not with major consonant changes: biblical Rabbat 'Ammon is present 'Ammān, Dibon is Dhiban, and so on.

Aelred Cody, O.S.B.

SIN AND ITS SEQUEL IN THE STORY OF
DAVID AND BATHSHEBA

The contributions to this volume of essays are, by agreement, to be fairly popular essays on something having to do with "sin, salvation, and the Spirit." The story of David's adultery with Bathsheba and its consequences in 2 Sam 11:2–12:25 is concerned with sin, and with a kind of national salvation in the long run. It is not concerned with Spirit, but from our vantage point here in the twentieth century, we might conceivably take something that was said in the intertestamental period and apply it to what we have seen in the story of David and Bathsheba in their earlier days together.

The story, although sin and its consequences are important concerns in it, has never been used much in formal treatises on such topics. The reason for that is surely that the author of a formal treatise on anything usually looks for biblical texts whose inspired authors have said something gnomic and sententious on the subject at hand. Concise, easily quotable sentences on sin and salvation are hardly to be found in 2 Sam 11:2–12:25. Such direct statements are foreign to the literary genre or genres chosen by the inspired author to say what he wants to say there; they are not suited to his purpose. But a story like that of David and Bathsheba, Uriah, Nathan, and the first two children born of the union of David and Bathsheba can be a theologian's delight, too. To it can aptly be applied what a theologian setting out to write a work of process theology says of the value of the Bible for such a task as his: "The Bible is there to show us what God is up to in the world, what human existence is about, and how we may be related to the reality of God in the immediate situations in which we find ourselves at whatever time and in whatever place we happen to live."[1] In the particular passage of the Bible with which we are now concerned, just what are we shown? What, in fact, are the purposes of the author?

We should look more accurately at different levels in the text and ask ourselves about the purposes of more than one author, each with his particular point of view. There is a general consensus among exegetes today that the scene in which the prophet Nathan figures (2 Sam 12:1-15a) is more recent than the rest of the story and that it was added in the process of what is commonly called the Deuteronomic redaction, the process in which the older material in a number of our present biblical books, including our two Books of Samuel, was being edited according to an ideological program that included a certain amount of theological emphasis and statement akin in spirit to what is found in the Book of Deuteronomy.[2] Since the "Deuteronomist" responsible for that editorial process does not prevent the older texts from speaking for themselves, we can profit by looking first at the older form of the story of David and Bathsheba before pondering it in the light of the encounter of Nathan and David.

The Old Succession Narrative

The older form of the story is itself part of a longer work, the so-called Succession Narrative, found in 2 Sam 9–20; 1 Kg 1–2, which recounts events leading from David's consolidation of his reign to the establishment of Solomon on the throne as his successor.[3] It is here in the episode that particularly occupies our attention at the moment, in fact, that Bathsheba, whose activity later assured her son Solomon's succession (1 Kg 1:11-31), is introduced, and it is here, at the end of our episode, that Solomon is born, after David's first son by Bathsheba has died soon after his birth.

Sin there is, in David's initial relations with Bathsheba, and for that matter there is a good bit of sin throughout the Succession Narrative — enough to raise the suspicion that the desire to show the often tragic consequences of sin was one subordinated purpose that the author of the Succession Narrative had throughout his work.[4] The story of David and Bathsheba, from David's first lustful glimpse of her until the birth of Solomon, prepares the reader for much that follows, because it clearly depicts David's character, with traits that will show up again, both in David and in some of his sons, always with fateful consequences. Some of those traits are of the kind that urge a man toward sin or that govern his reactions afterwards.

Is the purpose of the old pre-Deuteronomistic author of the story of David and Bathsheba historical, then, or moral? In the whole Succession Narrative, for that matter, does he mean to tell us about the history of a king and the people who loom large in the drama of his life, or is he really more interested in questions of right and wrong? Questions like this have been discussed over and over again, and the entire Succession Narrative is surely too subtle a work to be characterized neatly as purely historical in intent or purely moral. The author does surely have genuine historical interests, and his primary purpose is surely historiographical in some way, but he also shows himself to be an acute delineator of human character. He is a creative writer who uses his imagination to embellish historical fact and to conjure up the interior sentiments of the persons in his story, expressed usually in soliloquy or dialogue most probably composed by the author himself. In 2 Sam 11:2–12:25 there are many details that the author could have known as facts, but is anyone likely to have jotted down the dialogue between David and Uriah in 11:10-13, or to have seen both David on the roof and Bathsheba below? We may not be far from the mark if we call the episode in 2 Sam 11–12, like many others in the Succession Narrative, a historical exemplary novel.[5]

The author's historiographic purposes lie outside the pale of our present interests. When he includes in his work an episode that has the characteristics of an exemplary novel in which there is sin and deliverance, is his purpose that of a moralist? The author of a good exemplary novel does not make explicit pronouncements on what is right and wrong; he takes it for granted that the reader can make those basic judgments for himself, unaided. The author of an exemplary novel depicts character and motives on the basis of accurate observation of the human condition, and he does so in order to let his readers contemplate what he shows and thus grow a little in wisdom. In his story he may recount historical sinful actions and their results, as our author does here, but in any case he is free to use his imagination to embellish historical event and thus sharpen the psychological traits he wants to stress in the human characters he draws for us in words.

Such an author does not give us an abstract disquisition on sin and deliverance, with the intention of gaining our intellectual adherence to what he says about them. He does not even make explicit moral judgments. He shows us a vividly concrete example of a historically important man who happened to fall into sin and who realized that he had offended God. He does so in a way meant to engage our own imagination as we ponder the example, so that we can draw some thoughtful practical conclusions on the way a man can fall into sin and on his reactions when he at last faces the consequences before God. We are supposed to be helped in our own wise understanding of the human condition. The author's purpose, in other words, as far as this side of his complex set of intentions goes, is not that of the metaphysician or of the modern moralist but rather that of the Ancient Near Eastern wise man.[6]

David in our story may be the author's hero, but unlike most heroes in ancient literature, he is not bereft of the complex and passionate emotions found in sinning and in coping with the aftereffects of sin. By presenting David that way, the author can engage us in the challenge and the conflict he depicts in David's sinful designs, their execution, and their objective and subjective sequel. Far from being a banal literary moralizer, he lets actions and the motives behind them speak for themselves.

There is even a certain amount of subtle social commentary in what the author lets us see of the ease with which a man in high social position can achieve the goal of his self-seeking desires. David can arrange for a military expedition to take place in such a way that a man he wants to get out of the way will perish in the action. He has the facility a king in ancient times had in having his sexual way with women in a society that protected its women (see Gen 12:15f.; 20:2; Prov 31:3). The very fact that David, because he was a powerful man in his society, could so facilely achieve his sinful designs gives us something to think about, quite apart from any narrative elements that might indicate specifically moral conclusions to be drawn.

The author, in 2 Sam 11:11, lets us ponder the ironic contrast he draws between the attitude of Uriah, refusing to sleep with his lawful wife for reasons of religious custom effective when men are engaged in active military combat,[7] and David, who has no noticeable religious scruples either about his unlawful sleeping with Uriah's wife or about sending the hapless man to his death. The author does not point out the contrast explicitly. He draws it for us, making good use of the touching speech on religious conviction and devotion to duty that he puts in Uriah's mouth (11:11), and then leaving us to be moved by the example and the heightened contrast, and to draw our own conclusions about persons who sin passionately and heedlessly on the one hand, and persons whose fidelity to conviction leads them to abstain from legitimate sexual activity on the other. The contrast is poignantly heightened when Uriah's very fidelity to religious principle leads him to avoid a moment of bliss that paradoxically would have saved him from being sent to death in the service of the very man who violated his wife.

In David's behavior the author lets us see that hotheaded rashness that all too often leads a man into inept actions — sinful even — performed in the unrealistic hope that "it may work out all right." He commits adultery in the obvious hope that it will not lead to a pregnancy, but it does. We then see an example of the inept and somewhat frantic behavior that can often be ours as we try to conceal a wrong. The failure of David's frantic efforts to get Uriah to sleep with Bathsheba then escalates, as the failure of such attempts often does. In this case the next step lies in the king's murderous calculations, whose goal is attained. In our contemporary society it might well have been something like abortion. Our biblical author says nothing here about abortion, but he does have something to say to the modern wise man, or to the modern man who would be wise, about the way a frantic state of mind can double one mistake with another far more sinful one.

Nothing much is said directly about Bathsheba's personality and character, but if we read straight through the Succession Narrative, we get a mental picture of her as a woman who is a little too naive in her openness to suggestion. At the time of the adultery she comes and goes without saying anything at all in the description that the narrator gives us, until she sends David the message later about her pregnancy (11:4f.). When the succession to the throne is imminent, she does what she is told to do by Nathan, apparently without thought of the potential dangers that arise when one gets involved in palace intrigue (1 Kg 1:11-27). When Adonijah asks her to entreat Solomon to give him Abishag, she does so; Adonijah, the manipulatory intent of whose request Solomon senses, is put to death, a result that Bathsheba, had she been a little less ingenuous and a little more cautious, could have foreseen and avoided (1 Kg 2:13-25). Admittedly, a king could do many things that men less highly placed could not do, but in the Israelite ethos real adultery was not morally acceptable for a king either (see Gen 12:17-20; 20:3-10; 26:10f.).

The narrator, by letting Bathsheba say nothing in the adultery scene, and by painting her openness to suggestion when she appears in later episodes, has sketched a woman who could at least have protested against the king's adulterous proposal and whose failure to do so enabled the king to have his sinful way. David, like many a man in a similar moment of passion, had a conscience, but needed to be confronted with some opposition in which ethical and religious principles could have been cited. Had Bathsheba made such opposition, she might have avoided the tragic sequence of events that was to follow. She did not do so, and the narrator has portrayed her in such a way, both by what she says and does and by what she does not say and do, that the reader may suspect her to have been a bit seductive. A treatise on sin, or a sententious saying on sin, has all its value in what the author says; in a story about sin, a point can also be made by what a person in the story does *not* say or does not do.

So the author of the old Succession Narrative tells us about sin, but he uses the narrative art to do his subtle telling. He tells us about sin by telling us a story about sinners and innocent victims, about what they do and what goes on in their minds.

He also has something to show us of the aftermath of sin. For one thing, the child of the adulterous union dies. At this point in the story, in the old Succession Narrative,[8] God enters the drama, though not as one of the *dramatis personae* actually appearing on the scene and speaking. He does not even communicate a message through a prophet, as he will do in the passage added later to our story. He enters the drama in 11:27; 12:15b-16, 24f. as one watching what is going on and reacting to it. This is the role God plays throughout the Succession Narrative.

There are few if any miracles or marvelous divine interventions in the narrative, and natural causes lead to natural effects, but the reader is made aware of God's presiding over history and human destiny, including the destiny of David and those around him.[9] It is God who puts justice and retribution into the course of events. The wages of sin are indeed death, but here it is not David, the sinner, who dies, nor is it Bathsheba, although both parties to an act of adultery were supposed to be put to death if they were caught in the act (Dt 22:22), and Num 5:11-31 sets out the procedure for determining the guilt of a woman suspected of adultery, with the death penalty in view. It is rather the child of their first, adulterous encounter whom God strikes and who dies. This, to the mind of the old Israelites, was justice enough, since the sins of the fathers could still be visited upon their sons.[10]

It is also God, in the Succession Narrative, who puts purpose into the course of human events. Even sinful actions and death have their place in the divine purpose. Normally a treatise on sin and salvation, especially if it is hortatory in intent, will not talk about divine purpose behind and above positively sinful actions, but the wise man knows that it is there, and he can use that awareness in reassuring himself or others, when he or they have done something wrong in God's eyes, have repented sincerely, but still grieve for having produced a sad or even tragic effect that can never be canceled. The author of the Succession Narrative shows us that God, for some really inscrutable reason, meant for David's kingdom to pass to Solomon. He shows us that David's sin with Bathsheba was a prerequisite to Solomon's birth, as was Uriah's death, in a way, for only with Uriah out of the way could David take Bathsheba as one of his wives so that a second child might be born to them: Solomon himself, whom "God loved" (12:24).

In 12:16-24 the wise author has also given us an example of the way a man of some grandeur of personality might act in the face of the tragedy of his child's sickness and death: prayer and desperation before the child's death, but calm and manly resignation afterwards. May we also see in David's behavior after the child's death (12:20-24) that of a man who, already in the old Succession Narrative (before the addition of Nathan's explicit prophetic words), knew that his child's death was disposed by God as a punishment for his sin and had come to a sense of guilt?[11] If so, it is perhaps worth noting that David's behavior in this example given to us for our wise reflection suggests that a well-founded sense of guilt did not lead him into a state of needless anxiety; once the child was dead, the guilty king, contrary to the expectations of his courtiers, got on with his life.

The Encounter of David with Nathan

The author of the somewhat later Nathan scene in 2 Sam 12:1-15a has a purpose somewhat different from that of the person who composed the older Succession Narrative. In the Succession Narrative, God remained not only invisible but also inaudible, disposing events in his own inscrutable ways; in the Nathan scene, God intervenes directly with a message, communicated through his prophet Nathan, in order to confront David openly with the evil of his sin and to pass judgment on it, with the announcement of punishment.

Nathan's opening parable of the poor man whose much loved ewe lamb was snatched away by the rich man who already had plenty of lambs of his own leads David to pronounce judgment on himself before he realizes to whom the parable applies. In the oracle that follows in 12:7-12, we have something much more explicit on the significance of sin and on God's attitude toward it than we should ever expect to find in the Succession Narrative. In Nathan's oracle the Deuteronomistic editor has made sure that we see more clearly what the older author was content to leave implicit. The precise nature of David's sins is reviewed in 12:9, and the connection of the child's death with its father's sin is stated clearly in 12:14. In the older story we were allowed to presume David's repentance, but in Nathan's oracle the fact of his repentance is mentioned expressly (in 12:13). His repentance is given as the explanation for God's transferring the death penalty, which David had unwittingly declared fitting for himself as he reacted to the parable (12:5), to the child instead.

The author of the Nathan scene does not have the finesse of the author of the Succession Narrative. He seeks clarity rather than subtlety. What he tells us, he tells us more explicitly, but there is less there for us to contemplate in depth. He is at times even a little heavy-handed; David's exclamation that the rich man who took the poor man's little ewe lamb is a "son of death" (12:5, translating the Hebrew expression literally) is really out of proportion to the guilt of the man in the parable, but it fits what the later author wants to tell us about guilt and repentance and transferred punishment in David's own case.

The Deuteronomist who added the Nathan scene extends his view to other parts of the older historical work, too. Nathan's prophecy includes elements whose fulfillment will come later.[12] The prophetic statement that the sword will never depart from David's house (12:10) is fulfilled in much of what follows in the Succession Narrative as sons rebel and sons are killed.[13] The prophecy about David's wives having intercourse with other men is fulfilled in 16:22, with David's own son Absalom perpetrating the action foretold.

The crimes of violence and lust that brought sorrow to David afterwards are interpreted by the Deuteronomist as the result of God's determination to punish David's initial sins against Uriah, while the older narrator saw God's just vengeance satisfied adequately in the death of the first child of David and Bathsheba. For the older narrator, sin had to be punished, but once the sinner had repented and God had inflicted a penalty commensurate to the sin, that was the end of the matter. For the Deuteronomist, however, with his more synthetic view of things, events not directly connected with a given sin could still be the result of God's desire to punish that sin. We have before us two different views of God's way of dealing with sin and punishment. The Deuteronomist's view can be useful to anyone who wishes to stress the inadequacy of human repentance in averting the perduring wrath of God; the narrator of the Succession Narrative provides more hope and consolation for those who genuinely repent of their wrongdoing.

It may not be entirely beside the point to note that in the oracle of judgment and punishment delivered by Nathan, David's adultery is looked upon, not as a "sin against chastity" (a virtue significantly difficult to isolate conceptually, as such, in the books of the Old Testament), but as a species of theft. David has stolen Uriah's wife from him, and that is the basis of the analogy expressed in the opening parable of the rich man and the poor man and the latter's beloved ewe lamb. The idea of adultery as theft is somewhat foreign to our habitual way of classifying and cataloguing sins, but in the Old Testament, with its fairly positive attitude toward sexuality in general and toward sexual activity as long as it did not harm some person or profane what was somehow or other sacral, the sin of adultery was looked upon fundamentally as an act of injustice to one's neighbor. In the Decalogue, the prohibition of adultery and of the coveting that tends toward it are contextually associated with the prohibition of theft and of the coveting that easily leads to that.

In writing on sin and the Ten Commandments, a modern psychologist, Eugene Kennedy, who also brings a theological dimension to his work, considers all four of these commandments not separately but together. All four of them "are clearly related to the style and reality of our relationships with others," he says; "insisting on being No. 1, justifying any and all activities that gratify us personally, lead us to violate the lives, possessions, and relationships of others in a reckless and destructive manner. . . . Call the sin stealing or sexual thievery; they are species of the same poisoned fruit."[14] In writing that, he could well be commenting on David's sin against Uriah, in the light of Nathan's message.

Some Concluding Remarks

The story of David and Bathsheba and Uriah has plenty of value for us if we want to grow a little in wisdom as we ponder sin and that kind of immediate, personal salvation that is forgiveness after repentance. With the scene involving Nathan it has something even more explicit to show us about them. But the story, like other biblical stories, is not meant to reach us in the way a conceptual essay does. It is not abstract or theoretical but exemplary. It is meant to involve us, to confront us and elicit a reaction.

Just as Nathan's parable was designed to provoke a reaction on David's part that enabled him to be confronted with the real sense of what he had done in God's eyes, the whole story is designed to involve us and to let us grow by vicarious experience of what happens in the story, with our sense of sin heightened by our own reaction to Nathan's parable and oracle. David's reaction to Nathan's parable was one of unwitting judgment on himself, a judgment that struck home as soon as Nathan showed what he was getting at. We react to the whole story, perhaps not because we have done quite all that David did, but because we are capable of doing the same things, or similar things, and because we know that we stand to profit from seeing how such human actions are reacted to by God.

In essays on sin, the emphasis, naturally, is usually on sin itself, punishment, and, today, even on anxiety as one of the natural consequences of sin and punishment.[15] Attention is given somewhat less often to the other side of the coin: repentance and forgiveness, and freedom from anxiety as a fruit of repentance and forgiveness. In the story of David and Bathsheba, we see all of these things. The author of the Succession Narrative shows us the ugly side of David and the wrath of God, but in showing us the ever passionate David's heartbroken supplication of God and then, after the execution of divine punishment had been completed, David's lack of crippling anxiety, he also shows us the beautiful side of David and the forgiving side of God. In the Nathan scene, the Deuteronomist has emphasized the wrath of God, but he has also shown us more explicitly David's moment of repentance and God's forgiving response.

The Deuteronomist's view of history is such that God's punishment extends far beyond the death of the child. But if we read the older form of the story of David and Bathsheba as a part of the entire Succession Narrative, as it was originally meant to be read, then we can also see how God can dispose human events in such a way that something good ultimately comes even from sinful actions, just as he brought his own solution to the question of the succession to David out of the tragic chain of events set off by David's sinful decision on the roof of his house early one evening long ago.

An Epilogue on Spirit

The general theme set for all the essays in this collection is "Sin, Salvation, and the Spirit," but we have said nothing so far of Spirit. That is simply because there is nothing said of Spirit in the story of David and Bathsheba, and the ancient authors certainly did not have in their own minds a concept of Spirit that would have been relevant to their subject matter. We have been taking the ancient texts on their own terms. We may perhaps be not unworthy of the reader's benevolence if, in our desire to collaborate fully, we indulge in synthesis for a moment and integrate a reflection on the Spirit of God as it is found in the intertestamental period with what we have seen of the story of David and Bathsheba as it is actually set before us in the Second Book of Samuel.

The old author of the Succession Narrative quietly lets us be aware of the divine disposal of human history lying behind the events he narrates. If it is true that he was steeped in the tradition of the Ancient Near Eastern wise man, he probably saw God's own wisdom as the directive force governing the world, or at least as the quality of God with which God governed the world. The Deuteronomistic editor has a still more explicit "theology" of history. Much later, in the Book of Wisdom, or of the Wisdom of Solomon, written just before the Christian era began, the divine wisdom that governs the universe and the destinies of men is called "intelligent spirit" (Wis 7:22). That same wisdom is a "spirit which loves men" but will not leave unpunished men who sin, for it knows all our thoughts and words; it fills the universe and will bring justice to bear on the wicked (Wis 1:6-9).

If we apply this Hellenistic Jewish concept in the Book of Wisdom to our reflections on the sense of the story of David and Bathsheba, we can say that it was indeed the Spirit of God that was invisibly present as the sinful actions in the episode were taking place, that brought about the death of a child as punishment for the wrong done by his father, and that guided all the events toward a turning point in the history of David's kingdom.

NOTES

1. Norman Pittenger, *Cosmic Love and Human Wrong: The Reconception of the Meaning of Sin in the Light of Process Theology* (New York: Paulist Press, 1978) 11.

2. The consensus is built mainly upon the findings and interpretations of Martin Noth, *Überlieferungsgeschichtliche Studien* 1, 3rd ed. (Tübingen: Max Niemeyer, 1967; 1st ed., Königsberg, 1943); as with any consensus, various scholars have modifications of their own to make to it.

3. The establishment of this material as a connected document written by a man close to the court of David and Solomon who intended to show how Solomon succeeded to the throne is due originally to Leonhard Rost, *Die Überlieferung von der Thronnachfolge Davids*, Beiträge zur Wissenschaft vom Alten und Neuen Testament 3/6 (Stuttgart: W. Kohlhammer, 1926), reprinted in Rost, *Das Kleine Credo und Andere Studien zum Alten Testament* (Heidelberg: Quelle & Meyer, 1965) 119–253. Rost's view has been modified in some ways by subsequent scholars, of course. James W. Flanagan, "Court History or Succession Document? A Study of 2 Samuel 9–20 and 1 Kings 1–2," *JBL* 91 (1972) 172–181, for example, proposes an original court history that became a kind of succession narrative only when the story of David and Bathsheba in 2 Sam 11–12 and the account of Solomon's accession in 1 Kg 1–2 were added a little later.

4. This has been proposed most strongly by Morton Smith, "The So-Called 'Biography of David' in the Books of Samuel and Kings," *Harvard Theological Review* 44 (1951) 167–169, who sees 2 Sam 10–20 with 1 Kg 1–2, at least as it now stands, as a moral tract.

5. The expression "exemplary novel" comes to mind by analogy with Cervantes' *novelas ejemplares*, which is what he called a set of his own stories in Spanish. *Novela*, so used, is not the English "novel," of course, but the Renaissance Italian *novella*, a kind of short story. Cervantes in his *novelas ejemplares* portrays vice and brutality in an artistic manner, unifying human experience and prophetic vision into a whole in such a way that he gives the reader a picture of human behavior from whose contemplation one can draw positive lessons in addition to plain enjoyment; see Richard E. Chandler and Kessel Schwartz, *A New History of Spanish Literature* (Baton Rouge: Louisiana State University Press, 1961) 189f. The story of David and Bathsheba and other episodes in the Succession Narrative obviously differ in certain respects from Cervantes' *novelas ejemplares*, but the similarities of manner and, in some respects, intent are also clear. Just as fairly self-contained episodes like that of David and Bathsheba are embedded in the Succession Narrative and integrated with it as a literary whole, some of Cervantes' stories of the same type as his independent *novelas ejemplares* are found embedded as episodes in his *Don Quixote*; see R. O. Jones, *A Literary History of Spain: The Golden Age* (London: Ernest Benn, 1971) 169.

6. This aspect of the Succession Narrative, noted in passing by Gerhard von Rad in *Supplements to Vetus Testamentum*, I (Leiden: E. J. Brill, 1953), 120f., English translation in von Rad, *The Problem of the Hexateuch and Other Essays* (Edinburgh: Oliver and Boyd, 1966), 292f., has been developed especially by R. N. Whybray, *The Succession Narrative: a Study of II Sam. 9–20 and I Kings 1 and 2*, Studies in Biblical Theology, 2nd series, IX (London: SCM Press, 1968), 56–95.

7. See 1 Sam 21:5 and see Johannes Pedersen, *Israel: Its Life and Culture* 3–4 (London: Oxford University Press, 1940) 10; Gerhard von Rad, *Der Heilige Krieg im Alten Israel* (Zürich: Zwingli-Verlag, 1951) 7; Roland de Vaux, *Ancient Israel: Its Life and Institutions* (New York: McGraw-Hill, 1961) 258, 465.

8. 2 Sam 12:1-15a, as we have noted, belongs to a later level of the text (that of the Deuteronomic redactor).

9. See Whybray, 63f. Walter Brueggemann, "On Trust and Freedom: A Study of Faith in the Succession Narrative," *Interpretation* 26 (1972) 3–19, goes so far as to say that God, in

the Succession Narrative, "is much more the *creator of a context* for human freedom and responsibility than a *disruptor of events*" (18).

10. See the old text in Ex 20:5 and the announcement of a new and opposite view in Jer 31:29 and Ezek 18:2.

11. The author of the Succession Narrative lets *us* know, anyway, that the child's death was the result of God's displeasure. 12:15b, in which God strikes the child with mortal illness, must originally have followed immediately the statement that what David had done displeased God in 11:27, from which it is now separated by the Nathan scene inserted later.

12. On the Deuteronomist's historico-theological schema of prophetic prediction and later narrated fulfillment, arranged in the related pairs found throughout his edition of earlier sources, see Gerhard von Rad, *Studies in Deuteronomy*, SBT 9 (London: SCM Press, 1953) 78–82.

13. 2 Sam 12:10-12 has often been taken as an addition to the text, on the grounds that God's forgiveness in 12:13f. cancels the punishment that David declared right for himself in verses 5b-6, and so leaves little room for the punishment announced in verses 10-12. Against this one may set, among other arguments, those of R. A. Carlson, *David, the Chosen King: A Traditio-Historical Approach to the Second Book of Samuel* (Stockholm: Almqvist & Wiksell, 1964) 157, who shows that in verses 13-14 the death penalty is transferred to David's infant son. We may add that verses 10-12 have to do with the less immediate future, and that David's impetuous declaration that the rich man of Nathan's parable is a "son of death" (12:5) is ambivalent in Hebrew and does not mean exclusively that he ought to be put to death. It can be used to signify that, but for a man to be a "son" of anything abstract in Hebrew means that there is some close association between him and the abstract thing or quality in question. The Deuteronomist can use the expression's ambiguity to let it mean that David is worthy of death when it is related to verses 13-14, while letting it refer also to David's involvement in the death and violence affecting his family and followers announced in verse 10.

14. Eugene Kennedy, *A Sense of Life, A Sense of Sin* (Garden City, N.Y.: Doubleday & Co., 1975) 137f.

15. See, for example, the section on loneliness and anxiety in Piet Schoonenberg, *Man and Sin: A Theological View* (Notre Dame, Ind.: University of Notre Dame Press, 1965) 90–97, although "anxiety" there seems to be more or less the equivalent of the German *Angst*.

Walter Harrelson

CREATIVE SPIRIT IN THE OLD TESTAMENT: A STUDY OF THE LAST WORDS OF DAVID (2 SAM 23:1-7)

The many studies of the meaning of the Spirit of God or the Spirit of Yahweh in the Hebrew Scriptures have identified several basic uses of the term *ruach* in association with the Deity.[1] Basic to such usages is the notion of power, power that cannot fully be controlled by the one or ones upon whom it comes, and power that cannot be summoned by human activity designed to bring God's presence in times of need. It may well be the case that the use of singing and dancing and of other activities intended to induce ecstasy were used effectively to produce ecstatic seizure; indeed, it would be surprising if that were not the case. The stories of the coming of God's Spirit, however, seem to be at pains to show that human beings do not control and cannot force the hand of God in causing the Spirit to come to bring deliverance in battle or any other particular actions desired from God.

It is also pointed out in the studies of the term *ruach* that there is a heavy emphasis upon the moral dimensions of God's action by the Spirit, that the Spirit acts to effect righteousness on earth, calling God's people to account and establishing justice, integrity, and peace within the institutions of Israel. While in the descriptions of the Spirit's seizure of the ancient judges of Israel the action of the Spirit seems to consist largely of endowing warriors with superhuman strength and vigor, increasingly in the later references the Spirit acts to underscore the Deity's demand for public righteousness.

One action of the Spirit that came to be thought of as extremely important in later times was dealt with very carefully indeed in ancient Israel: the action of the Spirit to "inspire" prophets or visionaries, opening up for them a world which, without the gift of the Spirit, would have been closed to them. We know that such a notion was widespread in the ancient Near Eastern and the Mediterranean worlds and that it also was held by ancient Israel as well. God's breath is breathed into persons and gives them power to speak that they otherwise lack, just as in the early experiences of the priestess at Delphi the spirit entered into her very body and enabled her to speak the disclosures that prophets could then interpret.

Many of the critical stories of God's revelation of his special will and purpose, however, have no reference at all to the coming or the gift of the Spirit. Moses sees a bush aflame and hears a voice speaking to him from the bush (Ex 3); Elijah lives through massive storm phenomena at the mountain of revelation later on, but is presently addressed by God in a "sound of gentle stillness" (1 Kg 19:12). The prophets must surely have understood their revelations to have reached them through the action of the Spirit. A reference such as that by the prophet Zedekiah ben Chenanah (1 Kg 22:24), who asked Micaiah ben Imlah which way the Spirit went when it left Zedekiah and passed on to Micaiah is a case in point. Zedekiah is credited with believing that prophecy is done in the Spirit; it apparently involved singing and dancing at such locations as the threshing floors also (1 Kg 22:10; see v. 6 as well). But there is only one passage in all of the prophetic literature that seems to suggest that the prophets received their words by divine inspiration, a text that is itself somewhat awkward (Mic 3:8). Moreover, this text stresses the justice of God — God's standard that shows up Israel's sin for what it is — to be the special disclosure given by the Spirit.

The prophets and traditionists responsible for the present form of the prophetic traditions must have deliberately avoided claiming that the Spirit provided the revelation, on the premise that the community would not thereby honor the words spoken the more; any ecstatic could claim that the divine Spirit gave him or her the message being delivered. Jeremiah draws the contrast very sharply between those who prate of having had a dream and those who have heard the divine Word. Yet Jeremiah knows that the true prophet must have entered into the normally secret council-seat of God in order to receive God's authentic message; he knows that the divine Word is a burning, flaming, uncontainable fire (Jer 23:9-32; 20:9).

Only in portraying the coming day of consummation appointed by God are the prophets less restrained about the use of the term Spirit of God in connection with their speaking in God's name. In Is 11:1-9 and 61:1-3 we have the most explicit of such texts, but there are others as well. These two texts continue to show the connection of the gift of God's Spirit and the demand for public righteousness.

In the later literature in Judaism and in Christianity, the connection between the Spirit and inspiration is much closer but also quite varied. It

appears that the chief action of the Spirit for the early Christian community was to confirm as true the Word and Presence of God. While the
Spirit also gave comfort and offered reproof and guidance generally, it
was the Spirit that above all enabled the community to know that a
prophet's testimony was true and faithful, that the guidance provided
by God through any means whatever was in fact God's guidance (see 1
Cor 12:3).

There are a few references in the Hebrew Bible to another dimension of the action of God's Spirit, and it is with those that this paper is
concerned. I have in mind what can be called the action of the creative
Spirit of God. Apart from the use of *ruach* in Gen 1:2, a very difficult
passage to understand, two uses stand out. The first has to do with
God's endowment of Bezalel with the divine Spirit so that he could do
his part of the artistic work on the tabernacle in the wilderness (Ex 31:5;
see 35:31). It is wisdom, or craftsmanship, or technical and artistic skills
that are directly traced here to the work of God's Spirit. The fact that the
tabernacle is to be a representation, a copy as it were, of a design that
God is disclosing to Moses makes it all the more evident that Bezalel's
creative gifts are more than merely fine artisanship. He is to exercise his
own creative gifts, but he is to follow the pattern, the *tabnith*, revealed to
Moses (Ex 25:9).

The passage, however, on which we are to concentrate our attention is the remarkable poem found as one of the appendixes to the
Samuel tradition: 2 Sam 23:1-7. This short poem, which has affinities
with 2 Sam 7 and also with the Abimelech-Jotham tradition in Jg 9 (as we
shall see below), gives a distinctive vocation to the divine Spirit: that of
inspiring a poet to speak in the name of God.

It is true that the poem could have arisen as a speech in the name of
God uttered by a prophet in the court of the king; such oracles are well
known in the ancient Near East and in Israel. In the Psalter, Psalms 2,
45, 72, and 110 are particularly good examples. But our speech is
presented as David's own words, words concerning his kingship and
what will enable it to endure. They are not given as a promise that the
house will endure, in the manner of 2 Sam 7, or at least not primarily to
make the point that the dynasty will endure. The emphasis falls upon
the beauty of God's rule over a people when the king does his task
rightly and places his full trust in God. Indeed, we believe that the poet
responsible for this poem wishes his hearers to understand that God's
own Spirit has enabled him to see what a glorious thing it is for Israel to
be ruled by such a king.

In the lines that follow I wish to discuss this poem as an example of
Israel's understanding of the Spirit of God as a creative force, shaping
the artistry of the poet, disclosing dimensions of beauty that might

otherwise have been missed. For a similar example we could look to the description of the high priest Simon that is found in Sir 50, although there is no reference in that place to inspiration by the divine Spirit.

The difficult text may be translated as follows: [2]

1 These are David's last words.
   Utterance of David, son of Jesse,
       utterance of the one God exalted,
   the one anointed by the God of Jacob,
       the sweet singer of Israel:
2 "The Spirit of the LORD speaks through me,
       his word is upon my tongue;
3 The God of Jacob has spoken,
       to me has the Rock of Israel declared:
   'One who rules over people rightly,
       one who rules in God's fear,
4 is like the light of morning,
       as the sun arises
       on a cloudless morning,
       gleaming from the rain
       on the grassy land.'
5 Is not my house like that with God?
       for an enduring covenant he has made for me,
       established and guarded in every way.
   Does he not make prosper
       all my deliverance,
       all my delight?
6 But worthless ones are all like thorns
       cast up aimlessly;
   they cannot be grasped by the hand.
7 To touch them one uses an iron bar
       or a spear handle.
   Then in the fire they are consumed,
       entirely consumed,
       in a single sitting."

The structure of the poem is clear enough, even though the text presents very considerable problems to the translator. The center of the poem is a short oracular verse that describes the true king, the importance of such a king, and the sheer beauty of the king in question, or of the office of king (if it is permissible to speak in that way) as the poet envisages it (23:3b-4). Around this center we have a speech of the king himself, in two parts. The first part (23:2-3a) claims that the words of the king, or perhaps the central poem to follow, are inspired directly by God's Spirit. The second part (23:5-7), which falls into two parts, draws conclusions from the gift of kingship by God. The poet first claims that the kingship of David is just the kind of just kingship mentioned in the oracular poem, and that for this reason it will surely stand inviolate. Then he points to the opposite kind of kingship, one not founded on the basis of justice, and shows that it is good for nothing but destruction. The following outline of the poem's structure will make clear this nice balance and the artistry of it.

1. Introduction: Identification of poem, 23:1a*a*
2. Apostrophe identifying the speaker and praising him, 23:1a*b*-b
3. The king speaks, identifying his words as prompted by God himself, 23:2-3a
4. The poetic word or oracle, 23:3b-4
5. Resumption of the king's speech, in two parts:
    a. Rhetorical question claiming that the king's rule is of the sort approved by God, 23:5
    b. Declaration that unjust kings are to be shunned and cannot for long exercise rule, 23:6-7

There is no way of knowing just when to place this poem historically. If we are right in identifying the poet's reference to the Spirit's speaking by the king as a reference to poetic inspiration, then the idea would seem to be fairly late. Its nearest analogy would be the Priestly passages in Ex 31 and 35, referred to above, which are probably not earlier than the time of the Babylonian Exile and may be a century later than the return from exile.

I suspect that the poem should be related to a number of psalms that have the character of meditations or reflections on various aspects of life and the issues of life:[3] Psalms 104 (meditation on the creation); 139 (on the presence of God and the ambivalence felt regarding that presence); 73 (on the nearness of God); 23 (on the care of God, or God's goodness), etc. I date all of these meditations to the late seventh or the early sixth century B.C. Our poem probably belongs in the same general period of time. It does not, therefore, contain the actual words of David, in all probability, but has been attributed to David as Israel's great poet and great king. Both attributions are important, and the claim that the divine Spirit operated in the special way indicated is of particular importance, I believe.

Let us deal first with the picture of kingship contained in the poem and then say something about the notion of the creative work of the Spirit. Our poet probably has two events in view as he speaks about the proper rule of kings. The first is the actual rule of Josiah, king of Judah from 640 or 639 to 609, which ended with Josiah's tragic death at Megiddo and the eventual ascendancy of the king's wicked eldest son, Jehoiakim (see Jer 22:1-30 for a collection of the prophet's oracles in praise of Josiah and against his successors). Our poet probably lived during the reign of the reformer Josiah and on into the reign of

Jehoiakim. Placing his speech on David's lips, he is able to avoid the strictures that prophets suffered at Jehoiakim's hands (see Jer 36 and 26).

The other event appears to be the story of Abimelech's bloody reign at Shechem as related in Jg 9. While there are no direct quotations from the story, it is, I think, highly likely that the poet meditated upon the fable of Jotham found in Jg 9:7-21 and drew his contrast between a just king's rule (Gideon the judge, who also was clearly a king in some sense [see Jg 8:22–9:6]; and Josiah, the reformer-king) and the rule of the bramble-bush (Hebrew *'aṭad*) Abimelech, whose violence leads to his certain destruction. His readers will probably have called to their minds the career of Abimelech as the poet speaks of the thornbushes (Hebrew *qoṣ*) that one dare not even touch with the hand lest one be stung badly. One must bunch them up for burning by using a rod or a staff; they are of no account but for providing a very quick fire, soon burned out. Just so evanescent is the rule of any king of the sort Jehoiakim shows himself to be — another Abimelech, quickly to be swept away.

Our poet praises David as one who spoke at the direct inspiration of the Spirit of the LORD. He calls him the "sweet singer of Israel," if that is the best translation of the difficult Hebrew phrase (23:1b*b*). And he provides a short poem portraying the coming of a king to Israel as like the dawning of light in the morning, like sunrise on a day marked by no clouds at all, like the sun's glistening on grass damp from rain. For Israel to have a king who rules righteously, who is touched by the fear of God, is to have one in her midst who embodies qualities of God himself, glorious as Zion is glorious (Ps 48), surpassing all human beauty as the high priest surpasses human beauty when properly fitted out (Sir 50), gleaming from the sun that rules over the heavens at God's direction (Ps 19).

Our poet, therefore, sees in the just king like David one who transcends ordinary human beings, focuses in his person the qualities of God himself, of transcendent beauty and splendor. His vivid portrayal helps others to do so as well.

The portrayal of kingship in this fashion probably had another basis. By the end of the seventh century the question of the collecting of David's psalms may well have been alive. David may be presented as Israel's sweet singer, composing under the inspiration of God's Spirit, in order to support such a collection of Davidic psalms. But it is difficult to believe that the poet is very largely motivated by such an apologetic interest. The most striking thing about the poem is its sheer beauty. And that is where, I believe, the reference to the Spirit of God finally leads us.

The Spirit of the LORD is said to be speaking "in" or "through" the poet (Hebrew *bi*). This is a very bold claim indeed, and one very rarely made. I think that our poet understood himself to be in the tradition of

David the poet, the one who lamented over Abner and Jonathan and Saul (2 Sam 3:33-34; 1:19-27), who was heartbroken when told of the death of Absalom (2 Sam 18:33). He believed that David had in fact been given his words by the Spirit of God — where else could such a gift of poetic utterance have come from?

And yet the poet is also steeped in the prophetic tradition. He knows that kings who exercise arbitrary power, who care nothing for public justice, can be swept aside in a moment; that such persons are dangerous beings, to be avoided; they poison the society. What a difference, he shows us in this inspired and inspiring poem, a just ruler can make! Such a one not only exercises just rule and keeps wholesome the society but also inspires others, claims their loyalty, transports them with the splendor of such a leader.

The poem, then, is an example, I believe, of the sort of inspired poetry that fills the Psalter. Rarely indeed do Israel's ancient poets trace their products to the impulse of God's Spirit. This poet was unafraid to do so. He placed on David's lips a magnificent image of the beauty of a society led by those who are devoted to public justice. Such a society is agleam with righteousness. Its opposite, on the other hand, is aflame with a consuming fire.

NOTES

1. For what follows compare the lengthy treatments of "pneuma" and related terms in *TDNT* 6:332–455.

2. The text is often very difficult indeed. My translation includes a few readings that should be explained. In 1a, I read *meqim 'el* with one of the Dead Sea Scrolls Samuel manuscripts rather than the Massoretic *huqam 'al*. In 3a, I read "the God of Jacob" instead of the Massoretic "God of Israel," a reading that has some manuscript support. And my reading "in a single sitting" for the last word, *baššabeth*, is an effort to make sense of a most difficult text.

3. My ideas concerning these psalms, and others akin to them, as meditations will soon appear in a special study.

Joseph Jensen, O.S.B.

MOUNT ZION AND ARMAGEDDON:
A TALE OF TWO ESCHATOLOGIES

The second chapter of the Book of Isaiah is one of the most extraordinary passages in prophetic literature. It is extraordinary for its idyllic vision of what will come to pass "in the days to come," when the nations will flow to Mount Zion to receive instruction from the Lord, submit to his judgments, and beat their swords into plowshares (vv. 2-4); extraordinary for the powerful description of the "day of the Lord" that follows it (vv. 6-21); and extraordinary for the manner of the conjunction of these two so disparate oracles.

I have argued elsewhere[1] in detail that the placing of these two oracles together is deliberate and intelligible, and that the arrangement is early (the order imposed by exilic editors is regularly promise *after* judgment, not before). The first piece gives the promise for the future; the second piece, which refers (for Isaiah) to events not far distant, tells of the obstacles to the promise (human sin and pride) and how Yahweh will overcome them.

The presence of these two oracles in one chapter serves to emphasize a problem that we often pass over in silence, namely, the problem of two quite diverse visions of the future within the body of Scripture. That is to say, we are confronted with visions of fiery judgment from which but few escape, on the one hand, and of universal blessedness on the other.[2] To trace this problem and its implications is the purpose of the present study.

The Day of the Lord

The development of the theme of "the day of the Lord" in the Old Testament is well known and need not be presented in detail. Although it began, in the early prophets, as a day of Yahweh's judgment within history, in the later prophets, at the stage at which we can speak of eschatology in the strict sense, this judgment brings an end to history and the beginning of a new reality that lies beyond history, with "new heavens and a new earth" (Is 65:17; 66:22). Although the theme of Yahweh's day probably began within the tradition of Israel's Holy War,[3] it comes to stand so directly for judgment that Joel places the action in the Valley of Jehoshaphat (Jl 4:2), a name that pertains to no actual geographical site but is contrived simply to express the Lord's role as Judge; for Joel, the day is accompanied by prodigious signs in the heavens and on earth (3:3f.; 4:15) and is a day of liberation for Israel but a day of judgment for the nations (3:5–4:17).

Although the term may be used less frequently by the apocalyptists, the reality is there, now tailored to their special concerns. The succession of periods that mark our present reality will give way to the "age to come," and the great judgment will mark the transition, bringing an end to all evil and to every power hostile to God's kingdom. Far more than in the prophets, the world is divided into two camps. The "good guys" may be Israel or some faithful segment in Israel, but in any case all the others are the wicked and are marked for destruction. While the prophets preached repentance in the hope that judgment could be avoided, the apocalyptists generally wrote as though decisions had already been made and fates already determined.

Closely related to the day of judgment, whether in prophetic or apocalyptic thought, is the theme of the remnant.[4] While the concept underwent a good deal of development, long before the development reached its term, "the remnant" comes to identify the faithful who will be spared in the judgment. They are the elect, the "saved" in a theological sense, and the others are the reprobate.

Most of these elements are carried over into the New Testament, which is strongly influenced by apocalyptic in many of its parts. This is not surprising, since the career of Jesus, the emergence of Christianity, and the composition of the New Testament all took place wholly within the period during which the apocalyptic specially flourished, 200 B.C. to 135 A.D. Moreover, not only were Jesus, his early followers, and the others ultimately responsible for the New Testament strongly influenced by the apocalypticism of their milieu, but emergent Christianity was subject to the same kind of pressure that generated much of the Jewish apocalyptic, namely, persecution at the hands of those who ruled the power structure.

Many specifically Christian traits emerged: the "day of the Lord" could be identified as the day of the second coming of Jesus; incorporation into Jesus through faith and baptism numbered one among the remnant to be saved; since the Christian community rapidly came to consist primarily of Gentiles, the remnant was no longer identifiable as Israel except in the sense of a new Israel of faith. All people were called to the new Israel, but only those who responded would escape the day of wrath. Although the Book of Revelation carries a message of admonition and conversion for the Christian communities (especially chs. 2–3), little good is expected of the rest of mankind, the "inhabitants of the earth" upon whom plagues and judgment would fall. The harvest of the earth, thrown into the wine press of God's wrath, is trodden to produce a stream of blood as high as a horse's bridle for 1,600 stadia (14:17-20), and the final judgment scene depicts the great capital of the Roman Empire, symbolized as harlot Babylon, being destroyed in the fires of judgment, to the delight of all the elect (18:1–19:3).

Closely connected with all this and explicitly assigned to "the great day of God the Almighty" is the assembling of the nations at Armageddon, the "mountain of Megiddo," for the final battle in which they are defeated and destroyed. The scenario is rather undeveloped in Revelation (16:12-16), but the literary antecedents make it clear that the nations have come up against God's people and destruction of the nations means deliverance of the elect (see, e.g., Ezek 38–39); the theme is carried on in 19:17-21 and 20:7-9, though without reference to Armageddon.[5]

It is not difficult to see how incompatible this version of the end is with the vision of Is 2:2-4. What has happened is that the "day of Yahweh," which for Isaiah was a judgment and chastisement within history, has become the final act in the eschatological drama before the establishment of God's kingdom, a judgment that involves the destruction of God's enemies (mainly the gentile nations) — which may be called Armageddon eschatology. Does the other view (i.e., the one contained in Is 2:2-4) deserve to be called an eschatology? It does. First of all, it deserves the title in the broad sense in which the term is used by Clements, von Rad,[6] and others, that is, to refer to prophetic visions of a new order of salvation different from the present order, even though a succession of "ages" and the end of history are not involved. Secondly, to the extent that it is taken up by later authors as an element of the "end time," it deserves the title in the strict sense. For Isaiah, the vision of all the nations coming to Yahweh for instruction, accepting his judgments, destroying their weapons of war, and living in peace was not to be an interlude, after which things would return to "normal," any more than the reign of peace in Is 11:6-9 would be an interlude; rather, this was to be the final stage of God's rule, even though it was not conceived to lie outside of history. The "day of Yahweh" of verses 6-21 could precede it, but it cannot follow it.[7]

Mount Zion Eschatology

The vision of peace of Is 2:2-4 has not fared as well as the "day of the Lord" concept, but the theme of all the nations turning to Yahweh, sometimes with references to peace (or to the destruction of weapons) and often with Jerusalem as focus, occurs often enough to be one of the constants of Scripture.

Some of the relevant passages do not necessarily look to a new era or an end-time at all, but simply express the conviction of what should be now, given Yahweh's nature as universal Lord, and express the hope that it will be for the future. This is found in many of the psalms. For example, Psalm 87 says, with reference to people from the many nations, that "this person and that person were born in her" (i.e., in Zion), as all confess their relationship to her (vv. 5, 7). Although this is expressed as though it were a present reality, it could only have been "present" to the psalmist as an ideal. But such convictions concerning what is ideal can exercise strong influence on expectations of the future.[8] Psalm 67 not only contains refrain-like invitations to all the nations to praise God, but also speaks of God's ways and his salvation being made known to them and of his "judging" them in equity and guiding them. Psalm 47 opens with an invitation to all peoples to praise God with songs of joy and then later explains, "For God is king of all the earth; / . . . / God rules as king over the nations; / . . . / The princes of the peoples are gathered with the people of Abraham's God" (vv. 8-10).[9] In Psalm 96 the "families of the nations" are invited to offer Yahweh glory, to "bring an offering, and enter his courts! / worship the Lord in holy attire," and the conviction is expressed that he will come (or comes) to rule the earth and its peoples with justice (vv. 7-10, 13; see 99:1-3). In Psalm 102, Zion is in need of rebuilding, but when that has been done, it will be a place of worship for the Gentiles as well as for Israel:

> The nations will fear your name, O Lord,
>   and all the kings of the earth your glory.
>
> . . . .
>
> That they may declare the name of the Lord in Zion,
>   and his praise in Jerusalem,
> When peoples gather together,
>   and kingdoms, to serve the Lord (vv. 16, 22f.).

More directly concerned with the Lord's action to bring in a new age are a number of prophetic passages. Some of these can appear to be more particularistic than universalistic, in that the nations serve as a foil to exalt Israel herself, for example, coming to Zion as bearers of the returning exiles (Is 49:22f.; 60:8f.), as bringers of wealth (60:1-7), or as builders of Jerusalem and servants of the Israelites (60:10-14). Even here it should be noted that the nations come "proclaiming the Lord's praises" (60:6) and confessing Jerusalem to be "City of the Lord" and "Zion of the Holy One of Israel" (v. 14). But there are other passages where the gathering of the nations to Zion is simply the result of their conversion to Yahweh. For example, in Jer 3:17: "At that time they shall call Jerusalem the Lord's throne, and all nations shall gather there,[10] and they shall no more stubbornly follow their own wicked heart." Again in Zech 2:14f.:

> Sing and rejoice, daughter Zion! Behold I come to dwell in your midst, says the Lord. Many nations shall join themselves to the Lord on that day, and they shall be his people; and he will dwell in your midst, and you shall know the Lord of hosts has sent me to you.

So also in Zech 8:20-22:

> Thus says the Lord of hosts: Peoples shall yet come, the inhabitants of many cities; the inhabitants of one city shall come to those of another, saying, "Up! let us go . . . to entreat the favor of the Lord, and to seek the Lord of hosts." Many peoples and strong nations shall come to seek the Lord of hosts in Jerusalem and to entreat the favor of the Lord.

In Zech 9:9f., daughter Zion is addressed with the promise of a Savior King who is to be a bearer of peace:

> He shall cut off the chariot from Ephraim
>   and the war horse from Jerusalem;
> the battle bow shall be cut off,
>   and he shall proclaim peace to the nations.

Such visions of a blessed future are surely to be understood as descriptions of an ultimate goal of Yahweh's activity, not as steps along a road that leads to a final, fiery judgment. Occasionally the theme may indicate a previous (not final) judgment and include the remnant concept. Thus Zeph 2:9-11 speaks of the punishment meted out to Moab by the remnant of Israel and then adds:

> The Lord will be fearful against them
>   for he will cause all the gods of the earth to waste away.
> Then to him shall bow down, each one in its own place,
>   all the coastlands of the nations.

This is rare, however, though contexts may occasionally be misleading. Zeph 3:9f. says that the Lord will purify the lips of all the peoples from beyond the rivers of Ethiopia so that they can all call upon his name and serve him with one accord. The passage can have nothing to do with the judgment scene that immediately precedes it (vv. 6-8), a passage that speaks of destruction of nations for refusal to accept correction and of the fire of the Lord's jealousy by which all the earth shall be consumed. Zech 14:16-19 is a rare attempt to append the conversion of the nations to the eschatological judgment. Those who survive "of all the nations that came up against Jerusalem" shall now come up year after year to worship at the Feast of Booths. The attempt is hardly compatible with verse 12, which had the same nations rotting in flesh, eye, and tongue. Moreover, the spirit of the piece is quite different from the others we have looked at; in place of spontaneous praise and submission there is the threat of drought and plague for any "family" that misses the pilgrimage.

TWO ALTERNATIVE ESCHATOLOGIES

In spite of the many biblical texts that deal with what I am calling "Zion eschatology," it can hardly be considered the controlling vision in biblical eschatology. What has happened is that evolving biblical thought has erected into an eschatology the theme of the day of the Lord, which Isaiah saw as a step toward Yahweh's goal,[11] while the other theme in Is 2, which can be regarded as the goal itself, has largely fallen out of focus. And as pointed out above, these two themes can hardly be composed into one picture. The conversion of the nations is possibly compatible with a judgment that is corrective in nature, which it would follow (as is the case in the thought of Isaiah), and even with the remnant concept (though that element rarely occurs in these texts); but it is not compatible with a destructive judgment that is conceived as the final act in the eschatological drama, to be succeeded only by the full establishment of God's kingdom. There is no way it could follow such judgment, and no way such judgment could be visited on the nations that "no more stubbornly follow their own wicked heart" (Jer 3:17), that walk in Yahweh's ways, instructed by his *tôrâ* and accepting his judgments (Is 2:3f.), and to whom his messianic king has proclaimed peace (Zech 9:10).

We are therefore faced with two eschatologies; they cannot function in a "before/after" framework, but can only be regarded as alternatives — in terms of "either/or." It is of no little importance to realize this, and it should have some impact on the way we teach Scripture — not to mention on the way we live.

The realization that Scripture presents us with two models of the end should not lead to the question, "Which one is valid? Which one is authentic?" Both are valid and authentic because both could come to pass — not conjunctively taken but as alternatives. The proper question is, "Which model should we strive to see realized?" To pose the question in that way is to answer it, but the development of eschatological thought, whether within the Bible or outside it, has not left the matter all that obvious. A prior question might be, "To what extent do we have a choice?" But even though no human power can bring in the *eschaton*, the inspired tradition would not have presented us with alternatives except as a call to choice. There is no doubt that much of the Christian tradition, especially the more conservative sects (which usually display a special predilection for the apocalyptic writings), takes the "Armageddon eschatology," with its remnant theology and the righteous exclusivism it fosters, as norm and idea.

The importance of recognizing these models as alternatives, while it lies mainly in the motivation to create the sort of world that deserves one consummation rather than the other, lies also partly in the awesome power we have to approximate one or the other by human means — especially that of the Armageddon variety.[12] One might even ask to what extent the present potential to produce humanity's own Armageddon has been conditioned, subconsciously of course, by America's traditional Protestant ethic with its strong biblical orientation. When, moreover, the same ethic tends toward investing the country with a messianic mission of redemption and seeing its wars as righteous crusades against the forces of darkness and evil,[13] the apocalyptic vision of Armageddon runs the risk of becoming a self-fulfilling prophecy.

Earlier we spoke of Revelation, but this book is not the only apocalyptic part of the New Testament; we spoke, in fact, of the pervasive influence of apocalyptic in the New Testament. One thinks at once of the "apocalyptic discourse" of the synoptic Gospels (Mt 24; Mk 13; Lk 21:5-36), St. Paul's words in 1 Thess 4:13–5:3 and 2 Thess 2:3-12, and those of 2 Pet 3:3-10. These passages testify to the expectation of all the standard elements of judgment day: widespread rebellion against God, distress of God's elect, cosmic disturbances, the consummation of all things in fire, etc. Is there no conflict felt between this expectation and the potentially universal saving power of the gospel? No doubt the experience of the early Church, which learned that, after initial successes, there were many who resisted the message, came into play here. It is possibly in view of this experience that we have the formulation "the gospel must first be preached to all nations" (Mk 13:10; see Mt 24:14), words that strike a compromise between the ideally universal nature of the gospel message and the fact that far from all have accepted it.

Zion Eschatology in the New Testament

There are some parts of the New Testament, however, that seem far more favorable to our "Zion eschatology." For example, in St. Paul's treatment in Rom 9–11 of Israel's failure to receive the gospel, he describes the working-out of God's plan in this fashion: at present, although Israel by and large has rejected the gospel, a remnant of faith, as foreseen by the prophets, has accepted it; in the meantime, the Gentiles, as also foretold by the prophets, have accepted it; when the full number (*plērōma*) of the Gentiles has entered in, then all Israel will also be saved. Of course, it is difficult to know with certainty what Paul means here by *plērōma* (11:25), for it could conceivably mean "the full number of those destined to be saved." Nevertheless, it is interesting to note that in this passage Paul uses the remnant concept only of Israel (9:27, 29; 11:1, 4f., 7, 25), and it marks a temporary stage: only a remnant of Israel has accepted the message, but after the period of "hardening" is over, all Israel (*pas Israēl* — 11:25) will be saved; sandwiched between is the entrance of the *plērōma* of the Gentiles.

St. John's theme of Jesus as the new Temple culminates in a scene that I would judge to be a transposition of Is 2:2-4. Early in John's Gospel, Jesus identified his body as the Temple which, if destroyed, would be raised again in three days (2:19-22); from this identification the conclusion is drawn that in the new law Jesus' own person is the place of encounter with God, of worship, etc. This word of Jesus was given in response to the demand for a sign to prove he was empowered to purify the Temple. In John's Gospel this comes very early in the ministry, while in the Synoptics the incident comes at the very end of the ministry, for Jesus' cleansing of the Temple follows the triumphal procession of Palm Sunday. Whatever the historical merits of John's arrangement, it allows him a completely different conclusion to Palm Sunday. Jesus does not go to the Temple, as in the synoptic account; instead, his own person becomes the focus of attention. Greeks who had come up to worship seek out Jesus, and their coming is the sign to Jesus, apparently, that his "hour," so frequently referred to elsewhere in the Gospel, has come.

That the arrival of these Gentiles should be the signal to Jesus that his hour has come is explicable if we relate it to the theme of the pilgrimage of the nations, something expected to take place "in the latter days" (Is 2:2).[14] It is significant that no further mention is made of these Greeks; their function is exhausted in putting Jesus on notice that his hour has come. The long-heralded hour is the time of his glorification, of his being "lifted up" (*hypsoō*). Given some hints of a Temple context to this passage (i.e., that the Greeks had come up to worship and that the synoptic account of Palm Sunday culminated at the Temple), the Isaiah passage in which the mountain of Yahweh's house is lifted up (*hypsoō*) comes easily to mind. If we note that at the end of Jesus' long soliloquy he says, "and I, when I am lifted up from the earth, will draw all people to myself" (12:32), a reference to God's uplifted Temple to which all nations flow should not be difficult to accept. The Isaiah version of the oracle (though not Micah's) is followed by the exhortation, "O house of Jacob, come, let us walk in the light of the Lord" (Is 2:5), and Jesus' dialogue with the people contains an exhortation to "walk while you have the light" (Jn 12:35).

Finally, the over-all thrust of Luke-Acts encourages the conclusion that a similar theme is present. Well known is the emphasis Luke gives to Jerusalem. The central section of the Gospel is arranged as a "travel narrative" (9:51–19:27) that brings Jesus inexorably to the Holy City and his death there. But even afterwards, Luke keeps the action in Jerusalem, omitting all reference to the disciples' return to Galilee and post-resurrection appearances in Galilee. As a result, there is no shift of scene for the ascension of Jesus (recounted at the end of the Gospel and at the beginning of Acts) and for the descent of the Spirit at Pentecost. The Pentecost account, of course, emphasizes the universal character of the crowd gathered at Jerusalem; and while these all seem to have been adherents of Judaism, Acts 2:5 insists that they were "from every nation under heaven," and the narrative lists their origins in great detail (vv. 9-11).

It is probable, as many argue, that the account, with its emphasis on "tongues," takes the Tower of Babel narrative as a primary Old Testament background; but some allusion to Is 2:2-4 is also possible. While language has important symbolic value for depicting the unity and diversity of the human race, it should be remembered that the basic meaning of Pentecost relates much more directly to the sort of things involved in Is 2:2-4. In that text nations come to Jerusalem to learn to walk in the ways of the Lord, to receive his word and keep his *tôrâ*, and so to be enabled to live in peace.

In Acts, Luke keeps the action in Jerusalem, and there the first Christians receive the Spirit, whose function is certainly to lead people in God's ways and to impart his *tôrâ* — whether that be thought of in terms of law or instruction — with love and unity as the goal. The undoing of the Tower of Babel could happen anywhere, but only in Jerusalem could Is 2:2-4 find its fulfillment. Of course, Luke does not keep the apostles there forever; the movement to Jerusalem reverses itself as the good news goes out from there to "Judea, Samaria, and to the ends of the earth" (Acts 1:8), and the center of gravity passes from Jerusalem to Rome in the person of Paul, known as the Apostle to the Gentiles. The last words Luke attributes to him are "this salvation of God has been sent to the Gentiles, and they will listen" (28:28).

Conclusion

As a reasonable consequence of the thesis here presented, I would like to suggest — or rather urge — that the sort of vision we have in Is 2:2-4 be promoted in our teaching, not simply as a beautiful ideal, as a spur to social and political action, as a model for a statue outside the U.N. building, but as the goal of history, a true eschatology that would obviate the very possibility of what "judgment day" regularly means to the popular mind. That "Christ will come again" is an indispensable element of Christian faith; what is at issue here is the manner of his coming. Ultimately what is at issue is whether the gospel shall have reached its goal.

This proposal does not downgrade the Book of Revelation or the other New Testament apocalyptic sections. If we recognize that we have two eschatologies, that they are incompatible, that they stand in an "either/or" relationship, then Revelation acquires a better and more positive value than it has been accorded through most of our theological history. It will, of course, always be a source of consolation to those suffering for their faith under oppressive governments, and its promise that God delivers those who trust in him will always be true.[15] But more importantly for the mass of Christians who do not suffer such persecution, it can stand as a warning of what the alternative will resemble if we do not take Mount Zion eschatology as our model.

NOTES

1. A paper entitled "Weal and Woe in Isaiah: Consistency and Continuity," given at the 1977 Catholic Biblical Association annual meeting and now in preparation for publication. The argument is based, in part, on the antithesis and parallelism of the two pieces: on the antithesis of the exaltation of Yahweh's mountain (first piece) and the humbling of all things, human and natural (second piece), and on the parallelism between the exaltation of Yahweh's mountain (first piece) and of Yahweh himself (second piece).

2. The fact that these visions involve symbolism and mythological imagery should not be thought to invalidate them, for descriptions of God's relationship to the world, especially when they deal with so obscure a matter as the consummation of history, can hardly dispense with procedures of this sort. If we believe that Scripture has truth to teach us, then we are convinced that beneath the imagery something of truth and importance is being asserted. It is to be noted that the discussion of this article deals only with passages that relate to mankind as a whole or at least to significant groups, not to the fate of individuals, though this may also be termed eschatological.

3. For the arguments for this position, see especially G. von Rad, *Old Testament Theology* 2 (Edinburgh-London: Oliver and Boyd, 1965) 119–125.

4. The role of the remnant in the thought of Isaiah himself is very difficult to evaluate, and it is sometimes given a prominence that is difficult to justify. S. Herrmann, *Die prophetischen Heilserwartungen im Alten Testament* (Stuttgart: Kohlhammer, 1965) 127–130, lists it along with the Davidic and Zion traditions as a principal theme of hope in Isaiah. For a much fuller treatment, see G. Hasel, *The Remnant: The History and Theology of the Remnant Idea from Genesis to Isaiah*, 2nd ed., Andrews University Monographs 5 (Berrien Springs, Mich.: Andrews University, 1974). Difficulties arise from the circumstances that some of the relevant texts are textually doubtful (e.g., the conclusion of 6:13), of disputed authenticity (e.g., 10:20f.), or ambivalent as to meaning (e.g., the name of Isaiah's son in 7:3). That the concept is of some importance to Isaiah is suggested by the name of his son, Shear-yashub, and is positive at least to the extent that it indicates that the threatened punishment will not bring an end to the people; where there is life, there is hope. But the reference to the remnant in 1:9, which almost surely dates from the latest period of Isaiah's ministry, speaks only of those who had survived a disaster but had shown no sign of repentance.

5. Mount Zion does figure in Revelation, of course, for it is there the Lamb stands with the 144,000 who have been "redeemed from all the earth" (14:1-3) and the place of God's reign is symbolized as the "new Jerusalem" (21:1–22:5). There is also universalism in that the saved are redeemed "from every tribe and tongue and people and nation" (5:9). But this remains a remnant theology, and the redeemed form a separate kingdom that stands in opposition to every earthly kingdom. The teaching is quite intelligible in terms of its historical origin, namely, the persecution of Christians by a Roman Empire that claimed divine honors for its kings. What concerns us here, however, is the contradiction, real or potential, between this and the other view we are discussing.

6. R. E. Clements (*Prophecy and Covenant* [SBT 1/43; London: SCM, 1965], ch. 6), explicitly defends the use of the term "eschatology" in this broader sense, as does von Rad (*Old Testament Theology* 2, 113–116); the latter points out that "it is perfectly possible to say that the event which they [the prophets] foretell is a final one even if we . . . would describe it as still 'within history'" (115).

7. Note the earlier reference to the extraordinary manner of the collocation of the two parts of Is 2. What one would expect is the threat-promise sequence that is common in the broader arrangements of the prophetic books, an order that was often the work of exilic and post-exilic editors; but that is *not* what is found in Is 2. (One can argue, by inference, that the order is early.) Moreover, the sequence of the action described in the chapter as it now stands is chronologically impossible; verses 2-4 could follow verses 6-21, chronologically speaking, but it won't work the other way around. The nations might submit to Yahweh's rule after he had humbled all human pride, but there could be no "day of Yahweh" against the world depicted in verses 2-4. Assuming that some sort of logic dictated the order, one can argue as follows. What comes first is the vision of the future. Since it presupposes a completely different response to Yahweh and his instruction than any then in evidence, there follows an account of what stands as an obstacle to the realization of the vision (especially verses 6-8) and of what Yahweh intends to do about it (especially verses 11-21).

8. See the comments of A. Weiser, *The Psalms*, Old Testament Library (Philadelphia: Westminster Press, 1962) 374–76, concerning the relatedness of history, cult, and eschatology. Speaking of Psalm 47, he says that "consummation of *Heilsgeschichte*" (i.e., eschatology) was a theme of the cultic tradition, celebrated and experienced at Yahweh's feast as sacred event.

9. Taking '*am* as a haplography for '*im* '*am*; in any case, for the purposes of this article, the difference is not great if only '*am* is read.

10. Omitting *lĕšēm yhwh lîrûšālāim* with LXX. The phrase, literally, "to (or possibly: for the sake of) the name of the Lord in Jerusalem," is included by NAB ("to honor the name of the Lord at Jerusalem") and by RSV ("to the presence of the Lord in Jerusalem"). The import of the verse under discussion is not materially affected, at least for present purposes, by the manner in which this doubt is resolved.

11. Modern authors occasionally uncritically retroject the "final judgment" concept into Is 2:6-21; see, for example, E. J. Young, *The Book of Isaiah* 1, The New International Commentary on the Old Testament (Grand Rapids, Mich.: Eerdmans, 1965) 122–125, especially, "This is the last judgment, and to speak of the last judgment is to speak of eschatology" (125).

12. Few will feel this is an exaggeration. Even descriptions of the effects of modern conventional arms can take on, in accounts intended to be sober and objective, an apocalyptic coloring. For the final assault on Berlin, the Russians massed some 20,000 guns, and C. Ryan's description of the bombardment that opened this assault includes the following: "With an ear-splitting, earthshaking roar the front erupted in flame. . . . Guns . . . poured a storm of fire onto the German positions. . . . The German countryside beyond the western Küstrin bridgehead seemed to disappear before a rolling wall of

bursting shells. Whole villages disintegrated. Earth, concrete, steel, parts of trees spewed into the air and in the distance forests began to blaze. . . . The hurricane of explosives was so intense that an atmospheric disturbance was created. . . . They created a concussion so tremendous that troops and equipment alike shook uncontrollably from the shock." He quotes one Russian officer as likening the glare from searchlights and flares to "a thousand suns joined together," and another as being reminded of the words of his grandmother about the end of the world, "when the earth would burn and the bad ones would be devoured by fire." (From *The Last Battle* [New York: Simon and Schuster, 1966] 384f.). Beside the reality of a nuclear bombardment, the imaginative descriptions of even our apocalyptic writings would probably seem pale.

13. See, for example, E. L. Tuveson, *Redeemer Nation* (Chicago-London: University of Chicago Press, 1968), especially ch. 1, "Apocalyptic and History," and ch. 6, "'The Ennobling War'." The ethic referred to is Protestant in its origin, but has of course provided the ideological orientation for millions from Catholic and other backgrounds.

14. The shift to "in the last days" (*en tais eschatais hēmerais*) in the LXX version of this Isaiah passage makes it even more appropriate.

15. It is doubtful, however, whether any modern Christian can or ought to identify the hostile state as a demonic force, as Revelation did.

Carroll Stuhlmueller, C.P.

THE PAINFUL COST OF GREAT HOPES:
THE WITNESS OF ISAIAH 40–55

In writing this tribute to The Liturgical Press, many happy and grateful memories crowd into my mind and heart from twenty or more years of collaboration.

In fact, it was that many years ago that The Liturgical Press, through the creative ingenuity of Fr. William Heidt, O.S.B., planned the *New Testament Reading Guide*. This commentary series was to be up-to-date and popular in style, yet with firm scholarly underpinning, informative with data and cross references, yet all the while distributed at the unbelievable price of thirty-five cents a copy. Although I counted only a few publications to my name at that time, Father Heidt entrusted me with the Gospel of Luke. The first edition of one hundred and twenty-five thousand copies was published in 1960. The series became so successful that a second, expanded edition was already on the book stands by 1964!

Moreover, I count William Heidt among those scholars whose favorable reaction to one of my first presentations before the Catholic Biblical Association imparted the impetus to turn that research into a doctoral dissertation. Later when the dissertation was revised and published as *Creative Redemption in Deutero-Isaiah* (Rome: 1970), The Liturgical Press marketed the book within the United States.

These personal reminiscences, ranging from the Gospel of Luke to Second or Deutero-Isaiah, easily associate this present chapter with the focus of the entire book honoring The Liturgical Press's fifty years of publishing. The General Editor drew the theme of "Sin, Salvation, and the Spirit" from Luke's Gospel; I propose to exemplify it from chapters 40–55 in the prophecy of Isaiah.

For our purposes right now, the key verses in the Gospel of Luke read:

> Thus it is written that the *Christ must suffer* and on the third day rise from the dead, and that repentance and forgiveness of sins should be preached in his name *to all nations, beginning from Jerusalem* (Lk 24:46-47).

Second or Deutero-Isaiah, the author of chapters 40–55 in the Book of Isaiah, did not begin geographically with Jerusalem. God summoned this prophet around 550 B.C. to work among the Israelite exiles in Babylon. Eventually he reached out "to all nations." We want to trace how such a quantum leap took place.

The preaching of Deutero-Isaiah can be subdivided, according to the major periods of his career, between chapters 40 or 41 to 48, chapters 49 to 55, and the Songs of the Suffering Servant. In chapters 41–48 this author manifests a well-organized mind, integrating major themes, one with another, into a vigorous synthesis of salvation exclusively for Israel. In chapters 49–55 the interrelation of individual parts begins to break down; and in the Songs of the Suffering Servant, the prophet has moved away from his earlier buoyant hope to laments of faith, from Israel's salvation to an announcement that all nations can be saved.

Severe trials cut across the prophet's missionary career and separate the earlier period of preaching to Israel from the later period of calling the Gentiles to convert to the Lord. These same elements we find in Luke 24:46-47. The disciples began with *Galilee and Jerusalem*, first during Jesus' earthly life; then came *the rejection, suffering and death* of Jesus. After the resurrection, "repentance and forgiveness of sin should be preached . . . *to all nations.*"

To clarify our discussion, I will summarize my own perception of how the preaching of Deutero-Isaiah was finally edited into chapters 40–55 and then added to the pre-existing scroll of the earlier or First Isaiah:

> *Ch. 40.* The final editor (or the prophet himself) prepared an ensemble of major themes: a new exodus for Yahweh's chosen people from Babylon back to their homeland (vv. 3-11), gathering world attention (vv. 5, 28) across the universe of Yahweh's creation (vv. 21, 26, 28), in which foreign nations and other gods are reduced to "dust on a scale" (vv. 15-20, 25-26). Yahweh's judgments are manifest (vv. 14, 27), and Jerusalem is purified and renewed (vv. 2, 9).

> *Chs. 41–48.* Poems composed after Cyrus' initial victories (after 550 B.C.) but before the fall of Babylon. For the most part these are poems of hymnic exultation and of definitive victory for Yahweh as Redeemer and Holy One of Israel. The ultimate prophecy is to be fulfilled, through the victories of Cyrus; Israel, the elect one and the servant of the Lord, will be redeemed and recreated as she experiences the new exodus through the desert. The nations are rejected, or at best they stand in awe!

> *Chs. 49:1–55:11.* A much more somber tone pervades these chapters. The new exodus has begun, but it turns out to be a disappointment. The prophet experiences rejection and isolation, except for a few disciples around him. Yahweh is still Israel's Redeemer on the new exodus, but emphasis turns now to the end of the journey at Zion-Jerusalem and her consolation. Thus will the Lord's judgments be recognized.

> *Ch. 55:12-13.* A stylistic finale, corresponding to chapter 40.

A few more observations may clarify this explanation of the final, edited work of Deutero-Isaiah. Chapter 40 and chapters 41–48 form a closely knit synthesis of major themes and so qualify as "theology." The poems in chapters 49–55 were composed more rapidly, after the fall of Babylon and the first trickling of Israelites back to their homeland. Cyrus did not convert to the Lord; the new exodus did not lead to the fulfillment of all prophecies. While the chapters (41–48 and 49:1–55:11) form two distinct units, I myself cannot identify any order or plan for the arrangement of poems within each of the two sections. Later in this study we will treat a further stage in Deutero-Isaiah's prophetic career, dealing with the Songs of the Suffering Servant (42:1-4, 5-7; 49:1-9a; 50:4-9a; 52:13–53:12). These, in my judgment, were inserted at the time of the final editing of chapters 40–55 and did not belong to the initial collection of chapters 41–48 and 49:1–55:11.

Deutero-Isaiah's prophecy moves from jubilant, firm hope for Israel (41–48) to disappointment and subdued expectation (49–55) to persecution, possibly death, and a call for world salvation (Songs of Suffering Servant). The prophet's small hopes had to die before God's universal love could be perceived and announced. Hopes, therefore, carry a heavy mortgage of pain and must themselves be sacrificed to God's mysterious will. Only when the human perception of hopes is surrendered to God can God manifest those hopes in their full dimension.

It is the task of this study to investigate Deutero-Isaiah's hopes: first, in the way they hinted to a fulfillment beyond the prophet's words and comprehension; second, in the sequence by which these hopes precipitated pain and disappointment; and third, in the consistency of hopes remaining "hopes," that is, unfulfilled dreams. Hopes fulfilled can no longer be called by that name. Hopes must sustain a vision of the future, beyond the scope of the original expectation, beyond pain and confusion, into a future marked by trusting surrender.

Hopes, Intuitions of the Future

While Deutero-Isaiah drew upon Israel's earlier religious traditions for his announcement of a new exodus, he also incorporated into his poems some significant foreign, pagan, or secular ideas. For some unaccountable reason, he avoided technical, liturgical language and favored more "secular," everyday words and images. Finally, like his prophetic forebears, he recognized the absolute importance of world politics and military actions for the advancement of God's will for Israel. After investigating these aspects of Deutero-Isaiah's preaching, we will conclude that religious traditions provided him with a context of faith and continuity, but it was the secular forces that enabled him to recognize the universal scope and internal richness of these traditions. To put this conclusion very simply: religious tradition imparted continuity and survival; secular traditions made that survival worthwhile!

The opening chapter 40 has given the work of Deutero-Isaiah one of its most recognizable names, "The Book of Consolation," and at once we observe the tender concern and majestic sweep, the religious traditions in their secular setting, characteristic of this prophet. We find ourselves eavesdropping upon a divine assembly. The Lord Yahweh is speaking before his heavenly court, as the plural form of the Hebrew verbs makes clear. One after another the messengers respond to God's command that Israel be comforted. Each of their statements carries the force of a divine imperative. As P.-E. Bonnard wrote: the prophet insisted much less upon the identity of the consolers than upon the intensity of the consolation and upon its divine origin. We read in 40:1-11:

> *Yahweh speaks:*
> "Comfort! Oh, comfort my people!"
> your God is saying.
> "Speak tenderly to Jerusalem. . . ."
>
> *Members of the heavenly court and the prophet then speak out:*
>
> *First Voice:*
> A voice! It cries out:
> "In the steppe prepare the way of the Lord!
> Make straight in the desert the highway for our God.
> Every ravine shall be filled in,
> every mountain and hill shall be smoothed over. . . .
> Then the glory of the Lord shall be revealed,
> and all humankind shall see [it] together.
> Surely the mouth of the Lord has spoken.
>
> *Second Voice:*
> A voice!
> [It is] saying, "Cry out!"
>
> *Third Voice, that of the prophet:*
> And I said:
> "What shall I cry out?
> All humankind is but grass,
> and all its endurance like the wild flowers
> of the field.
> The grass withers, the flowers wilt,
> when the breath of the Lord blows upon them."
>
> *Fourth Voice:*
> "Yes! The grass does wither and the flowers do wilt,
> but the word of our God holds good forever."
>
> *Fifth Voice:*
> "Go up onto a high mountain,
> Zion, herald of glad tidings!

> Cry out with full voice,
> > Jerusalem, herald of glad tidings!
> Say to the cities of Judah:
> > 'Look! Your God!'
> Look! The Lord Yahweh!
> > With strength he comes,
> > With his regal arm he rules. . . .
> Like a shepherd he tends his sheep,
> > in his arms he gathers
> The lambs, and carries them against his breast,
> > and the ewes he gently leads."

The major theme here, garnered from Israel's traditions, is of course the *exodus* from foreign oppression back to the Promised Land. While the idea reaches as far back as Moses, the immediate inspiration for Deutero-Isaiah is to be located in the two great theologian-prophets of the northern tradition, Hosea and Jeremiah. Exodus becomes a type of future deliverance from oppression in such passages as Hos 7:16; 8:13; 9:3, 6; 11; 12:9; 13:4 and in Jer 2:2-3; 31:2-3, 7-14.

The appearance of the Lord's glory (Is 40:5) reminds us of another important tradition, this one closely associated with the *Jerusalem temple*. At its solemn dedication by King Solomon, the temple was filled with the Lord's glory (1 Kg 8:11). This chapter of First Kings carefully links the temple and its glory with the ark of the covenant and the days of Moses (Ex 40:34-38). This temple theme and the Lord's glory reappear during the exile, not only in Deutero-Isaiah but also in Ezekiel. This other prophet who preceded Deutero-Isaiah during the Babylonian captivity not only associated the glory of the Lord with his own inaugural vision (ch. 1) but he introduced it with many other important sermons or instructions (3:22; 8; 10; 37:1, 27-28; 43:1-9).

The references to Zion or Jerusalem (40:2, 9) also kept Deutero-Isaiah in close touch with the central unifying feature of biblical religion. The phrase "herald of good tidings" in verse 9 echoes happy announcements in such earlier passages as 1 Sam 31:9; 2 Sam 18:19; Jer 20:15; Nah 2:1.

Is 40:1-11, therefore, is redolent with tradition, particularly from Israel's liturgy. Yet, on closer scrutiny the section amazes us with its foreign, non-Israelite aspects, modeled upon the Babylonian *akitu*, or New Year's celebration. This spring festival of new life began with triumphal processions, when statues from neighboring, vassal cities were drawn along specially constructed roads to Babylon. These sacred journeys scintillated with light and splendor. The lesser or tutelary gods were placed in the central ziggurat or temple at Babylon, surrounding the chief god, Marduk. Other *akitu* ceremonies, like the determination of the year's destiny, the new coronation of Marduk, the recitation of the creation myth, the *Enuma elish*, the watering of the tree of life, the sacred marriage, all echo throughout the Book of Consolation.

While both Deutero-Isaiah and Ezekiel accepted the appearance of the Lord's glory outside the temple, even in a foreign "unclean land" (Am 7:17), still Ezekiel maintained an Israelite context, a sacred setting reminiscent of the Jerusalem temple with its cherubim and other symbolic touches. Deutero-Isaiah, for his part, kept the entire activity quite independent of the sanctuary. In fact, in all sixteen chapters of his prophecy, he never uses the word temple, except once in 44:28b, usually considered a later addition to his prophecy. In 40:5 the "glory of the Lord" is to be identified with the people Israel as they return liberated to their homeland, not with any sacred building or personnel.

Deutero-Isaiah, moreover, avoids sacred terminology. For instance, in the phrase "her iniquity is pardoned" (40:2), we would expect the liturgical word *kāpar* (origin of the phrase *yôm kippur*, Day of Atonement), but the prophet employed a secular word, *rāṣâ*. Again, in 43:23, a phrase that seems very liturgical, "sheep for burnt offering," turns out to be deliberately non-liturgical, because the prophet substituted a word for sheep different from the cultic passages in Ex 29:38-42 and Num 28:3-8. Deutero-Isaiah, therefore, strikes us as always in the process of "democratizing" and "de-sacralizing" the technical language and sacred imagery of his religious tradition. Without consciously realizing it, the prophet was opening the sanctuary doors to foreigners, or better, he was identifying the sacred precinct with all the world.

Deutero-Isaiah's *conscious* reaction, however, was quite different. In this new exodus he was separating God's chosen, covenanted people from all other peoples and was leading them back to their own city. At best, the foreigners stood in awe at this manifestation of the Lord's glory within the people Israel. Yet, at the same time, by removing the walls and barriers of the temple and transforming the homeland of the Gentiles into a sanctuary, he was preparing for God's invitation to them and for himself to be a "light to the nations" (Is 49:6).

In many other ways the Book of Consolation hints that God's call must someday reach to the world. One simple piece of statistics says very much. The Hebrew word *'ereṣ* can mean both "land" (i.e., the land of Israel, Moab, or any other particular nation) and "earth" (i.e., the planet at its farthest reaches). The prophet Ezekiel introduced the word *'ereṣ* 198 times, and in all but three contexts (Ez 7:21; 38:20; 14:13-19) he intends the very restricted meaning of land of Israel (a country the size of New Jersey). Deutero-Isaiah, on the contrary, applies the word *'ereṣ* to the entire world or to all humankind (as in 54:9, destroyed by the waters of Noah's flood) or the rulers of the earth (40:23-24). When Deutero-Isaiah used *'ereṣ* for a specific geographical area, the term remained vague (45:19, in a dark place of the earth). Finally, on only three occasions does *'ereṣ* refer to the land of Israel, and each time the reference is not nearly as clear-cut as in Ezekiel (Is 40:9; 49:9, 19).

When Deutero-Isaiah enhanced *'ereṣ* with such a large scope of meaning, did he also dilute its theological significance as compared with Ezekiel? Dieter Baltzer thinks so, and he may be right. But in my judgment it is more correct to state that *subconsciously* Deutero-Isaiah is arriving at a different religious meaning in *'ereṣ*, namely, Yahweh's control of the universal *'ereṣ* in fulfilling his promises to Israel.

Another interesting fact surfaces. Deutero-Isaiah lived not only immediately before but even during the return to the Promised Land. We would expect a more limited vision of *'ereṣ* in him than in Ezekiel. The reason why Deutero-Isaiah took a panoramic view may lie in the dismal reality of the return. This fact may have turned the nationalist into a universalist, but he was being prepared for such a transition.

Besides *'ereṣ*, Deutero-Isaiah made use of a series of words, all of which, in the statement of Norman M. Snaith, are "poetic language for the whole world." These synonyms include expressions like "nations," "peoples," "ends of the earth," "coastlands" or "isles," "far corners," "the sea," "the steppe and its cities," "mountains and hills," "deserts," "wastelands," "forests," "heavens," "skies." The list is long, but still not exhaustive, indicative of the continual sweep and grandeur of his preaching.

These examples strike some scholars as rhetorical exaggeration, and such a tendency was certainly present in a poet as brilliant as Deutero-Isaiah. What seems to be emerging, however, is the prophet's concern with Israelites scattered to the farthest corners of the then known world (see 43:1-7). According to some authors, Deutero-Isaiah ordinarily did not mean the Gentile nations at all in these expansive statements but only Israel. This position has been further nuanced by D. E. Hollenberg. He rightly subdivided the terms "Israel" and "nations." "Israel" can refer to "the Servant, the 'righteous remnant,' the prophetic nucleus," Israel par excellence; or it can mean "Israel as a whole" without the fervor of the former group, discouraged, ready to give up, but for the moment still loyal to Yahweh and their national traditions. "Nations" can be subdivided between crypto-Israelites who for all external purposes have dissociated themselves from Israel and have gone over to other nations and other gods, and the Gentile nations, always separate from Israel. If Deutero-Isaiah worked vigorously to win back the crypto-Israelites whom he called "the nations," then he was being prepared, again subconsciously, for the conversion of the other "nations," namely, the Gentiles.

Deutero-Isaiah was moving outward in his thinking and imagery at the very moment when Israel was moving inward, away from the nations toward the Promised Land. Unlike Ezekiel, Deutero-Isaiah maintained a more open, international perspective. He was being prepared for an evolutionary leap by which the nationalist could become the universalist.

Hopes, the Source of Suffering

Chapters 41–48, as we have just tried to show, manifest many signs of a well-integrated theology. Before the fall of Babylon in 539 B.C., Deutero-Isaiah had the time to think through a complex situation and to wrestle many ancient traditions into a new theological synthesis. At its heart this new presentation summoned Israel, God's elect people, to the fulfillment of the ultimate prophecy, to leave behind the non-elect foreigners and to seek out their own Promised Land. Yet, as we have already pointed out, we can also identify certain elements within Deutero-Isaiah's thinking that drew the prophet in the opposite direction and extended his interests favorably toward the non-elect "nations." These subconscious factors, full of hope for both Israel and the nations, needed a severe crisis before leaping visibly into the open arena. At that point they would demand a settlement. They would either achieve a fulfillment beyond everyone's expectations, even those of the prophet, or they would splinter the theological synthesis and seemingly destroy its main hopes, even for Israel.

Within a series of poems in chapters 41–48 on First and Last, the prophet was anticipating the ultimate fulfillment of all prophecy in Cyrus the Great. This extraordinary Persian had already absorbed the kingdom of the Medes (500 B.C.) and in a lightning stroke across snow-covered mountains in central Turkey, he had conquered the golden kingdom of Croesus at Sardis (546 B.C.). Deutero-Isaiah wrote about him:

> Listen to me in silence, O coastlands;
>   let the peoples renew their strength;
> let them approach, then let them speak;
>   let us together draw near for judgment.
> Who stirred up one from the east
>   whom victory meets at every step?
> He gives up nations before him,
>   so that he tramples kings underfoot;
> he makes them like dust with his sword,
>   like driven stubble with his bow.
> He pursues them and passes on safely
>   by paths his feet have not trod.
> Who has performed and done this,
>   calling the generations from the beginning?
> I, the Lord, the first,
>   and with the last; I am He.
> The coastlands have seen and are afraid,

>the ends of the earth tremble;
>they have drawn near and come (41:1-5).

Deutero-Isaiah considered Cyrus to be the Lord's anointed (45:1), a new Moses, called by name to lead the people Israel to freedom in their own land. Whether or not the prophet expected Cyrus to convert to Yahweh remains a bit vague, but Deutero-Isaiah saw in Cyrus a convergence of the Lord's eternal plans for creation. Cyrus' main role or vocation was to be centered on Israel's redemption. Deutero-Isaiah bestowed the title of "the anointed one" on Cyrus and invested him with a world mission within a poem that began and ended with the Lord's power and purpose throughout creation. The Lord, Israel's Redeemer, who makes all things, stretching out the heavens all by himself and spreading the earth for human habitation (44:24), this Lord is the one God

>. . . and there is no other
>forming light and creating darkness,
>   making peace and creating woe.
>I am the Lord, doing all these things (45:7).

This mighty confluence of creation and world history in Cyrus for the sake of Israel's redemption and new exodus disintegrated. Israel could not accept a pagan foreigner in the role of Moses. Deutero-Isaiah did not understand how Israel would reject the obvious. If Yahweh controlled world history, then he and no one else

>stirred up one from the east
>   whom victory meets at every step (41:2).

Still, Israel refused and so resisted the Lord's prophet. Deutero-Isaiah reacted with a mixture of sarcasm, disbelief, anger, and frustration against his people Israel:

>Foolish that one who strives against his Maker,
>   an earthen vessel against the potter of earthen vessels.
>Does clay say to the potter: what are you doing? . . .
>Foolish that one who says to a man begetting a child,
>   What are you begetting?
>Or to a woman,
>   What are you conceiving? . . .
>Do you question me about my children,
>   and argue against the work of my hands?
>I made the earth
>   and created humankind upon it. . . .
>I, yes I raise up one for the victory of my righteousness,
>   I make straight all his ways.
>He rebuilds my city . . . (45:9-13).

The people's response seemed irresponsible, faithless, and

downright foolish to a prophet who had learned to look upon the world as the Lord's temple and had come to appreciate, subconsciously yet all the more firmly at the core of himself, how everything secular was contributing to Yahweh's will for his people. Yet, the prophet's clear new insight, for a long time sharpening within his mind and heart, isolated him from the people and then caused them to turn against him.

The next period of the prophet's ministry evinces the high cost of pain he had to pay for his great hopes of world involvement in Israel's salvation and even of world salvation along with Israel. This new "age" began with the fall of Babylon in 539 and Cyrus' edict allowing all exiled peoples, Israel included, to return to their homeland. It seems that only a small straggling group of Israelites decided to return, while most people preferred to remain in the more prosperous country of Babylon.

Even if one excludes from consideration the mournful Songs of the Suffering Servant, chapters 49–55 are cast in a much darker and sadder mood than the first section of the Book of Consolation. We encounter a number of lines like:

> But Zion said, "The Lord has forgotten me. . . ."
> The children born in the time of your bereavement
>   will yet say [a message of hope] in your ears.
> "Where is your mother's bill of divorce
>   with which I put her away?"
> Rouse yourself, rouse yourself, . . .
> You who have drunk at the hand of the Lord
>   the cup of his wrath.
> Therefore, hear this, you who are afflicted.
> Fear not, for you will not be ashamed.
> For the Lord has called you
>   like a wife forsaken and grieved in spirit.
> Seek the Lord while he may be found, . . .
> Let the wicked forsake their ways.

And in the very last verse of the Book of Consolation (55:13), we feel the hurt and pain from briers and thorns. Although hope is not lost, still its buoyant joy seems dampened. The prophet's vision of a new creation has narrowed and no longer emerges with the same spontaneity as in chapters 41–48.

Rejected for the most part by his own people, struggling to keep their hopes and his own afloat, confronted with the loss of world possibilities, unable to accept the minuscle fulfillment of a few returnees reinhabiting the devastated area around Jerusalem, the prophet faced a serious personal crisis. To sustain his faith, he started writing down the sounds and the mysteries of his sorrow. He began with fragmentary attempts at laments, which combined ideas from the earlier Book of Consolation, usually hymnic in style, with a new, untried medium.

These "fragments" or "orphan verses" found their way into the Book of Consolation and were placed after the first three Servant Songs. Scholars will include or reject them from the Servant Songs. In any case, the literary edges around the Servant Songs appear ragged and upset. I am suggesting that the final editor added the "fragments," like appendices, when he inserted the Servant Songs into the Book of Consolation.

We propose the following arrangement of material where the Servant Songs appear. It is based upon earlier study by myself and other scholars, especially Ernst Vogt, S.J.

1) The Book of Consolation forms a continuous development if the Servant Songs and the fragments are removed:

41:21-29 + 42:8-9	Spoken against false gods in favor of Yahweh, First and Last.
48:20-21 + 49:9b-12	New Exodus
50:1-3 + 50:9b	Image of sackcloth

2) The fragments consist of:

42:5-7	Yahweh is praised as Savior of Israel, the same as in chapters 41–48, and also as Creator of the world. The relation of Israel with the nations is highlighted.
48:22	a stray verse, which actually belongs at 57:21, where it reappears.
49:7	properly belongs in style and thought with the other poems of the Book of Consolation rather than with the Servant Songs.
49:8, 5a, 6	the prophet almost shouted these verses in desperation. He had worked all his life for Israel and now at the end he saw clearly for the first time that Yahweh wanted the salvation of all the world.
50:10-11	a later editor's admonition to obey the voice of the Lord's servant.

3) The fully developed Servant Songs:

42:1-4	Solemn investiture of the Servant before the divine assembly.
49:1-4 + 5c	Autobiographical account of the Servant's call.
50:4-9a	Autobiographical lament over personal suffering.
52:13–53:12	Collective lament over the Servant [now dead?].

According to the explanation being proposed here, the dramatic leap from exclusive concern over Israel's redemption to a vision of world salvation happened in a flash. The deepest, subconscious movements of the prophet's soul suddenly swept to the surface and overwhelmed every other inhibition and consideration. In one of the fragments Deutero-Isaiah recorded this "call" from the Lord:

> It is such a small thing, too small indeed,
>   for you to be my servant,

[simply] to raise up the [fallen] tribes of Jacob,
and to restore the dispersed [children of] Israel.
Look! I make you a light to the nations
that you may bring my salvation to the end of
the earth (49:6).

The prophet realized that there is a universe created and loved by God, and that Israel was chosen with a mission to share her election with the entire world of all men and women. Yet, Deutero-Isaiah came to this conclusion too late — or so it seemed to him. His life was over and his energy was spent. Events had passed him by. He was left only with his hopes.

Now he was paying the high price of these hopes. Earlier, because of the wondrous expansiveness, resting subconsciously beneath the surface of his mind, he was able to speak in ways that surprised even himself and that produced the golden poetry of the Book of Consolation. The universe had become the Lord's temple; all peoples, pagans as well as Israelites, performed "liturgical" roles as the Lord's instruments within this temple. God was mustering all the world for the enactment of Israel's salvation. Plans hidden in the world from past ages were now reaching a moment of fulfillment for Israel's sake. Hopes, however, that were responsible, subconsciously, for this extraordinary vista of Israel's salvation now demand their payment. They must be shared in the act of their fulfillment or be lost! To have restricted this vision to a single people turned out to be "such a small thing." The prophet was now liberated to give these hopes to the world, but no one was ready to receive them, neither in Israel nor among the nations.

So his hopes remained hopes, and a new generation must pick them up, suffer for them, and wait.

They who wait [with hope] upon the Lord
renew their strength (40:31).

Sustaining the Pain of One's Hopes

Deutero-Isaiah, I am suggesting, composed the Songs of the Suffering Servant, not so much to predict the future nor even to describe the lamentable plight of Israel at this time, but simply to brace himself against overwhelming disappointment and to hang on to his hopes. In the words of a later saint who turned to the Book of Consolation for inspiration and direction, the prophet was "hoping against hope" (Rom 4:18). Jesus, too, returned repeatedly to this same section of sacred tradition to appreciate and to communicate the mystery of God's will for himself in his own rejection, death, and renewed hope. In this way a chain of prophecy-fulfillment was forged.

We, too, direct attention to the Songs of the Suffering Servant that we may be guided in sustaining hopes even in the midst of sin, our own and others', in seeking salvation with no compromise of hopes, and so in being led by the Spirit to the fulfillment of mysteries, planted deeply within us by God before our birth. From the witness of Is 40–55 we will reckon the painful cost of great hopes and realize how worthwhile the price. Perhaps, at this point, the title of this particular chapter will begin to match up with the theme of the entire book, "Sin, Salvation, and the Spirit."

The *first major Song of the Suffering Servant* (42:1-4) presents the solemn investiture before God's heavenly court. The scene takes place in the same setting as 40:1-11. The Lord God publicly declares to the divine assembly: "Behold my servant!" In a very true sense Deutero-Isaiah has been swung back to the moment when he was first called to be a prophet. The hopes, embedded within his spirit from the very start, are now enunciated openly and clearly, perhaps for the first time.

These ideals were not to be achieved by military might nor by sound and fury.

> He will not cry out nor lift up his voice.

No one is to be hurt or trambled down in any blind rush to fulfillment:

> a bruised reed he will not break,
> and a dimly burning wick he will not quench.

The prophet learned the meaning of those words "bruised reed" and "dimly burning wick" in the school of life with its great disappointments. The first quality about a hopeful person, then, is patient perseverance, waiting not only upon the Lord but also upon others.

Hopes, too, must be dissociated from personal ambition and secular careers. At least, hopes are not to be identified that closely with the limits and expectations of this earth. Hopes come from God and belong always to the Lord who pronounced these other words over the Servant:

> I will place my spirit upon him.

Sometimes to appreciate how jealously God cares for his hopes within us, we must lose all our human resources. Then we can truly say: What exists is from the Lord and returns to the Lord, as another distant disciple of Deutero-Isaiah confessed:

> The Lord gave, and the Lord has taken away (Job 1:21).

Finally, in the first Song, an almost contradictory position emerges: the people already possess what they are to receive through the Servant. This paradox serves to reinforce the gracious respect due to all other persons. When God says about the Servant:

> The coastlands wait for his instruction,

the Hebrew word for "wait" implies that they already possess, like a pregnant mother, what they hope to receive. The Servant, then, deals with hope in himself and in others, like a midwife who enables new life, implanted mysteriously by God, to come to birth. The painful cost of hopes are the birthpangs of new life.

The Second Song (49:1-4 + 5c) in many ways is a meditation upon the prophecy of Jeremiah. Life, especially at the end, has become so mixed up and its hopes so self-destructive that the prophet, like Jeremiah, could find no other refuge but God who summoned him into life with a secret mission, determined before birth and even before conception:

> The Lord called me from the womb.

At times God's servants felt the anguish of a wasted life. The Song then set up a pathetic interchange:

> But he [the Lord] said to me,
> You are my Servant, . . .
> But I [felt compelled to] reply:
> I have wearied myself uselessly. . . .

Perhaps at the heart of this anguish lay the all–important lesson: hope, like true love, does not exist to be used, nor to be bartered and exchanged, nor to be gauged by accomplishments. Hope and love are attitudes far more precious than any way to measure them. They are the compelling way of reuniting one with God in a mystic embrace where all is absorbed in wonder:

> My justification is with the Lord [alone],
>   my accomplishment is with my God.
> I am honored in the eyes of the Lord,
>   my God is my strength.

It seems that such ecstatic experiences of love are possible only if hopes *remain* hopes, seemingly unfulfilled with little or nothing to show and yet consummated as hopes beyond hopes in God. As such, hopes reach back to the wellsprings or to the womb of life; for beneath the surface of the conscious direction of one's energies and at the end when everything else disappears, these secret hopes bring us to the fullness of life in God.

In *the Third Song* (50:4-9a) the Suffering Servant combines paradoxical attitudes of shame and nobility, of oppression and independence, of discipleship and authority.

> The Lord God has given me
>   the tongue of one who is taught
> that I may know how to sustain the weary
>   with a rousing word. . . .
> I did not hide my face

> from the shame of being spit upon. . . .
> Yet I was not put to shame.

The Servant has first experienced what he imparts to others. He is convinced, from personal crises and profound disappointment, from the endurance of ridicule and isolation, that no amount of external abuse can touch the goodness and nobility of one's character. Therefore, though bent over from pain and shame, the Servant still stands erect and calls for a legal process before all the world.

> Look! The Lord God helps me!
> Who can impeach me?

Hopes, therefore, must run the gauntlet of selfish expectations and political maneuvering, of compromise and belittlement, in hostile surroundings, and so to reach their goal. Only then is one able to speak the language that echoes the groans of God's oppressed children.

The *Fourth Song* (52:13–53:12) defies every attempt to repeat or summarize its message:

> Who has believed what we have heard?

More than any other song, this one baffles the reader with its paradox and seeming contradiction:

> Behold! My servant prospers [like a sage],
> and many are appalled at you!

These opening lines combine the wisdom of the sages with a word — "appalled" — normally applied to a conquered and devastated city, foolish enough to have resisted the enemy. Wondrous exaltation overlaps with disappointing shame. A word about the Servant is abruptly switched into direct address: " . . . appalled at *you*!"

This poem, like any song, is to be *heard*, and the sounds of the Hebrew verse carry the haunting resonance of pain, with a continuous pitch of *u* and *o* vowels, or of consonants combining liquid *l*'s and guttural *ch*'s. Yet, the song summons us much more to silent contemplation than to active listening. Repeatedly such words as "appearance," "see," "look at," "revealed," "hiding," "consider," etc., occur. Hopes elude imagination; one can only remain silent in amazement. Yet one contemplates what seems absent! While, in one sense, the Servant is always intensely present, he is never mentioned in the main section of the Song (53:1-11a). Our gaze is attracted beyond the Servant to the Person of God, who is saying, "Behold! My Servant!" While the Song has been written in the style of a community lament over the rejected, silent, and possibly dead Servant, still the pervasive tone is one of triumph. Hopes lost in God are hopes regained in a new and greater life with God.

When Deutero-Isaiah disappeared from history, we were bequeathed a legacy of hope that enabled Jesus to accept the burden of his own mission, through death, to resurrection. We, too, can continue "hoping beyond hope." We will discover the cost to be small, indeed, compared to the ecstatic joy of living beyond the boundaries of this life and its pain and so to reach the instinctive purpose of our conception and birth.

> The Lord called me from the womb (49:1).

Conclusion

The theme of *sin, salvation, and the Spirit* in Luke 24:46-47 summarizes not only Luke's Gospel but also the prophecy of Deutero-Isaiah. Both Jesus and the Great Unknown Prophet of the Babylonian Exile began their ministry and devoted almost all, if not all, their activity to the conversion of their own people Israel. Each was highly gifted, brimming over with enthusiasm, talents, hopes, and the Holy Spirit. They saw, each in his own way, the convergence of prophetical tradition upon an unique moment of world history.

As Jesus and Deutero-Isaiah labored vigorously for the removal of sin and the salvation of their own people, subconsciously they introduced ideas or acted even impulsively in ways that hinted at something far beyond the confines or limits of their tradition or people. Deutero-Isaiah's imagery extended round the universe and soared among the stars, as mountains collapsed and valleys were lifted up. John the Baptist called upon this very text in Is 40 to announce the One to come after him (Lk 3:4-6, 15-17). Jesus broke the shackles of tradition, touching lepers and the bier of a dead man, speaking with prostitutes and oppressed groups, dining with tax collectors and foreigners — and all the while he was amazed at their faith.

Both Jesus and Deutero-Isaiah carried hopes that reached beyond their articulated message and somehow tended to rend the seams of their carefully integrated theology. These hopes lay deep in their pysche, where people groan in the spirit and sense a life beyond the borders of their consciousness. These hopes were to renew the spirit of men and women everywhere, purify religion, and produce a more adequate theology of sin and salvation. Strangely enough, these hopes seemed to spring forward most naturally in the *secular* arena of daily life, particularly in the midst of the poor and the oppressed.

Dark clouds settled upon Deutero-Isaiah and upon Jesus. The people could not tolerate a theology of such bounding hope, on such a world perspective. The prophet's preaching began to reflect a more persistent note of gloom and discouragement. He appeared in conflict with the people. He became ever more isolated. For strength and perseverance he began to compose, at first in fragmentary sketches, the songs or laments of the Suffering Servant. In one of these, the dramatic turning point occurred: it was too small a thing to labor simply for Israel. Look! (God declared) I make you a light to the nations. Jesus too began ever more earnestly to set his face toward Jerusalem and the cross (Lk 9:51).

Finally, in the four Songs of the Suffering Servant, Deutero-Isaiah relinquished into the Lord's hands the most precious gift ever received from the Lord. He returned to their rightful owner the hopes that had inspired and led him up this moment. He thus paid the highest cost for hopes this sublime. He gave them back as "hopes," and therefore as a vision of the future, personally unfulfilled. By returning to God these ideals, more pure and more illuminating than they ever were at the beginning of the prophet's career, these hopes lived in one generation after another until all men and women would find the ultimate fulfillment of prophecy in Jesus, dying and rising to new life.

The first of the Servant Songs began with the breathing of God's spirit upon the servant. Jesus, the Servant of the Lord, ended, committing his spirit to the Father. The cycle of sin-salvation-spirit was complete.

A. Joseph Everson

EZEKIEL AND THE GLORY OF
THE LORD TRADITION

Preface

The common text that unites this collection of essays is found in the final chapter of St. Luke's Gospel. In this concluding chapter, St. Luke recalls the ways in which people were confronted by the reality of the risen Christ. Mary of Magdala and Joanna, together with Mary, the mother of James, and certain other women, discovered the empty tomb and were met by two strangers in brilliant clothing who declared to them the resurrection of the Lord (24:1-11). On hearing this news, Peter ran to the empty grave and returned in amazement (24:12). Later, two disciples met a stranger on the road to Emmaus and felt deeply moved as they talked and broke bread together; only afterwards did they fully realize that they had been with the risen Lord (24:13-35). Then, when the Lord appeared in their midst, the disciples were simply filled with fear and wonder until someone had the presence of mind to offer him a piece of grilled fish (24:36-43).

The resurrection stories convey Luke's deep belief that in a dramatic and personal way the God of Israel was present in and through Jesus of Nazareth. For this reason the Torah, the prophets, and the Psalter all find fulfillment and unity in the risen Christ (24:44-47). For this reason the Scriptures add depth and richness to our understanding of the presence of Christ in our world.

This essay focuses on the biblical tradition of the Glory of the Lord. It is an ancient temple tradition, one used by priestly and prophetic writers for the specific purpose of declaring the dramatic and personal presence of the Lord God of Israel in specific times and places. More than any other writer, the prophet Ezekiel uses vivid imagery to declare God's particular presence in history with this tradition. In his writing, the Glory of the Lord exposes sin and evil in the world, and on other occasions heralds marvelous salvation and new life for people.

163

When Luke concludes his Gospel with an account of the ascension, he declares that the disciples returned joyously to Jerusalem and went regularly to the Temple to worship. ". . . they worshipped him, and returned to Jerusalem with great joy, and they were continually in the temple praising and blessing God" (Lk 24:52-53).

Why, we might ask, did they go to the Temple? And what does it mean that they were filled with joy so that they were continually praising and blessing God? A study of Ezekiel and the Glory of the Lord tradition suggests a possible answer. The disciples knew that for centuries the Temple had been the dwelling place of the Glory of the Lord. The Temple was the place where the spirit and presence of God seemed most real for them. Like Ezekiel long before them, the disciples had experienced events that convinced them that they had been in the presence of the living God. Like Ezekiel, they must have been almost overwhelmed with awe as they reflected on the events they had experienced. But like Ezekiel, they also were led to a clearer understanding of their purpose and direction in life.

In a most striking way, Luke suggests in his Gospel that with the birth, life, death, and resurrection of Christ, the Glory of the Lord has appeared in new form among people on earth. But the purpose of the Glory remains the same: people are called to renounce sin and evil, to hear the new word of salvation, and to live as people of the Spirit.

God's Particular Presence

"Dad, where is God?" The question from an eight-year-old daughter is asked with a mood of great curiosity, mystery, and intrigue. Yet her question is also very old. It is a question that people of faith have asked down through the ages. What imagery shall we use to speak of God, particularly when we feel or experience the presence of God on a particularly important or sacred occasion? And how shall we continue to affirm with biblical writers both the transcendent power of God as Lord of all the world and yet proclaim the Lord's particular presence in certain places or situations?

This tension is addressed in a variety of ways in the Bible. In the creation story in Gen 2, the Lord God is portrayed almost in human form — as a gardener and as a potter — working the ground, planting a garden, shaping Adam from the dust of the ground after it has become moist, and later calling, "Adam, where are you?" as though the Lord really did not know where Adam was at that moment. In striking contrast, the creation account in Gen 1 suggests that God commanded the creation of the world from some lofty heavenly throneroom through his divine decree and powerful word. The Deuteronomic writer speaks of the Lord God dwelling in the heavens, but affirms his earthly presence as he causes his Name to dwell in the Temple among the people.

In all of the Scriptures, however, there is probably no more dramatic imagery used to express God's particular presence among people on earth than is found in the stories of the Glory of the Lord tradition. While references are found in various traditions, including Isaiah and the Psalter,[1] it is particularly in the Priestly tradition and in the Book of Ezekiel that we see the fullness of the tradition. These two sources will be considered in detail in this essay.

The most important factor to realize about the Glory of the Lord tradition is that when the word *kabod* ("glory") appears in construct with the name of the Lord God, it is not simply intended as an attribute or descriptive word about God; rather, the word *kabod* describes an observable phenomenon, something that is actually seen by people.[2] Our concern is to survey the tradition of *kabod Jahweh* ("glory of the Lord") when the word is used in this manner in the Priestly tradition and when it is appropriated with this meaning by the prophet Ezekiel.

The Glory of the Lord in the Priestly Tradition

In the Priestly writings of the post-exilic era, the *kabod Jahweh* is remembered most clearly in direct connection with Sinai and the reception of the Torah by Moses, with the ark and tabernacle in the wilderness, and with traditions of the Temple of Solomon. Four biblical texts help us focus the memories preserved by the Priestly tradition.

We consider first the account found in Ex 24:15-18, where the Priestly writer may in fact only be adding his own comment to an earlier memory of Sinai. However that may be, the Glory of the Lord is remembered here as an awesome cloud that settled on the mountain with fire at the top,[3] visible to all the people:

> Then Moses went up on the mountain, and the cloud covered the mountain. The glory of the Lord settled on Mount Sinai and the cloud covered it six days; and on the seventh day he called to Moses out of the midst of the cloud. Now the appearance of the glory of the Lord was like a devouring fire on the top of the mountain in the sight of the people of Israel. And Moses entered the cloud and went up on the mountain (Ex 24:15-18a).

In the text the author is emphasizing that the Lord is present in the mystery of the fire and smoke, from which he speaks to his servant Moses. The Torah is received, and Moses is also given directions for the construction of an ark and a tabernacle that will be a suitable dwelling place.[4] Because of the golden calf incident and the infidelity of the people, Moses again takes two tablets of stone to the top of the mountain. When he returns from the mountain, his face is radiant, obviously caused by his proximity to the Glory of the Lord:

> When Moses came down from Mount Sinai, with the two tablets of the

testimony in his hand as he came down from the mountain, Moses did not know that the skin of his face shone because he had been talking with God. And when Aaron and all the people of Israel saw Moses, behold, the skin of his face shone, and they were afraid to come near him (Ex 34:29-30).

The Book of Exodus concludes with the Glory of the Lord settling on the newly constructed tabernacle. This final story in Exodus preserves for later generations the deeply religious conviction that the Lord of heaven and earth whom they have encountered at Sinai in a very particular way will continue to be among them. Through the Torah and through the services of worship at the tabernacle, people may trust that the Lord is among them in a very particular and special way.

> Then the cloud covered the tent of meeting, and the glory of the Lord filled the tabernacle. And Moses was not able to enter the tent of meeting because the cloud abode upon it, and the glory of the Lord filled the tabernacle. Throughout all their journeys, whenever the cloud was taken up from over the tabernacle, the people of Israel would go onward; but if the cloud was not taken up, then they did not go onward till the day that it was taken up. For throughout all their journeys the cloud of the Lord was upon the tabernacle by day, and fire was in it by night, in the sight of all the house of Israel (Ex 40:34-38).

Here again, we see the *kabod* described in terms of cloud and fire, visible to all the people. The *kabod* gives guidance and direction for people who travel in the wilderness. And the pilgrims who traveled across the difficult terrain were invited again and again to trust in the presence of God in their midst to bring security and meaning in their lives.[5]

One further memory is important for an understanding of how the Glory of the Lord tradition was remembered by people in the post-exilic era. Throughout the time of the judges and the time of David, the *kabod* was remembered as dwelling with the ark and the portable tabernacle.[6] Then a new home was built for the ark. Amid great ritual and pageantry, the Temple built by Solomon was dedicated with countless sacrifices of sheep and oxen. The ark was brought up to the new Temple, where it was placed in the innermost sanctuary. The Priestly tradition preserves the memory of the Glory of the Lord now settling upon the Temple in this way:[7]

> Now when the priests came out of the holy place (for all the priests who were present had sanctified themselves, without regard to their divisions; and all the Levitical singers, Asaph, Heman, and Jeduthun, their sons and kinsmen, arrayed in fine linen, with cymbals, harps and lyres, stood east of the altar with a hundred and twenty priests who were trumpeters; and it was the duty of the trumpeters and singers to make themselves heard in unison in praise and thanksgiving to the Lord), and

when the song was raised, with trumpets and cymbals and other musical instruments, in praise to the Lord, "For he is good, for his steadfast love endures forever," the house, the house of the Lord, was filled with a cloud, so that the priests could not stand to minister because of the cloud; for the glory of the Lord filled the house of God.

Then Solomon said, "The Lord has said that he would dwell in thick darkness. I have built thee an exalted house, a place for thee to dwell in forever" (2 Chr 5:11–6:2).

From 922 down to 587 B.C., from Solomon's era to the fall of Jerusalem, it seems probable that among the priests in Jerusalem the Glory of the Lord was thought of as the cloud, smoke, and fire present within the Temple in Jerusalem, the visible sign of the presence of the Lord in his dwelling place.

It is in this setting in Jerusalem that the prophet Ezekiel received his training as a priest. He evidently grew up with an awareness of this substantive understanding of the Glory of the Lord. For it seems quite certain that long before the Priestly accounts were written down, they were preserved in Jerusalem in oral fashion from generation to generation. Thus, when Ezekiel experiences his visions in exile in Babylon, he is not without prior knowledge of the awesome scene that appears before him. How Ezekiel draws from this stream of tradition and appropriates it into his own life and message is our present concern.

Ezekiel and the Glory of the Lord Tradition

According to the references included within the text of his book (1:1; 33:21; 40:1), Ezekiel was among the exiles who were deported from Jerusalem to Babylon in the year 598. Judah had weathered a very difficult era from 609 to 598, during which time King Jehoiachim served as a vassal first to Egypt and then to Babylon. In the last years of his reign, rebellion broke out and became rather widespread, probably with the support of the king. By 598, Babylonian authorities were able to move to put down the revolt. Jehoiachim either died or was killed and his eighteen-year-old son, Jehoiachin, soon paid the price. Shortly after becoming king, he and a number of officials and their families were deported.[8] Ezekiel was evidently part of that group.

Ezekiel's Call-Vision

Ezekiel does not tell us exactly where he was when the visions recorded in chapters 1–3 came to him. Were these dreams that came to him while he was sleeping? Was he lost in deep prayer and contemplation among other people? Or was he out in some remote wilderness place or along the river Chebar? Wherever he was, he recalls a strong wind coming from the north and a bright cloud. Around the cloud was fire, flashing continually, and in the midst of the fire something that appeared like gleaming bronze. As it drew closer, Ezekiel discerned that at the center of the cloud was a four-wheeled chariot, like the chariot of a king in battle. Strange creatures, each with four heads, were at each of the four wheels; they served as throne-bearers.[9] Over their heads was a firmament, a covering that glistened like crystal, and there was a roaring sound as the chariot moved. Then Ezekiel described the throne that was above the firmament:

> And above the firmament over their heads there was the likeness of a throne, in appearance like sapphire; and seated above the likeness of a throne was a likeness as it were of a human form. And upwards from what had the appearance of his loins I saw as it were gleaming bronze, like the appearance of fire enclosed round about; and downward from what had the appearance of his loins I saw as it were the appearance of fire, and there was brightness round about him. Like the appearance of the bow that is in the cloud on the day of rain, so was the appearance of the brightness round about.
>
> Such was the appearance of the likeness of the glory of the Lord. And when I saw it, I fell upon my face, and I heard the voice of one speaking (Ezek 1:26-28).

Like the prophet Isaiah,[10] Ezekiel is confronted by the Lord of Israel in a vision of overwhelming divine presence. From his throne, amid fire, clouds, and awesome light, the Lord speaks to one whom he has now called to be his messenger and servant. In contrast to earlier memories of the *kabod*, the divine theophany appearance here is private. Only Ezekiel has seen this vision, which he now feels compelled to share and to follow. Like earlier portraits, there is little question but that Ezekiel felt an intense awareness of the personal presence of the Lord in the moment of his vision. In the third chapter of Ezekiel, a further memory of the *kabod* vision is preserved:

> . . . the Spirit lifted me up, and as the glory of the Lord arose from its place, I heard behind me the sound of a great earthquake; it was the sound of wings of the living creatures as they touched one another, and the sound of the wheels beside them, that sounded like a great earthquake. The Spirit lifted me up and took me away, and I went in bitterness in the heat of my spirit, the hand of the Lord being strong upon me; and I came to the exiles at Tel Abib who dwelt by the river Chebar. And I sat there overwhelmed among them seven days.
>
> And at the end of seven days, the word of the Lord came to me: "Son of man, I have made you a watchman for the house of Israel; whenever you hear a word from my mouth, you shall give them warning from me" (Ezek 3:12-17).

Significant is the direct connection between Ezekiel's vision and his sense of calling. A new dimension is added here to the traditional understanding of the prophet as a messenger for the Lord. Here Ezekiel uses the imagery of a watchman to explain the work that the Lord has given him. He is to sound a warning for an endangered city and people. Because of the imminent danger to Jerusalem, he must speak if he is to be responsible and faithful to his Lord.

The striking aspect of Ezekiel's calling with the imagery of the *kabod* is, of course, that he does not see the Glory of the Lord tied in any way to the Temple in Jerusalem; it has made its appearance to him in Babylon. We will see that when Ezekiel understands the tradition in this manner, he is not breaking with the tradition, but is actually understanding it in a deep and profound manner consistent with earlier portrayals.

Ezekiel's Vision of the Glory of the Lord Departing from Jerusalem

It is in the visions in chapters 8–11 that we see how Ezekiel uses the Glory of the Lord tradition to sound a warning and pronounce judgment on the people of Jerusalem. In the vision in chapter 8, Ezekiel finds himself at the north-gate entrance to Jerusalem. The *kabod* appears like a great light illuminating the abominations and evil deeds of the people who still live in Jerusalem.[11] What becomes obvious throughout this text is the deep conviction on the part of the author that the Lord still wants very much to dwell among his people. There is a plaintive, almost tragic mood present as the Lord inquires of Ezekiel: "Son of man, do you see what they are doing, the great abominations that the house of Israel are committing here, to drive me far from my sanctuary? But you will see still greater abominations" (Ezek 8:6).

In chapter 9, Ezekiel portrays the actual drama as the *kabod* begins its departure from the traditional dwelling place in the Jerusalem Temple. The *kabod* rises up from the cherubim and the throne to the entrance or "threshold" of the Temple (v. 3). A messenger, clothed in linen and carrying a scroll, is sent out throughout the city to mark out those who are in sorrow for the evils that are being committed. Those who have no sorrow are also noted, and it is clear that this latter group will soon be visited for their crimes.

In chapter 10, the *kabod* is again seen moving from the inner court up to the threshold and then up into the air, where it hovers over the eastern gate of the Temple:

> Now the cherubim were standing on the south side of the house, when the man went in; and a cloud filled the inner court. And the glory of the Lord went up from the cherubim to the threshold of the house; and the house was filled with the cloud and the court was full of the brightness of the glory of the Lord. And the sound of the wings of the cherubim was heard as far as the outer court, like the voice of God Almighty when he speaks (Ezek 10:3-5).

After a lengthy description of the cherubim and their functions with the four-wheeled chariot (the same chariot that Ezekiel saw in his call-vision), the second stage of the movement is described:

> Then the glory of the Lord went forth from the threshold of the house, and stood over the cherubim. And the cherubim lifted up their wings and mounted up from the earth in my sight as they went forth, with the wheels beside them; and they stood at the door of the east gate of the house of the Lord; and the glory of the God of Israel was with them (Ezek 10:18-19).

With this portrait, we can become more precise in our understanding of Ezekiel's vision of the *kabod*. Here the *kabod* clearly is understood as something separate even from the cherubim and the chariot-throne. On several occasions,[12] Ezekiel declares that he saw the Lord God in human-like form, although the figure is obscured by the fire, cloud, and dazzling light. While this picture may be influenced by Persian apocalyptic thinking, it is even more probable that Ezekiel is here depicting the Lord as the divine Warrior of Israel, her King who is resplendent in battle array.[13]

In fact, the warrior imagery is quite restrained in the portraits in Ezek 8-11, but the military context seems quite evident. The commander of the heavenly armies and his royal messenger have taken account of the situation in Jerusalem, and the fire of divine judgment will follow soon after his departure from the Temple sanctuary.

Chapter 11, which probably contains two originally separate visions (vv. 1-13 and 14-21), forms the capstone for these four chapters that describe the departure of the *kabod*. From the east gate, Ezekiel sees the assembly of corrupt officials and hears again the reasons why God is about to remove his presence: the princes have devised plots and given wicked counsel to the city (v. 2); the people have feared the sword, but now the Lord himself will bring the sword upon them and they will be given into the hands of foreigners or will die by the sword (vv. 9-10). Using the recognition formula found so often throughout this writing, "then you will know that I am the Lord," the writer declares that the impending time of punishment will be the occasion when the people remaining in Jerusalem will experience a personal encounter with their Lord (v. 10).

The second oracle (vv. 14-21) is most interesting because of the sharp contrast set out between the group in Jerusalem and those who are already in exile. The group in Jerusalem thinks that the people in exile have "gone far from the Lord" (v. 15), while they are the secure ones who dwell in the land of promise and in close proximity to the Temple, where the Lord certainly dwells. The Lord now declares that the opposite situation is in fact the case. The Lord is a sanctuary for those who are scattered; those who live in the land of promise and near the sanctuary are the ones who face imminent catastrophe.[14] The chapter then concludes with a description of the *kabod* departing from the Temple mountain eastward to the Mount of Olives:

> Then the cherubim lifted up their wings, with the wheels beside them; and the glory of the Lord was over them. And the glory of the Lord went up from the midst of the city, and stood upon the mountain which is on the east side of the city. And the Spirit lifted me up and brought me in the vision by the Spirit of God into Chaldea, to the exiles. Then the vision that I had seen went up from me. And I told the exiles all the things that the Lord had showed me (Ezek 11:22-25).

In these ways Ezekiel incorporates the Glory of the Lord tradition to give theological meaning to the fall of Jerusalem. It seems clear that he had anticipated and struggled with a conviction that Jerusalem would soon fall, even as he was beset by his visions. His deepest conviction is that the people have literally driven their Lord from them by their evil actions and deeds. For Ezekiel, the causes of Jerusalem's fall are not merely a matter of political intrigue; the catastrophe is a moral and spiritual concern. The destruction comes because people in Jerusalem have forgotten their calling and the Lord who has been their sustenance through the ages. The people have forgotten their primary charge to look to the welfare of all their people as would be expected in true worship and trust in their Lord's commands.

Ezekiel's Vision of the Glory of the Lord Returning to Jerusalem

In chapters 40–48, the Glory of the Lord tradition functions for a purpose quite in contrast to chapters 8–11. Instead of being the focal point of a message of impending judgment for Jerusalem, now the *kabod* is at the heart of a message of salvation and future hope. This final section of Ezekiel is dated in 573, some fourteen years after the fall of Jerusalem. In these chapters Ezekiel's visions of the future are recorded. He sees the time when Jerusalem will once again be restored, and with that restoration, the rebuilding of the Temple, the reinstitution of the Temple ordinances, and the return of the tribal territories. In chapter 40, an architect is seen going throughout the city indicating the exact measurements for the restoration — the gates, the Temple areas, and the chambers that will again be set in order. Everything in the ideal new Jerusalem is to be prepared because of the dramatic announcement of chapter 43:1-12. The *kabod Jahweh*, "the glory of the Lord," is going to return to Jerusalem!

> Afterward he brought me to the gate, the gate facing east. And behold, the glory of the God of Israel came from the east; and the sound of his coming was like the sound of many waters; and the earth shone with his

glory. And the vision I saw was like the vision which I had seen when he came to destroy the city, and like the vision which I had seen by the river Chebar; and I fell upon my face. As the glory of the Lord entered the temple by the gate facing east, the Spirit lifted me up, and brought me into the inner court; and behold, the glory of the Lord filled the temple (Ezek 43:1-5).

It is the desire of the Lord to dwell among his people. It is his desire that they should be a holy people. And it is his desire that people should know him, not in moments of judgment or in the destruction of war, but rather through his abiding presence among them. By their actions and the purity of their hearts (11:17-21), people demonstrate their holiness. In their life together, they are called to reverence, awe, and wonder, remembering that the Lord is present among them and that it is his Law that brings holiness, light, life, and health to all in the community.[15]

Ezekiel and the Priestly Tradition

How did Ezekiel dare to use the tradition of the *kabod* in this awesome manner? How did he feel enough freedom to break with the established understanding that the Glory of the Lord was only present with the ark of the covenant? As we have seen in this essay, Ezekiel did not create the concept of the *kabod*, but rather appropriated it from an oral and, perhaps, written tradition among the priests of the Jerusalem Temple.

The answer to these questions certainly is to be found in Ezekiel's own deep understanding of biblical faith. By that we mean that he was a man of keen mind, one who obviously had studied and reflected on the history and religious heritage of his people. At the same time, it seems equally obvious that he was a man of profound conscience, one who struggled and agonized over questions of good and evil and the Lordship of Yahweh over the earth and especially over his people. Ezekiel knew the stories of the wilderness era recalled in the Priestly tradition. In that tradition, there is a story that happened well before Sinai and the reception of the Torah. After fleeing from Egypt, the Hebrew people crossed the sea to the wilderness of Sin. There they were tired and hungry; murmuring against Moses had become the dominant mood of the day. There the Lord graciously provided manna for the complaining people. Amid their grumbling and complaining, Moses called the people together and commanded Aaron to speak to them. Then, it is recorded, ". . . as Aaron spoke to the whole congregation of the people of Israel, they looked toward the wilderness, and behold, the glory of the Lord appeared in the cloud" (Ex 16:10).

As in the account in Ex 40, where the *kabod* leads the tabernacle from day to day, so also here the Lord's *kabod* was not bound to the ark or

Temple. The Glory of the Lord was present before either the ark or the Temple was constructed.

These memories provide a basic key for understanding Ezekiel. He found himself among a group of people who were once again in exile far from their homeland. Like those who were with Moses, this exiled band was once again in a wilderness setting. Like Moses, Ezekiel understood his own calling to be an obedient messenger and a watchman, sounding warnings and giving help to a homeless people. In this deep historical sense, Ezekiel uses the tradition of the Glory of the Lord in a way that is totally consistent with earlier memories.

In chapter 43:6-9, after the declaration has been given that the *kabod* will return to Jerusalem, the Lord declares: "Son of man, this is the place of my throne and the place of the soles of my feet, where I will dwell in the midst of the people of Israel forever" (Ezek 43:6-9). We have seen, however, that such a statement cannot be understood in a rigid or literalistic way. For at the heart of Ezekiel's theology is the profound knowledge that God can be present with people wherever they are. The awesome presence of God has been experienced amid the splendor of a temple; it has also been experienced in the barrenness of a foreign wilderness.

The Glory of the Lord and the Church

In classical Greek usage, the term *doxa* ("glory") had the basic meaning of an "opinion" or "what one thinks."[16] In the New Testament writings, this understanding has almost totally disappeared. In a few places the term is used to mean "repute" or "reputation." But when we encounter a phrase such as *doxa Kyriou* ("glory of the Lord") in New Testament writings, we may be quite certain that the author was thinking of the ancient tradition of the Glory of the Lord. Space does not allow consideration of all the places where the term "glory" appears in the New Testament. Here we will consider only three texts from St. Luke.

In the Christmas story, angels appear to the shepherds out in the fields and the Glory of the Lord appears.

> And in that region there were shepherds out in the field, keeping watch over their flock by night. And an angel of the Lord appeared to them, and the glory of the Lord shone around them, and they were filled with fear. And the angel said to them, "Be not afraid, for behold, I bring you good news of a great joy which will come to all the people. . . ." (Lk 2:8-10).

Luke was not simply describing the brilliance of a night sky over Bethlehem. Like Ezekiel, he was drawing from the ancient theological tradition to declare that again in a very special and personal way, the

Lord of heaven and earth was present this night in the birth of Christ in Bethlehem.[17] The Glory of the Lord tradition is used by Luke here to add depth and richness to the proclamation that Christ's birth heralds a new era of salvation for all people.

In the description of the crucifixion of Jesus, Luke joins both Mark and Matthew in preserving the memory that at the moment of death, the Temple curtain was rent from top to bottom.

> It was now about the sixth hour, and there was darkness over the whole land until the ninth hour, while the sun's light failed, and the curtain of the temple was torn in two (Lk 23:44-45).

Again, this brief reference is not simply included as a strange coincidence. The evangelists declare that in the event of the death of the Messiah, the holy of holies is made visible before all people. The dwelling place of the Glory of the Lord is now exposed as people reflect on what has happened among them. The Glory exposes the sin and the evil that has taken place.

Finally, we return again to the story of the disciples on the Emmaus road. They join in prayers of blessing and break bread with a stranger whom they have met along the way, only to discover that he is their risen Lord. It seems certain that this was a story told in the early Church to emphasize how Christ is present with his people in the Eucharist.

> And he [Jesus] said to them, "O foolish men, and slow of heart to believe all that the prophets have spoken! Was it not necessary that the Christ should suffer these things and enter into his glory?" And beginning with Moses and all the prophets, he interpreted to them in all the Scriptures the things concerning himself.
>
> So they drew near to the village to which they were going. He appeared to be going further, but they constrained him, saying, "Stay with us, for it is toward evening and the day is now far spent." So he went in to stay with them. When he was at the table with them, he took the bread and blessed, and broke it, and gave it to them. And their eyes were opened and they recognized him; and he vanished out of their sight (Lk 24:25-31).

While there is not a specific reference to the Glory of the Lord tradition here, it is appropriate for us to make the connection. In the earliest story, the *kabod* is remembered with the manna provided by the Lord God for the nourishment and sustenance of his people. We have seen how Luke uses the tradition to declare the presence of the Glory of the Lord at the birth and death of Christ. It is in the celebration of the Eucharist that people of faith gather today to be nourished in a particular place. In the breaking of bread, the Church proclaims the particular presence of God among us. Where the Lordship of Christ is declared, sin and evil must be exposed and judged by the sacred traditions of the

Scriptures. In worship, people speak, hear, and act by the word of God; in the simple acts of eating and drinking together, the Christian community continues to proclaim the particular presence of the Glory of the Lord among people alive today — and the promise of salvation, new life sustained by the Spirit.

NOTES

1. See Pss 104:31; 138:5, and especially Is 40:5; 58:8; 60:1.

2. Frequently in Scripture, the word *kabod* can serve as a descriptive adjective, such as when it refers to the "honor, importance, wealth or material substance" of people. Abraham was *kabod* (wealthy) in cattle, silver, and gold; Jacob was *kabod* (wealthy) in goods. See G. von Rad, "Kabod in the Old Testament," *TDNT* 2:238ff. Even more frequently, the word appears in praise of God, such as in Ps 29:1-2: "Ascribe to the Lord the *kabod* ("glory, majesty") of his name; worship the Lord in holy array."

3. Debate concerning the exact location of Mount Sinai has focused on this text, in which the description seems to suggest a volcanic mountain. Jebel Musa, the traditional site in southern Sinai, is not a volcanic mountain, in contrast to some possible mountain sites in the northern regions of the Sinai. But other scholars argue that it would be unlikely for people to assemble at the foot of a volcanic mountain, and contend that the description is much more characteristic of a storm. It is also interesting to note in this text the reference to the Sabbath-day tradition, which here appears to pre-date Sinai.

4. See the elaborate descriptions in Ex 25–40.

5. See further the marvelous story in Ex 33:17-23 and references to the *kabod Jahweh* in Lev 9:6, 23; Num 14:10, 21; 16:19; 20:6.

6. See 1 Sam 4–6 and the account of the trauma when the ark was captured by the Philistines, and the difficulties involved in bringing the ark to Jerusalem in 2 Sam 6–7.

7. See the parallel account in 1 Kg 8:1-11; in the longer description in 2 Chr 5, is it possible that the dedication hymn quoted could be Ps 136?

8. See 2 Sam 24 and 2 Chr 36.

9. Compare portraits of the cherubim in 1 Sam 4:4; 2 Sam 6:2; 2 Kg 19:14, and the construction in Ex 25:10-22 and 37:1-9.

10. See Is 6:1-13.

11. In chapter 8 reference seems to be made to syncretistic worship practices involving the cult of Tammuz and to the inner-court sun-worship practices by the government or religious officials, who at the same time are charged with "filling the land with violence."

12. See especially 1:26-27 and 8:2-3.

13. See Ezek 25–32 and collections of oracles addressed to other nations in other prophetic collections, Am 1–2, Is 13–23 and Jer 46–51. Particularly vivid portraits of the Lord as divine Warrior are found in Is 34; 63:1-6; and Ezek 7. See P. D. Miller, *The Divine Warrior in Early Israel* (Cambridge: Harvard University Press, 1973) 135ff.

14. See Walter Zimmerli, *Biblischer Kommentar Altes Testament* (Neukirchen-Vluyn: Neukirchener Verlag, 1969) 241ff. This work is probably the most comprehensive study of Ezekiel available today.

15. See further the parallel motif in Is 40:5, where a highway is prepared for the return

of the *kabod*. In the Targums and in later rabbinic writing, the term "Shekinah" is used to express much the same meaning as *kabod*, emphasizing the conviction of God dwelling in a personal way among his people. See further D. Moody, "Shekinah," *Interpreter's Dictionary of the Bible*, 317–319.

16. G. Kittel, "Doxa," *TDNT* 2:233–237.

17. See further Lk 9:31-32; 21:27; Mt 16:27; 25:31; Mk 8:38ff.; 13:26; Jn 1:14; 13:31-38; 2 Cor 4:6; Heb 1:1-4; 9:1-5; Rev 15:8; 21:11, 23.

Roland E. Murphy, O. Carm.

WISDOM AND SALVATION

The juxtaposition of the words in the title may seem questionable to many. Biblical wisdom is notoriously innocent of any proclamation of the great saving events of salvation history. The chapters in Sirach (44–50) and in the Wisdom of Solomon (11–19) are hardly an exception. For even here, as we shall see, the wisdom approach, as opposed to the historical, is uppermost. Biblical theology has long struggled with the place of wisdom within the Hebrew Bible, and indeed within Israel's faith.[1] When salvation and faith are narrowly defined and are understood solely in terms of the divine intervention in the history of Israel (ultimately climaxing, for the Christian, in God's action in Christ), the problem persists. But the definition of salvation needs to be reconsidered. Is there another nuance, equally biblical, that deserves theological treatment? We propose to sketch here such a broad understanding of wisdom that will allow for its salvific aspect.

1. Wisdom and Life

The kerygma of wisdom is life.[2] Such is the message of personified wisdom in Prov 8:32-36:

> So now, O children, listen to me;
>
> . . . .
>
> For he who finds me finds life,
>   and wins favor from the Lord;
> But he who misses me harms himself;
>   all who hate me love death.

The doctrine of the biblical sages pivoted about life and death. The fear of the Lord, so frequently proclaimed as the beginning of wisdom (Prov 1:7; 9:10; 15:33), is hailed as "an aid to life," so that one is not visited by misfortune (Prov 19:23); "the teaching of the wise is a fountain of life" (Prov 13:14). This image of the fountain of life is used to characterize the mouth of the just (Prov 10:11), the fear of the Lord (Prov 14:27), and plain good sense (Prov 18:22). Prov 22:4 proclaims that "the reward of humility and fear of the Lord is riches, honor and life." Life is more often explicitly associated with justice or virtue ($s^e d\bar{a}q\bar{a}h$), which is practically interchangeable with wisdom ($hokm\bar{a}h$). Thus, it is virtue that "saves from death" (Prov 10:2; 11:4), and "in the path of justice there is life" (Prov 12:28).

In the biblical view, life is an elastic concept. The quality of life is determined by length (Prov 3:16; 28:16), a good name (Prov 10:7; 22:1), riches and honor (Prov 22:4). This is far from being "materialistic," since it included union with the Lord; the temporalities were viewed sacramentally, as blessings from the Lord (Prov 10:22). This emphasis was shared by the Deuteronomic school (Dt 30:19): "I have set before you life and death . . . Choose life!" The urging of the prophets is in the same vein: "Seek good and not evil, that you may live; then truly will the Lord, the God of hosts, be with you as you claim!" (Am 5:14; see Ezek 33:10; Is 55:1-3).

Opposed to life is death. Because the sages cultivated antithetic parallelism (especially in Prov 10-15), there is frequent mention of death (Prov 12:28) and death's "snares" (Prov 13:14). Death is to be understood in a dynamic sense, as life itself is. Life is more than prolongation of one's days; it is also a good life of prosperity and well-being. Death is more than drawing one's final breath before departing for Sheol; it is also the ever-present enemy of human beings, in that it dogs them as long as they live. It pursues every living being, and to the extent that one experiences any adversity or distress, one dies. Death is non-life, and its most expressive synonym is Sheol, or the nether world. This image of Death/Sheol is particularly developed in the psalms (18:5; 49:14; 89:48). The psalmist can praise the Lord for having delivered him from Sheol (Ps 30:4). And praise is precisely the proper reaction, for there is no praise of God, no contact with him, in the "real" Sheol (Pss 6:5; 88:10-12).

This wisdom perspective shows that there is a soteriological dimension to wisdom in its task of coping with daily existence. At every turn life and non-life are the choices confronting the worshipper of Yahweh. It is not a question of "saving one's soul" or of an eschatological heaven or hell — all this is beyond the Old Testament perspective. But the issues are just as imposing. They have to do with the way life is lived, with the blessings of the Lord or their absence (often interpreted as an indication of sinfulness), with well-being or adversity. These were the issues of Job. In chapter 29 he describes the days of his prosperity as "the days when God watched over me":

> While he kept his lamp shining above my head,
> and by his light I walked through darkness;
> As I was in my flourishing days,
> when God sheltered my tent. . . .

> When my footsteps were bathed in milk,
>   and the rock flowed with streams of oil. . . .
> I wore my honesty like a garment;
>   justice was my robe and my turban (Job 29:3-14).

In most of the book, Job is complaining about the non-life that has been visited upon him; indeed, in relation to it, Sheol would seem to provide respite (3:11-19; 14:13).

When Job appeals to the Lord as his "redeemer" (Job 19:25, *gōʾēl*, better "vindicator"), the sense is that Yahweh will be his defender, as in a lawsuit. But the term has a coloring, as one can see from Ex 6:6, where the verb is used in the context of the deliverance from slavery in Egypt (see Ex 15:13; Ps 106:10). And in Is 40ff., *gōʾēl* is used as an epithet of the Lord to indicate the divine activity in the release from Babylon, a second Exodus. Hence one may conclude that Israel did not separate the experiences of redemption and deliverance in daily life, which is the domain of wisdom, from the experiences of the entire people in the realm of salvation-history.

To the tasks that Israelite wisdom understood herself to meet, there corresponds the prayer of the psalmist. With no less faith than that of the sage, the psalmist awaits the word of the Lord: "'Now will I arise,' says the Lord; "'I will grant safety (*yēšaʿ*, or 'salvation') to him who longs for it'" (Ps 12:6). There is also the assurance of Ps 91:16 (see 85:8): "With length of days I [Yahweh] will gratify him and will show my salvation (*yᵉšûāʿtî*)." Salvation is played out in this world, and wisdom is a means to it: "I [Yahweh] will instruct you and show you the way you should walk; I will counsel you, keeping my eye on you" (Ps 32:8; see Pss 33:18-19; 34:12-23). Hence the psalmist prays: "Say to my soul, 'I am your salvation'" (Ps 35:3).

Nowhere is wisdom's life-giving qualities more to the fore than in the remarkable passages in which she is personified: Job 28; Prov 8; Sir 24. It should be stressed that she is not a person; the literary device of personification (and as a woman!) is at work here. In Job 28 one learns that although it is possible for humans to discover precious minerals in the earth, the realm of wisdom lies beyond them. She is with God:

> Whence, then, comes wisdom,
>   and where is the place of understanding?
> It is hid from the eyes of any beast;
>   from the birds of the air it is concealed. . . .
> God knows the way to it;
>   it is he who is familiar with its place. . . .
> When he made the rules for the rain
>   and a path for the thunderbolts,
> Then he saw wisdom and appraised it,
>   gave it its setting, knew it through and through (Job 28:23-27).

And yet, wisdom is somewhere! According to Sirach, the Lord "poured her forth upon all his works, upon every living thing according to his bounty; he has lavished her upon his friends" (Sir 1:9-10). In Prov 8, wisdom is presented as a teacher, describing her own value and all that she has to offer to those who will heed her (8:1-21). She then describes her divine origins and presence with God before creation as a craftsman (8:30, 'āmôn, also translated as "nursling"). Finally, as in the passage quoted at the outset above (Prov 8:32-36), she offers life to those who will seek her.[3] Again, it appears that wisdom has the power to transform human existence. She confronts human beings in the nitty-gritty of daily life, offering prosperity, even under the threat of death (Prov 2:20-33). Ironically enough, it is to death that Dame Folly invites her followers, although they realize it not: "Little he knows that the shades are there [in the house of Dame Folly], that in the depths of the nether world are her guests" (Prov 9:18).

2. Wisdom and Salvation

We have seen that the real gift of biblical wisdom is life in the here and now, deliverance from the evils that afflict human beings, in short, *shalom* or salvation. But wisdom is seen also in another perspective, that of salvation-history itself. This association is described most clearly in chapter 24 of Sirach, where wisdom is again personified. As in chapter 8 of Proverbs, wisdom once more describes herself, her origins from God, and dominion over creation. She asked herself where she should abide;

> Then the Creator of all gave me his command,
>   and he who formed me chose the spot for my tent,
> Saying, 'In Jacob make your dwelling,
>   in Israel your inheritance. . . .'
> In the holy tent I ministered before him,
>   and in Zion I fixed my abode.
> Thus in the chosen city he has given me rest,
>   in Jerusalem is my domain (Sir 24:8-11).

Ben Sira then identifies wisdom with the Law: "All this is true of the book of the Most High's covenant, the law which Moses commanded us as an inheritance for the community of Jacob" (24:23). The Law is, of course, an essential ingredient in the Lord's dealing with his people, a component of the salvation-history. Here it is seen as the gift of wisdom, in the same way as Israel is told in Dt 4:6, "thus will you give evidence of your wisdom and intelligence to the nations, who will hear of all these statutes and say, 'This great nation is truly a wise and intelligent people.'"

G. von Rad has pointed out that wisdom, not Torah, is uppermost in the mind of Ben Sira.[4] His point of view is that of a wisdom teacher, not a lawgiver. In other words, we are dealing with a kind of wisdom imperialism. Covenant and Torah are not seen in themselves so much as they have been subordinated to wisdom thought.

The same emphasis appears in the famous "Praise of the Fathers" (44–50), which summarizes Israelite history by presenting its great personalities. It begins:

> Now I will praise these godly men,
>   our ancestors, each in his own time:
> The abounding glory of the Most High's portion,
>   his own part, since the days of old.
> Subduers of the land in kingly fashion,
>   men of renown for their might,
> Or counselors in their prudence,
>   or seers of all things in prophecy;
> Resolute princes of the flock,
>   and governors with their staves;
> Authors skilled in composition,
>   and forgers of epigrams with their spikes; . . .
> At gatherings their wisdom is retold,
>   and the assembly proclaims their praise (Sir 44:1-4, 15).

Again, wisdom has dictated the point of view. In contrast to the classic expressions of salvation-history, in which God and his actions are always in steady focus, Ben Sira simply presents great men whose human virtues are a source of inspiration and admiration. As von Rad remarks, "One wanders through history here as through the rooms of a hall of fame."[5]

The Wisdom of Solomon was written in Greek, probably in Alexandria, in the first century B.C. It is a striking synthesis of biblical and Greek ideas. For the first time in biblical writings, "body" and "soul" appear in parallelism (Wis 1:4), and the four cardinal virtues are mentioned in 8:7. Yet the author remains true to his Jewish wisdom heritage. If the message of older wisdom could be expressed as wisdom=life (in the here and now), the author expands it into wisdom=life eternal. For him, immortality is rooted in wisdom, or justice: "for justice is undying" (Wis 1:15). The relationship established between God and humans is seen as perduring. Sheol is not the end; one's true destiny is to be "accounted among the sons of God"; one's lot is "with the saints" (Wis 5:5). Eschatological salvation is the achievement of wisdom:

> Because into a soul that plots evil wisdom enters not,
>   nor dwells she in a body under debt of sin.
> For the holy spirit of discipline flees deceit
>   and withdraws from senseless counsels;
>   and when injustice occurs it is rebuked.
> For wisdom is a kindly spirit,

> yet she acquits not the blasphemer of his guilty lips;
> Because God is the witness of his inmost self
> and the sure observer of his heart
> and the listener to his tongue (Wis 1:4-6).

> For there is nought God loves,
> be it not one who dwells with Wisdom (Wis 7:28).

But wisdom's saving role is oriented not only to eternal life; she is very much involved in this life as well. The author portrays Solomon as praying for wisdom, who has saved those who courted her:

> Or who ever knew your counsel, except you had given Wisdom
> and sent your holy spirit from on high?
> And thus were the paths of those on earth made straight,
> and men learned what was your pleasure,
> and were saved by Wisdom (Wis 9:17-18).

Chapter 10 is a long discourse concerning wisdom's saving activity in the lives of Adam, Noah, Abraham, Jacob, and Joseph. The verbs "deliver" (*ruomai*) and "preserve" (*phylassō*) are continually repeated. Even the cardinal event of salvation-history, the deliverance from Egypt, is attributed to wisdom:

> The holy people and blameless race — it was she
> who delivered them from the nation that oppressed them.
> She entered the soul of the Lord's servant,
> and withstood fearsome kings with signs and portents;
> she gave the holy ones the recompense of their labors,
> Conducted them by a wondrous road,
> and became a shelter for them by day
> and a starry flame by night.
> She took them across the Red Sea
> and brought them through the deep waters —
> But their enemies she overwhelmed,
> and cast them up from the bottom of the depths (Wis 10:15-19).

Wisdom has ended up by becoming a savior-figure!

3. Conclusion

We have sketched briefly the soteriological dimension of wisdom in the Old Testament. For the Christian, the soteriological doctrine of the New Testament might seem to dwarf it. Hence it may be simply smothered by a "fulfillment" mentality that remains satisfied that Christ is the "wisdom of God" (1 Cor 1:24) and goes on from there. Yet, there is much to be learned from the wisdom approach of the Old Testament.[6] It takes human beings where they are — in their daily experiences of truth, integrity, relationship with neighbor, priority of values, etc. In this practical wisdom a relationship to God is worked out for salvation or destruction, life or death. Through the various areas of human activity runs the possibility of a saving response in faith to the creator.

NOTES

1. The classical example is afforded by G. E. Wright, who writes, "it is the wisdom literature which offers the chief difficulty because it does not fit into the type of faith exhibited in the historical and prophetic literatures" (*God Who Acts* [London: SCM, 1952] 103). Some have gone so far as to deny the theological relationship of wisdom literature to the "real" Old Testament; see the discussion by R. E. Murphy, "Wisdom and Yahwism," in *No Famine in the Land*, John L. McKenzie Festschrift ed. J. W. Flanagan and A. W. Robinson (Missoula, Mont.: Scholars Press, 1975) 117–126.

2. See R. E. Murphy, "The Kerygma of the Book of Proverbs," *Interpretation* 20, no. 1 (January 1966) 3–14.

3. For a study of wisdom in the tradition of von Rad's concept of the "self-revelation of creation," see R. E. Murphy, "What and Where Is Wisdom?" *Currents in Theology and Mission* 4, no. 1 (October 1977) 283–287.

4. See *Wisdom in Israel* (Nashville: Abingdon, 1972) 244–246. Of Sir 24:12-20 he writes: "Notice that it is wisdom who speaks here, not Torah, and this is where Sirach's heart beats. Primeval wisdom is here regarded as a fascinating, aesthetic phenomenon. Where Torah is concerned, Sirach does not rise to such enthusiastic statements" (246).

5. *Ibid.* 258.

6. It is intriguing to balance the wisdom data against the patristic development of salvation as described by J. Patout Burns, S. J., "Salvation: Two Patristic Traditions," *Theological Studies* 37, no. 4 (December 1976) 598–619. He presents two different approaches to the economy of salvation, Greek and Latin, as represented in Gregory of Nyssa and Augustine. It is the Greek tradition, as it relates to contemporary theology, that presents points of comparison with wisdom. On the basis of Gregory, Burns generalizes to a salvation theory that he calls the "developmental" model: "In this schema [developmental] human effort is effective in every stage of the process of attaining perfection. Divine grace co-operates with but never replaces human action. Thus the stages in the process are intrinsically and continuously related by the functioning of created means. As attained in such a process beatitude will be the product of human effort and co-operative divine grace rather than of the intervention of an operative grace. If the means of growth toward perfection are neither exclusively contained within the created nature of each person nor given only by unmediated interior graces, then the economy of salvation will include social institutions which foster religious growth. . . . The social institutions which constitute the cultural context of an individual's life would help his religious growth to the extent that they encourage and provide means for it" (617–618).

PART THREE

New Testament Studies

Monika E. Hellwig

THE CENTRAL SCANDAL OF THE CROSS:
FROM SIN TO SALVATION

It is axiomatic in the Christian tradition from apostolic times that the Cross of Jesus is a scandal, but this scandal has been compounded in the course of centuries in ways not always recognized. The intent of this essay is to explore some implications for Christian spirituality of a suggestion of J. B. Metz: The Cross must be seen as a challenge to write history upside down from the perspective of the vanquished and excluded, for it is only in this perspective that the unfinished agenda of history (of the ongoing task of salvation) can be discerned.[1]

Paul writes with dogged determination (1 Cor 1:18-24) of the proclamation of the crucified Christ as scandal to those who understand the implications of it and sheer folly to those who do not. He writes, however, in a context in which crucifixion has a concrete social, political, and criminal meaning. The beginning of our contemporary problem is the fact that the Cross has lost such contextual meaning. More than this, it may have acquired a considerably distorted meaning. Paradoxically, the Cross as liturgical symbol seems to undergird the distortion of meaning.

The problem to which this essay addresses itself is the fact that the Cross of Jesus has become, for Christians and others, one of the supreme symbols of respectability and of endorsement of existing structures of power and authority in the world. This is not the original, historical sense of the Cross. It is not the synoptic nor the Pauline sense of the Cross. It is not even the Johannine sense; though the crucified Jesus of John's Gospel is certainly a triumphant figure exalted by God, it is not coherent with John's juxtaposition of Jesus and "the world" to see the Crucified blending into the picture to become, henceforth, the figurehead of the power structures of the world. If, therefore, the Cross does not have this sense of endorsement of existing power structures for the apostolic witnesses,[2] there has certainly been an important shift of meaning, carrying far-reaching implications. As Anabaptist and other

187

radical Christian groups have long pointed out, such a shift of meaning must justify itself as consistent within the Christian gospel of salvation or stand convicted as a distortion.

Any analysis of the question, no matter how brief, must address itself to the history of the shift in meaning, to the issues of Christian spirituality involved in the shift, and to the theological implications of the shift. The history is so well known that it may be summarized very briefly. In the New Testament and the earliest Christian centuries, the image of the crucified Jesus is central in verbal representations and in ritual (that is, Eucharist and baptism), though it may be argued that what is represented is the complex paschal mystery, with its double aspect of death and resurrection and its levels of interpretation by reference to the Exodus and Passover *seder*. In verbal and ritual representation in these earliest times, the Cross of Jesus remains the sign of contradiction that questions all worldly power and righteousness in the name of the wholly other power of the redeeming God. As a visual, that is, graphic representation, the form of a cross appears sparsely and elusively in the earliest centuries, and the figure of the Crucified does not appear in a single extant example. As is well known, the use of a cross-shaped symbol by Constantine on his way to the imperial throne in the early fourth century became identified with the invocation of the divine champion of the Christians and developed into the symbolization of Christ in the chi-rho.[3]

Constantine moved from the protection of *sol invictus* to that of the Christ of Christians, as demonstrated on his coins. The parallel positioning suggests the chi-rho seen as a resurrection symbol rather than a representation of the crucifixion. However, by the sixth century, when we finally see representations of the crucified Jesus, he is portrayed as utterly different from the thieves who flank him. He is robed and reigning.[4] This can be accounted for in a number of ways in the hermeneutics of graphic pictorial symbols. It can be seen as a dramatization of the inner reality of the redemption; Christ is represented visually as he is inwardly: not the outcast but the center, the one who holds all things together, not the abandoned of God but the chosen. It can also be seen as a telescoping of history whereby the eschatological fulfillment is seen as already breaking through in the moment of the crucifixion. Be this as it may, the effect of seeing one composite scene, rather than a diptych representing both an unqualified criminal execution and a divine vindication, is to eliminate conflict and tension from the symbol.

If the extant crucifixion scenes from the ancient East represent a triumphant, undisgraced and, in effect, non-conflictual crucified Jesus, the crucifixes of the West since the medieval era have more usually represented a totally passive, usually quite lifeless, tortured human body without any hint of resurrection or vindication. This latter is also a non-conflictual crucified Jesus whose position is rendered unproblematic by his utter passivity. This is underscored in many famous paintings by the fact that the painter's wealthy and powerful patrons are incorporated into the picture, standing respectfully by as at a dignified and well-conducted liturgical ceremony. More recently we have experienced a swing back to an undisturbed and undisturbing figure who presides from the Cross over the present order of things in the world with benignly permissive detachment.

It would seem that the history of Eucharistic piety and of devotional practices is consistent with the changing visual representations, though it would be a lengthy project to demonstrate this. Certainly soteriology has followed a pattern of detachment from the concrete political conflict implied in the historical Cross from the third or fourth century. The reference point for the explanation of the death of Jesus as redemptive came to be simply the eternal will of the Father, contingent upon sin in a general and quite abstract sense. Indeed, in much of our soteriological discussion, as for instance in Leo's Tome and in Anselm's *Cur Deus homo*, the actual context and issues of the criminal execution of Jesus are of no interest or relevance to the discussion, having been conveniently provided so that Jesus could die the death divinely foreordained for him outside the context of any concrete human social or political situation. In most of our soteriological discussion, it has not been considered necessary to ask who really killed Jesus and why — certainly not to ask this with the exigent scrutiny of the historian. It was convenient enough to assume that the Jews killed him for blasphemy, because the more pertinent explanation was that the will of the Father killed him, and the more pertinent question was what divine exigence demanded the death of the innocent Son of God, and what exactly was accomplished by it — if it was a redeeming death, to whom it was that the ransom must be paid.

This history of the changing meaning of the Cross of Jesus poses a fundamental and inescapable question for Christian spirituality, which may be considered from the point of view of the problems raised by quietism or from the point of view of what constitutes transformation in charity. If we take the symbol of the Cross of Jesus, key to the mystery of redemption, in its concrete historical setting, the one who redeems and is held up for our imitation appears as the very negation of all that is respectable in the society. He appears as the negation of all that is reliable and trustworthy in the social institutions.

There is, to be sure, much room for debate concerning the sense in which Jesus may be seen as a political figure. There is even more room for debate as to the sense in which imitation of Jesus in our times involves the Christian in political action. However, there is really no room for debate as to *whether* a man who was crucified is a political figure if we take history seriously at all. As is well known, crucifixion was not a punishment for blasphemy or unorthodox religious teachings; it was a punishment for seditious or revolutionary activities, as the Church has frequently been obliged to remember in celebrating the deaths of martyrs. One may argue that those who executed Jesus were quite wrong in seeing him as a threat to the good order of society, but one cannot historically argue away the fact that he suffered the execution intended for those who were judged to be a revolutionary threat to society.[5]

In its historical essentials, the symbol of the Cross poses the ultimate question in spirituality. It presents the breakthrough to salvation as happening in an utterly unexpected way: through failure, rejection, and the discrediting of the bearer of salvation by those charged with the discernment of what is authentically salvific. The problem, however, is that this can be apprehended and appropriated in two radically opposed ways in Christian spirituality. It can be seen as the challenge to "write history upside down." It can also be interpreted in a fully quietist sense — a message that human effort and initiative are irrelevant in the journey from sin to salvation, from alienation to union with God. In this interpretation, salvation has entered the world by the Cross, the crucifixion took place entirely by divine initiative, and the only part played by Jesus was essentially to wait and let his divinely ordained destiny overtake him. In reward for his willing passivity, grace has entered into circulation in the human community, but this does not and need not change the existing order, except perhaps to render individuals less aggressive and cruel in playing their already determined roles within the society. What the individual must do, then, is to fulfill his role in the society peacefully and uncritically, and to imitate Jesus in renouncing personal initiatives toward salvation and waiting for divine initiative to overtake him.

Quietism as a mode of spirituality has, of course, been condemned as un-Christian in the official teaching of the Catholic Church.[6] Moreover, quietism as a mode of spirituality is difficult to reconcile with Paul's treatment of the scandal of the Cross or with the evangelists' unfolding of the tactical confrontations between Jesus and the powers holding sway in his society. Yet it may be questioned whether in a subtle way quietism has not in fact continued in Christian spirituality despite official condemnations. If the Cross of Jesus no longer symbolizes the legitimacy of the current order of earthly rule, as it apparently did under Constantine and his successors, it does at least symbolize utter passivity in unjust and ungodly situations and the renunciation of personal initiative — and therefore of personal responsibility — in reconstructing human affairs to be in harmony with God's exigent call. In the many and complex patterns of relationship that constitute human lives, the sign of the Cross appears often as the symbol for "letting God do it," the symbol that signifies that conversion in the practical arena of human institutions is not necessary.

The same ultimate issue in spirituality may be considered from the point of view of charity. It is axiomatic in Christian teaching that the journey from sin to salvation is by love of God and fellowmen. The Cross is the great symbol and example of that saving love. That it is the symbol of total and ultimate gift of self to God and others is indisputable. What this calls for in Christian faith and imitation, however, is subject to sharply variant interpretations. It can be seen as the ultimate word in permissiveness and acceptance of whatever is in the world as God's will. In other words, it can be so interpreted that the most loving response of the creature to God is the one that exerts the least creativity, accepts the least responsibility, and refuses to see the structures of the world as conflictual.

On the other hand, the Cross can be seen as the symbol of a love that is necessarily expressed in ultimate personal protest against whatever is not Godward. It would then be so interpreted that the most loving response of the creature to God is the one that exerts the most creativity, accepts the most responsibility, and frankly sees the structures of the world as bitterly conflictual. This certainly is charity and surrender to the will of God in the spirituality of the martyrs and of Christian churches in times of persecution directed against them as Christian. This is also the spirituality of the Ignatian *Spiritual Exercises*, in which love of God is not seen as passivity in the world and the surrender of one's freedom to God is not the abdication of creativity and initiative, but their passionate dedication to a highly conflictual undertaking in which the Cross is the symbol of the conflict.[7]

This issue in Christian spirituality is not just a matter of academic speculation, but is a commonplace matter of the everyday business of formation of Christian consciousness, discernment in practical decisions, and focus in preaching and exhortation. However, it does carry far-reaching theological implications. Intertwined with the spiritual issue are conceptual models of God, the understanding of salvation-history, and the perception of the human person in general, and of Jesus in particular, as image of God.

Christian faith finds the definitive revelation of God as merciful, faithful, and all-powerful in the crucified Jesus seen retrospectively in the light of the resurrection. This also, however, is seen in two curiously different ways. God may appear as the inscrutably just and holy, who foresees all, weighs all, plans all, and implements the details of the plan, showing himself master of the situation no matter what the perversity of human agents, for they serve his secret plan in spite of themselves. God is seen as the supreme ruler, the mastermind, even (perhaps) the conjurer who can always make conflicting patterns of behavior move toward his intended goals by pulling out his trump cards.

However, the scandal of the Cross seems to be precisely that this image of God collapses with a great thud when Jesus dies. God appears as powerless to achieve his purpose alongside and independently of human action. The forces of evil and destruction appear to triumph. The just one calls on God and is abandoned to die ignominiously. His followers wait expectantly for the thunderous intervention of God to vindicate the person and the way of Jesus, and they are left holding a corpse and a shattered dream.

The crucial question, of course, is how the resurrection is to be interpreted in this context. It might be interpreted to mean that the thunderous intervention indeed came, but they had to wait a few days longer for it. God paused, so to speak, for dramatic effect; to prevent the death of Jesus would have been less spectacular than to let him die and bring him back from the dead in triumph. Sober reflection on the testimony of the earliest witnesses suggests a very different interpretation.[8] It suggests that whatever the apostolic community's experience of the resurrection may literally have been — and they were unable to tell us in so many words — it did not represent a cancellation of the death and its scandal. It did not promise the followers of the Way that the master conjurer would play the trump cards for them. It seems rather that, whatever the experience of the resurrection was, in the light of that experience and vision the death takes on a wholly different meaning. God appears not as less powerful, but as powerful in a quite different way from the expected manner of the supreme ruler. The power of God appears no longer as a power acting alongside human creativity, but rather within it. It appears not as a power overwhelming human power, but as one summoning the inner resources of human freedom in modes that have nothing to do with bullying.

Corresponding to this is the question of the understanding of salvation-history. In its crudest terms, it is the question whether we conceptualize or picture salvation-history as mapped out in eternity by divine foreknowledge and predestination independently of human decision-making, or whether the fashioning of salvation-history is a historical process. If salvation-history is seen as forecast from eternity, then God is moving us as pawns in the game — to our merit if we cooperate willingly and to our condemnation and ultimate shame if we are simply being outmaneuvered. In this view, historical action, political action, critical activity in the public sphere is no more than exercise in a squirrel cage with a revolving drum; its value is in its intention, not in anything that may in fact be accomplished in the bettering of the conditions of life for the needy. Moreover, in this perspective, the significant action of salvation-history is in the past and ended with the death of Jesus and the witnessing of the resurrection.

If salvation-history is seen as a historical process, then the symbol of the Cross points our attention toward the actual circumstances and confrontations that brought Jesus to his death, and forces us to ask why the grace and power of God should break through precisely in the person of the condemned, the marginated, the powerless, and the silent. It forces us to see that Jesus did not occupy this position by circumstances that overtook him and were beyond his control, but rather by deliberate choices and stances that unveiled the sinfulness of the respectable order of things in society and unveiled salvation in the re-emergence of the divinely created human freedom. In the concrete circumstances of the Cross, Jesus not only unmasks the real structure of sin and salvation but becomes in his person the bridge from sin to salvation — becomes, in other words, the Way in the actual context of a highly conflictual political situation.

Involved in this question of the understanding of salvation-history is the understanding of the human person in general and of Jesus in particular as the image of God. Christian faith acknowledges that the human person and the human community are made in the image and likeness of God, that the project usually fails in greater or less degree, and that in Jesus the human image of God is surpassingly realized. The face of God, which it is not given to us to see directly, is shown to us in the face of the crucified Jesus. The question that arises, however, would seem to be not the one that used to grace the catechisms, namely, whether the likeness of God is chiefly in the body or in the soul, but rather whether the divine image is seen chiefly in the passivity or in the creativity of the human person.

The relation between the divine and human creativity might be seen mainly as one of limitation of the weaker by the stronger, or even as one of conquest and manipulation of the weaker by the stronger. The divine might be envisaged as appearing in the human like an imprint in an inert and pliable material. This, however, is not the representation suggested by the biblical theme of sonship, which proposes a living, not an inert, human image of the divine. In other words, it would not seem that the creature is most receptive to God and therefore to the divine image when he or she is least critical and most permissively acquiescent in the way things are, no matter what this may be doing to people.

To conclude, the symbol of the Cross is today readily discerned as a symbol of powerlessness in suffering. Placed in its historical setting, with all the economic, social, and political factors operative at the time, the symbol of the Cross is rather the symbol of power in non-violent protest on behalf of the authentically human, the crushed, and the excluded that makes up the unfinished agenda of salvation-history and points the Way from sin to salvation.

NOTES

1. J. B. Metz, "The Future in the Memory of Suffering," *New Questions on God*, Concilium 76, ed. J. B. Metz (New York: Herder, 1972) 9–25.

2. Some would argue that the *Haustafeln* would suggest a different interpretation, but see J. H. Yoder, *The Politics of Jesus* (Grand Rapids, Mich.: Eerdmans, 1972), particularly chapter 9, "Revolutionary Subordination," 163–192.

3. The sequence of symbolizations and interpretations as seen in the historical setting of Constantine's reign is discussed in detail in Francine Cardman, "The Emperor's New Clothes," in the forthcoming volume *The Kingship of Christ and Social Systems*, ed. Thomas Clarke (New York: Paulist Press).

4. A brief overview of extant sixth-century representations is given by Henri Marrou, in his commentary on Plates 19–36, in Jean Daniélou and Henri Marrou, *The Christian Centuries: The First 600 Years* (London: Darton, 1964).

5. For detailed discussion see, for example, Oscar Cullmann, *Jesus and the Revolutionaries* (New York: Harper, 1970); Jon Sobrino, *Christology at the Crossroads* (Maryknoll, N.Y.: Orbis Books, 1978), *passim*, but particularly chapter 6; J. H. Yoder, *op. cit.*

6. The principal official statements are from the seventeenth century. See, for example, Denzinger-Schonmetzer, *Enchiridion Symbolorum* (Freiburg: Herder, 1965) nos. 1221–1288 and 1327–1349.

7. See, for example, *The Spiritual Exercises of St. Ignatius*, trans. Anthony Mottola (New York: Doubleday, 1964): "The Kingdom of Christ," 67–68, and "Meditation on Two Standards," 75–76. See also Philip Land, "Justice, Development, Liberation and the Exercises," *Studies in the International Apostolate of the Jesuits* 5, no. 1 (June 1976).

8. For a discussion of different perspectives on the mystery of the resurrection, see, for example, Willi Marxsen, *The Resurrection of Jesus of Nazareth* (Philadelphia: Fortress Press, 1970); F. X. Durrwell, *The Resurrection: A Biblical Study* (New York: Sheed & Ward, 1960); G.W.H. Lampe and D. M. MacKinnon, *The Resurrection: A Dialogue* (Philadelphia: Westminster Press, 1966); H. A. Williams, *True Resurrection* (New York: Harper, 1972).

Jack Dean Kingsbury

THE SPIRIT AND THE SON OF GOD
IN MARK'S GOSPEL   *Study of the Prologue of Mark.*

In a dramatic scene in the synagogue at Nazareth, Luke depicts Jesus as identifying himself with the Servant of God by declaring in the words of Isaiah that he has been anointed with the Spirit of God (4:18-19). So anointed, Jesus is portrayed as the agent through whom God will grant salvation to all humankind (Lk 2:30-32). As a concrete manifestation of such salvation, Jesus is described as forgiving sins (Lk 5:20-24; 7:48-50). In the passage 24:44-49, which gives unity to the present volume of essays, Luke gathers up these themes and at the same time underlines the abiding importance of Jesus in God's plan of salvation by writing that "repentance for forgiveness of sins should be preached in his name to all the nations" (24:47). In addition, Luke also shows in the Acts of the Apostles that God, in confirmation of his gracious disposition toward humankind, pours out his Holy Spirit upon those who do in truth repent at the proclamation of the name of Jesus Christ (see, for example, 2:37-42; 5:29-32; 10:34-45).

When one comes to Mark's Gospel from the twin works of Luke, one is struck by the comparative absence of references to the Holy Spirit. Indeed, whereas Mark refers some eleven times to "unclean spirit(s)" (1:23, 26, 27; 3:11, 30; 5:2, 8, 13; 6:7; 7:25; 9:25), he refers only six times to the Holy Spirit (1:8, 10, 12; 3:29; 12:36; 13:11). Still, these statistics can be deceptive, for a careful look at Mark's Gospel reveals that his initial references to the Spirit (1:8, 10, 12) play a key role in the development of his Gospel narrative. The purpose of this article is to examine these references and, in this connection, to explore briefly the role the Spirit plays in Mark's presentation of the mission of Jesus.

I

Mark's Gospel divides itself roughly into a prologue (1:1-13 [15]) and two main parts (1:14–8:26; 8:27–16:8). The prologue has to do with the "beginning of the gospel of Jesus Christ" (1:1). Except for the inaugural appearance of Jesus in Galilee (1:14-15), this "beginning" encompasses the ministry of John the Baptist (1:2-8) on the one hand, and the baptism (1:9-11) and the temptation (1:12-13) of Jesus on the other.

Mark describes John the Baptist in the words of Malachi as "my messenger," i.e., the messenger of God (cf. Mk 1:2 to Mal 3:1). As God's messenger, John is also called "Elijah," in echo of Mal 4:5-6 (LXX: Mal 3:22-23; cf. Mk 9:11-13; also 1:6 to 2 Kg 1:8). But although John is, to be sure, the messenger of God, it is only as he relates to Jesus that Mark regards him as a figure of singular importance. This is clear already from the circumstance that Mark, as we just saw, relegates the ministry of John to the beginning of the gospel of Jesus Christ (1:1). But this is likewise clear from the Isaianic quotation that Mark cites in 1:3. Thus, the voice that cries in the desert in Isaiah does so in order to summon Israel to "make straight the paths *of our God*" (LXX: Is 40:3). By contrast, in Mark's rendering of this passage the voice is said to summon Israel to "make straight *his* paths," i.e., the paths of Jesus Christ (1:1). Accordingly, if in Isaiah the voice is that of the herald of God, in Mark's Gospel it is that of the herald of Jesus. Who, then, is John the Baptist in Mark's Gospel? He is Elijah redivivus, the "messenger of God" who, significantly, is the "forerunner of Jesus Christ."

As the forerunner of Jesus, John's mission in Mark's Gospel is to inaugurate the "eschatological age of fulfillment" (1:2-3; cf. 1:15), which is at the same time the "age of the gospel" (1:1). He does this by preparing Israel, through a "baptism of repentance for the forgiveness of sins" (1:4), for the coming of Jesus, whom John designates as the "Mightier One" (1:7). In predicting the coming of the Mightier One, John announces that he will baptize Israel, not with water, as John himself has done, but "with the Holy Spirit" (1:8). How is the expression "baptizing with the Holy Spirit" to be understood?

Excluded, it would seem, is some type of "charismatic experience" associated with what is commonly known today as "speaking in tongues." On this kind of activity Mark is silent. More plausibly, some scholars believe that this expression alludes to Christian baptism as practiced by the church of Mark.[1] They base their argument on the fact that Jesus stands out in the primitive document of Q as one who "will baptize with the Holy Spirit *and with fire*" (Mt 4:11 // Lk 3:16). This imagery, they note, is apocalyptic, and it characterizes Jesus as the eschatological figure (Son of Man) who will preside over the great judgment at the end of the age that will issue in salvation or damnation for all humankind.[2] Since Mark makes mention only of a "baptism with the Holy Spirit," it seems likely, they reason, that he has adapted an earlier saying to make it refer to the rite of baptism that people underwent on becoming members of his church.

The problem with this argument, however, is that it appears to be incapable of corroboration. Unlike Matthew, for example, Mark nowhere speaks pointedly about the rite of Christian baptism (see Mt 28:19). The one passage that comes into question, Mk 16:16, is spurious on textual grounds. Consequently, one does better to interpret the Marcan clause "he will baptize you with the Holy Spirit" (1:8) in line with such passages as Jl 3:1-2 (RSV: 2:28-29) and Num 11:29. These passages gave rise in Judaism to the expectation that a mark of the end-time salvation that God will accomplish in Israel is the outpouring of his Spirit.[3] In this view, therefore, Mark would have understood the expression "baptizing with the Holy Spirit" to refer in a broad sense to the eschatological salvation that God achieves through the agency of Jesus, the Mightier One.

II

The story of the baptism of Jesus (Mk 1:9-11) is central to our study. Mark emphasizes in the opening line that "Jesus came" (*ēlthen Iēsous*) to John from Nazareth of Galilee (1:9). This ostensibly insignificant notation serves a dual purpose of no little importance: it documents the fulfillment of John's prophecy that after him the Mightier One would "come" (*erchetai*, 1:7); and it identifies the Mightier One with Jesus. Once Jesus is on the scene, John recedes into the background (1:9), in keeping with his own words that the Mightier One is incomparably superior to him (1:7). Indeed, the actual baptism of Jesus by John is merely asserted and not described (1:9). Also, it is Jesus alone who, following the baptism, sees the vision and hears the voice (1:10-11), which are the events that constitute the heart of the baptismal story.

Mark reports that Jesus "ascends" (*anabainōn*) from the water (1:10). This observation, too, serves a twofold function: the "ascent" of Jesus from the water prepares the way for the "descent" (*katabainon*) of the Spirit from heaven (1:10); and this "ascent" is likewise a signal to the reader that he can anticipate the occurrence of a supernatural event, in this case the communication to Jesus of divine revelation (see Acts 10:9-16; also 8:39).

In the initial revelatory event, Jesus sees the heavens split apart and the Spirit in the form of a dove descend upon him (1:10). What this signifies is Jesus' empowerment by God with his Holy Spirit, as a number of Old Testament and intertestamental passages make plain (Is 11:1-3; 42:1; 61:1; 1 Enoch 49:2-3; Ps Sol 17:42; Testament of Levi 18:2-14; Testament of Judah 24:1-6).

In the second revelatory event, Jesus hears the voice from heaven, i.e., God himself, declare: "You are my beloved Son, in you I am well pleased" (1:11). The meaning of these words can be ascertained in large part from the Old Testament passages from which they have been drawn. Thus, the adjective "beloved" (*agapētos*) underlines the truth that Jesus is God's "only," or unique, Son (cf. Gen 22:2); the verb "to be well pleased" (*eudokēsa*) alludes to the circumstance that Jesus is the one whom God has "chosen" for messianic ministry in Israel (cf. Is 42:1); and the term "my Son," in the mouth of God, refers to the fact that Jesus is the Son of God (cf. Ps. 2:7). In addition, the double stress on the pronoun "you" (*sy*, *soi*) calls further attention to the great discrepancy in station between John and Jesus: whereas John is, again, the "messenger of God" ("my messenger," 1:2), Jesus is the "Son of God" ("my Son," 1:11).

On the basis of the preceding, this much can be said: Mark brings the story of the baptism in order to describe Jesus, who far surpasses John, as the unique Son of God whom God has chosen for messianic ministry in Israel and whom, to that end, he has empowered with his Holy Spirit. At the same time, in need of further specification in this summary statement is the designation "my Son," or the "Son of God" (*hyios tou theou*). Because Mark's source for this title is Psalm 2, we begin there.

Mark employs the designation "my Son" (Son of God) from Ps 2:7 at two key places: here in the story of the baptism of Jesus at the beginning of his Gospel (1:11) and in the story of the transfiguration of Jesus in the middle of his Gospel (9:7). This indicates that this designation, which Mark received from the tradition, is one that he affirms.

Of interest is the fact that Psalm 2 is a royal psalm with prophetic overtones.[4] It describes, in verse 7, God's "adoption" of a royal figure ("I have begotten you") to be his son.[5] This adoption takes place on the day of enthronement, when God appoints this son to be ruler over the kingdom of Judah and, proleptically, over the nations (vv. 6-8).[6] In addition, this son of God is also said to be God's "anointed" ("messiah"; LXX: "christ"; v. 2), the "king" from the house of David (v. 6).

Now Mark, we observed, finds in the story of the baptism of Jesus the fulfillment of John's prophecy concerning the coming of the Mightier One (1:7). This means that, to Mark's way of thinking, Jesus does not first become something at his baptism, namely, the Mightier One, or the Son of God, which he has not been before. Hence, the story of the baptism functions in Mark's Gospel not, strictly speaking, to set forth the "adoption" of Jesus as the Son of God, but to depict his "presentation" as the Son of God.[7]

Significantly, Mark also applies to Jesus, presented at his baptism as the Son of God, the other royal predications that occur in Psalm 2. This suggests that Mark sees the expectations associated with this psalm as coming to their eschatological fulfillment in Jesus Son of God (see also the related passages, Ps 89:19-37; 2 Sam 7:12-16). Thus, Mark likewise designates Jesus Son of God as God's "Anointed" ("Messiah," "Christ"; 1:1; 8:29; 14:61) and as the "King of the Jews (Israel)" (see 15:2, 9, 12, 18, 26, 32–39) from the house of David ("Son of David"; see 10:47-48; 11:1-11; 12:35-37). What is more, Mark, too, asserts that the kingdom he establishes will extend to both Israel and the nations (4:30-32; 13:10; 14:9). On balance, then, if the question is raised as to who this unique Son of God is whom Mark presents at his baptism as being chosen by God and empowered by his Holy Spirit for messianic ministry, the answer is: He is the royal Messiah, the King of the Jews (Israel) from the house of David, whom God has appointed to establish his kingdom over Israel and the Gentiles.

III

The third time Mark makes reference to the Holy Spirit in the prologue of his Gospel is in the story of the temptation of Jesus (1:12-13). In this story Jesus, endowed with the Spirit, is led, or perhaps driven,[8] by the Spirit out into the desert, where he encounters Satan. Satan, in Mark's view, is the "prince of demons" (3:22-24), the supernatural antagonist of Jesus Christ, the Son of God. He, like demons in general, is at home in the "desert."[9] By subjecting Jesus to temptation for forty days, which is a classic period of time in the Old Testament and underscores the momentous nature of the event taking place (Ex 24:18; 34:28; Dt 9:9; 10:10; 1 Kg 19:8), Satan endeavors to "turn Jesus from the task which God has laid upon him in His baptism, and therewith to render His mission [cross] impossible."[10]

The three terse statements, "And he was . . . tempted by Satan; and he was with the wild beasts; and the angels were ministering to him" (1:13), tend to be interpreted by scholars in one of two ways. If, on the one hand, it is thought that the wild beasts are to be construed as being hostile to Jesus (cf. Pss 22:12-21; 92:11-13; Testament of Issachar 7:7; Testament of Naphtali 8:4), then it is held that Satan and the wild beasts are to be seen as ranging themselves in opposition against Jesus and the angels who are ministering to him.[11] But if, on the other hand, it is thought that the presence of Jesus with the wild beasts is meant to convey the notion that harmony has been created between the worlds of nature and of humankind (cf. Is 11:6-9; 65:25), then it is held that Jesus, in having overcome the temptation of Satan, is to be regarded as having restored the conditions of paradise: the Messiah Son of God lives at peace with the wild beasts and feeds on the foods of heaven administered to him by angels.[12] But either way, the point the story of the temptation makes remains the same: in the power of God's Spirit, Jesus Messiah, the Son of God, confronts Satan in his own stronghold and withstands temptation, decisively defeating him.

IV

Mark, therefore, presents Jesus in his prologue as the Messiah, the Son of God, the one whom God has empowered with his Spirit and chosen to be his agent of salvation and who is stronger even than Satan. Throughout the rest of his Gospel, Mark depicts Jesus as carrying out his mission of salvation. The striking thing about his ministry is the unparalleled "authority" (*exousia*) with which he acts. The source of this authority is, of course, God himself (11:27-33), and it is to stress this very fact that Mark has so arranged the prologue that it reaches its culmination in the story of Jesus' baptism, in which, again, the Holy Spirit descends and the voice calls down from heaven (1:9-11). The point is this: Mark traces the unparalleled authority on which Jesus acts in the course of his public ministry to his divine sonship and empowerment with the Holy Spirit. Hence, although the story of the baptism is remarkably brief and Mark otherwise makes exceedingly few references to the Spirit, this story is foundational to the whole of his Gospel narrative because it treats of the origins of that transcendent authority that manifests itself in all phases of his ministry.

Marcan examples of the divine authority with which the powerful Son of God speaks and acts are ready at hand. Thus, in 1:14-15, a passage that belongs at once to the prologue of the Gospel and to the first main part, Jesus is described as arriving in Galilee and publicly proclaiming, "The time is fulfilled, and the kingdom of God is at hand; repent, and believe in the gospel." It is a sign of his authority that the Marcan Jesus simply announces his message in Israel and is portrayed as making no effort whatever to validate it in the eyes of his hearers.

In a similar vein, the teaching of the Marcan Jesus, too, is with divine authority (1:22; 11:17, 28-33). Indeed, teaching is the "customary" activity in which Jesus engages during his public ministry (see, for example, 10:1), and it is as "Teacher," or "Rabbi," that persons address him (see 4:38; 9:17, 38; 10:17, 20, 35; 12:14, 19, 32; 13:1; 9:5; 10:51; 11:21; 14:45). In principle, Mark understands the content of Jesus' teaching to be a "new," i.e., an eschatological, word of revelation from God (1:27; 11:27-33). This notion, cast in the form of a negative comparison, is also stated by Mark as follows: "And they were astonished at his teaching, for he taught them as one who had authority, and not as the scribes" (1:22).

Third, the Marcan Jesus furthermore exorcises demons and heals with divine authority (1:27, 32-34; 3:10-12; 6:54-56). Through mighty acts such as these he works to overthrow the kingdom of Satan (1:13). By releasing people held to be in bondage to Satan from their afflictions (see, for example, Lk 13:16), Jesus is pictured as "plundering" the house of Satan (3:24-27).

Again, the Marcan Jesus authoritatively calls disciples to follow him (1:16-20). With an unconditional word of command, he "orders" Simon, Andrew, James, and John to "Come after me!" (1:17), and the text reads that "immediately" they "left" their profession and former way of life and began following him (1:18, 20).

Finally, the same divine authority that Mark writes so large across the public activity of Jesus also reflects itself in Jesus' resolve to suffer and die in Jerusalem (8:27–16:8). When Jesus sets out on the road that ultimately ends at the cross, he employs the authority he has been given to fulfill divine necessity (8:31). In so doing, he accomplishes the whole of that mission of salvation (10:45; 14:24) for which God had initially chosen him and equipped him with his Holy Spirit.

Summary

It is apparent from this brief study that Mark operates with what is basically an Old Testament and Jewish understanding of the Holy Spirit.[13] For Mark, the Holy Spirit stands for the power and presence of God. To depict Jesus Christ as receiving the Holy Spirit at his baptism is, in Mark's perspective, to see him as being equipped by God with his divine power and to see God as being fully active in him. It belongs to such a one that God should declare to him that he is his unique Son, the one whom he has chosen for messianic ministry in Israel. Consequently, as Mark depicts Jesus Christ, the Son of God, as preaching, calling disciples, teaching, exorcising and healing, and going the way of the cross, he intends that he should be looked upon as one who acts on divine authority and in full accord with the will of God. If Mark holds that Jesus is God's eschatological agent of salvation, he also affirms that God is the author of salvation. To show that the two act in concert, he describes the one as empowering the other with his Holy Spirit.

NOTES

1. See, for example, Vincent Taylor, *The Gospel According to St. Mark* (London: Macmillan & Co., 1952) 157; Ernst Haenchen, *Der Weg Jesu* (Berlin: A. Töpelmann, 1966) 45; Rudolf Pesch, *Das Markusevangelium*, 2 vols., Herders Theologischer Kommentar zum Neuen Testament 2 (Freiburg: Herder, 1976–77) 1:83.

2. See Eduard Schweizer, *"pneuma,"* in *TDNT* 6:398–399.

3. See further C. K. Barrett, *The Holy Spirit and the Gospel Tradition* (London: S.P.C.K., 1947) 153.

4. See Hans-Joachim Kraus, *Psalmen*, 2 vols., Biblischer Kommentar: Altes Testament 15 (Neukirchen: Neukirchener Verlag, 1960) 1:14, 17–19.

5. *Ibid.*, 1:19.

6. *Ibid.*, 1:13–16, 20.

7. See Fritzleo Lentzen-Deis, *Die Taufe Jesu nach den Synoptikern*, Frankfurter Theologische Studien 4 (Frankfurt am Main: Joseph Knecht, 1970) 269, 277, 282.

8. See William F. Arndt and F. Wilbur Gingrich, *A Greek-English Lexicon of the New Testament and Other Early Christian Literature* (Chicago: The University of Chicago Press, 1957) 236–237.

9. See Hermann L. Strack and Paul Billerbeck, *Kommentar zum Neuen Testament aus Talmud und Midrasch*, 6 vols. (München: C. H. Beck'sche Verlagsbuchhandlung, 1926–61) 4:515.

10. Heinrich Seesemann, *"peira,"* in *TDNT* 6:34.

11. See, for example, Ernest Best, *The Temptation and the Passion*, Society for New Testament Studies Monograph Series 2 (Cambridge: Cambridge University Press, 1965) 8–10.

12. See, for example, Pesch, 1:96–97.

13. See also Schweizer, 404.

Neal Flanagan, O.S.M.

THE WHAT AND HOW OF SALVATION
IN LUKE-ACTS

"Today *salvation* has come to this house . . . ," said Jesus to Zac-chaeus as the latter descended in haste from his branch on the sycamore tree and stood before him. "For the Son of Man came to seek and *to save* the lost" (Lk 19:9-10). This story is surely one of the most appealing in the Gospels. It is human, graphic, dramatic, even enigmatic. Zacchaeus seems to be the seeker (v. 3), but in reality he is the one being sought (v. 10) by the Son of Man. It is enigmatic, too, because of its emphasis on *salvation* and *save*. These are words that Christians cast about lightly. But what do they mean? More precisely, what do they mean in the writings of Luke? This article will study this question, beginning with a word study of Luke's *salvation*-vocabulary, and then proceeding into a resumé of some recent work done on the subject.

I. *Word Study*

The Lucan salvation vocabulary includes two words for salvation = *sōtēria* and *sōtērion*, one word for savior = *sōtēr*, and two verbs for save = *sōzō* and *diasōzō*.[1] They are distributed in Luke according to the following categories:

1) physical well-being, e.g., saved from sickness, danger, etc.
   a) in general,
   b) through faith;
2) transcendent salvation
   a) in general,
   b) specifically from sin,
   c) through faith.

What I would like to do now is simply lay out the pertinent passages in Luke-Acts, indicating in each which of the five Greek words given above is being used. The translation is that of the RSV, even in those places where "save" does not appear, e.g., ". . . your faith *has made you well*" (literal translation, "your faith has saved you") as in Lk 7:50; 8:48; 17:19; 18:42. It is only by reading carefully through this long list that the variety of Luke's use of salvation-vocabulary becomes evident.

1) Physical well-being
   a) in general
   . . . that we should be saved (*sōtēria*) from our enemies (Lk 1:71).

   I ask you, is it lawful on the Sabbath to do good or to do harm, to save (*sōzō*) life or to destroy it? (Lk 6:9)

   When he (centurion) heard of Jesus, he sent to him elders of the Jews, asking him to come and heal (*diasōzō*) his slave (Lk 7:3).

   And those who had seen it told them how he (Gerasene demoniac) who had been possessed with demons was healed (*sōzō*) (Lk 8:36).

   He saved others; let him save (*sōzō*) himself, if he is the Christ of God, his chosen one! (Lk 23:35)

   If you are the king of the Jews, save (*sōzō*) yourself (Lk 23:37).

   Are you not the Christ? Save (*sōzō*) yourself and us (Lk 23:39).

   . . . if we are being examined today concerning a good deed done to a cripple, by what means this man has been healed (*sōzō*) . . . (Acts 4:9).

   He (Moses) supposed that his brethren understood that God was giving them deliverance (*sōtēria*) by his hand, but they did not understand (Acts 7:25).

   Also provide mounts for Paul to ride, and bring him safely (*diasōzō*) to Felix the governor (Acts 23:24).

   . . . all hope (in storm) of our being saved (*sōzō*) was at last abandoned (Acts 27:20).

   Unless these men stay in the ship, you cannot be saved (*sōzō*) (Acts 27:31).

   Therefore, I (Paul) urge you to take some food; it will give you strength (*sōtēria*), since not a hair is to perish from the head of any of you (Acts 27:34).

   . . . but the centurion, wishing to save (*diasōzō*) Paul. . . . And so it was that all escaped (*diasōzō*) to land (Acts 27:43-44).

   After we had escaped (*diasōzō*), we then learned that the island was called Malta (Acts 28:1).

No doubt this man is a murderer. Though he has escaped (*diasōzō*) from the sea, justice has not allowed him to live (Acts 28:4).

These sixteen brief citations make it evident that Luke's salvation-vocabulary often includes physical healing. Healing of the whole person, not merely of the soul or spirit, is part of salvation.

b) through faith

Daughter, your faith has made you well (*sōzō*); go in peace (Lk 8:48).

Do not fear; only believe, and she (Jairus' daughter) shall be well (*sōzō*) (Lk 8:50).

Rise and go your way; your faith (Samaritan leper) has made you well (*sōzō*) (Lk 17:19).

Receive your sight (blind man at Jericho); your faith has made you well (*sōzō*) (Lk 18:42).

. . . and Paul, looking intently at him (cripple at Lystra) and seeing that he had faith to be made well (*sōzō*) . . . (Acts 14:9).

Luke uses what seems to be almost a technical formula, "Your faith has made you well = has saved you," to tie physical salvation to its faith agent. But salvation, for Luke, encompasses far more than the physical. The following examples speak certainly, if not distinctly, of a broader, transcendental type of salvation that does, indeed, encompass *the whole person*, and *for all time*.

2) Transcendent salvation

a) in general

My soul magnifies the Lord, and my spirit rejoices in God my Savior (*sōtēr*) (Lk 1:46-47).

. . . and has raised up a horn of salvation (*sōtēria*) for us in the house of his servant David (Lk 1:69).

. . . for to you is born this day in the city of David a Savior (*sōtēr*) who is Christ the Lord (Lk 2:11).

For whoever would save (*sōzō*) his life will lose it; and whoever loses his life for my sake, he will save (*sōzō*) it (Lk 9:24).

And someone said to him, "Lord, will those who are saved (*sōzō*) be few?" (Lk 13:23)

Then (speaking about the rich) who can be saved (*sōzō*)? (Lk 18:26)

And Jesus said to him (Zacchaeus), "Today salvation (*sōtēria*) has come to this house, since he also is a son of Abraham. For the Son of Man came to seek and to save (*sōzō*) the lost" (Lk 19:9-10).

Save (*sōzō*) yourselves from this crooked generation (Acts 2:40).

And the Lord added to their number day by day those who were being saved (*sōzō*) (Acts 2:47).

And there is salvation in no one else, for there is no other name under heaven given among men by which we must be saved (*sōzō*) (Acts 4:12).

God exalted him at his right hand as Leader and Savior (*sōtēr*) to give repentance to Israel and forgiveness of sins (Acts 5:31).

. . . he will declare to you (Cornelius) a message by which you will be saved (*sōzō*) (Acts 11:14).

Of this man's (David's) posterity God has brought to Israel a Savior (*sōtēr*), Jesus, as he promised (Acts 13:23).

Brethren (at Pisidian Antioch), sons of the family of Abraham, and those among you that fear God, to us has been sent the message of this salvation (*sōtēria*) (Acts 13:26).

For so the Lord has commanded us, saying, "I have set you to be a light for the Gentiles, that you may bring salvation (*sōtēria*) to the uttermost parts of the earth" (Acts 13:47).

Unless you were circumcised according to the custom of Moses, you cannot be saved (*sōzō*) (Acts 15:1).

She (slave girl at Philippi) followed Paul and us crying, "These men are servants of the Most High God, who proclaim to you the way of salvation" (*sōtēria*) (Acts 16:17).

The salvation of which Luke writes in these seventeen examples is clearly more than, and superior to, physical well-being. It is a salvation which originates with God (Lk 1:47), is effected by Christ the Lord (Lk 2:11), and extended not only to the sons of Abraham (Lk 19:9; Acts 13:23, 26), but also to the Gentiles and to the ends of the earth (Acts 13:47). It is connected in some special fashion to the forgiveness of sins and to the act of faith, as we can see in the following two sets of citations:

b) specifically, from sin
. . . to give knowledge of salvation (*sōtēria*) to his people in the forgiveness of their sins (Lk 1:77).

God exalted him at his right hand as Leader and Savior (*sōtēr*) to give repentance to Israel and forgiveness of sins (Acts 5:31).

c) through faith

Your (sinful woman) faith has saved (*sōzō*) you; go in peace (Lk 7:50).

The ones along the path are those who have heard; then the devil comes and takes away the word from their hearts, that they may not believe and be saved (*sōzō*) (Lk 8:12).

. . . whoever calls on the name of the Lord shall be saved (*sōzō*) (Acts 2:21).

. . . for there is no other name under heaven given among men by which we must be saved (*sōzō*) (Acts 4:12).

But we believe that we shall be saved (*sōzō*) through the grace of the Lord Jesus, just as they will (Acts 15:11).

"Men, what must I (jailor at Philippi) do to be saved (*sōzō*)?" And they said, "Believe in the Lord Jesus, and you will be saved (*sōzō*)" (Acts 16:30-31).

This total collection of Lucan citations leads to the following initial conclusions:

i) Luke's salvation vocabulary is used to cover a wide span of activities and effects.

ii) Luke gives considerable attention to *physical* salvation. People are not simply healed (*therapeuō*), they are saved (*sōzō*). God's salvation reaches out to the whole person. And this physical salvation is frequently tied to faith: ". . . your faith has made you well" (Lk 8:48; 17:19; 18:42). Salvation, consequently, is a wholeness that affects the entire person.

iii) But Luke speaks especially of a more encompassing salvation without, however, defining it while using this vocabulary. He does, though, relate it to the forgiveness of sins (Lk 1:77; Acts 5:31), to the reception of the word (Lk 8:12) and, most of all, to faith, to faith in Jesus, or faith in the name of the Lord (Lk 7:50; 8:12; Acts 2:21; 4:12; 15:11; 16:30-31).

II. *Contributions from Recent Studies*

Recent literature concerning Luke's theology of salvation has been fairly prolific. The second part of this article will consider four authors who have made excellent contributions in this field: H. Conzelmann, I. H. Marshall, B. H. Throckmorton and R. Martin.[2] In an effort to be clear, and following the actual steps through which this article came into being, I will (1) compare Conzelmann and Marshall, and then will (2) add further insights from (a) Martin and (b) Throckmorton. At the very end (III) I will attempt to pull together the results of this whole study.

1) Conzelmann and Marshall

a) Both agree that Luke gives curtailed emphasis to the soteriological meaning of the passion as act of "redemption," "expiation," "liberation," or "salvation." The most striking proof for this comes from the absence in Luke of Mk 10:45 (Mt 20:28), "For the Son of Man also came, not to be served but to serve, and *to give his life as a ransom (lutron) for many.*" It is certainly surprising to find this verse missing in Luke. On the other hand, Luke does contain passages which indicate the soteriological value of Jesus' death, though he neither emphasizes nor develops this theme (Marshall, 175).

Thus:

i) — Acts 8:32ff. speak of Philip converting the Ethiopian through an exegesis of Is 53:7-8, "sheep led to slaughter," etc. (Marshall, 171), an Isaian passage devoted completely to expiatory death. And Acts 3:13 probably refers to Is 52:13's glorification of the servant (Marshall, 171). Further "servant" terminology is found in Lk 22:37's use of Is 53:12, "And he was reckoned with transgressors." Still further usage of this motif may be present in the "just man = *dikaios*" of Acts 3:14; 7:52; 22:14 which seems to reflect the use of the term in Is 53:11 (Marshall, 171).

ii) — Acts 20:28, moreover, has Paul speak in strongly soteriological language of Jesus' death: "Take heed to yourselves and to all the flock in which the Holy Spirit has made you guardians (*episkopous*) to feed the Church of the Lord which he obtained with his own blood."

iii) — The complete Eucharistic text[3] of Lk 22:19-20 states that "This cup which is poured out for you is the new covenant in my blood."

iv) — Luke, in his passion narrative (22:37) applies to Jesus the words of Is 53:12, "And he was reckoned with transgressors."

b) Both agree that, for Luke, salvation is mediated through the Church by means of *word* and *sacrament*, accepted through *faith*, gifted by the *Spirit* (Conzelmann, 208–209, Marshall, 181).

i) — The word is the Church's message, consisting of its proclamation of the resurrection-exaltation of the Lord and its tradition of the words and deeds of Jesus, and backed by the authority of the witnesses. Church and word are so intimately related that as *the Church* grows, *the word* grows (Acts 6:7; 12:24; 19:20).

ii) — Baptism confers both forgiveness of sins and the Spirit (practically synonymous with the notion of salvation), while the Eucharist keeps the Christian fellowship in being. In so doing they span the gulf between the present and the Christian beginnings (Conzelmann, 200, 218). It is word and sacrament which tie the Church of the present to the Jesus of the past, which tie the Acts to the Gospel.

iii) — Through faith, the saving power of word and sacrament are accepted into the believer's life.

iv) — Integral to the whole process of salvation is the gift of the Spirit, present and operative in the Christian's life — as already in the life of Jesus (Gospel) and in the life of the earliest Christian communities (Acts). This Spirit is the Spirit of Jesus: "And when they had come opposite Mysia, they attempted to go into Bithynia, but the *Spirit of Jesus* did not allow them" (Acts 16:7).

c) Marshall is more specific in spelling out the elements and the process of salvation.

i) — Basic to every consideration is the divine initiative (Marshall, 102–115, 166, 188–192). God stands behind the whole process and, indeed, is the object of Luke's initial reference to salvation: "My soul magnifies the Lord and my spirit rejoices in *God my Savior*" (Lk 1:46-47). God sends Jesus "to seek and to save the lost" (Lk 19:10). This uniquely Lucan passage seems to be Luke's substitute for Mk 10:45.

ii) — The central point of the saving kerygma is not the passion of Jesus, but rather his *resurrection and exaltation* (Marshall, 174). These certify Jesus' Lordship and put him in position to send out the Spirit with a consequent forgiveness of sins (Marshall, 169, 181f.). This means that salvation is *now* (Marshall, 178), available through the name of Jesus (Marshall, 179). Even in his lifetime Jesus was savior (Marshall, 170). His healing ministry is definitely part of, sign of, his broader power to save. Consequently, there is no essential difference between what Jesus did before and after exaltation (Marshall, 170).

iii) — The *word*, the message, the good news is *preached*. Salvation depends on reaction to the preaching, to the word (Marshall, 192). Belief means acceptance of the message together with commitment to Jesus the Savior (see Lk 8:11-15).

iv) — With this is allied repentance, i.e., confession of sins and the beginning of a new life (Marshall, 193–195). (The Zacchaeus account in 19:1-10 is an excellent example of a saving event.)

v) — *Baptism* in the name of Jesus confers salvation itself, i.e., the *forgiveness of sins* and the *gift of the Spirit* (Marshall, 181, 197) which constitutes Christians as witnesses to Jesus (Marshall, 200). This gift of the Spirit is both continuous and renewable in the life of every believer (Marshall, 181, 201f.).

vi) — This simultaneously incorporates the believer into the *Christian community, the Church*. Those who hear the word of God and do it become Jesus' family (Lk 8:21) (Marshall, 202).

vii) — From this conversion follow *joy, praise of God, prayer* (Marshall, 202–204).

viii) — In the *breaking of bread* Jesus himself is present, though unrecognized as at Emmaus (Marshall, 205). The *breaking* of the bread and the *pouring* of the blood signal Jesus' death and constitute its sacrificial character (Marshall, 206).

ix) — From all this follows the necessary movement toward *sharing*: a sharing of goods (Marshall, 206), a sharing of prayer, of life, of love (Acts 2:42, 44-47; 4:32-35). Luke's stress, therefore, is on the blessings which Jesus brings as Savior (Marshall, 169f.).[4]

x) — The notion of salvation, itself, is the main theme of Luke's theology, the main theme of both his Gospel and Acts (Marshall, 92, 116).

2) Further Insights from Martin and Throckmorton

a) Martin, of necessity, shares many of the notions about Lucan salvation already seen in Conzelmann and Marshall. He gives special emphasis to the following points:

i) — Salvation is the dominant idea of the whole Lucan message (Martin, 366–367). This appears clearly in the infancy narrative (1:47, 69, 71, 77; 2:11, 30), in the repeated use of the set formula, "Your faith has saved you" (7:50; 8:48; 17:19; 18:42), and in the Zacchaeus story (19:1–10). It is intimately connected to the person of Jesus.

ii) — Salvation was initiated in practice by the *earthly* Jesus who, as Spirit–anointed (Messiah), offered salvation to all (4:18–19). Jesus, as Messiah, is a Moses figure (transfiguration of 9:28-36), a deliverer and savior of his people (Martin, 368–370).

iii) — Luke's special — and frequent — use of *Kyrios* for both the earthly Jesus and risen Lord stresses continuity between these two phases of Jesus' existence while, at the same time, conveying the sense of personal bond uniting Jesus and his disciples. The same Lord is as active now as he was during his earthly life (Martin, 371–72).

iv) — Salvation was extended by Jesus through his ministry of exorcism and healing — an overthrow of Satan's kingdom — and through his offer of forgiveness of sins (Martin, 373–74). Salvation was open even to non-Jews (Martin, 375) and involved Jesus' passion in Jerusalem. Though Luke does not emphasize Jesus' death as atonement, he still sees it as a sacrificial offering (his *exodos* of 9:31) set within a Passover time-frame (22:1). But Luke's insistence is on Jesus' death as the establishment of the covenant of Jer 31:31-34 with its concluding offer of forgiveness: " . . . for I will forgive their iniquity and I will remember their sin no more" (Martin, 376–78).

v) — Sharing in salvation means a response to the exalted Lord who has sent the Spirit and now lives on in the Spirit. This presence anticipates the parousia, yet the end is still to come. It is imminent, if not immediate. In the meantime the disciples live in a time of temptation, even of apostasy. The demands of discipleship are severe, total, and may lead to martyrdom. "Through many tribulations we must enter the kingdom of God" (Acts 14:22). Yet as the suffering Christ has been exalted, the faithful Christian may expect no less (Martin, 378–80).

b) Throckmorton initiates his presentation by stating — what is now clear for the reader of this article — that the meaning of the word *salvation* "is not at all obvious" (Throckmorton, 515). His own treatment insists on the following points:

i) — Luke's salvation-vocabulary designates *past* and *present*, what the saving God and saving Lord have done or are doing. In contrast to Paul's concept, salvation is not future, not reserved to the end-time, but now, in the historical present. This, I judge, is Throckmorton's main insistence (Throckmorton, 515–17, 522–25).

ii) — Many of Luke's references to salvation concern healing (Throckmorton, 516–517).

iii) — Salvation is frequently tied intimately to faith, to belief. The precise formula, "Your faith has saved you" occurs four times in the Gospel (7:50; 8:48; 17:19; 18:42), with substantially the same phrasing found also in 8:50. *Belief* leads to *salvation, now* (Throckmorton, 517–18).

iv) — An all-important component of Luke's concept of salvation is forgiveness of sins. The two are tied together repeatedly in Luke-Acts, are joined to baptism, and presuppose repentance (518–519).

v) — A final element in Luke's presentation is the hearing of the word. Salvation arrives as the word is accepted in faith. This word, preached first to the Jews, is now available to and for the world, available to the ends of the earth (523–24).

III. *Conclusion*

This article presents itself as a study of the *what* and *how* of salvation according to Luke–Acts. And so, having finished the word study of Luke's salvation-vocabulary, and having gathered together the contributions of some recent scholars on the subject, it is time to pull together the final conclusions.

1) The *What* of Salvation

Essentially, and very simply, *Lucan salvation is a healing*. It *can* include physical healing, it *must* include the deeper, more pervasive healing which is forgiveness of sins (Lk 1:77; Acts 5:31). Jesus' physical healings are sign, symbol, sacrament, manifestation, and proof of the spiritual healing with which they are allied. Luke's vocabulary happily embraces both.

2) The *How* of Salvation

How salvation takes place is, in Luke's theology, at least a double question. How it was *effected* by Jesus is one aspect, how it is *received* by us is another.

a) Jesus and salvation

i) — It is true that Luke places no major emphasis on Jesus' death as expiatory, as a ransom or deliverance. Yet this concept does play some part in his thinking as is evident from his use of the Isaian Servant songs (Acts 8:32 ff.; Lk 22:37; Acts 3:14; 7:52; 22:14), from his bold soteriological statement in Acts 20:28, from the complete Eucharistic text of Lk 22:19–20, and from his reference to redemption (*lutrōsin*) in Lk 2:38. It is this same Greek root (*lutr*) which is found in Mk 10:45.

ii) — Yet Luke's main emphasis is on *salvation as a gift* which Jesus gives us through the Spirit. It is this factor which makes healing such a practical notion for Luke as he describes the effect of salvation in the world. God our savior, and Jesus our saving Lord, give healing. Another way of saying this is that the gift of the Spirit (Acts 2:38) bestows healing, the forgiveness of sins. The risen and exalted Lord pours out this gift of the Spirit and, in so doing, effects our salvation.

b) Salvation and us. If Jesus gives, how do we receive?

i) — We receive, primarily, by accepting the word in faith, by believing the word and, consequently, commiting ourselves in personal bond to Jesus. This accounts for Luke's clear and pervasive insistence on the word, on belief, on discipleship.

ii) — Baptism is an external sign of this commitment, of this union with the personal Lord and with his followers who compose his spiritual family (Lk 8:21), his Church. Baptism is intimately related to both forgiveness of sins and the gift of the Spirit (Acts 2:38).

iii) — Eucharist keeps us in personal contact with the risen — yet hidden — Lord (Emmaus), and is the constant renewal of our covenant with him (Lk 22:20).

3) To the *What* and the *How* must be added, finally, the *When* and the *Where*.

a) Primarily, the *when* is now. Jesus' saving work does, of course, have a past, the past of his earthly life. Even more important for Luke and his readers is the *now*, the *present*. Jesus, who saved–healed in the past, saves–heals at this moment. Lord of his first disciples, he is equally our Lord, ever ready to bestow his greatest of gifts, the Spirit (Lk 11:13). Luke's theological perspective does view the future. There will be a parousia, the ultimate coming of the Lord. Nevertheless, salvation is God's gift of the moment, the time of salvation is now.

b) And the *where? Everywhere*, for whoever will hear the word, believe and be saved (Lk 8:12,15). Luke does show some interest in the expiatory theology of the Servant Songs, but he shows immeasurably more in the universalism that is evident in the first two songs (Is 42:1-7; 49:1-6), particularly in Is 49:6. "I will give you as a light to the nations," says the Lord in the prophet's song, "that my salvation may reach to the end of the earth." Here is the center, the core, the heart of Luke's theological interest: salvation (*sōtēria*), to all, to the ends of the earth (Acts 1:8; 13:47).

NOTES

1. *Sōzō* occurs thirty times in Luke-Acts, fifteen in Matthew, fourteen in Mark, six in John. *Sōtēr, sōtēria* and *sōtērion* occur seventeen times in Luke-Acts, but are not found at all in Matthew and Mark. *Diasōzō* is used six times in Luke-Acts, but elsewhere in the Synoptics only once in Matthew. Luke clearly has a special interest in this vocabulary.

2. H. Conzelmann, *The Theology of St. Luke* (1960) 199–231; I. H. Marshall, *Luke: Historian and Theologian* (1970) 77–215; R. Martin, "Salvation and Discipleship in Luke's Gospel," *Interpretation* 30 (October 1976) 366–380; B. H. Throckmorton, "*Sōzein, sōtēria* in Luke-Acts," *Studia Evangelica* (4th International Congress on N.T. Studies: Oxford, 1969), Akademie–Verlag–Berlin (1973) 515–526.

3. Both Conzelmann, 199, and Marshall, 170f., believe that the longer text is the original.

4. See the similar position of F. Danker: "For Luke, the Father, as the great benefactor of mankind, gives Jesus to the world, so that there is no need to speak of a ransom" (*Luke*, Proclamation Commentaries, 1976, 32).

Reginald H. Fuller

LUKE AND THE THEOLOGIA CRUCIS

It is a widely held view among scholars that Luke had no conception of the cross as saving event. Hans Conzelmann writes: "Nor is there any direct soteriological significance drawn from Jesus' suffering and death. There is no suggestion of a connection with the forgiveness of sins.[1] Even as cautious and conservative a scholar as F. F. Bruce has recently written: "The soteriological significance of the death of Christ is not emphasized in Luke's writings."[2]

At first sight there is much to support this point of view. Luke omits the important conclusion to Jesus' saying on service as this is recorded in Mk 10:45: "and to give his life as a ransom for many." His parallel in Lk 22:27 has only the first part of the saying, the part about service. The kerygmatic speeches, in Acts, regarded by Conzelmann and many others primarily if not exclusively as expressions of Lucan theology, present the cross not as a saving event, but as Jesus' contemporaries' rejection of him, now reversed by the Easter event as God's vindication of his mission:

> This Jesus, delivered up according to the definite plan and foreknow-ledge of God, *you* crucified and killed by the hands of lawless men. But *God* raised him up (Acts 2:23-24).

> The *God* of Abraham and of Isaac and of Jacob, the God of our fathers, glorified his servant Jesus, whom *you* delivered up and denied in the presence of Pilate, when he had decided to release him. But *you* denied the Holy and Righteous One, and asked for a murderer to be granted to you, and killed the Author of life, whom *God* raised from the dead (Acts 3:13-14).

> . . . Jesus Christ of Nazareth, whom *you* crucified, whom *God* raised from the dead . . . (Acts 4:10).

> . . . the Righteous One, whom *you* have now betrayed and murdered . . . (Acts 7:52).

They [the inhabitants of Judea and Jerusalem] put him to death by hanging him on a tree; but God raised him on the third day . . . (Acts 10:39-40).

Those who live in Jerusalem and their rulers . . . fulfilled [the scriptures] by condemning him. Though they could charge him with nothing deserving death, yet they asked Pilate to have him killed. And when they had fulfilled all that was written of him, they took him down from the tree, and laid him in a tomb. But *God* raised him from the dead (Acts 13:27-30).

These forms of the kerygma, including even that attributed to Paul in Acts 13, stand in marked contrast to Paul's kerygma:

I delivered to you as of first importance . . . that Christ died *for our sins* in accordance with the scriptures (1 Cor 15:3).

But there is something to be said on the other side. One of the most important shifts of opinion in the textual criticism of Luke has been the recent tendency to prefer the longer text of the institution narrative at the Last Supper.[3] Thus the first edition of the Revised Standard Version had relegated verses 19b-20 of chapter 22 to the margin. But the revised edition of 1971 has restored them to the text, simply noting in the margin that some ancient manuscripts omit them. The words in question read:

". . . which is given for you. Do this in remembrance of me." And likewise the cup after supper, saying, "This cup which is poured out for you is the new covenant in my blood."

Here the key phrase, *hyper hymōn*, occurs not just once in the cup-word, as in Mark's supper account, but twice, in the bread-word as well as in the cup-word. Given the authenticity of the longer text, it is arguable that at this point Luke stresses the salvific significance of Jesus' death even more strongly than Mark, who features it only in the cup-word.

It follows from this that Luke's omission of Mk 10:45 must be accounted for on grounds other than a desire to play down or obliterate any reference to the salvific significance of Jesus' death. Now if Luke had reproduced Mk 10:45a in its Marcan context (i.e., without the ransom saying), there would be some weight to the argument that he had suppressed it for theological reasons. However, he omits the whole Marcan pericope of the sons of Zebedee and precedence among the disciples (Mk 10:35-45). Why did he do this? To some of the material he clearly had no theological objection but considered the material there adequately covered by 12:50 and 22:24-27. Of course, in these days of redaction criticism the explanation that Luke was sometimes concerned with what, on his principles, was a faithful use of his sources and not always with some ulterior theological motive is often laughed out of court. Every change, however minute, has to be attributed to some subtle theological motivation[4] rather than to the use of earlier sources, whether written or oral. One can only say that while redaction criticism is a legitimate form of Gospel study, it is a method which is in its infancy and which, like most methods and movements in their early stages, tends to run to excess.

One could, of course, argue that had Luke wished to underline the salvific significance of the cross, he would have attached Mk 10:45b to the end of Lk 22:27. It is, however, debatable whether such a procedure can be in accordance with Luke's normal editorial techniques. Some would hold with Joachim Jeremias that it is not Luke's practice to rearrange the order of pericopes.[5] His procedure of producing an order (*kath' hexēs*, as he promised in his preface) seems to be to follow one source at a time. Admittedly such a view is not popular among the redaction critics, neither the German nor the new British variety.[6] But of course that is not to say that it is wrong. However that may be, there was really no need for Luke to shift Mk 10:45, since he had adequately compensated for its omission in the supper context by the repeated *hyper hymōn* over the elements.

The longer text of Luke also varies from Mark in another important regard. Both evangelists have a cup-word that alludes to the covenant established by the salvific event of the cross. But whereas Mark's wording is "this cup is my blood-of-the-covenant," thus replacing the Mosaic covenant of Ex 24:8, Luke has "This cup which is poured out for you is the new covenant in my blood" (Lk 22:20). This is generally recognized as an allusion to Jer 31:31-34. Now this pericope of Jeremiah concludes with the promise: "I will forgive their iniquity, and I will remember their sin no more."

Of course, Luke does not call attention to this, but it is at least implicit in this text.

This implicit allusion to the remission of sins[7] becomes quite explicit in Luke's Easter narrative. In the missionary charge to the Eleven in Lk 24:46-47, we read:

> Thus it is written, that the Christ should suffer and on the third day rise [be raised from] the dead, and that repentance and forgiveness of sins (*aphesis hamartiōn*) should be preached in his name to all nations.

Two points should be noticed here. The first is that the proclamation of remission of sins follows directly upon the proclamation of the passion and resurrection of Christ. Luke thus intends us to understand that the remission of sins is the consequence of passion and resurrection. If we are asked what is the role of the resurrection in this regard, our reply would be that the resurrection vindicates the salvific significance of the passion. For Luke invariably interprets the resurrection as vindication. The Emmaus disciples saw the salvific significance of the mission of Jesus radically called into question by the passion: "we had hoped that he was the one to redeem Israel" (Lk 24:21). By expounding the scriptures to them, the risen One showed that it was "necessary that the Christ should suffer these things and enter into his glory" (v. 25). Thus the resurrection had vindicated and the Christophany had manifested the redemptive significance of the earthly mission of the Christ which culminated in his passion.

The second point about Lk 24:47 is that the *aphesis hamartiōn* is baptismal language. Luke agrees with Mark that John had preached a baptism of repentance for the remission of sins (Lk 3:3). Like Mark, too, Luke had made John promise a coming One would baptize with the Holy Spirit (Lk 3:15). The programmatic sermon that Luke (4:16-30) has Jesus deliver at the inauguration of his ministry in his home town of Nazareth includes the *aphesis*, setting free of captives and oppressed. All this is now definitively achieved as a result of the ministry, passion, and resurrection, and because of that it can be proclaimed to the new world by the witnesses who have been with him from the time of John the Baptist until the day that he was taken up (Acts 1:22). Then after Pentecost, when the disciples themselves have received their baptism with the Spirit (Acts 1:5), all others who come after them are brought within the orbit of the redemptive event by hearing the kerygma, responding with repentance and belief, and receiving baptism. As a result they receive remission of sins and the Holy Spirit. Hence the charge in Lk 24:47 to proclaim *aphesis hamartiōn* implicitly included the charge to baptize. This becomes explicit in the Matthean and Pseudo-Marcan versions of the charge (Mt 28:19; Pseud-Mk 16:16). From these two points we infer, therefore, that Luke accepted and transmitted a tradition which identified with the belief that the passion effected remission of sins and that this salvific event was made available through baptism.

Luke can hardly be accused of downplaying the remission of sins as the outcome of the Christ-event (and more specifically, as we have argued, of the passion) when he comes to present the kerygma of the post-Easter Church. Sometimes he includes it within the kerygmatic core of the speech:

> The God of our fathers raised Jesus whom you killed by hanging him on a tree. God exalted him at his right hand as Leader and Savior, to give repentance to Israel and *forgiveness of sins* (Acts 5:30-31).
>
> To him [the one whom his fellow countrymen killed, but whom God raised from the dead] all the prophets bear witness that every one who believes in him receives *forgiveness of sins* through his name (Acts 10:43).
>
> Let it be known to you therefore, brethren, that through this man [the one whom the inhabitants of Jerusalem and their rulers persuaded Pilate to kill, whom they took down from the tree and laid in a tomb, but

whom God raised from the dead] *forgiveness of sins* is proclaimed to you, and by him every one that believes is freed from everything from which you could not be freed by the law of Moses (Acts 13:38-39).

There are three other speeches in Acts in which the reference to the remission of sins occurs, but outside of the kerygmatic core. The first is in the sermon Luke puts in the mouth of Peter on the day of Pentecost. Here the remission of sins comes up after the speech itself in answer to the audience's reaction. They inquire, "What shall we do?" To this Peter replies: "Repent, and be baptized every one of you in the name of Jesus Christ for the *forgiveness of your sins*" (Acts 2:38).

It is clear that this speech, like the others, regards the remission of sins as the outcome of the work of Christ, including his death, which was proclaimed in the kerygmatic core of the speech. Notice the close association of remission of sins with baptism.

The speech in Acts 3 likewise does not include the remission of sins as part of the central core of the kerygma (vv. 13-15). There is, however, a concluding summary and a challenge to repentance with a promise of forgiveness:

> And now, brethren, I know that you acted in ignorance, as did also your rulers [in killing the Author of life]. But what God foretold by the mouth of all the prophets, that his Christ should suffer, he thus fulfilled. Repent therefore, and turn again, that your sins may be blotted out . . . (Acts 3:17-19).

Note the "therefore" in verse 19. It is precisely because the Christ has suffered that the blotting out of sins is offered on condition of repentance. Presumably their sins will be "blotted out" in baptism.

In chapter 4 there is an apology of Peter before the Sanhedrin which, while not strictly speaking an example of kerygma, employs kerygmatic language. This does not speak at all of the remission or blotting out of sins. Probably this is because baptism is not being offered in response to faith. But it does speak in general terms of the offer of salvation through the name of Christ: "And there is salvation in no one else, for there is no other name under heaven given among men by which we must be saved" (Acts 4:12). If "name" stands for the Christ-event in its totality, including his death, and if salvation stands as an equivalent for, or a term that includes, the remission of sins, this speech preaches the salvific significance of the cross as much as any of the other speeches. Also, the reference to the "name" suggests baptism in the name of Christ.

Lastly, there is the speech by Paul to the Ephesian elders. This contains the following exhortation:

> Take heed to yourselves and to all the flock, in which the Holy Spirit has made you the guardians [*episkopos*], to feed the church of God,[8] which he obtained by his own blood (Acts 20:28).

F. F. Bruce, who, as we have seen, is at pains to minimize Luke's theology of the cross, discounts this passage as evidence for the theology of the author of Acts on the ground that this speech was spoken by Paul and represents Pauline rather than Lucan theology.[9] Quite apart from this rather uncritical attitude to this speech in Acts[10] as *ipsissima verbi Pauli*, and even if the author of Luke-Acts is here adopting a traditional formula (which would be the present writer's view) into a speech that he has composed himself, the very fact that he has chosen to incorporate this formula into his composition suggests that he has given its soteriology his stamp of approval.

In sum, it seems a little unfair to the author of Luke-Acts to contrast him unfavorably with Mark as regards his soteriology. It is true that the cross *per se* is not as central to his theology as it is for Mark. But for Mark the cross is central, not because he presents it as a salvific event (only two passages, both of them from the pre-Marcan tradition, Mk 10:45b and 14:24, actually do this), but because it serves as a corrective to the inadequate Christology of his opponents.[11] Statistically, Luke has exactly the same number of explicit references to the cross as salvific event as does Mark, the *hyper hymōn* and the new covenant in the cup-word. And there are references to the remission of sins in connection with baptism that imply it. Luke passes on traditions that connect a soteriology through the cross with baptism and Eucharist. He does not elaborate that theology, any more than Mark does, but by passing it on he affirms it, no less than Mark does.

NOTES

1. Hans Conzelmann, *The Theology of St. Luke* (New York: Harper & Row, 1960) 201.

2. F. F. Bruce, *The Time Is Fulfilled: Five Aspects of the Fulfillment of the Old Testament in the New* (Grand Rapids: Eerdmans, 1978) 31 n. 34.

3. While the textual theories of Westcott and Hort were dominant, the longer text was rejected as a "Western Non-Interpolation." The credit for the indication of the longer text seems to belong to J. Jeremias, *The Eucharistic Words of Jesus*, trans. N. Perrin from 3rd German ed. (New York: Scribner's, 1965) 138–159. The arguments on both sides are summarized in B. Metzger, *A Textual Commentary on the Greek New Testament* (London and New York: United Bible Societies, 1971) ad loc. Those on the committee who still favored the shorter text were in a minority.

4. The *reductio ad absurdum* of this methodological tendency is the attitude of the two pioneers in the redaction criticism of Mark and Luke respectively (Marxsen and Conzelmann) toward the location of the post-resurrectional appearances. Marxsen attributed Mark's Galilean location to the redaction and regarded Jerusalem as the traditional loca-

tion, while Conzelmann attributed Luke's Jerusalem location to the redaction and regarded Galilee as the traditional location!

5. J. Jeremias, "Perikopen-Umstellungen bei Lukas?" *NTS* 4 (1957–58) 115–119.

6. See J. Drury, *Tradition and Design in Luke's Gospel* (Atlanta: Knox, 1977). Drury follows A. Farrer in dropping the Q hypothesis and attributing everything that Luke did not find in Matthew and Mark to his editorial composition.

7. The favored translation of *aphesis* in this context is "forgiveness." This rendering was vigorously attacked by E. C. Hoskyns in his Cambridge Lectures on "The Theology and Ethics of the New Testament" (1936–37) on the basis of papyrus evidence for *aphesis* used of the discharging of the waters of the Nile to irrigate the fields. He contended that *aphesis* presupposed that sin was a power that held man in bondage rather than merely guilt that needed forgiveness, and that it meant a release from that power — a much more forceful concept than forgiveness.

8. RSV reads "Lord" (with A, D) here. The reading "God," which is better attested (B Vg), is probably to be preferred as the more difficult reading. See Metzger, *A Textual Commentary*, ad loc.; also R. E. Brown, *Jesus God and Man* (Milwaukee: Bruce, 1967).

9. F. F. Bruce, *The Time*, 31 n. 4.

10. No speech in Acts gives such a clear view of the early Catholic *Sitz im Leben* of Luke's Church: The apostle has left the scene. The episcopal-presbyterial order of ministry has replaced the charismatic order of the Pauline churches. The Church is threatened by heresy, and the order of the day is to hold fast to the apostolic tradition. All of this suggests a situation similar to that which led to the composition of the deutero-Pauline Pastoral Epistles.

11. One does not have to subscribe to the thesis of Weeden, Perrin, and others that Mark regards that Christology as false or that he sets up the Twelve as the mouthpiece of it. See my article, "The Son of Man Came to Serve, Not to be Served," in *Ministering in a Servant Church*, Proceedings of the Theology Institute of Villanova University, ed. F. A. Eigo (Villanova, Pa.: University Press, 1978) 45–77, esp. 67–68. A further point about Mark's theology of the cross that is worth noting is that the Son of man suffering-predictions (Mk 8:31; 9:31; 10:33) draw upon traditional materials that present the cross as Israel's rejection of the Messiah and the resurrection as God's vindication of him, i.e., precisely the same type of theology we find in the kerygmatic speeches in Luke-Acts.

Jerome Kodell, O.S.B.

LUKE'S THEOLOGY OF THE DEATH OF JESUS

There is probably no conviction more deeply embedded in the hearts of Christian believers than the doctrine that Christ died for our sins. We have forgiveness through the blood of Jesus. The *Crux Fidelis* of Good Friday expresses this traditional faith:

> From his open side
> Blood and water flow
> To cleanse all creation.

This doctrine of the saving death is a key for understanding Jesus' mission and for personal Christian spirituality. Its centrality for Catholics is symbolized in the celebration of the Eucharist as the "holy sacrifice."

The most thorough New Testament statement of the expiatory or atoning death of Jesus is found in the letters of Paul. He "was put to death for our trespasses" (Rom 4:25; see 3:25; 5:8); he "gave himself for our sins to deliver us from the present evil age, according to the will of our God and Father" (Gal 1:4). Some critics have said that Paul "created" this doctrine of expiation, but Paul tells us that he learned it from the Christian teachers after his conversion: "I delivered to you as of first importance what I also received, that Christ died for our sins in accordance with the scriptures" (1 Cor 15:3).

The doctrine is strongly witnessed in other important places in the New Testament, in both the Gospels and other writings. In the Gospel of John, Jesus is identified as "the Lamb of God, who takes away the sin of the world" (1:29). Matthew's account of Jesus' words at the Last Supper specifies what is implicit in the narrative in Mark: "This is my blood of the covenant, which is poured out for many *for the forgiveness of sins*" (Mt 26:28; cf. Mk 14:24; Matthew's addition in italics). Mark and Matthew also preserve the important ransom-saying of Jesus: "The Son of man also came not to be served but to serve, and to give his life as a ransom for many" (Mk 10:45; Mt 20:28). In other writings: Jesus "appeared once for all at the end of the age to put away sin by the sacrifice of himself"

(Heb 9:26); "He himself bore our sins in his body on the tree" (1 Pet 2:24); his blood "cleanses us from all sin" (1 Jn 1:7); he has "freed us from our sins by his blood" (Rev 1:5).

The Writings of Luke

It stands out as truly remarkable, then, that the doctrine of the expiatory death of Jesus is missing from the writings of Luke (the Gospel and the Acts of the Apostles). There is abundant evidence that this omission is intended. A good test is a comparison of Luke's handling of the dispute over greatness in the kingdom (Lk 22:24-27) with that of Mark, his source, and Matthew, who also followed Mark (Mk 10:41-45; Mt 20:24-28). Mark and Matthew conclude the passage with Jesus' description of his life as a ransom (quoted above). Luke, though he sets the episode in a different context, follows the received text closely until this verse; then he develops the theme of service, avoiding the idea of a life given in ransom.

The early Christian sermons of Peter and Paul in Acts bear similar evidence (2:14-40; 3:12-16; 4:3-12; 5:29-32; 10:34-43; 13:16-41). Though these sermons contain authentic reflections of the earliest preaching, it is generally accepted that Luke is responsible for their present form. The forgiveness of sin is a primary theme in these sermons (2:38; 3:19; 5:31; 13:38), and the death of Jesus is mentioned in each of them, but forgiveness through Jesus is not connected to his death. This is most noteworthy in the sermon in Acts 13 attributed to Paul, who in his letters is so emphatic on this issue. Peter calls for baptism (2:38), but without relating it to the death of Jesus (cf. Rom 6:1-4; 1 Pet 3:18-21).

Another telltale discrepancy is Luke's use of the fourth Servant-song from Is 52:13–53:12. The New Testament writers found this Old Testament passage a great help in explaining Jesus' saving mission, as a glance at the biblical cross-references will show. The Isaian idea of the Suffering Servant is the seed of the New Testament teaching of the atoning death of Jesus. Luke used this important traditional source, but was careful to avoid any mention of atoning death in his quotations. At the Last Supper, Jesus recalls the saying of Is 53:12, "He was numbered with the transgressors," but stops short before the next line, "yet he bore the sin of many" (Lk 22:37). In Acts 8, the Ethiopian eunuch is reading Is 53; verses 7 and 8 are quoted, mentioning the humiliation of the Servant, "like a lamb that is led to the slaughter." The words of verse 6, "The Lord has laid on him the iniquity of us all," are avoided.

Are there any texts at all in the Lucan writings that allude to the death of Jesus as atoning? Yes, there are two such texts, but they do very little to change the impression of Luke's overall attitude. At the Last Supper, Jesus took bread, and when he had given thanks he broke it and gave it to them, saying, "This is my body which is given for you. Do this in remembrance of me." And likewise the cup after supper, saying, "This cup which is poured out for you is the new covenant in my blood" (Lk 22:19-20).

This narrative (closer to Paul's account in 1 Cor 11:24-25 than to the synoptic parallels) contains atonement language, but two points minimize its significance for Luke's theology. The words following "This is my body" are the subject of a classic textual dispute. They are absent from ancient texts in the Western tradition; this, coupled with the fact that the cup has already been offered once (v. 17), has led many to doubt their authenticity. The second point is that even if the words in verses 19b-20 are authentic,[1] they may have been included by the author only because they belong to a liturgical formula that he did not feel free to tamper with.[2]

The other text is Acts 20:28. Paul is speaking to the Ephesian elders, admonishing them: "Feed the church of God which he obtained with his own blood." The saving efficacy of the death is indicated, but here too the significance for Luke's theology is inconclusive. Luke may be either quoting Paul exactly or attributing to him a statement known to be consonant with Paul's theology.[3] Further, the connection between the death of Jesus and individual salvation is vague.

Interpreting Luke

Luke does not proclaim the saving death of Jesus the way it is understood by Paul. Does he understand the death of Jesus as instrumental in our salvation at all, or has he put all the salvific emphasis on something else, for example, the resurrection or ascension? Ernst Käsemann believes that Luke has replaced a *theologia crucis* (theology of the cross) with a *theologia gloriae* (theology of glory).[4] It is more common among scholars to find in Luke's writing a theology that includes the death of Jesus in the work of salvation, but one that is different from Paul's and significant in its own right. The descriptions of Luke's thought on this point fall into two general categories. We will present these two theories and then a third recent explanation that incorporates them in a new analysis.

A Martyr's Death

When the expiatory overtones are omitted, Jesus' death as presented in the Gospels is that of an innocent man condemned by an unjust council. This is the death of a martyr. Martin Dibelius first pointed out how Luke has highlighted this aspect of the passion.[5] Jesus is a martyr (or rather *the* martyr) whose death confirms and climaxes his life. It does not cause forgiveness of sin and salvation in itself, but it is the final witness to Jesus' true dedication to the will of God in carrying out the mission of salvation.

The suffering Jesus is the model for all the faithful witnesses who will follow him: "If any man would come after me, let him deny himself and take up his cross daily and follow me" (Lk 9:23). The first Christian to follow Jesus all the way to death is Stephen; his death is presented in striking parallel to that of the Master. Both are killed without a fair trial and die praying for their executioners and commending their spirit to the Lord (Lk 23:34, 46; Acts 7:54-60).

Several alterations in the passion narrative throw into sharp relief the theme of Jesus' innocence. Pilate mentions his own not-guilty verdict three times (Lk 23:4, 14, 22) and refers once to the similar judgment by Herod (v. 15). Even one of those crucified with Jesus defends his innocence (v. 41). When the centurion witnesses Jesus' death, his exclamation is not "Truly this man was the Son of God" (Mk 15:39; Mt 27:54), but "Certainly this man was innocent" (v. 47). The contrast between Barabbas' murderous guilt and Jesus' innocence (v. 25) is continued in Acts (3:14). Peter, Stephen, and Paul refer to Jesus as the Righteous or Just One (3:14; 7:52; 22:14);[6] at Pisidian Antioch, Paul summarizes tersely Jewish guilt and Gentile instrumentality in the martyrdom of the innocent: "Though they could charge him with nothing deserving death, yet they asked Pilate to have him killed" (13:28).

Luke treats Jesus in his role as martyr as the successor of the Old Testament prophets who were persecuted and martyred by their own people. Though there are allusions to Jesus' identity as a prophet in the other Gospels (e.g., Mk 6:14-15; Mt 16:14; Jn 6:14), Luke reinforces this theme in various ways. He mentions unique instances of Jesus' acclamation as a prophet by the people (Lk 7:16; 24:19), and records his identification as the prophet-like-Moses in the speeches of Peter and Stephen (Acts 3:22; 7:37; see Dt 18:18). To the Q references concerning the murder of the ancient prophets by "your fathers" (Lk 6:23; 11:48; Mt 5:12; 23:32), Luke adds the remark of Stephen: "Was there ever any prophet whom your fathers did not persecute? In their day, they put to death those who foretold the coming of the Just One; now you in your turn have become his betrayers and murderers" (Acts 7:52). He changes the wording of Mark to emphasize the speculation that Jesus is not just a prophet, but "one of the prophets of old" (Mk 6:15; 8:28; Lk 9:8, 19).

Jesus' identity as the Isaian Servant of Yahweh, as remarked earlier, is not focused on his vicarious suffering for sin, as elsewhere in the New Testament, but on the humiliation and rejection of the "Holy and Righteous One" (Acts 3:13-14; cf. Lk 22:37; Acts 8:32-33). Luke stresses Jesus' prophetic anointing and the guidance of the Spirit (Lk 4:1, 14, 18; Acts 10:38). When Jesus is on the Mount of Transfiguration with Moses and

Elijah, only Luke of the Synoptics mentions that they are speaking of his *exodos* to be accomplished in Jerusalem (Lk 9:30-31). Finally, in another text unique to Luke that may be taken as the martyr's own description of his role, Jesus responds to Herod's threats: "I must go on my way today and tomorrow and the day following; for it cannot be that a prophet should perish away from Jerusalem" (Lk 13:33). Jesus as martyr is the suffering just man, a model of obedience and faithfulness, who is put to death by the malevolence and ignorance of his own people, just as were the prophets of old.[7]

Prelude to Exaltation

Another approach (often only a difference of emphasis from the preceding one) is to interpret the death of Jesus in Luke as the necessary prelude to his exaltation, which unleashes the Spirit as the source of forgiveness and salvation (Acts 2:33). Here it is the exaltation through resurrection and ascension that brings redemption, with the death sharing the saving role as a crucial link in the chain of events, a *sine qua non* on the way to glory.

The sense of a foreordained plan irresistibly unfolding in the mission of Jesus is strong in Luke-Acts. As in many other special Lucan emphases, the author is only developing a theme already present in the synoptic tradition. In the first prediction of the passion, Jesus speaks of his divinely ordained destiny: "The Son of man must suffer many things, and be rejected by the elders and the chief priests and the scribes, and be killed, and after three days rise again" (Mk 8:31; cf. Mt 16:21; Lk 9:22). The pivotal Greek word here is *dei*, "it is necessary, it must happen." Luke employs this word to show the divine plan behind all Jesus' actions (Lk 2:49; 4:43); but he emphasizes the destiny especially in regard to Jesus' suffering and death.

We can imagine that the Christian preachers faced many questions about the death of Jesus from the Greek-speaking audiences of Luke's time, a generation after the Gospel events. If Jesus is our Savior, the Messiah and Lord, why did he die? Luke's answer was to stress the traditional notion of fulfillment: Jesus' death was part of the plan foretold from of old, the necessary prelude to Jesus' glorification and our salvation. There was a "definite plan" (Acts 2:23; see Lk 13:33; 22:22) that was promised and "must be fulfilled" (Lk 24:44; see 18:32-33; 22:37; Acts 13:27); first would come suffering (Lk 17:25; 24:7), but it would result in resurrection and glory (Lk 24:26). Jesus has been established Lord because of his complete obedience certified by his death; God exalted him and made him the source of salvation. The death of Jesus thus has only "mediate influence" on our salvation, as the necessary step toward glorification.[8]

Recent Research

A recent dissertation by a German Dominican has found a new avenue in the study of Luke's theology of Jesus' death. In *Luke's Proclamation of Salvation*, Richard Glöckner devotes a lengthy section to the "Salvific Meaning of the Death of Jesus."[9] His treatment of the subject incorporates the elements mentioned above, but discovers different insights through consideration of Luke's theme of salvation as the raising of the lowly.

Lowliness is the biblical posture of availability and openness to salvation, readiness for "raising" at the hand of God (1 Sam 2:8; Job 29:12; Pss 72:12-13; 149:4; Is 11:4; Zeph 2:3). Luke emphasizes this theme from the beginning of his Gospel. Mary prays in her canticle: "My spirit rejoices in God my Savior, for he has regarded the low estate of his handmaiden. . . . He has put down the mighty from their thrones, and exalted those of low degree" (1:48, 52). To be "mighty" here means to be self-sufficient, in no need of salvation. God raises the lowly, but the mighty do not recognize their lowliness; they desire to raise themselves up. This spirit of self-exaltation is the key to sinfulness for Luke.[10] Simeon recognizes that true judgment has come into the world with the infant he holds in his arms: "Behold this child is set for the fall and rising of many in Israel" (2:34).

The Lowly and the Mighty

The contrast between lowly and mighty is carried also by the term "righteous" (*dikaios*) and its opposite, unrighteous or self-righteous. Zechariah and Elizabeth are lowly, ready for the Lord's action, "righteous before God, walking in all the commandments and ordinances of the Lord blameless" (1:6). Simeon is righteous (2:25), as are Joseph of Arimathea (23:50) and Cornelius (Acts 10:22). John the Baptist will "turn the disobedient to the wisdom of the righteous" (Lk 1:17). His birth is a sign of the promised deliverance; now all will be able to serve God "in holiness and righteousness before him all the days of our life" (1:75).

But there is a self-righteousness that rebels against this gift of God. "You are those who justify yourselves before men," Jesus tells the Pharisees, "but God knows your hearts; for what is exalted among men is an abomination in the sight of God" (Lk 16:15). He did not come to call the (self-)righteous but sinners (5:32) and announces that there is more joy in heaven over one repentant sinner than over "ninety-nine righteous persons who need no repentance" (15:7). Two of the parables recorded only by Luke are directed to the self-righteous. A lawyer "desiring to justify himself" hears the story of the Good Samaritan (10:29-37); a group "who trusted in themselves that they were righteous and despised others" are told the parable of the Pharisee and the publican

(18:9-14). To climax this latter story, Luke uses the pointed saying from Q: "Every one who exalts himself will be humbled, and he who humbles himself will be exalted" (18:14; see 14:11; Mt 23:12).

It is within this tension between righteous and self-righteous, this struggle in each human heart between lowliness and might, that Glöckner locates Luke's theology of the death of Jesus. God wants to raise mankind to a life of glory, but human sinfulness seeks self-glorification. The climax of this divine-human conflict is the death of Jesus. From within humanity Jesus overcomes the desire for self-exaltation. He is lowly and serves the lowly; he announces salvation for the poor, the captive, the blind, the oppressed (Lk 4:18); he defeats sinfulness by accepting the thorough humiliation of his passion and death, which prepares the way for his exaltation by God and opens the door of salvation to all.

Jesus' Lowliness

Jesus' lowliness is essential to his saving mission. Luke stresses the humble condition of Jesus' birth. In Matthew's account the mother and child are in a house (Mt 2:11), but in Luke's account Mary "wrapped him in swaddling cloths, and laid him in a manger, because there was no place for them in the inn" (Lk 2:7). At age twelve, Jesus is already making a mark before men, but at the word of his parents he went home to Nazareth "and was obedient to them" (2:51). Though he speaks of justice and righteousness during his public ministry, Jesus does not speak of his own righteousness. The Father will reveal this at the proper time. And it is at the moment of death that the centurion exclaims: "Certainly this man was innocent [= righteous]" (23:47). The Christian preachers name him the "Righteous One" (Acts 3:14; 7:52; 22:14); by him the world will be judged "in righteousness" (17:31).

Jesus, the lowly one, carries God's good news to the lowly and outcast. He ministers to the "tax collectors and sinners" (Lk 15:1), such as Zacchaeus (19:1-10) and the repentant woman (7:37-50). Besides the teaching found in the other Gospels, Luke's Jesus tells stories about the prodigal son (15:11-32), the Good Samaritan (10:30-37), the rich man and Lazarus (16:19-31), the Pharisee and the publican (18:10-14). His healing of a woman "whom Satan bound for eighteen years" (13:11-16) is typical and symbolic of his overall mission of raising the lowly.[11]

Suffering and death is Jesus' destiny by the foreordained plan of God (Mk 8:31; Mt 16:21; Lk 9:22). This synoptic theme of destiny is broadened in Luke to embrace all of Jesus' life: "I must be in my Father's house" (Lk 2:49); "I must preach the good news" (4:43); "I must go on my way" (13:33; see 19:5; 22:22; 24:44). But ultimately his life and mission funnel into the passion as the focus of the way of salvation decreed by God: "Was it not necessary that the Christ should suffer these things and enter into his glory?" (Lk 24:26). But why was it necessary? Why did death have to intervene before glory? In Glöckner's view, Luke wasn't satisfied with the answer "God willed it" in some arbitrary decree.

Jesus, sent as "a prophet mighty in deed and word before God and all the people" (Lk 24:19), must go to Jerusalem to suffer a prophet's fate (13:33). He is not just any prophet, but the one anointed (Acts 10:38), the servant who preaches to the lowly and walks the way of humiliation (Lk 4:18; Acts 3:13). God's answer to the sinful self-exaltation of mankind is the self-emptying life and death of Jesus. In his death, humiliation and lowliness taken to the extreme, the power of sin is undermined. Jesus pursued his saving mission right into the jaws of human sinfulness, and by suffering unjust violence without resistance and without swerving from his appointed task, he revealed God's unconditional saving will. God's love emerged undaunted by the evil that men could produce. The offer of salvation remained intact, even for the executioners: "Father, forgive them; for they know not what they do" (Lk 23:34).[12]

Defeat of Satan

As the climax of his life as prophet and servant in lowliness, Jesus' death overturns the power of sin, not simply by "taking away" human guilt but by breaking the hold of sin from within. Jesus is driven to death by Satan, acting through human agents (Lk 22:3). The devil had tried earlier to upset Jesus' way of lowliness (Lk 4:1-13). He returned at the passion, "an opportune time" (v. 13), in order to destroy Jesus. The same temptation to power and might, like one last thrust to break Jesus' commitment to God's will, emerges from the bystanders at the cross (23:35-37). In Luke's Gospel, the passion is not "my hour," the moment of fulfillment as in John (2:4; 17:1), but "your hour, and the power of darkness" (22:53).[13] The great irony here lies in the fact that by causing Jesus' death, Satan is fulfilling the Father's will and causing his own reign of sin to be shattered. The death of Jesus is a crime of men, but it is also, and more importantly, an achievement of God (Acts 2:23).

By God's plan Jesus became vulnerable to the power of sinfulness and guilt, but it could not overcome him. In fact, guilt succumbed to Jesus by putting him to death; for this was the most that it could do, and when God's forgiving love was not extinguished, it became evident that the bonds of condemnation could not hold against his desire to save: "God raised him up, having loosed the pangs of death, because it was not possible for him to be held by it" (Acts 2:24). What was possible for Jesus, the Author of life (Acts 3:15), would also be possible for his followers. The humble death of Jesus exposed the emptiness and ultimate powerlessness of human self-exaltation.

Conclusion

Jesus's death, in Luke's theology, is indeed a martyrdom, patterned on and climaxing the suffering of prophets in times past. His way of the cross is an example for his followers, but more than that, his death has meaning in itself as the confrontation of human sinfulness by lowliness, which in God's plan is the state of openness to divine salvation.

The death of Jesus is the prelude to exaltation, but it is not a mere *sine qua non*. Because of its particular content as the obedient humiliation of the anointed Servant, this death sets the stage for the exaltation of Jesus and all his lowly ones. The forgiveness of sin is not connected with the death as such, but with the "raising of the lowly" that it makes possible (Acts 5:30-31). The gift of the Spirit flows from this exaltation (2:33).

And so we return to the question posed at the beginning of this article: Does Luke have a doctrine of saving death, and if so, how does it relate to Paul's doctrine of expiation? Our study has shown that the death of Jesus is definitely integral to Luke's theology of salvation. His understanding of this, however, is not the same as Paul's. In Luke's theology, forgiveness is available in the "name" of Jesus (Acts 2:38; 3:12), who as risen Lord (2:36) is the giver of the Spirit (2:33). The saving power of Jesus' name is the consequence of his exaltation, not directly of his death. But it is because of the kind of death he suffered that God raised him and, with him, all the lowly who would follow him to glory.

NOTES

1. These verses are treated as authentic in the critical text established by the team of scholars working for the United Bible Societies: Kurt Aland et. al., *The Greek New Testament*, 3rd ed. (Stuttgart: Württemberg Bible Society, 1975).

2. In post-resurrection meals with Eucharistic overtones recorded by Luke (Lk 24:30-35; Acts 20:7-11; 27:35), there is no connection between the breaking of bread and Jesus' death.

3. T. E. Bleiben, "The Synoptists' Interpretation of the Death of Christ," *Expository Times* 54 (1942–43) 148; G. W. H. Lampe, in *Peake's Commentary on the Bible* (London: Nelson, 1962), par. 797k.

4. Ernst Käsemann, "Ministry and Community in the New Testament," in *Essays on New Testament Themes* (London: SCM, 1964) 91–94.

5. Martin Dibelius, *Die Formgeschichte des Evangeliums* (Tübingen, 1919) = *From Tradition to Gospel* (London, 1934); see C. H. Talbert, *Luke and the Gnostics* (Nashville: Abingdon, 1966) 71–76.

6. Behind the RSV "righteous" and "just" in these texts and "innocent" in Lk 23:47 is the single Greek adjective *dikaios*.

7. Augustin George, "Le Sens de la Mort de Jesus pour Luc," *Revue Biblique* 80 (1973) 207–209; Gerhard Friedrich, "prophētēs," in *TDNT* 6:841–848.

8. Richard Zehnle, "The Salvific Character of Jesus' Death in Lucan Soteriology," *Theological Studies* 30 (1969) 431–432. This "death as prelude" theme is recognizable in other New Testament traditions, e.g., Jn 12:24; Phil 2:6-10; Heb 5:8-9.

9. Richard Glöckner, *Die Verkündigung des Heils beim Evangelisten Lukas*, Walberberger Studien 9 (Mainz: Matthias-Grünewald Verlag, 1976) 155–195.

10. Here there is a noticeable similarity to Paul's understanding of *sarx* (Glöckner, 140–141).

11. Glöckner, 136.

12. Glöckner, 193–95.

13. The goal of Jesus' journey in Luke's writing is the ascension, *analēmpsis* (Lk 9:51; see Acts 2:1, 11, 22).

Demetrius R. Dumm, O.S.B.

LUKE 24:44-49 AND HOSPITALITY

Luke's version of the final words of Jesus to the apostles derives its significance from the fact that it is both a summary of his Gospel and a preparation for Acts. As such it is a hinge-text between these two works of Luke and can be properly understood only if one reads it in the larger context of Luke-Acts.

I. SOME FEATURES OF LUKE-ACTS

Table-fellowship

It has long been recognized that there is a movement or flow in Luke's Gospel toward Jerusalem and the paschal events and then, in Acts, from Jerusalem to all the world. More important than the simple recognition of this fact, however, is an awareness of the dynamic that propels and guides this extraordinary movement. There is, of course, the will of God dominating everything. But this divine will makes room for human freedom, so that the presence of God is felt more as an invitation than a command. In such an atmosphere of free personal exchange, one should look for shy signs and subtle clues rather than an obvious and obtrusive display of power. No evangelist is better than Luke at creating this kind of gospel climate.

When one begins to take note of the details of Luke's narrative, it is immediately evident that he is extraordinarily attracted to scenes of table-fellowship. In the immediate context of the passage under consideration, there is the classic breaking of bread with the disciples of Emmaus (24:30, 35) whereby Jesus reveals his identity to them. Then he eats in the presence of the apostles to remove their doubts about the reality of his presence (24:41-43).

Luke's Gospel is full of table scenarios. Simon's mother-in-law is cured and waits on her guests (4:39); Levi is called and prepares a great feast for Jesus (5:29), who is later anointed by the penitent woman while

231

at table (7:36ff.) and feeds five thousand through the miracle of the loaves and fishes (9:12ff.). The seventy-two disciples are instructed to accept hospitality from those whom they visit (10:7); Martha and Mary eat with their friend and master (10:38ff.); Jesus discusses ritual law while dining with a Pharisee (11:37ff.); the reward of the faithful disciple will be a feast in the kingdom of God (13:29). Jesus is eating in a Pharisee's house when the dropsical man is brought to him (14:1ff.); this occasion also provides him with an opportunity to comment on humility and generosity (14:7ff.); and Luke gives an ample version of the great supper parable (14:15ff.). The prodigal son is welcomed home with a feast (15:23); the rich man at table ignores the need of Lazarus (16:19ff.); and Jesus accepts the hospitality of Zacchaeus (19:5ff.). While some of these scenes are found in the other Gospels, there is an evident emphasis in Luke that is hard to miss. As John Drury has noted: "Luke's editing of Mark shows a particular fondness for the dinner table as a setting."[1]

The same feature is notable in Acts also. The first Christians celebrate their unity by breaking bread together (2:42, 46), as they share everything they possess (4:32ff.). The first deacons are chosen to serve at the table of the needy (6:1ff.); Paul's blindness is cured by Ananias, and he immediately takes food (9:19); Peter is prepared for the conversion of Cornelius by a vision of food (10:9ff.), and he entertains the messengers from Cornelius (10:23) and is entertained in turn at Cornelius' house (10:48; 11:3). Lydia, once converted, provides hospitality for Paul (16:15), and the jailer whom Paul rescued from suicide sets food before Paul and Silas, though it must have been the wee hours of the morning (16:34). After curing the young man who fell from the window, Paul takes a meal, though it is again after midnight (20:7, 11). Finally, Paul insists that all take food as they prepare for shipwreck off Malta (27:33ff.). Some of these references to food are so unexpected and unusual that they can scarcely be dismissed as normal narrative details.

A Spirit of Tolerance

The table-fellowship that is highlighted in Luke-Acts is noteworthy not only because it manifests a spirit of generosity but also because it frequently serves as an occasion for association with companions who would not normally be invited to table. This is particularly true in the case of Jesus. "The actions and parables of Jesus in Luke are consonant with a concern for the social and religious outcasts of his day, particularly in his offer of table-fellowship to 'publicans and prostitutes' (5:29-32; 15:1-2; 19:5-7)."[2]

One sees everywhere in Luke's writings a gentle and temperate spirit that finds good in unlikely places and is not scandalized by the imperfect and the unclear. Drury refers to Luke's "whole rogues' gallery" of Gospel characters, noting in particular the unjust steward (Lk 16:1-8): "This resourceful villain would be at home in no other gospel: and here he is very much at home."[3]

Luke seems to be keenly aware of the fact that good and evil are rarely found in a pure state. One senses in him a man of deep conviction but of equally wide experience. This accounts for a certain mundane realism that sees "God's traces not only in the epic sweep of history but also in the roadside inn, the steward's office, at the evening dinner table and in the courts."[4] When one compares Luke with Matthew and Mark, he appears much less absolute and apocalyptic; there is in his judgments a definite spirit of tolerance and understanding.[5]

Fulfillment-Theology

Luke's hospitable disposition toward the pluralism that he found in the wide world of his experience was hardly just a feature of his personality. It derived rather from a profound insight that he gradually acquired as he pondered the meaning of what Jesus had done. Most authors tend to agree with Conzelmann[6] when he points out that Luke represents a transition from the view that Jesus was the end of history to the more realistic conclusion that there would be an era of the Church. A modern Christian finds it difficult to understand how painful it must have been for those earliest believers to deal with this conclusion that was being imposed upon them by history.

No doubt Luke's own more cosmopolitan background was a significant factor here. But it was still a major creative initiative for him to attempt in Acts a sequel to the Gospel. The need to cope with an unexpected new epoch enabled him to see implications in all of salvation history that had been somewhat obscured. No longer was it simply a matter of the messianic fulfillment of Israel's authentic aspirations with the ringing finality of apocalyptic judgment on all the world; now there was a historical future to be considered. This would mean evaluation and accommodation rather than condemnation and rejection.

If history has not been completed, it can only mean that the religion of Israel is meant for the whole world. To be a true Israelite now is to "make room," to show hospitality to the Gentile. Moreover, this new openness to the future leads to a new understanding of the past. Suddenly the tradition of Israel is full of new meaning, for the Messiah and for the world. No wonder the hearts of the disciples on the way to Emmaus were burning within them as Luke's Jesus, "beginning with Moses and with all the prophets, interpreted to them in all the Scriptures the things concerning himself" (Lk 24:27). Jesus is "the centre of the story of salvation. . . . This 'centre' divides the first epoch, that of

Israel, from the third and last epoch, that of the Church."[7] Moreover, this is a dynamic center from which the believer is asked to rediscover the meaning of the Old Testament as well as to be prepared for the adventure of unfolding history.[8]

The Final Banquet

Israel was justly proud of the promises that God had entrusted to her; she nurtured them and kept them alive by her faith. These promises spoke of a final victory, an era of peace and prosperity and a messianic banquet of joyful fellowship. All the evangelists see in Jesus the fulfillment conceived by God, not man. It went so far beyond human expectations that for one frightening moment it seemed to be no fulfillment at all. Israel looked for a Messiah; God gave her a Lord (Acts 2:36).

Luke is particularly sensitive to the implications of this fulfillment-beyond-fulfillment, because he sees with a special clarity that Jesus is the Lord of history and not just the Messiah of Israel. The era of the Church unfolds as the time of the Lord Jesus who works creatively in and through the Spirit.

All of this reveals profound new implications for the meaning of the messianic promises. They are enriched as they reach beyond national and earthly goals to the victory and fellowship that belong to divine dreams. The believers who can put aside their good but narrow hopes and allow themselves to entertain God's dreams will see both past and future illuminated and transformed. They are asked to make room endlessly for God's plans; they are challenged to show hospitality to a God turned stranger (Lk 24:16). But in the end it is God who becomes the host and spreads a banquet that eclipses the most daring human expectations. This banquet is large enough to embrace all, and its host is gracious enough to accommodate all possible varieties and disparities, both worldwide and ages long.[9]

II. LUKE 24:44-49

Tradition Reconsidered

"Then he said to them, 'These are my words which I spoke to you, while I was still with you, that everything written about me in the law of Moses and the prophets and the psalms must be fulfilled'" (Lk 24:44).

This text recapitulates the past, not only in the sense that it gathers the entire Old Testament together under its three classic headings but also because it summarizes all the teachings of Jesus while he was with them, that is, up to the time of his death. It is clear then that his presence with them now belongs to a new era. The meaning of this new presence is critical and decisive, but for the moment the focus of attention is on the past.

The challenge that Jesus places before his disciples is to reconsider the biblical tradition. This had been the familiar basis for their conversing with God. It was dominated by promise and thus had given meaning and direction to life. But it had turned stranger in these recent days. The disciples on the road to Emmaus summed it up poignantly: "We had hoped that he was the one to redeem Israel" (Lk 24:21). Popular and readily nurtured hopes of messianic salvation had been revived and enhanced by the eloquence and power of Jesus, only to be dashed. The brilliant flare of his early ministry died down and left them more in the darkness than ever.

But this tradition must be considered anew. It is like a friend who has been taken for granted and is assumed to have no surprises left. Both the old friend and the old scriptures must be entertained once more and allowed to reveal those deeper meanings. The past, too, has its own mystery but will divulge its secrets only if welcomed and treated hospitably. The "law of Moses and the prophets and the psalms" had much more to say about the Messiah than the disciples had ever suspected. It was an old friend who had not yet told all his stories.

The Scriptures Explained

"Then he opened their minds to understand the scriptures, and said to them, 'Thus it is written, that the Christ should suffer and on the third day rise from the dead . . .'" (Lk 24:45-46).

The Scriptures are full of surprises. But the greatest surprise of all is centered in Jesus. This man from Nazareth was singled out by God "with mighty works and wonders and signs" (Acts 2:22). Peter spoke for all of them when he drew the conclusion, "You are the Messiah" (Mk 8:29). But then began the abandoning and the suffering and the dying. Luke does not say simply that Jesus must suffer and die — that would have been bad enough. It is the Messiah, the Christ, who must die.

The Messiah was the point of convergence for all the hopes of Israel. He was the center of the promise. It was in the Messiah more than anywhere that God's fidelity was committed. It was unthinkable, then, that the Messiah should fail. But the facts, though unacceptable, were equally undeniable. When Jesus, on the way to Emmaus, pleaded ignorance about recent happenings, the disciples enlightened him, "Concerning Jesus of Nazareth, who was a prophet mighty in deed and word before God and all the people, and how our chief priests and rulers delivered him up to be condemned to death, and crucified him" (Lk 24:19-20). For Israel and the disciples, the word "Christ" could only mean hope and life. But now it was joined with that other word, "died," and they were stunned.

When Jesus now reminds the disciples that the suffering and dying of the Messiah was foretold by the Scriptures, he is not drawing attention to some forgotten or neglected texts of the Old Testament; he is pointing rather to the central message of all the Scriptures concerning the sovereignty of God that constantly challenges the faith and obedience of man. The dying of the Messiah was "necessary" because it was God's free choice. As such, it was a uniquely divine act; indeed he was "delivered up according to the definite plan and foreknowledge of God" (Acts 2:23). From God's side, this was intended to be and was a supreme act of love. But from the side of the disciples it was a disaster. "We had hoped that he was the one to redeem Israel" (Lk 24:21).

Jesus invites them to see this as mystery rather than tragedy. Their expectations have been dashed. God has become a stranger. It is time to practice a radical new hospitality! Jesus challenges them to make room for mystery, to entertain the "impossible." From a later perspective, it may appear that he simply asked them to look beyond the death to resurrection. Such a facile solution destroys the essential point. First there must be a radical opening to God in trust and an acceptance of mystery, and only then is that hospitality rewarded by God's resurrection surprise. At Emmaus, it was only *after* the disciples had offered hospitality to the stranger that he was revealed to them (Lk 24:29-31).[10]

Not only the disciples are involved here. All those who encounter mystery, which is mostly associated with the experience of human suffering and death, and make room for this unwanted stranger are thereby preparing themselves for recognition of the risen Lord. *The ultimate hospitality is, then, an entertainment of divine mystery in human life.* Table hospitality is but a sign and sacrament of this.

The Gentile Mission

". . . and that repentance and forgiveness of sins should be preached in his name to all nations, beginning from Jerusalem" (Lk 24:47).

If the condition for receiving God's resurrection gift is the accepting of God's dying Messiah, the proclamation must first be concerned with repentance, not primarily in the sense of regret, but rather as a renunciation of narrow and sectarian and merely human views that are not large enough for God's plans and God's mystery. Luke skillfully highlights the contrast between the rigid and scrupulous Pharisees and Jesus, who eats and drinks with sinners. And when Stephen sums up the sinfulness of Israel, he says that they have been "a stiff-necked people" (Acts 7:51). Repentance, then, means to turn away from a stubborn and obdurate position that cannot accept what is new and different and therefore cannot entertain God's mysterious ways.[11] It is ironic that this obduracy, as in the case of the Pharisees, is frequently a "religious" stance that turns out to be radically irreligious. Repentance is proclaimed, therefore, as the primary condition for receiving the gift of God.

The other side of the coin of salvation is forgiveness of sins. Just as sin in the Scriptures is never simply limited to sinful acts but embraces the whole condition and experience of bondage, so also does forgiveness or remission of sins represent an experience of release and liberation. It is God's hospitality as he responds to the new openness and readiness of man. God turns host as he entertains and nourishes those who embrace mystery with trust and courage.[12]

In the context of Israel as custodian of the promises, the classic sign of man's acceptance of God's mystery is welcoming and making room for the Gentiles. Israel is thus challenged to move beyond a narrow, sectarian view of her mission. Henceforth the whole world must share in the precious promises. This is asking for extraordinary openness and generosity, but it is the condition that will permit God to fulfill the promises in a way that far surpasses the best human expectations. It is not a question of Israel in some sense adopting the Gentiles; rather, the Gentiles have become, from God's perspective, an integral part of Israel, and this has been revealed in the dying and rising of the Messiah.[13]

It is not surprising that this proclamation of repentance and forgiveness is to go forth "from Jerusalem." It is well known that Luke is prejudiced in favor of Jerusalem. The reason is theological. It is in Jerusalem, where the Messiah is crucified, that the mystery of God in human history is most sharply portrayed. The crucifixion has become the decisive and paradigmatic sign of God challenging human faith, trust, and obedience, just as the resurrection has become the decisive and paradigmatic sign of God's gift of freedom and victory where divine sovereignty is accepted. In Luke's Gospel, Jesus moves obediently toward Jerusalem and sacrifice. After the testing and the victory, it is from Jerusalem that the Good News must go forth to all the world.[14]

"You are witnesses of these things. And behold, I send the promise of my Father upon you; but stay in the city, until you are clothed with power from on high" (Lk 24:48-49). The message of salvation that tells what happened at Jerusalem is entrusted to the apostles. They had been most sorely tested by the mystery, the strangeness of God, and they were now joyfully aware of the victory, the friendship of God. But their witness must be more than just an attesting to this fact of God's victory in Jesus; it must testify to the trustworthiness of all manifestations of the mystery that is God's presence in human history. Indeed, their witness declares that man must not only tolerate the strange and new and unwanted elements of life but that he must cheerfully greet them and search expectantly for the good in them. Like Abraham, the model believer, he must be a gracious and generous host for all the strangers in life (Gen 18). The apostles bear personal witness to the wisdom of practicing this most fundamental kind of hospitality.

Since the witnessing of the apostles is so much more than just the recounting of a personal experience, it requires the continuous and creative presence of the Father's promise, that is, of the Spirit. They are instructed to stay in the city until this power of the Spirit is conferred upon them to emphasize the fact that it is God's story, not some personal adventure, that is being entrusted to them. And precisely because it is God's story, its telling is controlled by God's calendar and its "director" will always be God's Spirit. For this story is more about God than man and can never therefore be controlled by man.

The mystery in the story derives from the fact that it is a story that is only partially completed. The sovereignty of God continues to challenge human courage and trust, and man's hospitality to this mystery in life continues to be vindicated and rewarded by the extraordinary hospitality of God. Jesus continues to be both paradigm and proof of the reality of both testing and victory. But it is no longer Jesus in the flesh; it is now Jesus in the Spirit.

Conclusion

Luke shows a special sensitivity for table-fellowship, not just for its own sake but also because it is a sign of a deeper kind of hospitality that entertains the strange and alien elements in life and looks for good everywhere. This large and generous spirit derives from his faith-understanding of the profound goodness hidden in the mystery of God.

God's mystery had been softened by attractive promises. Men eagerly claimed the promises and quickly defined them according to human expectations. But in the suffering and dying Messiah the mystery of God was reasserted in a dramatic and decisive way. To make room for this turn of events required great courage and much trust. This demanded a new kind of hospitality. Israel must henceforth make room for the Gentiles, not because they are Gentiles but because this is part of God's mysterious plan. And the people of God in all ages must entertain the sovereignty of God expressed in the events of life which, whether joyful or tragic, are never lacking in opportunity for faith and trust.

Man's best hospitality, however, is only a meager preparation for the lavish hospitality of God, first in the resurrection and Lordship of the Messiah, and finally in the heavenly banquet, where table-fellowship becomes a sign of definitive fulfillment and ultimate freedom.

NOTES

1. John Drury, *Tradition and Design in Luke's Gospel* (London: Darton, Longman and Todd, 1976) 146.

2. Ralph P. Martin, "Salvation and Discipleship in Luke's Gospel," *Interpretation* 30, no. 4 (October 1976) 374.

3. Drury, 78.

4. *Ibid.*, 175.

5. *Ibid.*, 182.

6. Hans Conzelmann, *The Theology of St. Luke*, trans. G. Buswell (New York: Harper & Row, 1960) 131–132.

7. *Ibid.*, 170.

8. Drury, 45.

9. John Navone, "The Lucan Banquet Community," *The Bible Today*, no. 51 (December 1970) 158.

10. Paul Schubert, "The Structure and Significance of Luke 24," *Neutestamentliche Studien für Rudolf Bultmann*, Beiheft 21 zur *ZNTW* (Berlin: A. Töpelmann, 1957) 172.

11. Jacob Jervell, *Luke and the People of God* (Minneapolis: Augsburg Publishing House, 1972) 42–43.

12. Drury, 153.

13. Jervell, 56–64.

14. Arland J. Hultgren, "Interpreting the Gospel of Luke," *Interpretation* 30, no. 4 (October 1976) 362.

Richard J. Dillon

EASTER REVELATION AND MISSION
PROGRAM IN LUKE 24:46-48

1. Introduction: Three Easter Episodes,
One Easter Story

St. Luke's Easter story is the literary and thematic intersection of his two volumes.[1] It works as a kind of axis in the structure of the sweeping history told to Theophilus, since it demonstrated to him the central concerns that the two books have in common and showed how these were to be pursued from the first book into the second. After the full story of "the third day" is told in the Gospel's twenty-fourth chapter, it gets a summary repetition in the first verses of Acts (1:1-11) — and not really a repetition at that, but a "flashback" fully characteristic of this author, with variation of detail, a noticeable shift of perspective, and admission of certain traditions that were not heard in the story's first telling.[2] Such an "axis" position of the story, at one book's end and the other's beginning, bespeaks the fusion of contents and argument that it effects between the two. It is at Easter, after all, that Luke's reader can join the Lord's historic following to experience the crucial point of connection between his ministry on earth and the mission to be carried out by others in his name. And these sequential ministries define the contents, respectively, of the Gospel and the Acts.

The Gospel's Easter narrative consists of three pericopes: one that is based mainly upon the empty-tomb account in Mark (Lk 24:1-12/ = Mk 16:1-8);[3] another that is a Lucan property altogether (Lk 24:13-35, the Emmaus story);[4] and a third that is partially based on a tradition shared with John's Gospel (Lk 24:36-53; cf. vv. 36-49 with Jn 20:19-29).[5] The three pericopes represent separate traditions that our evangelist has molded together into a single Easter story,[6] with an integral argument and a unified objective. This means that those factors in the narrative

240

that blend the three episodes into an internally consistent sequence are most likely the contribution of the evangelist to his traditional raw materials.[7]

To be specific: it serves the unity of argument in Lk 24 that a uniform framework of *time, place,* and *persons* has been superimposed upon the three pericopes, and this with the byproduct of conflict with other accounts of the sacred triduum, even Luke's own (Acts 1)![8] To show Easter's unity as the focal point of all sacred history before and after it, Luke has situated all three episodes on the same day, "the third day" of the Lord's own prophecies.[9] Correspondingly, he has localized all three in or close to Jerusalem, sacred history's geographical center; and to carry this out, of course, he had to exclude pointedly the resurrected Christ's appearances in Galilee, which were promised in Mk 16:7 and narrated in Mt 28:16ff. and Jn 21.[10] Needless to say, these are not adjustments motivated by the chronicler's passion for accuracy of fact and detail. Chronology and geography are determined by the sense of the events in Luke-Acts; they never become independent factors important in their own right.[11]

Finally, as the last and perhaps the most important ingredient of our chapter's framework, it all unfolds before a fixed gallery of *Easter observers* — we cannot call them "witnesses" till the end, Lk 24:48! — some of whom are brought out for trips to the tomb or the Emmaus repast, but all of whom are carefully regrouped at 24:33 for the story's finale. This paschal "gallery" was first taken note of back on Calvary, at Lk 23:49, where we heard that "all his acquaintances and the women who had followed him from Galilee stood at a distance and saw these things" (cp. Mk 15:40f.). Recall that Luke had not recorded the flight of the disciples from the scene of Jesus' arrest (as in Mk 14:50); rather, he kept all on hand to the end, and from their ranks he can now draw the *dramatis personae* of the triduum sequence. First, there is Joseph, who carries out the burial. Then come the women, who seem to cooperate with Joseph in the burial proceedings, rather than coming on as an afterthought, as in Mk 15:47. Indeed, the women are doing their part by preparing materials for the embalming when the sabbath overtakes them (Lk 23:56); and thus Luke explains the two-day hiatus between the burial and the great discovery.[12] After the women have made their stunning discovery, they return to the "gallery" at 24:9, reporting the news to "the Eleven and the rest"; but the group treats the story of the empty tomb as "womanly prattle" and disbelieves it (24:11). The textually uncertain verse 12 has Peter verifying the women's tale but uncertain of what to make of it.[13] Next, at 24:13, we are introduced to the obscure travelers of the Emmaus story, designated first as merely "two of them," that is, two from the "gallery." After their marvelous experience, they too rejoin "the Eleven and those with them," who were gathered at Jerusalem (24:33). Not the wayfarers' tale is told first, however, but the report of Peter, formerly the chief doubter, now the leading eyewitness of the risen Kyrios.

While the travelers are telling their story in turn, the final appearance occurs in a manner that belies all that has gone before it. The same sequence of incomprehension and revelation now unfolds before the plenary group, just as we followed it first in the company of the Emmaus pilgrims. And finally, at the conclusion of the group appearance, which is also, of course, the climax of the chapter, we hear the fully reassembled "gallery" appointed "witnesses of these things" (24:48). And suddenly we know why the group has been kept together since Calvary; indeed, we know what the whole Lucan Easter story is about. It is dedicated to telling us not just how perplexed observers became Easter believers, but how uncomprehending eyewitnesses were made *witnesses* of the risen Christ — sharers of his messianic destiny[14] and spokesmen of the word of forgiveness in his name to all the nations (24:47). The process of this recruitment of the missionary Church *in partu* is the story that Lk 24 tells, or better, the story it concludes. It is a story of frustrated human perceptions and the unconditional gift of Easter revelation.[15] It is thus a story with counterpoint motifs, with a dialectic of physical evidence and meta-physical disclosure, and with leading themes that develop concurrently and cumulatively.

We wish to concentrate, in this essay, upon the words of the risen Lord that comprise the final and conclusive instruction of "Easter day," Lk 24:46-48.[16] We are interested specifically in the logic that unites verses 46 and 47, and the logic that can sum up both those verses in the *toutōn* of verse 48. If we can discover the links in the arguments of these verses, we shall have every chance of laying hold of the basic idea of the whole Easter story, of which they form the obvious climax. And with the Easter story, of course, we shall have grasped the vital connective tissue between the two books of St. Luke.

2. Tradition-Analysis of the Third Pericope (Lk 24:36-53)

The appearance before the assembled disciples, Luke's third Easter pericope, consists of a narrative of the apparition (vv. 36-43), words of instruction by the still unacknowledged Kyrios (vv. 44-49), and a concluding scene in which joyous adoration is finally accorded the ascending Christ (vv. 50-53).[17] It is widely recognized that the appearance *narrative* is a fairly close rendering by Luke of a prior tradition that the fourth evangelist also utilized.[18] The rest of the pericope seems mostly Lucan, on the other hand, especially the words of instruction,[19] but probably the solemn concluding scene as well.[20]

It would be wrong to overlook the traditional basis for Luke's commissioning words, however, under the hasty assumption that only narrative details of the group appearance unite his Easter story with John's. First of all, the appearance to the full circle of disciples has been recounted according to a common schema in three of the Gospels: Mt 28:16ff. ("the Eleven"), Jn 20:19ff., and Lk 24:36ff. A standard sequence of "vision" and "audition" is followed in all three accounts,[21] and each shows the risen One overcoming his followers' uncertainty of his identity and commissioning them to carry out a mission for which he endows (or will endow) them. The three accounts differ enough that no single ancestor can explain them; and yet the stability of the two elements, the identity-motif and the mission mandate, persuades us of a traditional matrix whose varied developments have resulted from either oral tradition's reflexes or the evangelists' literary adjustments.[22] It stands to reason that the words spoken by the risen Lord to his astonished followers were prime opportunities of self-expression by the evangelists, and at least in the cases of Matthew and Luke, this seems to have involved the commissioning words above all.[23]

We have to modify this judgment with respect to Luke, however. Two basic components of the commissioning words are, in fact, part of the common material of Lk 24 and Jn 20: the forgiveness of sins as the mandated ministry, and the Holy Spirit as the enabling endowment for it (cf. Lk 24:47, 49; Jn 20:22-23). It is not very difficult to judge which version of this common tradition renders it more closely to its original form. The language and focus of the Johannine commission are quite uncharacteristic of the Fourth Gospel,[24] whereas nearly everyone recognizes the heavy hand of Luke in his version of the mission prospect.[25] What makes this passage inalienably Lucan is, first of all, its relation to the fact and plan of Luke's two volumes. The "commission" is really only an appointment, and the Spirit is promised, not bestowed. In this way, the actual inauguration of the mission, the very *raison d'être* for the Church, is postponed to the second book. The ascension will close out the days of Jesus, and the book of the Gospel therewith.[26] The actual Spirit-outpouring will inaugurate the life of the Church, and the proper subject matter of Acts therewith. Consequently, the "economy" of the risen Lord's mission program in Luke's version is inspired by "deliberate and controlling elements" of his overall literary plan.[27] Following these signals, we can now examine the editorial motifs in 24:44f. more closely.

3. Concerns of Luke's Composition in 24:44ff.

Distinctively Lucan also, of course, is the fact that the mission program is part of an instruction by the risen Christ that is devoted to exposition of the Scriptures (24:44ff.), and indeed, to the unveiling of their testimony in its totality. The same instruction, with a similar function in the recognition process, was recorded in the Emmaus story, at Lk

24:25-27. In each instance, the pathos of non-recognition is protracted and left unresolved prior to the Lord's words of instruction,[28] so that these obtain a special moment in the onlookers-to-believers' transformation that is the basic twist of both narratives. Both times, too, the instruction offers nothing new, but only repeats what the Master had announced to his followers during his lifetime (v. 44), implying a reproach of their disappointment and confusion on this "third day" (v. 25).

The words spoken are, in fact, the same as the perplexed women had heard from the angels at the tomb (v. 7); and there, too, they were merely a reminder of instructions already given (v. 6).[29] The words are those of Jesus' own prophecies of his passion (Lk 9:22; 9:44; 18:32f.), which are replayed no less than three times in the Easter story, as centerpieces of as many episodes (24:7, 26, 46).[30] They express the divinely appointed necessity (dei) of the Messiah's passion, wherein they locate the central truth of all the Scriptures. So it is that the Emmaus travelers are reproached for not having grasped "all that the prophets have spoken," namely: "Was it not necessary that the Christ should suffer these things, and enter into his glory?" (vv. 25f.). So too, at verses 44ff., an instruction on "everything written about me . . ." is captured in the sentence: "Thus it is written[31] that the Christ should suffer, and on the third day rise from the dead," — only here, the Scriptures' provision for a universal preaching of the forgiveness of sins is joined to the passion formula to express the total scriptural truth.[32]

Obviously, Easter revelation in Luke consists in a lifting of the veil of mystery that hung over the teaching of the earthly Jesus concerning his destiny. His death at men's hands is simply beyond the grasp of anyone who does not stand with the resurrected Christ, under his personal instruction, to view the whole dominical mission with his retrospect. As soon as a person does this, he is inevitably committed to the mission of an Easter *witness*, which will involve the appropriation of the Master's destiny and the carrying forward of his message of "release" for the sinner (see Lk 4:18; Acts 5:31; 10:43; 13:38; 26:18).

Thus the mystery of Jesus' passion, the one ingredient of Mark's "messianic secret" that Luke emphatically develops,[33] is featured in the Easter story on a precise schedule of concealment and disclosure. The editorial statements accompanying the second and third passion prophecies, in Lk 9:45 and 18:34, had already suggested that the veil was drawn over the Messiah's fate by God's own will and design.[34] Correspondingly, the moments of blindness and perception in the Easter witnesses are signaled by passive-voice expressions that clearly imply divine action as decisive of both.[35] At 24:16, for instance, we learn that the travelers' eyes *"were held* so that they did not recognize him," a sentence of parallel structure to Lk 9:45, attached to the second passion forecast: ". . . this word . . . *was concealed* from them, so that they should not perceive it." Accordingly, in 24:31, following the instruction and breaking of the bread by the Stranger,[36] the travelers' eyes *"were opened"* to recognize him, and they could subsequently relate how he *"was made known* to them in the breaking of the bread" (24:35). These evocative expressions find their complement in 24:45: "then *he opened their minds* to understand the scriptures," highlighting the same threshold of human blindness, even before overpowering physical evidence (vv. 39-43),[37] over which the Easter revelation made its entrance as unconditioned gift and rescue!

We sense that the delay of recognition in each appearance story is a Lucan editorial device for pinpointing the center and substance of the Easter revelation, and to show that faith was conceived as God's gift, not as a conclusion drawn from the evidence by human faculties unaided. Indeed, the victory of the Crucified is a truth that no human faculty can grasp, except through the faith that affirms the "righteous man's" victory on Calvary itself (Lk 23:46-48).[38] The Lucan "schedule" for the unveiling of this deepest of Christian mysteries was already implied in our evangelist's version of the concealment of the transfiguration experience, with its celestial dialogue, proper to Luke, concerning the Jerusalem "departure" to follow: "And they kept silence and told no one *in those days* any of the things they had seen" (Lk 9:36b/ *diff.* Mk 9:9).[39] So it is that the Easter disclosure of the "messianic secret," which Mark's Gospel anticipated (9:9) but left in the offing (16:8), Luke's Gospel fully records as its last word and climax.

Let us recall how this deep "secret" about the Messiah functioned in Luke prior to the last chapter. When it was declared for the first time, in Jesus' first passion prediction (Lk 9:22), it soon received both existential application to the lives of his disciples (9:23ff.; also 9:64ff.) and heavenly confirmation in the dialogue of the heavenly figures (9:30f.). Thus far, Luke was basing the presentation on Mark. On the other hand, when his enormous addition of non-Marcan materials began at 9:51, he gave it the faithfully Marcan framework of a continuous *journey to Jerusalem*, an expression of the messianic destiny in terms of a travelogue.[40] Here, the existential implications of the messianic destiny for the followers were brought to the fore consistently. The "journey" is conceived as a steady preparation of the "fellow travelers" for its appointed destination;[41] and expressive of this conception are not only the passion predictions bordering the travelogue-section at either end (9:44; 18:31ff.), but the exclusively Lucan thematic statement that comes in the middle of it: *"it is necessary* (dei) *that I travel onward today, tomorrow, and the next day, for it is inconceivable that a prophet should perish outside Jerusalem"* (Lk 13:33).

In view of this important structural plan of the Gospel's composition, it is surely no coincidence that the Emmaus disciples encountered the Stranger on an Easter *journey* (Lk 24:13, 15); that they express to him their befuddled disappointment over a mighty *prophet*, a prospective Savior, whom the leaders have put to death at Jerusalem (24:18-21); and that he dispels their misapprehension with a version of the passion formula that expresses the messianic destiny as the conclusion of a *journey*: "[it was] necessary that the Christ should suffer these things and enter into his glory" (24:26). The "entry" of this verse is a clear reminder of the "exit" foreseen at 9:31, in that the Greek prefixes are complementary: *eis-elthein* and *ex-odus*. Jesus' fulfillment of the Messiah's role is conceived in terms of a journey, and the heavenly destination of the journey was already announced at its inception (Lk 9:51: "the days of his being taken up"[42]). Christ, as fellow traveler to Emmaus, is nearing the journey's completion and explaining its necessity from the Scriptures. Moreover, the existential meaning of the journey for his disciples will be made explicit by Paul and Barnabas in words of consolation spoken after their dire circumstances at Lystra: ". . . it is through many afflictions that we *must* (dei) *enter into the Kingdom of God*" (Acts 14:22). The resemblance of this statement to Lk 24:26 is clear enough to convince us of the ultimate relevance of the Lucan "journey" pattern to the ideals of discipleship and mission.[43]

If Luke's "travel" patterns and terms thus have an ultimately ecclesiological (or better, missiological) point of reference, so also do the passion formulas, which are so closely related to them. This is the basic logic that brings the passion-mystery disclosure and the universal mission program together in the risen Lord's final instruction, Lk 24:46ff.

4. Passion, Resurrection, and Mission (Lk 24:46-47)

The third transcription of the passion formula in the Easter story is typical of Lucan "repetition and variation."[44] Over the course of their threefold rehearsal in Lk 24, the formulas have been augmented in a cumulative fashion, and a "conscious climactic effect" has been instilled in the ensemble.[45] First, the messianic enigma has gradually yielded to the messianic revelation, and this decisive turn in Luke's story is betokened by the shift from the mysterious "Son of Man" (v. 7) to the *Christos* (vv. 26, 46) as subject of the formulas.[46] Secondly, Luke's definition of the messianic "necessity" (*dei*) in terms of Scripture fulfillment has been brought out progressively and is now fully clear in the combination of the formulas in verses 44 and 46. And the "necessity" documented in *all* the Scriptures — Moses and the prophets and the psalms[47] — is that the Christ must "suffer" (v. 46a = v. 26a) and "rise from the dead on the third day" (v. 46b = v. 7b). Thirdly, the two phases of suffering and resurrection, previously expounded, are now augmented by a third, the universal proclamation of forgiveness in the

Lord's name, which has been foreshadowed in earlier passages of the Gospel[48] but never explicitly scheduled.

An instructive parallel passage to put next to the one before us is Acts 26:23, which is also the last word of a cumulative Lucan argument concerning the vocation of St. Paul. Recent studies have traced the editorial process by which, through the repetition of the Pauline conversion story in two *apologiae* later in Acts, the author has refashioned a legend of "the notorious persecutor subdued" into the story of a full-fledged vocation, on the same level with that of the first Easter witnesses.[49] This has been an overdue correction of the tendency to charge Luke with a systematic reduction of the stature of Paul over against the original "apostles" of Jerusalem.[50] Although the narrative of Acts 9 told of a blinding apparition that subdued the persecutor but withheld information on his future course from him temporarily,[51] the two speeches gradually diminish the intermediary role of Ananias (he disappears from 26:12ff.) and bring the conversion and commission aspects of Paul's vision into one single exchange with the risen One. The speech before King Agrippa, in Acts 26, brings this progressive argument to full statement; hence it rejoins Paul's own explanations of his calling (1 Cor 15; Gal 1) as a revelation by the Easter Christ equivalent to those he made to earlier witnesses.[52] As if to demonstrate that the last word is spoken on the subject as the Agrippa speech ends, we hear Paul's assertion there that, in obedience to the risen Christ's direct instruction, he stands *"bearing witness (martyromenos)* to small and great alike, saying nothing other than what *the prophets and Moses said* would come to pass: that *the Christ would undergo suffering*, and that, as first in the *rising from the dead*, he would *announce light both to the people and to the Gentiles"* (Acts 26:22-23). What could be clearer evidence that the "bottom line" of the speech is coequal association of Paul with the Easter-day assembly in the "witness" mandate? These lines are a restatement, typically transposed, of the very text that we are studying! All the ingredients are there: the disclosure of passion mystery and universal mission as the message of *tota Scriptura*, and the "witness" status of the Lord's draftee. The announcement to be borne abroad is only the unspecific "light," but just a few verses before, on the Lord's own lips, it was to "open the eyes" of the Gentiles: ". . . that they may turn from darkness to *light* . . . , that they may receive *forgiveness of sins* . . ." (Acts 26:18; see also 13:38 for the combination of "forgiveness of sins" and the verb *kataggelein*.)

There is one rather startling novelty about the Agrippa peroration, and that is that the risen Christ himself is represented as making the proclamation to humanity following upon his passion and rising. It is really he who speaks to the world in the mission and offers it forgiveness. The only other text in which this idea gets aired is Acts 3:26, the conclusion of an exegesis of Deuteronomy 18:15ff. in which Peter, preaching in the temple, proclaimed the risen Christ as the fulfillment of Moses' promise of a prophet like himself, to be "raised up" by God in days to come (see Acts 3:22-26).[53] In Peter's sermon, the Deuteronomy text is used to motivate the call to repentance, with the Messiah's persecutors being enjoined to heed the voice of the prophet like Moses lest they be excluded from the people of election (v. 23). That voice is Jesus' own, now heard through his preaching spokesmen. It is the voice of the risen Lord, the key to the truth of all the Scriptures.[54] Apparently it is the Easter event, in Luke's schema, that makes it possible to identify Jesus with the eschatological prophet, in Moses' image, in whom all the prophetic words of Scripture come to realization (see Acts 3:24f.; 7:37).[55] It is this thought that underlies the sequence of the Emmaus disciple's impression ("a prophet mighty in work and word . . . ," Lk 24:19; cf. the Moses description in Acts 7:22) and the instruction of the still hidden Master (Lk 24:25-27).[56] Even on the completion of his path to glory (Lk 24:26), the Messiah remains also "the prophet," to whom the *anastēsei* of Dt 18:15 belongs in a full and proper sense. His voice, and no other's, is the voice of the Christian mission!

Eschatological prophecy, therefore, is an important component of Lucan Christology, albeit an understated one.[57] The "prophet" designation is unmistakably applied to Jesus, but never in the kind of direct, credal affirmation that credits him with the messianic titles of *Christos* and *Kyrios* in, say, Acts 2:36. Its role is subordinate, but important nevertheless, since it offers Luke the key to the mystery of why, as Messiah, Jesus had to go to his death. It was, in fact, an odd tradition that helped him find this key, but the tradition's influence on his books is substantial. It is the tradition of the *prophets' violent fate at the hands of the Israelites*,[58] which Luke found in transmitted sayings of Jesus and to which he gave independent adaptations in the course of his sweeping history.

The tradition of the prophets' violent destiny is not a chronicle of Israel's rejection of her prophets. It is rather a pattern of reproachful exhortation to repentance, based on a Deuteronomic motif alleging that Israel had always rejected the messengers whom God had sent to urge her to change her ways.[59] Post-exilic embroideries of the Deuteronomic pattern began to accuse the Israelites of putting their prophets to death as well as repudiating their message, even though prophet-murder can hardly be documented in the prophetic or the historical books. Nehemiah 9:26 is actually the first instance of the prophet-murder accusation, after which Jubilees (1:12), Josephus,[60] and some apocalypses show that it gained currency in the intertestamental period.[61] Given its post-exilic emergence, the idea may well have been part of an attempt to interpret the tragedy of the Babylonian captivity and to learn its harsh lessons.

In any case, the accusation of prophet-murder by the Israelites had an ample background in Jewish tradition by the time it came into the sayings of Jesus, particularly those Matthew and Luke jointly drew from the source-stratum designated "Q." These include one where rejection is cited but murder is not (Lk 6:22-23/Mt 5:11-12), and then two major statements where Israel and Jerusalem are reproached as prophet-murderers. In Lk 11:49-51 (Mt 23:34-36), the Wisdom of God is quoted as mistress of the prophets: "I will send them prophets and apostles, some of whom they will kill and persecute, so that the blood of the prophets shed from the foundation of the world will be required of this generation. . . ." Here the solidarity between Israel's prophets and the latter-day messengers of Jesus is that of the persecuted and murdered spokesmen of the divine word. — In Lk 13:34f. (Mt 23:37f.), the murderess is Jerusalem, capital of the rebellious nation, and Luke joins to the "Q" passage his own proper logion to the effect that Jerusalem is the destined place of every prophet's demise (Lk 13:33, wanting in Mt).

Lk 13:33, the theme-statement of the "journey" section of Luke (see note 42), attests our evangelist's considerable interest in the old theme of ill-fated prophets on Israel. His interest is already evident in the sequence of the Nazareth episode (Lk 4:16-30), which everyone knows to be a passage of programmatic importance to the Third Gospel.[62] Pursuant to the rejected-prophet maxim of Lk 4:24, shared with Mk 6:4, one reads an exclusively Lucan passage that ends in the near-murder of Jesus by his compatriots. Hearing of the estrangement of Elijah and Elisha from their countrymen long ago (Lk 4:25-27), the Nazarenes presented an instance of prophet-rejection gone to the lengths of attempted prophet-*murder*! Indeed, the violent conclusion of the Nazareth scene makes the whole episode, with its prophetic proclamation, its references to Jesus' charisma, and its augury of his violent end, something of a condensed version of the Gospel story as a whole. "In a certain sense, it contains the whole of the Gospel already" (Schürmann).[63]

Turning to Acts, we find an important reservoir of traditions that influenced the Lucan vision of sacred history in the lengthy speech of the protomartyr, Stephen, in Acts 7.[64] His argument traces the maltreatment of Israel's prophets all the way back to Moses, the "prophet mighty in words and deeds" (7:22), whom the Israelites challenged and resisted before he could carry out his appointed role as their "leader and deliverer" (7:35; cf. 7:27ff.). At the end of his speech, Stephen arouses the lynch-mob by summing up his sweeping historical argument with a nearly perfect restatement of the Deuteronomic prophet-rejection schema[65]: "You stiff-necked people . . . , as your fathers did, so you do. Which of the prophets did your fathers not persecute? They killed those who announced beforehand the coming of the Righteous One, whom you have now betrayed and murdered" (7:51-52). After that, amidst his vision of the One whose passion furnished the (literary) model of his own,[66] Stephen himself comes to experience the inevitable fate of a prophet in Jerusalem (cf. Lk 13:33)!

It is clear that Luke found in the prophet-murder theme a major continuum of sacred history. As such, of course, it could not lie outside the divine intention, inscrutable as this might remain for the student of sacred history (cf. Lk 18:31-34/ *diff.* Mk 10:32-34). The fate of *all* God's prophets at the hands of God's people — which, according to Stephen, not even Moses escaped! — forms the unanimous testimony of *all* the Scriptures as to the necessary fate of the Messiah. His destined passion at Jerusalem was the realization of "all that was written by the *prophets* concerning the Son of Man" (Lk 18:31), and it is to be understood that Moses' testimony is part of that unison chorus (Lk 24:25, 27, 44; Acts 26:22f.).[67] A drastically schematized view of the testimony of biblical prophecy, to be sure. Yet Luke found in it the key to the mystery that came to light on Easter — the mystery of the fate of Jesus as Messiah; and not of Jesus only, but of those whom he commissioned as his witnesses and missionaries.

One naturally wonders what hermeneutical value might be found in the peculiar motif of Israel's perennial prophet-murder. We suggest it might be greater than appears at first sight. The tradition understood the rejected prophet to stand in the breach between God's realm and man's; God certifies and vindicates him, while men repudiate and seek to destroy him.[68] The nerve of this encounter, according to the Deuteronomic texts, was the prophets' call to repentance, warning Israel to turn away from her habitual disobedience of the Law.[69] Stephen could demonstrate Israel's rejection of the call to repentance both at the beginning (Acts 7:26-28) and the end (Acts 7:52f.) of her dealings with the prophets; and nevertheless, the mission of the resurrected Christ was again "to give to Israel repentance and forgiveness of sins" (Acts 5:31).[70] That is finally what makes the sorry prophet-history still a redemption-history, and not a history of unredemption. Brought to its climax in Jesus and his messengers, the prophets' tradition attests, not the incorrigible perversity of mankind, but the dauntless persistence of the divine will to forgive![71] This is the message, ultimately and essentially, that the risen Christ "announces" to the world through his "witnesses" (Lk 24:47f.; Acts 26:22f.; 13:38). Moreover, what surpasses the earlier prophetic messages in that of the risen One is precisely the gift of forgiveness, announced as a gift of the last days by all the prophets (Acts 3:19-26; 10:43), more effective and extensive, Paul would claim, than could ever have been obtained under Moses' Law (Acts 13:38).

In the last analysis, therefore, the word of forgiveness is the "eschatological prophecy" of Jesus. But his passion and resurrection partake of that prophecy in that they bring to a climax the long history of conflict between God's and man's designs, through all of which the divine will to forgive emerges triumphant. Rising up in victory to proclaim God's forgiveness, Christ brings to fruition all those earlier messages that called for reform but could only anticipate the forgiveness to come. By contrast, Christ's summons is "repentance *unto*[72] *the forgiveness of sins*" (Lk 24:47), and as such, it displays the final triumph of God over the persistent malice of men. In a full sense, therefore, *God rules* in the message of the risen Christ.[73] His death and resurrection are conclusive moments of this eschatological prophecy.

And with this, we hope to have explained how the messianic passion and resurrection came to be joined to the announcement of forgiveness in Lk 24:46-47 as correlative aspects of the fulfillment of *tota Scriptura*. All three belong to Jesus' conclusive prophecy, which both resumes and exceeds the experiences of all prophets before him. Moreover, given Jerusalem's role in the prophets' dire fate — at least as Luke has emphasized it (Lk 13:33; 18:31ff., etc.) — one can see that the last part of verse 47 belongs to the sentence structure depending on "thus it is written," no less than the rest of the two verses.[74] The Christian mission's "beginning from Jerusalem" is a substantive, keynote "beginning," not just a matter of geographical fact.[75] His ambassadors must share the destiny of Jesus as prophet; hence they can expect the path of their mission to be defined by its origin in Jerusalem, perennial prophet-murderess, just as the Master's path was defined by its destination in the city!

5. *The Word of Forgiveness (Lk 24:47)*

To show how the logic of Lk 24:46-47 serves the overall argument of Luke's two-part historiography, we must turn to the mission sermons of Acts, which illustrate the birth of the Christian Church in response to the apostolic preaching. The anticipation of the Acts' sermon-patterns in our verses has been pointed out often enough,[76] but we wish to take particular note of the fact that the logic of the sermons is already the logic of the passage at hand.

The focal point of the Acts oratory is precisely the collision of divine and human designs on the person of the Messiah, similar to what we found to be the basic assertion of the Deuteronomic tradition concerning the rejected prophets.[77] In the sermon-structure that the author repeatedly uses, the collision either motivates a final call to repentance (unto) forgiveness (Acts 2:38f.; 3:19) or — depending on the special narrative framework of a sermon — forges a direct link between Jesus' fate and the bestowal of forgiveness in an integral, divinely fixed protocol of salvation (Acts 5:31; 10:42f.; 13:38; cf. 17:30f.). In all cases, the forgiveness announcement constitutes the discursive goal of the mission sermon.[78]

The example of the premier mission sermon, Peter's Pentecost discourse, is the most effective for bringing out this pattern of argument (see Acts 2:22-39). Peter, addressing the Jews of Jerusalem, identifies the object of his audience's murderous rejection: "a man certified by God among you by powerful deeds and wonders and signs" (2:22). The syntax of the long sentence thus inaugurated, verses 22-24, shows that its main clause is the accusation of the audience, not the action of God: "*you killed him* by hanging him aloft. . . ."! The preceding reference to accrediting miracles and the subsequent resurrection statement (v. 24) are merely subordinate clauses to the accusation. Such an unorthodox kerygma, featuring men's action as its central thought, could only result from a thought-structure controlled by the concluding summons to the audience. And indeed, the powerful contrast between men's action against Jesus and God's action in him, first established in verses 22-24, returns in the climactic summation of 2:36: "*God has made* both Lord and Christ this Jesus whom *you crucified!*" And from here, the summons to repentance follows without any intermediate step (vv. 37ff.). The summons thus fully qualifies as the goal of the speech, and the dialectic of divine and human action is the discursive thrust towards the goal.[79]

It is important to remember that these sermon compositions of Acts are not direct messages from the author to his reader. That is to say, their purpose is not to convey the accusation of the Jews to the reader, but to illustrate the historical process that was served by the sermon and its argument.[80] The sermons' function is historiographical, therefore. For the most part, they illustrate the birth and formation of the Christian Church as *a forgiven people*, comprised of those who answered the missionaries' call to abandon a sinful past and receive forgiveness in Jesus' name. In the case of the Jews of Jerusalem, this meant turning from their perennial sin of prophet-rejection — indeed, the gravest instance thereof — to take their place in a chastened, forgiven Israel.[81] According to Luke, the Church did not lay claim to Israel's status as an outsider, but rather developed organically and gradually from the womb of Israel, as the result of a separation of repentant and obstinate Israelites that is still going on when the Book of Acts closes (see the last sundering at Rome in Acts 28:24!).[82]

The process of the ingathering can be observed already in Luke's passion story.[83] Jesus was brought to his death by a condemnation in which the people and their leaders were united (Lk 23:4f., 13). However, the two groups became disunited under the cross, the folk looking on while the leaders mocked (23:35). Finally, at Lk 23:48, the multitude is shown beating its breast and returning home as Luke rings down the curtain on the scene of the crucifixion. Does not this subtle process foreshadow both the apostolic preachers' accusation of the people and the repentance to which they called them? And does it not also account for the distinction made in two sermons between a hardened leadership and a public still susceptible to the call to repent (Acts 3:17; 13:27)?

It seems correct to say, with G. Lohfink,[84] that the apostolic summons to repentance, recorded in the first Acts sermons, began the process of assembling a forgiven Israel, a "true Israel," from the masses of homeland Jewry. Those who responded to the summons entered the chastened people, whereas those who resisted lost their right to the ancient title of election, "Israel." And thus does Luke explain, through the nexus of his two volumes, the birth of the Christian Church as a forgiven people,[85] heir to the status of God's people through his gracious gift.

We are now in a position to understand the unique importance of the forgiveness of sins in Luke's understanding of the continuity of salvation-history. The expression itself, *aphesis hamartiōn*, can be equivalent to "salvation" (Lk 1:77) or "being justified" (Acts 13:38f.) *simpliciter*.[86] Moreover, the fact that "forgiveness of sins" was the precise content of all the prophets' expectation about Christ is the final word of Peter's sermon in the first Gentile-Christian household, Acts 10:43. As early as Jesus' programmatic instruction in the synagogue of Nazareth, forgiveness (*aphesis*) proved to be the keyword of his reading from the prophet's book, as if to show one prophet saying what they all had to say. When we look closely at the tailoring of the text read by Jesus to his compatriots (Lk 4:18), we find an interesting conflation of two late Isaian passages that featured the word "release" (LXX: *aphesis*), Is 61:1f. and Is 58:6. The first text, which is the main one, contained the word but once: "to proclaim release to the captives." Reading on, we find the word a second time in a phrase brought in from Is 58:6: "to send forth the oppressed in release." This conflation could surely not be read in any "scroll" of the synagogue collection; it represents a Christian "splicing" of separate passages to form a doubly emphatic testimony to the messianic "release" offered by Jesus.[87] Whatever "release" the post-exilic "Isaiah" had in mind, there is only one sense that noun ever has in New Testament usage: it always means God's "release" of men from sin's bondage, hence his "forgiveness."[88]

Understood in this way, the prophet's *aphesis* proves to be a prolepsis of the message to be carried forth to the world in Jesus' name (Lk 24:47), as well as a summation of all that the prophets had to say about the messianic salvation (Acts 10:43). When Acts documents the carrying forward of this message in Jesus' name, it does so by showing that the offer of forgiveness was the constant focus of the missionary preaching, and that the preachers argued its basis in the unanimous testimony of the prophets about Christ. Peter argued thus in the temple sermon, for example, moving from the offer to its basis in Scripture (Acts 3:19-21/ 22-26) and declaring the arrival of the days of the prophet like Moses. Indeed, as we now know, the same Jesus who spoke out over the prophet's scroll to his kinsfolk and countrymen is also the speaker who proclaims the fulfillment of Scripture in the kerygma of the apostles. The voice is that of the eschatological prophet,[89] Moses' counterpart, end and fruition of the prophets' line, bestower of the gift of forgiveness just as they all had foretold.

6. The "Witness" Mandate (Lk 24:48)

Having discovered the logic that unites the passion and resurrection with the forgiveness of sins in the scriptural instruction of the risen Christ, we now inquire after the sense that the witness-mandate has right on the heels of that instruction. The short statement, "you are witnesses of these things," clearly makes the demonstrative pronoun, *toutōn*, refer to the whole statement of 24:46-47, not just to the "facts" of verse 46. This is already good reason to challenge the widespread view that Luke's "witnesses" are primarily "guarantors of the facts" on which the Christian message is based.[90] We are convinced that, to sustain the logic of the discourse in these verses, verse 48 has to commission some kind of integral representation to the world of what has been taught in verses 46-47, *in toto*.[91] But let us argue this in orderly steps.

a) First, total exposure to empirical fact in the present pericope, no less than in the preceding ones in Lk 24, led only to perplexity and "disbelief" (v. 41), not yet to the Easter faith. The latter comes only under elucidation of the "facts" by the risen Lord expounding the Scriptures; hence its witnesses had to be, above all, faithful exponents of his prophetic argument.[92] It is that argument, after all, that Luke has made the center of the Easter revelation.

b) The fact that the Easter "witness" was primarily an exponent of the Lord's "opening" of the Scriptures is confirmed by the assertions of apostolic "witness" status in the Acts sermons. One will notice that the assertions are usually made following the Scripture argument that interprets the paschal happenings (as in Acts 2:32; 3:15).[93] Especially instructive among the Acts statements is 10:42f., which places the "testifying" of the disciples (*diamartyresthai*) in conjunction with the "witnessing" (*martyrein*) of the biblical prophets to Christ.

c) It is perhaps most important to point out that, as exponents of the risen Christ's elucidation of the Scriptures, the Easter assembly became committed to "testimony" that was not to be rendered in word alone. Here is where our analysis of the prophet-rejection motif as Luke's hermeneutical key to the Old Testament's Christology can come to our assistance. We have already observed how Stephen cites the tradition of prophet-murder in Israel to explain the death of the Messiah and prepare for his own death (Acts 7:52ff.). It is, then, quite appropriate for Paul, entering the lists at Jerusalem, to refer back to Stephen as the risen Lord's "witness" (Acts 22:20). Not the mere fact of his death, of course, but the fact of his scriptural "testimony" to the perennial enemies of the prophets is what founds Stephen's claim to the "witness" designation.

And that is why Paul, too, can obtain the same title in a similar setting (Acts 22:15; 26:16).[94]

The association of the dominical "journey" to Jerusalem with the witness-status of the original followers, made in the famous "Pauline" statement of Acts 13:31, is probably to be explained along similar lines. The "journey," we recall, was a literary expression of the messianic destiny, pursued by Jesus out of a necessity (Lk 13:33) that the Scriptures attested (Lk 18:31ff.). The fact that this formative Christological experience was undergone by the disciples *with* Jesus (*synanabasin*, Acts 13:31) means they were prepared to embrace the "Jerusalem destiny" as their own. And once the risen Lord's instruction lifted the veil of mystery that hid the journey's meaning till its end, these fellow travelers could become his witnesses in this fullest sense.[95]

Some linguistic features of the tradition of the rejected prophets may explain Luke's association of it with the "witness" status of Jesus' followers. In the texts that belong to our prophet-tradition, the Hebrew word depicting the ministration of the prophets to Israel which she rejected — "admonishing" (to repentance) — was usually translated by the Septuagint with the Greek verb *diamartyresthai*,[96] which can also mean "testify," "bear witness." This trend of translation may account for the fact that when the tradition turns up in the second-century (B.C.) Book of Jubilees (1:12),[97] the Ethiopic translation of the book, which is the most reliable, designates God's spokesmen "witnesses" instead of "prophets." In view of this, can it be without reference to the same tradition that the function of "bearing witness" (*martyrein*) is ascribed to all the prophets in Peter's peroration, Acts 10:43? Chances are that Luke took the suggestion for the nature of testimony he ascribes to his Easter "witnesses" from the tradition of the prophets' violent fate in Israel, and particularly from the expressions of that tradition which came to him in his own Greek language and Greek Bible. The Christian *martyrium* before an obstinate and vindictive people could thus be shown to be the continuation of a classic trend of salvation-history. Our conclusion is that, for Luke, Easter witness meant the transmission of the risen Lord's "opening up" of all the Scriptures by a total reenactment of his "journey" on the part of the witness (see Acts 10:39). The existential corollaries of this in the mission were brought out by Luke's editing of Jesus' apocalyptic prophecies. Providing for the tribulations of his followers in the time before the end, Jesus foresaw the necessity of confession before hostile human magistrates — in Mark's words, "for my sake as a testimony to them" (Mk 13:9). Luke, in turn, devotes a separate sentence to the "testimony" and switches its focus from the recipients to the witnesses: *"This will befall you as testimony"* (Lk 21:13). The confessors' sufferings thus enter into the content of their testimony.[98] Moreover, a definite connection between Lk 21:12ff. and 24:46ff. is indicated by the fact that Mk 13:10 was dropped from that earlier context and saved for Lk 24:47, which seems to be our evangelist's version of it.[99] Lk 21:13 is thus found to make much the same affirmation as we find in 24:48; and Lk 21:12-19 qualifies as a commentary on the risen Lord's commission from the standpoint of the *ecclesia pressa*. Indeed, the redactional insertion of Lk 21:18 brings out the confessor's passage through death to salvation in the footsteps of the Master (see Acts 14:22; 27:34). Salvation "through Jesus' name" is, in essence and by necessity, passage through death, and so it must be that passion and death — and the integral course of which they are part — belong to the structure of Christian "witness."[100] In what possible sense can this be called resurrection-witness, on the other hand (see Acts 1:22)? It cannot be, of course, if one is bent on separating Jesus' death from his resurrection, supposing that Luke considered the death a mere "malfunction of world history" that "God repaired at Easter. . . ."[101] But does not our evangelist emphatically argue that Christ's passion was in full accordance with God's will, and that its meaning was the center of the revelation of Easter day? It followed a recurrent pattern of the prophets' fortunes that God willed, not as a mere negative moment in the historical process, but as positive testimony of his undaunted mercy and purpose to forgive, which become all the more effective where man's resistance is mightiest! The embattled prophets gave this testimony with their unheeded calls for repentance; and Jesus completed their testimony with a call to "repentance unto the forgiveness of sins," which he continues to make through his emissaries. His was consequently the eschatological prophecy, and Lk 24:47 makes it the essence of every Christian preacher's witness.

Here is where, in my opinion, the death of Jesus obtains its positive theological moment in Luke.[102] It was the most powerful of the historical Jesus' "prophecies," fully continuous with the ministry of forgiveness-proclamation that he inaugurated at Nazareth. The fact that he, against whom the greatest human wickedness was unleashed, *lives* to speak the word of forgiveness to sinful humanity (Acts 3:26; 26:23) — this is the conclusive testimony of God's love, the eschatological prophecy of his rule!

There is the basic logic that makes our passage coherent. It fully explains why Jesus' death, resurrection, and message of forgiveness stand together as both the Easter fulfillment of the Scriptures and the total commitment of Easter witness.

NOTES

1. Literature is surprisingly small and disparate. The following list is for the convenience of subsequent citation, which will be abbreviated. Entries fall into five categories.

(A) STUDIES OF LUKE 24 AND ITS SINGLE EPISODES: The only monograph on the whole
chapter is this author's *From Eye-Witnesses to Ministers of the Word. Tradition and Composition
in Luke 24*, Analecta Biblica 82 (Rome: Biblical Institute Press, 1978). — Other studies are:
Max Brändle, "Auferstehung nach Lukas," *Orientierung* 24 (1960) 85–89; Jacques Dupont,
"Les discours de Pierre dans les Actes et le chapitre XXIV de l'évangile de Luc," in Frans
Neirynck, ed., *L'évangile de Luc: Problèmes littéraires et théologiques*, Bibliotheca Eph. theol.
Lov. 32 (Gembloux: J. Duculot, 1973) 329–374; Jacques Dupont, "Les pèlerins d'Emmaüs
(Luc xxiv, 13-35)," in *Miscellanea Biblica B. Ubach*, Scripta et documenta I (Montserrat, 1953)
349–374; Jacques Dupont, "La portée christologique de l'évangélisation des nations d'après
Luc 24, 47," in J. Gnilka, ed., *Neues Testament und Kirche, für Rudolf Schnackenburg* (Freiburg
and Basel: Herder, 1974) 125–143; Josef Ernst, "Schriftauslegung und Au-
ferstehungsglaube bei Lukas," in J. Ernst, ed., *Schriftauslegung. Beiträge zur Hermeneutik des
Neuen Testaments und im Neuen Testament* (Paderborn: F. Schöningh, 1972) 177–192; Augus-
tin George, "The Accounts of the Appearances to the Eleven from Luke 24, 36-53," in P. de
Surgy et al., *The Resurrection and Modern Biblical Thought*, trans. C. U. Quinn (New York:
Corpus Books, 1970) 49–73; Robert Leaney, "The Resurrection Narratives in Luke (XXIV,
12-53)," *New Testament Studies* 2 (1955–56) 110–114; Gerhard Lohfink, *Die Himmelfahrt Jesu.
Untersuchungen zu den Himmelfahrts- und Erhöhungstexten bei Lukas*, Studien zum Alten und
Neuen Testament 26 (Munich: Kösel, 1971); Eduard Lohse, *Die Auferstehung Jesu Christi im
Zeugnis des Lukasevangeliums*, Bibl. Stud. 31 (Neukirchen: Neukirchener Verlag, 1961); I.
Howard Marshall, "The Resurrection of Jesus in Luke," *Tyndale Bulletin* 24 (1973) 55–98; C.
M. Martini, "L'apparizione agli Apostoli in Lc 24, 36-43 nel complesso dell'opera lucana,"
in É. Dhanis, ed., *Resurrexit. Actes du symposium international sur la résurrection de Jésus*
(Rome: Libreria Editrice Vaticana, 1974) 230–245; Heinrich Schlier, "Jesu Himmelfahrt nach
den Schriften des Lukas," in Schlier, *Besinnung auf das Neue Testament. Exegetische Aufsätze und
Vorträge* II (Freiburg and Basel: Herder, 1964) 227–241; Joseph Schmitt, "Le récit de la
résurrection dans l'évangile de Luc: Étude de critique littéraire," *Revue des sciences re-
ligieuses* 25 (1951) 119–137, 219–242; Paul Schubert, "The Structure and Significance of
Luke 24," in W. Eltester, ed., *Neutestamentliche Studien für Rudolf Bultmann*, Beiheft 21 zur
ZNTW (Berlin: A. Töpelmann, 1954) 165–186; Joachim Wanke, *Die Emmauserzählung: Eine
redaktionsgeschichtliche Untersuchung zu Lk 24, 13-35* (Leipzig: St. Benno-Verlag, 1973);
Joachim Wanke, "'. . . wie sie ihn beim Brotbrechen erkannten': Zur Auslegung der
Emmauserzählung Lk 24, 13-35," *Biblische Zeitschrift* 18 (1974) 180–192.

(B) COMMENTARIES ON LUKE'S GOSPEL: The situation in this category is scarcity and, in
the English language, downright drought. In English, after 1930, only two are scientific:
John Martin Creed (London: Macmillan, 1930; reprint ed. 1957), and A. R. C. Leaney,
Harpers N.T. Commentaries (New York: Harper & Row, 1958).

Of German-language commentaries, only two are complete and reasonably up-to-
date: Josef Ernst, Regensburger N.T. (Regensburg: F. Pustet, 1977), and Gerhard
Schneider, Ökumenischer Taschenbuch-Kommentar zum N.T. 3, 2 vols. (Gütersloh: Gerd
Mohn, 1977). Among older German commentaries, we make reference especially to Walter
Grundmann, Theol. Handkommentar zum N.T. 3 (Berlin: Evangelischer Verlagsanstalt,
²1961); Erich Klostermann, Handbuch zum N.T. (Tübingen: J. C. B. Mohr, ³1975); Josef
Schmid, Regensburger N.T., older series (Regensburg: F. Pustet, ³1955). Still incomplete
is the commentary of Heinz Schürmann, Herders theologischer Kommentar zum N.T. III
(Freiburg and Basel: Herder, 1969), of which only the first volume, Lk 1:1–9:50, is presently
available.

(C) STUDIES OF ST. LUKE AS REDACTOR AND THEOLOGIAN: Those better known to the

English-speaking reader offer meager instruction on Lk 24. They include: C. K. Barrett, *Luke the Historian in Recent Study*, Facet Books, Biblical Series 24 (Philadelphia: Fortress Press, 1970); Henry J. Cadbury, *The Making of Luke-Acts* (London: S.P.C.K., ²1958); Hans Conzelmann, *The Theology of St. Luke*, trans. G. Buswell (New York: Harper & Row, 1960); Helmut Flender, *St. Luke: Theologian of Redemptive History*, trans. R. H. and Ilse Fuller (Philadelphia: Fortress, 1967); Eric Franklin, *Christ the Lord: A Study in the Purpose and Theology of Luke-Acts* (Philadelphia: Westminster, 1975); Adrian Hastings, *Prophet and Witness in Jerusalem: A Study in the Teaching of Luke* (London: Longmans, 1958); Jacob Jervell, *Luke and the People of God: A New Look at Luke-Acts* (Minneapolis: Augsburg, 1972); Leander E. Keck and J. Louis Martyn, eds., *Studies in Luke-Acts: Essays Presented in Honor of Paul Schubert* (Nashville: Abingdon, 1966); I. Howard Marshall, *Luke, Historian and Theologian* (Grand Rapids: Zondervan, 1971); Charles H. Talbert, *Luke and the Gnostics: An Examination of the Lukan Purpose* (Nashville: Abingdon, 1966); S. G. Wilson, *The Gentiles and the Gentile Mission in Luke-Acts*, Society for N.T. Studies Monograph Series 23 (Cambridge: Cambridge University Press, 1973).

Of Lucan treatises in foreign languages, I list only those which are cited frequently in the present study: Hans-Werner Bartsch, *Wachet aber zu jeder Zeit: Entwurf einer Auslegung des Lukas-Evangeliums* (Hamburg-Bergstedt: Herbert Reich, 1965); Georg Braumann, ed., *Das Lukas-Evangelium: Die redaktions- und kompositionsgeschichtliche Forschung*, Wege der Forschung 280; (Darmstadt: Wissenschaftliche Buchgesellschaft, 1974); Michael Dömer, *Das Heil Gottes: Studien zur Theologie des lukanischen Doppelwerkes* (Cologne and Bonn: Hanstein, 1978); J. Dupont, *Études sur les Actes des Apôtres* (Paris: Editions du Cerf, 1967); Walther Eltester, "Israel im lukanischen Werk und die Nazarethperikope," in E. Grässer et al., *Jesus in Nazareth*, Beiheft 40 zur *ZNTW* (Berlin: W. de Gruyter, 1972) 76–147; Augustin George, "Tradition et rédaction chez Luc: La construction du troisième évangile," in I. de la Potterie, ed., *De Jésus aux évangiles: Tradition et rédaction dans les évangiles synoptiques*, Bibliotheca Eph. theol. Lov. 25 (Gembloux: J. Duculot, 1967) 100–129; Augustin George, "Israel dans l'oeuvre de Luc," and "Le sens de la mort de Jésus pour Luc," in *Revue biblique* 75 (1968) 481–525, and 80 (1973) 186–217, respectively; Richard Glöckner, *Die Verkündigung des Heils beim Evangelisten Lukas* (Mainz: Matthias-Grünewald Verlag, 1975); Gerhard Lohfink, *Die Sammlung Israels: Eine Untersuchung zur lukanischen Ekklesiologie*, Studien zum Alten und Neuen Testament 39 (Munich: Kösel, 1975); Peter von der Osten-Sacken, "Zur Christologie des lukanischen Reiseberichts," *Evangelische Theologie* 33 (1973) 476–496; Martin Rese, *Alttestamentliche Motive in der Christologie des Lukas*, Studien zum N.T. 1 (Gütersloh: Gerd Mohn, 1969); William C. Robinson, *Der Weg des Herrn: Studien zur Geschichte und Eschatologie im Lukas-Evangelium*, Theol. Forschung 36 (Hamburg-Bergstedt: Herbert Reich, 1964); Gerhard Schneider, *Verleugnung, Verspottung und Verhör Jesu nach Lukas 22, 54–71: Studien zur lukanischen Darstellung der Passion*, Studien zum Alten und Neuen Testament 22 (Munich: Kösel, 1969); Frieder Schütz, *Der leidende Christus: Die angefochtene Gemeinde und das Christuskerygma der lukanischen Schriften*, Beiträge zur Wissenschaft des A./N.T. 89 (Stuttgart: Kohlhammer, 1969); Ulrich Wilckens, *Die Missionsreden der Apostelgeschichte: Form- und Traditionsgeschichtliche Untersuchungen*, Wissenschaftliche Monographien zum A./N.T. 5 (Neukirchen: Neukirchener Verlag, ³1974); Josef Zmijewski, *Die Eschatologiereden des Lukas-Evangeliums: Eine traditions- und redaktionsgeschichtliche Untersuchung zu Lk 21, 5-36 und Lk 17, 20-37* (Cologne and Bonn: Hanstein, 1972).

(D) MONOGRAPHS ON THE RESURRECTION: The number of these is legion, and their fruits for the study of Lk 24 are widely varying. Among the more useful, I would list: John E. Alsup, *The Post-Resurrection Appearance Stories of the Gospel Tradition: A History-of-Tradition Analysis*, Calwer theol. Monagr. 5 (Stuttgart: Calwer-Verlag, 1975); Lyder Brun, *Die Auferstehung Christi in der urchristlichen Überlieferung* (Giessen: A Töpelmann, 1925); C. F. Evans, *Resurrection and the New Testament*, Stud. Bibl. Theol. II/12 (Chicago: Allenson, 1970); Reginald H. Fuller, *The Formation of the Resurrection Narratives* (New York: Macmillan,

1971); Hans Grass, *Ostergeschehen und Osterberichte* (Göttingen: Vandenhoeck und Ruprecht, ⁴1970); Jacob Kremer, *Die Osterevangelien: Geschichten um Geschichte* (Stuttgart: Katholisches Bibelwerk, 1977); and earlier Kremer, *Die Osterbotschaft der vier Evangelien* (same publisher, ³1969); Xavier Léon-Dufour, *Resurrection and the Message of Easter*, trans. R. N. Wilson (New York: Rinehart, Holt & Winston, 1971); Willi Marxsen, *The Resurrection of Jesus of Nazareth*, trans. Margaret Kohl (Philadelphia: Fortress, 1970); Ulrich Wilckens, *Resurrection. Biblical Testimony to the Resurrection: An Historical Examination and Explanation*, trans. A. M. Stewart (Atlanta: John Knox, 1978).

(E) MONOGRAPHS ON TOPICS PERTINENT TO OUR DISCUSSION: Norbert Brox, *Zeuge und Märtyrer: Untersuchungen zur frühchristlichen Zeugnis-Terminologie*, Stud. zum A./N.T. 5 (Munich: Kösel, 1961); Christoph Burchard, *Der dreizehnte Zeuge: Traditions- und kompositionsgeschichtliche Untersuchungen zu Lukas Darstellung der Frühzeit des Paulus*, FRLANT 103 (Göttingen: Vandenhoeck und Ruprecht, 1970); J. G. Davies, *He Ascended into Heaven: A Study in the History of Doctrine* (New York: Association Press, 1958); Daniel P. Fuller, *Easter Faith and History* (Grand Rapids: Eerdmans, 1965); Heinrich Kasting, *Die Anfänge der christlichen Mission: Eine historische Untersuchung*, Beitr. zur ev. Theol. 55 (Munich: Kaiser, 1969); Emmeram Kränkl, *Jesus, der Knecht Gottes: Die heilsgeschichtliche Stellung Jesu in den Reden der Apostelgeschichte*, Bibl. Unt. 8 (Regensburg: F. Pustet, 1972); Karl Löning, *Die Saulustradition in der Apostelgeschichte*, N.T. Abh. 9 (Münster: Aschendorff, 1973); Otto Michel, "Zeuge und Zeugnis: Zur neutestamentlichen Traditionsgeschichte," in H. Baltensweiler and Bo Reicke, eds., *Neues Testament und Geschichte . . . (für) Oscar Cullmann* (Zürich: Theol. Verlag, 1972); Ernst Nellessen, *Zeugnis für Jesus und das Wort: Exegetische Untersuchungen zum lukanischen Zeugnisbegriff* (Cologne and Bonn: Hanstein, 1976); Walter Radl, *Paulus und Jesus im lukanischen Doppelwerk: Untersuchungen zur Parallelmotiven im Lukas-evangelium und der Apostelgeschichte* (Bern and Frankfurt: Lang, 1975); Jürgen Roloff, *Apostolat-Verkündigung-Kirche* (Gütersloh: Gerd Mohn, 1965); Franz Schnider, *Jesus der Prophet*, Orbis bibl. et orient. 2 (Göttingen: Vandenhoeck und Ruprecht, 1973); Odil Hannes Steck, *Israel und das gewaltsame Geschick der Propheten*, Wiss. Monagr. zum A./N.T. 23 (Neukirchen: Neukirchener Verlag, 1967); Volker Stolle, *Der Zeuge als Angeklagter: Untersuchungen zum Paulusbild des Lukas*, Beitr. Wiss. A./N.T. 102 (Stuttgart: Kohlhammer, 1973); Allison A. Trites, *The New Testament Concept of Witness*, Society for N.T. Studies Monograph Series 31 (Cambridge: Cambridge University Press, 1977).

— N.B. Listings made in footnote 1 will be abbreviated in subsequent citations.

2. Instances: the "forty-day" perspective of Acts 1:3; the Baptist logion of 1:5; a delayed version of Mk 13:32 in 1:6f.; an alternate version of the ascension scene, 1:9-11. See Rudolf Pesch, "Der Anfang der Apostelgeschichte: Apg. 1, 1-11. Kommentarstudie," *Evangelisch-katholischer Kommentar, Vorarbeiten* III (Zürich: Benziger, 1971) 7–35.

3. Assuming the authenticity of the non-Western readings of Lk 24, according to a newly forged consensus of leading textual critics and exegetes. Lk 24:12 seems to have been omitted in the Western manuscript tradition because it conflicted with *both* Jn 20:3-10 and Lk 24:24! See Bruce M. Metzger, *A Textual Commentary on the Greek New Testament* (London and New York: United Bible Societies, 1971) 183f., 186f., 189–193; and for an excellent survey of the discussion which, nevertheless, reaches the opposite conclusion, Robert Mahoney, *Two Disciples at the Tomb: The Background and Message of John 20, 1-10* (Bern and Frankfurt: Lang, 1974) 41–69.

4. Beside the studies listed in note 1 above, an essay that deals effectively with the thought-structure of the Emmaus account, and sheds light on the overall *argumentum* of Lk 24 in so doing, is Hans Dieter Betz, "The Origin and Nature of Christian Faith According to the Emmaus Legend (Luke 24:13-35)," *Interpretation* 23 (1969) 32–46.

5. We understand the third pericope to include the ascension scene (vv. 50-53) as its organic and required conclusion. G. Lohfink has argued brilliantly and conclusively on this, in our opinion (see *Himmelfahrt*, 114, 147 ff.).

6. The underlying tradition is hardest to trace in the Emmaus story, where the structure and overall argument of the pericope are manifest products of Lucan theology. On the other hand, the pericope cannot be reduced to a Lucan creation from whole cloth (see J. Wanke, *Emmauserzählung*, 122 ff.; R. J. Dillon, *Lk 24*, 149ff.).

7. As J. M. Creed rightly comments (289), the Easter episodes' order and interconnection have been "imposed by the historian upon his materials, and the links are the least original part of the story."

8. The single day of Lk 24 versus the "forty days" of Acts 1 is only the most obvious of the conflicts. Luke's systematic revision of Mark with respect to the flight of the disciples (Mk 14:27, 50) and the provision for appearances in Galilee (cf. Lk 24:6f. and Mk 16:7) creates a conflict between the two books that admits of scarcely any resolution (cf. Lk 24:49; Acts 1:4!). — On the conspicuous Lucan "framing" of the Easter story, aimed at drawing the episodes into an integral picture, see L. Brun, *Auferstehung*, 85ff.; H. Grass, *Ostergeschehen*, 114; J. Kremer, *Osterbotschaft*, 80; A. George, "Tradition et rédaction chez Luc," 117–119; C. F. Evans, *Resurrection*, 95ff.; J. Wanke, "'. . . wie sie ihn beim Brotbrechen erkannten,'" 187.

9. Lk 9:22; 18:33, drawn from Mk 8:31 and 10:34. See also Lk 13:32f., from Luke's special material.

10. Luke's purposeful revision of Mk 16:6f., the angelic message at the tomb (see note 8 above), is a matter of nearly universal consensus among exegetes. See the commentaries, and P. Schubert, "Luke 24," 168; M. Brändle, "Auferstehung nach Lukas," 86, 89; U. Wilckens, *Missionsreden*, 116; E. Lohse, *Auferstehung . . . Lukas*, 18f.; H.-W. Bartsch, *Wachet*, 20–21; C. F. Evans, *Resurrection*, 103; R. H. Fuller, *Resurrection Narratives*, 97–98; Béda Rigaux, *Dieu l'a ressuscité: Exégèse et théologie biblique* (Gembloux: Duculot, 1973) 207; J. Kremer, *Osterevangelien*, 107f.

11. See H. Conzelmann, *St. Luke*, 27, 33, etc.; and in specific reference to Lk 24, J. Schmitt, "Le récit de la rés. dans . . . Luc," 238; G. Lohfink, *Himmelfahrt*, 115; A. Descamps, "La structure des récits évangéliques de la résurrection," *Biblica* 40 (1959) 726–741 (738).

12. Whereas, of course, Mark had the would-be embalmers starting out on the first day of the week, a rather implausible project to conceive on the third day after a death in the Palestinian climate (as Mark's critics have always pointed out). See Mk 16:1ff. — As against R. H. Fuller, however (*Res. Narratives*, 96), I do not think it is sufficient to explain Luke's editing as "an attempt to wrestle with the difficulties of the Marcan version." See R. J. Dillon, *Luke 24*, 12f.

13. On verse 12, see again note 3.

14. As this essay will attempt to show, there is an existential implication to the fact that the mystery of Christ's passion (24:26, 46) is made the focus of the Easter revelation by Luke. The solidarity between the Master and his disciples in the destiny of the passion is expressed, for example, in the parallelism between Lk 24:26 and Acts 14:22, and between the passion of Jesus in the Gospel and the harsh experiences of Stephen and Paul in Acts. The landmark in the career of Jesus that Lk 9:51 creates has its counterpart in Paul's career, at Acts 19:21.

15. I have tried to argue this case in my thesis on Lk 24, *From Eye-Witnesses to Ministers of the Word*. The title is based on the "becoming" that I believe to be expressed in the *genomenoi* of Lk 1:2, which is therefore not to be taken as uniting the two designations in an equalizing "were" (see *op. cit.*, 271, note 114).

16. Treatments of these verses, like J. Dupont, ". . . Luc 24, 47," tend to treat the elements separately and not to argue their coherence and interrelationship. Passion, resurrection, and mission are not isolated promises of the Scriptures that happen to come to realization together. They are a coherent unity constituting the central truth of all the

Scriptures; and Lk 24, with its unification of three separate pericopes, means to bring the coherence of the three moments of fulfillment to effective expression.

17. See G. Lohfink, *Himmelfahrt*, 114, and note 5 above.

18. This is *opinio communis* among the John commentators (see Bultmann, Brown, Schnackenburg), and students of the resurrection narratives as well. See J. Schmitt, "Le récit de la rés. dans . . . Luc," 230f.; P. Schubert, "Luke 24," 172; H.-W. Bartsch, *Wachet*, 26f.; J. Kremer, *Osterbotschaft*, 111; U. Wilckens, *Resurrection*, 50; R. H. Fuller, *Res. Narratives*, 139; X. Léon-Dufour, *Resurrection*, 82ff., 89ff.; B. Rigaux, *op cit.* (n. 10) 262f., 269f.; I. H. Marshall, "Resurrection . . . in Luke," 91. J. E. Alsup (*Appearance Stories*, 173) seems to lean towards a "common source" in writing (so also R. Leaney, "Resurrection . . . in Luke," 111; A. George, ". . . Lk 24, 36-53," 64, 67), but the difficulties of reconstructing any uniform account underlying the two (see J. Kremer, *Osterevangelien*, 198) leave the oral-tradition hypothesis as the solution acceptable to most.

19. The decidedly Lucan character of 24:44ff. was recognized even before the days of "redaction criticism" (see Rudolf Bultmann, *History of the Synoptic Tradition*, trans. John Marsh [New York: Harper & Row, ²1968] 286; Julius Schniewind, *Die Parallelperikopen bei Lukas und Johannes* [Hildesheim: Olms, ²1958] 92; J. Schmitt, "Le récit de la rés. dans . . . Luc," 231–232; H. Grass, *Ostergeschehen*, 292), and it needs no demonstration these days (see H. Conzelmann, *St. Luke*, 157ff.; U. Wilckens, *Missionsreden*, 98, note 1, and *Resurrection*, 53; J. Kremer, *Osterbotschaft*, 83, and *Osterevangelien*, 142, 152; G. Lohfink, *Himmelfahrt*, 149; H. Kasting, *Mission*, 43f.; R. H. Fuller, *Res. Narratives*, 116ff.; Chr. Burchard, *Zeuge*, 130f.; B. Rigaux, *op. cit.* [note 10 above], 260; I. H. Marshall, "Resurrection . . . in Luke," 91; E. Nellessen, *Zeugnis*, 111–117, esp. 117; M. Dömer, *Heil*, 99, 106). — It is only with mechanical vocabulary-analysis and supposition that J. E. Alsup resists this consensus and posits substantial "non-Lukan" material in the words of instruction and commission (*Appearance Stories*, 184ff.). His work is innocent of any acquaintance with Luke's mind and method that has been won by redaction criticism.

20. As against R. Pesch (*art. cit.* [note 2 above], 15), I feel the case for pre-Lucan tradition in the final scene is too meager to win the day. G. Lohfink's arguments for Lucan conception and authorship are convincing, to my mind (see esp. *Himmelfahrt*, 147–151).

21. L. Brun, *Auferstehung*, 54–64. See also C. H. Dodd, "The Appearances of the Risen Christ: An Essay in Form-Criticism of the Gospels," in Dodd, *More New Testament Studies* (Manchester: Manchester University Press, 1963) 104ff., 111, 113; A. Descamps, *art. cit.* (note 11 above), 739ff.; W. Marxsen, *Resurrection*, 79f., 83; A. George," . . . Lk 24, 36–53," 50, 59–64; H. Kasting, *Mission*, 46; J. E. Alsup, *Appearance Stories*, 173ff., 189f.

22. It is easy to see, for example, how the narrators became increasingly concerned to set the witnesses' doubt aside, given that their accounts run the gamut between no demonstration (Mt) and massive demonstration (Lk/Jn) of the apparition's physical reality. This development continues in the post-canonical literature, e.g., *Epistula Apostolorum* 12; Ignatius, *Smyrn.* 3, 2. — However, when we find bodily demonstration occurring in John's version of the appearance story (20:20) without being motivated by the doubt factor, we suspect that this is due to a postponement of the doubt by the evangelist himself, who makes it thematic of the subsequent Thomas episode, a Johannine vehicle of protest against the kind of faith that insists on supporting evidence. See J. Kremer, *Osterbotschaft*, 108ff.; W. Marxsen, *Resurrection*, 62; U. Wilckens, *Resurrection*, 51ff.; C. F. Evans, *Resurrection*, 117f., 125f.; R. H. Fuller, *Res. Narratives*, 141f.; J. E. Alsup, *Appearance Stories*, 173f. See the recent and convincing literary criticism of the Johannine narrative by Rudolf Schnackenburg, *Das Johannesevangelium* III, Herders theol. Kommentar zum N.T. IV/3 (Freiburg and Basel: Herder, 1975) 381, 390–391, 395, 398–399.

23. Whatever basis the final Matthean scene might have in prior tradition — R. H. Fuller thinks it was scant (*Res. Narratives*, 91) — it is clear that the words of the commission (28:18-20) express ideas that are basic to the rationale of his composition.

24. H. Grass, *Ostergeschehen*, 68; R. Schnackenburg, *op. cit.* (note 22 above), 385, 387f.; Gert Hartmann, "Die Vorlage der Osterberichte in Joh 20," *ZNTW* 55 (1964) 215.

25. I say "everyone" (see note 19 above), with J. E. Alsup the exception that proves the rule.

26. I avoid saying the "epoch of Jesus" in order not to imply support for the artificial division of Luke's historical perspective into three separate epochs, *pace* H. Conzelmann, *St. Luke*, 12ff., 16f.

27. Chr. Burchard, *Zeuge*, 131. See also W. Marxsen, *Resurrection*, 170ff.; R. H. Fuller, *Res. Narratives*, 118f., 140; H. Kasting, *Mission*, 42; J. E. Alsup, *Appearance Stories*, 186f.; J. Kremer, *Pfingstbericht und Pfingstgeschehen: Eine exegetische Untersuchung* (Stuttgart: Katholisches Bibelwerk, 1973) 226f.

28. Instance the recital of Cleopas in 24:19-24. Everything is correct. The observers had missed no essential information. And yet they had missed everything! Nothing had meaning for them, since only the light of Easter, illumining the Scriptures, could bring the disconnected, enigmatic facts together (see H. D. Betz, *art. cit.* [note 4 above], 35, 36). — The same situation prevails in the third pericope. Total physical display of the risen Lord cannot dispel the doubt of those who, up until a moment previous, had been discussing the experiences of Peter and the Emmaus travelers. In its curious way, verse 41 shows that belief did not follow the physical display, despite the mitigating expression "disbelieving for joy" (see J. Kremer, *Osterevangelien*, 141). And no notice of the inception of belief accompanies the risen Lord's taking of food (v. 43), which is at least ostensibly a probative measure (cf. Lk 8:55 and Mk 5:43). — As against those who consider the Visitor's repast in verse 43 to be a proof *ne plus ultra* of his physical reality and identity, it must be insisted that the evangelist awards it no such function in the course of his narrative, for no belief is recorded in its wake. Rightly insisting that the narrative of verses 36-43 makes no case by itself, apart from the instruction to follow, is C. M. Martini, "L'apparizione agli Apostoli. . . ," 231ff.

29. It is wrong, therefore, to consider the women's "remembering" in 24:8 to be an assertion of their *belief* in the angels' message (as, e.g., J. Schmitt, "Le récit de la rés. dans . . . Luc," 123, 125; H. Grass, *Ostergeschehen*, 33; C. F. Evans, *Resurrection*, 104). What is "remembered" by the women is an announcement whose content lay completely concealed from the followers when it was made by the Master; and this according to the emphatic statements of Lk 9:45 and 18:34.

30. It is to establish the continuity between the instruction of the earthly Jesus and the kerygma of the risen Lord that the prediction-formula recurs as revelatory proclamation in each of the Easter episodes. See U. Wilckens, *Missionsreden*, 98; and now M. Dömer, *Heil*, 90ff.

31. Luke firmly and explicitly equates "*it is necessary*" with "*it is written*" (cf. Lk 24:44, 46; 22:37; see H. Conzelmann, *St. Luke*, 153 [with note 3] 158; U. Wilckens, *Missionsreden*, 158f.; I. H. Marshall, *Luke*, 111).

32. There is no syntactical or hermeneutical reason to doubt that the universal preaching of repentance and (or unto) forgiveness is being presented as part of the Easter fulfillment of Scripture. See the commentaries, especially J. M. Creed (301) and E. Klostermann (242); also H. Kasting, *Mission*, 43; J. Jervell, *Luke*, 56; S. G. Wilson, *Gentiles*, 48; J. Dupont, *Études. . .* , 404, and ". . . Luc 24, 47," 128ff. The strikingly parallel passages in Acts 26:22f. and 10:43 say it with the fullest clarity: passion, resurrection, *and universal mission* of preaching (forgiveness), are the sequential stages of the realization of all prophecies by the risen Christ.

33. William Wrede already observed that the "messianic secret" of Mark had become a "passion secret" (*Leidensgeheimnis*) in Luke. See *Das Messiasgeheimnis in den Evangelien* (Göttingen: Vandenhoeck und Ruprecht, ³1963) 166ff.; also H. Conzelmann, *St. Luke*, 56, 64f., 197f.; W. Grundmann, *Lk.*, 189; H. Flender, *St. Luke*, 31, 41f.; J. Wanke, *Emmauser-*

zählung, 88; R. Glöckner, *Verkündigung* . . . *Lukas*, 156f.; F. Schütz, *Christus*, 65; M. Dömer, *Heil*, 81, 91f.

34. On the divine agency implied in the passive-voice expressions in Lk 9:45 and 18:34, see A. George, "Le sens de la mort . . . pour Luc," 206f., and the commentaries of A. Loisy, K. H. Rengstorf, J. Schmid, W. Grundmann, and J. Ernst, on the two passages (near unanimity on the issue, so far as we can see). See also, most recently, M. Dömer, *Heil*, 83.

35. Among the commentators, J. Ernst (508) joins E. Klostermann (183) in suggesting a relationship between the divinely willed enigma of the passion prophecies and the disclosure on the road to Emmaus. On the force of the passive-voice forms in verses 16 and 31, see H. Grass, *Ostergeschehen*, 37f.; E. Lohse, *Auferstehung* . . . *Lukasev.*, 30; C. F. Evans, *Resurrection*, 106; J. E. Alsup, *Appearance Stories*, 196f.; J. Ernst, *Lk.*, 659, 663f.

36. The Scripture instruction and "breaking of the bread" in the Emmaus story are not separate moments of the revelation by the Easter Christ but, according to Lucan conception, a coherent unity wherein the sacramental gesture completes the disclosure by word. This is not an exegete's "eisegesis," I insist, but is based on the pattern established on the two previous occasions where "breaking of the bread" occurs in the Gospel, i.e., Lk 9:12-17 and Lk 22:14-20. In each instance, the *fractio panis* was prelude to instruction by the Master concerning his harsh destiny and his disciples' participation therein (Lk 9:18-27; 22:21-38). Since the sequence has been achieved, in both cases, by decisive editing of his sources by Luke, we can take it as an intended Lucan statement that "breaking of the bread" is the sacramental expression of Jesus' sharing of his mysterious passion-destiny with his disciples. No wonder that recognition, based on the elucidation of this prior instruction, had to include both scriptural instruction and communion in the bread before it was complete. Note that instruction and *fractio* are now in inverse order vis-à-vis Lk 9 and Lk 22.

37. See again note 28 and its case against finding any successful issue of the physical demonstration in 24:36-43, apart from the instruction that follows.

38. This has seemed to me to be the import of Luke's novel employment of Psalm 31 at the crucifixion scene, in place of Psalm 22 (Mk). Not only are the words of the Crucified drawn from Ps 31:6 (=Lk 23:46), but the subsequent recognition of "the Righteous Man" by the centurion (23:47/ *diff.* Mk 15:39) seems to reflect the designation of the praying sufferer in the same psalm (31:19). See R. J. Dillon, *Luke 24*, 100f., n. 91; Anton Büchele, *Der Tod Jesu in Lukasevangelium: Eine redaktionsgeschichtliche Untersuchung zu Lk 23* (Frankfurt: J. Knecht, 1978) 53f., 83f., 87.

39. See W. Wrede, *op. cit.* (note 33 above), 167f., 175, 176; also H. Schürmann, *Lk.* I, 563. Notice that in Lk 9:36b, in contrast to Mk 9:9, it is not Jesus who imposes the silence, but rather the *time*, which simply did not permit as yet the understanding of the Messiah's destiny (cf. Lk 9:45; 18:34). In interpreting the messianic *krypsis* as thus a phase in the historical process, willed and controlled by God, Luke removes from it the overtones of strain and disharmony between Master and disciples over his fate (as in Mk 8:33).

40. Rightly H. Conzelmann, *St. Luke*, 65; W. Grundmann, *Lk.*, 199; M. Dömer, *Heil*, 83–89.

41. See H. Flender, *St. Luke*, 73ff.; W. Eltester, "Nazarethperikope," 85; G. Schneider, *Lukas 22*, 54-71, 199; P. von der Osten-Sacken, "Zur Christologie des lk. Reiseberichts," 479, 484, 495; David Gill, "Observations on the Lukan Travel Narrative and Some Related Passages," *Harvard Theological Review* 63 (1970) 213–214, 218–221; A. Büchele, *op. cit.* (note 38 above), 161ff.

42. The word *analēmpsis* in Lk 9:51 (cf. Acts 1:2, 11, 22) indicates that the "journey" commencing at Lk 9:51 does not reach its goal until the ascension, and that death and resurrection are stations on the one itinerary of the Messiah. So rightly E. Lohse, "Lukas als Theologe der Heilsgeschichte," in G. Braumann, *Lukasevangelium*, 72f.; J. G. Davies, *He*

Ascended, 40; E. Klostermann, *Lk.*, 111; H. Schlier, "Himmelfahrt," 227; H. Flender, *St. Luke*, 33, 95; J. Dupont, *Études*, 479; D. Gill, *art. cit.* (note 41 above), 202; P. von der Osten-Sacken, "Zur Christologie des lk. Reiseberichts," 479f.; E. Kränkl, *Jesus*, 166; W. Radl, *Paulus und Jesus*, 122f.; Michi Miyoshi, *Der Anfang des Reiseberichts Lk 9: 51–10: 24:Eine redaktionsgeschichtliche Untersuchung*, Analecta Bibl. 60 (Rome: Biblical Institute Press, 1974) 19. — It is wrong, therefore, to make *analēmpsis* in 9:51 refer either to Jesus' death exclusively (*pace* G. Lohfink, *Himmelfahrt*, 220) or to the heavenly ascension exclusively (*pace* P. Schubert, "Luke 24," 184f.). As "the days" indicates, the word should be understood as a designation of the "journey" in its totality.

43. P. von der Osten-Sacken, "Zur Christologie des lk. Reiseberichts," 495 (with note 80); W. C. Robinson, *Weg*, 38f.

44. See H. J. Cadbury, "Four Features of Lucan Style," in Keck-Martyn, *Studies in Luke-Acts*, 88–97.

45. P. Schubert, "Luke 24," 177. See also C. F. Evans, *Resurrection*, 109, and, on the climax pattern in the chapter, also J. Roloff, *Apostolat*, 188; G. Lohfink, *Himmelfahrt*, 113–114.

46. On the importance of *Christos* as title of the passion formula, see M. Dömer, *Heil*, 70ff., 78f., who finds in the destination to suffering the essential element of the Lucan portrait of Christ.

47. Luke views all of the old Scriptures as *prophecy*. This was clear from the citation of Moses in the company of "all the prophets" in 24:27 (cf. 24:25). Luke's varying formulas for citing all of Scripture — "the prophets," "the prophets and Moses," "the Law and the Prophets," "the scriptures" — are dedicated to expressing the unity and harmony of all sacred writ, never to singling out any of its components (so J. Ernst, "Schriftauslegung . . . bei Lukas," 178–179; cf. H. Conzelmann, *St. Luke*, 158f.). — The psalms, specified in 24:44 presumably because they will be crucial to the Lucan Christological hermeneutic of the Old Testament (especially in the Acts sermons), likewise fall into the category of prophecy, since David, understood to be the author of all of them (Lk 20:42 *diff*. Mk; Acts 1:16; 2:25, 34; 4:24), was a "prophet" before all else (Acts 2:30), thus author of songs that are a "repository of prophecy" (J. Dupont, *Études*, 265; also Conzelmann, *St. Luke*, 158 n. 1).

48. The universality of the mission has been foreshadowed in the admonition to the Nazarenes (Lk 4:25ff.), the mission of the symbolic Seventy(-two) (Lk 10:1-20), and the allegorical touches to the parable of the Great Supper (Lk 14:16-24, esp. 21ff.). See the study of these passages in S. G. Wilson, *Gentiles*. — So far as "forgiveness" as the mission's content is concerned, this, too, has been intimated in the choice of Scripture to be read by Jesus at Nazareth (Lk 4:18; see note 87 below).

49. Chr. Burchard, *Zeuge*, 120f., 129ff.; K. Löning, *Saulustradition*, 86f., 127.

50. It seems, for example, that G. Lohfink is still under the sway of this criticism in *The Conversion of St. Paul: Narrative and History in Acts*, trans. B. J. Malina (Chicago: Franciscan Herald Press, 1976) 98f.

51. The model for the account in Acts 9 is best represented in the Heolidorus legend in 2 Macc 3 (esp. 27–29), according to Burchard (*Zeuge*, 55ff.) and Löning (*Saulustradition*, 64ff.). Saul's counterquestion, "who are you. . . ?" is true to the literary form and underscores the non-revelatory character of the heavenly light according to that form (see Acts 9:5; 22:8; 26:15).

52. The reunion of apparition and revelation in the Agrippa speech has been prepared for in the two previous accounts: in Acts 9:17, by the introduction of the technical term of the Easter-appearance traditon, *ōphthē*; and in 22:17ff., by the separate, revelatory temple vision.

53. I tend to agree with J. Dupont (*Études*, 249) and F. Schnider (*Prophet*, 93) on the intended reference to Jesus' resurrection in the *anastēsas* of 3:26. Others prefer to make the

earthly mission of Jesus the point of reference (so U. Wilckens, *Missionsreden*, 43, 137, 163; J. Ernst, "Schriftauslegung. . . bei Lukas," 182f.; M. Rese, *Christologie des Lukas*, 70 n. 19).

54. Rightly Ernst Haenchen, *The Acts of the Apostles: A Commentary* trans. B. Noble & G. Shinn (Philadelphia: Westminster, 1971) 209: "Everything he says must be heeded — and he is now speaking through his Apostles. . . ." Why Haenchen then applies verse 26 to the earthly Jesus (209f.), I do not understand. Rightly F. Schnider, *Prophet*, 91f.

55. The introduction to Acts 3:22 — *Mōüsēs men*, etc., with corresponding *de* in verse 24 — shows clearly that Moses is to be reckoned with the "holy prophets from of old," already spoken of in verses 18 and 21 (see M. Rese, *Christologie des Lukas*, 68). Understandably, in the period prior to Easter — say, when the crowds acclaimed the miracle-worker (Lk 7:16) or a divided public opinion was recorded (Lk 9:7f.19) — the *Mosaic* dimension of Jesus' prophecy could not yet be brought out. The "prophet like Moses" is he who finally "opens" all the Scriptures and reveals their meaning.

56. Therefore, the disciple's retrospect in Lk 24:19ff. is not inaccurate nor expressive of some lesser, archaic Christology, *pace* R. H. Fuller, *Res. Narratives*, 110; I. H. Marshall, *Luke*, 125f.; J. Ernst, *Lk.*, 657, 660.

57. On the "prophet" motif as an important ingredient of Lucan Christology, see A. Hastings, *Prophet and Witness*, 50–75; Gerhard Voss, *Die Christologie des lukanischen Schriften in Grundzügen*, Stud. Neotest., studia II (Paris and Bruges: Desclée de Brouwer, 1965) 155–170; F. Schnider, *Prophet*, 237f.; W. Radl, *Paulus und Jesus*, 281ff.; R. Glöckner, *Verkündigung . . . Lukas*, 164ff.; E. Franklin, *Christ the Lord*, 67ff.; A. Büchele, *op. cit.* (note 38 above), 88–92.

58. Studied in detail by O. H. Steck, *Israel. . .* ; see digests of his analysis in U. Wilckens, *Missionsreden*, ³202ff.; F. Schnider, *Prophet*, 130ff.; R. J. Dillon, *Luke 24*, 257ff.

59. Old Testament texts, in which the murder element has not yet developed, are 2 Kg 17:13ff.; Jer 44:4-6; 2 Chr 36:14-16; Ezra 9:10ff.

60. The rejection statement shows a gradual development to the point where, in order to express the pre-exilic people's total resistance to Yahweh, she is made murderess of the prophets (see O. H. Steck, *Israel*, 79f.). A reflex of that development can be observed between the two texts in which Josephus employs the schema and the Old Testament texts on which he depends: *Antiquities* IX, 13, 2 (2 Chr 30:6-10) and *Antiquities* IX, 14, 1 (2 Kg 17:7-20). In the first text, the schema emerges in Josephus vis-à-vis his source, and prophet-rejection becomes prophet-*murder* in his writing (cf. *Ant.* X, 3, 1); in the second text, the historian respects his source and there is no violent-fate statement.

61. Obviously, the *novum* of Neh 9:26 has become self-understood by the time the schema is used in the New Testament (Jesus' sayings, and Acts 7:51ff.). On Nehemiah, see O. H. Steck, *Israel*, 71).

62. It is not necessary to decide whether Luke refashioned his Nazareth pericope out of Mk 6:1-6a (so R. Bultmann, *op. cit.* [note 19 above], 31f.; H. Flender, *St. Luke*, 146–147; W. Eltester, "Nazarethperikope," 135; M. Rese, *Christologie des Lukas*, 153f.; Ernst Haenchen, "Historie und Verkündigung bei Markus und Lukas," in *Die Bibel und wir. Gesammelte Aufsätze* II [Tübingen: J. C. B. Mohr, 1968] 167–169; M. Dömer, *Heil*, 57f.; Ulrich Busse, *Das Nazareth-Manifest Jesu: Eine Einführung in das lukanische Jesusbild nach Lk 4, 16-30*, Stuttgarter Bibelstudien 91 [Stuttgart: Katholisches Bibelwerk, 1977] 66f.) or whether, on the other hand, he drew it integrally from pre-existent source-material (so W. Grundmann, *Lk.*, 119; G. Lohfink, *Sammlung Israels*, 45, and others). Following the lead of H. Conzelmann (*St. Luke*, 35f. n. 2), R. C. Tannehill seems to judge sensibly: "Even if Luke found the text in some source in nearly the same form as he presents it to us, it is Luke who has interrupted Mark's order in order to place this scene at the beginning of Jesus' ministry, and it is within the context of Luke's work as a whole that themes from this scene are developed and interpreted" ("The Mission of Jesus according to Luke IV 16-30," in E. Grässer et al., *Jesus in Nazareth*, Beiheft 40 zur *ZNTW*; [Berlin: W. de Gruyter, 1972] 51). In

the same sense: E. Klostermann, *Lk.*, 61f.; J. Ernst, *Lk.*, 168–169; I. H. Marshall, *Luke*, 118f.; R. Glöckner, *Verkündigung . . . Lukas*, 126–127 n. 29.

63. H. Schürmann, *Lk.* 1:225.

64. As in the case of the Nazareth pericope, the question of Luke's sources arises with unusual urgency. It is undoubtedly oversimplified here to speak of a whole-cloth creation of the speech by Luke (so Johannes Bihler, *Die Stephanusgeschichte im Zusammenhang der Apostelgeschichte* [Munich: Max Hueber, 1963] 86; John Kilgallen, *The Stephen Speech: A Literary and Redactional Study of Acts 7, 2-53*, Anal. Bibl. 67 [Rome: Biblical Institute Press, 1976] 121, 163; apparently also S. G. Wilson, *Gentiles*, 149; *e contra*, and rightly, Martin Hengel, "Zwischen Jesus und Paulus. Die 'Hellenisten', die 'Sieben' und Stephanus [Apg. 6, 1-15; 7, 54-8, 3]," *Zeitschrift für Theologie und Kirche* 72 [1975] 186).

On the other hand, however, it may be too simple also to speak of a source-composition adopted without infusion of Lucan interests (so U. Wilckens, *Missionsreden*, ³208ff.; O. H. Steck, *Israel*, 265–269). I am inclined, however, to rule with these scholars, H. Conzelmann (*Die Apostelgeschichte*,² Handbuch zum N.T. 7 [Tübingen: J. C. B. Mohr, 1972] 57), E. Haenchen (*op. cit.* [note 54 above] 289), M. Hengel (*loc. cit.*), and others, in favor of a solid tissue of pre-Lucan tradition taken over in the Stephen speech. This tradition probably included the application of the Deuteronomic prophet-murder parenesis to Christian purposes (Acts 7:51ff., *contra* Haenchen).

65. See O. H. Steck, *Israel*, 265–269, also 99ff.; U. Wilckens, *Missionsreden*, ³215f.

66. So E. Lohse, "Lukas als Theologe der Heilsgeschichte," in G. Braumann, *Lukasevangelium*, 86; W. Grundmann, *Lk.*, 388; J. Bihler, *op. cit.* [note 64 above], 18f.; H. Flender, *St. Luke*, 54; M. Hengel, *art. cit.* [note 64 above], 190. See the reservations of Chr. Burchard, *Zeuge*, 29f.

67. See note 47 above, and note the parallel appeals to "the prophets" and "Moses and all the prophets" in Lk 24, 25, 27.

68. Thus is the whole career of Jesus resumed in the Pentecost speech, Acts 2:22ff. (echoing the Emmaus dialogue, Lk 24:19-27). You will recall that Pentecost was the day when the spirit of prophecy took hold of the whole *ecclesia in partu*, according to Peter's exegesis of Jl 3:1-5 LXX (esp. Acts 2:17-18, with the added *kai prophēteusousin* in 2:18).

69. See 2 Kg 17:13; 2 Chr 24:19; Neh 9:26, 29f. The schema's purpose in post-exilic Judaism was clearly to urge conversion upon the audience of the present, lest they continue the cycle of unredemption in which their forefathers were caught up (O. H. Steck, *Israel*, 321). The addressee of the futile prophetic missions and the audience of the prophet-rejection preaching are thus the same: all Israel. Conforming to this usage, Stephen's concluding words identify the audience with their ancestors' misdeeds and summarize the latter under disobedience to the Law (Acts 7:53; Steck, *op. cit.*, 266 n. 2).

70. Moses and Jesus are thus seen in the Stephen speech as terminal figures of the prophets' line. Luke is manifestly heir of this pattern of thinking. His adaptation of it appears in a crisp sentence of the Petrine kerygma, Acts 5:31, where the exalted Christ is endowed with "Mosaic" titles of "leader" and "savior" (see Acts 7:25, 35), whose effect is simply that Israel is given "repentance . . . and forgiveness of sins." What makes Jesus' ministry eschatological, vis-à-vis Moses, is apparently the offer of forgiveness, announced as a gift of the last days by all the prophets from Moses on (Acts 3:19-26), more extensive than could have been obtained under the Law of Moses (Acts 13:38).

71. R. J. Dillon, *Luke 24*, 286.

72. The reading *eis*, instead of *kai*, has the authoritative support now of P⁷⁵ as well as Codex B (Vaticanus). It may just be a scribal rationalization of *kai*, however, and one supposes this is why it was not adopted by K. Aland for the Bible Societies' *Greek N.T.*, or the forthcoming (Sept. 1979) Nestle-Aland²⁶.

73. See R. Glöckner, *Verkündigung . . . Lukas*, 185–187, 194f.; V. Stolle, *Zeuge*, 150. The "Kingdom of God" is the object of Paul's *diamartyresthai* in Acts 28:23, where we have

arrived at the world-capital, yet Jews are still being challenged and divided by the message (28:24). The story told in Acts is not of the rejection of Israel and the access of the Gentiles to salvation; rather, it is of the gradual emergence of a universal people of God, comprised of believers of every stock, won over to the message of forgiveness through the instrumentality of its embattled harbingers.

74. "Beginning," *arxamenoi*, is taken almost adverbially, but the masculine plural form accentuates that the "beginning" is for the missionaries and their destiny, not just for the mission as such. In other words, Luke's interest in Jerusalem as the prophet's city of doom best accounts for the unattached and ungrammatical participle. — For similar uses of the verb *archomai*, "begin," see Lk 23:5; Acts 1:22; and especially Acts 10:37 (and J. Dupont, ". . . Luc 24, 47," 126f., with n. 7).

75. Rightly E. Lohse, *Auferstehung . . . Lukasev.*, 37. — On the matter of Old Testament prophecy involving Jerusalem in this connection, see G. Lohfink, *Himmelfahrt*, 264, citing Is 2:3 as typical.

76. For example, U. Wilckens, *Missionsreden*, 98; A. George, "Lk 24, 36-53," 54f., and "Tradition et rédaction chez Luc," 119, 125, 126; J. Kremer, *Osterbotschaft*, 76; C. M. Martini, "L'apparizione agli Apostoli . . . ," 239ff. Detailed comparisons are displayed in J. Dupont, "Les discours de Pierre . . . et le chapitre XXIV. . . ," 332–345, 353; and the argument is resumed in Dupont, ". . . Luc 24, 47," 130f.

77. U. Wilckens believes that the prophet-murder schema, known to Luke from the Q tradition and his special sources (Acts 7:52), was adapted by him to the mission sermons attributed to the apostles before Jewish audiences (see *Missionsreden*, ³221, 223f., following O. H. Steck, *Israel*, 268). Whether or not this is a correct assessment of the tradition-history of the Acts sermons, there is no doubting the similarity of structure and affirmation between the apostles of the Acts and the preachers of repentance to Israel in the Deuteronomic tradition.

78. See Martin Dibelius, *From Tradition to Gospel*, trans. B. H. Woolfe (New York: Scribner, paperback 1965) 17, and *Studies in the Acts of the Apostles*, ed. H. Greeven, trans. M. Ling (New York: Scribner, 1956) 111, 165; H. Conzelmann, *St. Luke*, 227 with n. 3; J. Dupont, *Études*, 433–440, 460–465; U. Wilckens, *Missionsreden*, 54, 87ff., 98–100, 119–121.

79. On the clash of divine and human designs captured in 2:36, the climax of the speech, see U. Wilckens, *Missionsreden*, 34. — On the reference of "God has made . . ." in 2:36 to the whole kerygmatic portion preceding it, 2:22-35, and not just to its immediate context, rightly U. Wilckens, *op. cit.*, 36, 173, ³238, as against E. Haenchen, *op. cit.* (note 54 above), 187; J. Dupont, *Études*, 147ff.; J. Kremer, *Pfingstbericht* (cited in 27) 175, 208; E. Kränkl, *Jesus*, 159ff. Despite this widespread explanation of 2:36 with reference only to the heavenly exaltation (vv. 33ff.), we are convinced that Wilckens has better understood the thought-structure of the sermon (so also H. Conzelmann, *St. Luke*, 174 n. 3; M. Rese, *Christologie des Lukas*, 65f. with n. 96; apparently also G. Voss, *op. cit.* [note 57 above], 143f.). We had formerly subscribed to the other viewpoint (*Jerome Biblical Commentary*, 45:21).

80. I do not mean to contradict the renowned criticism of the Acts speeches made by Martin Dibelius, who saw that the speeches were not to be measured by the historical context to which Luke attached them, but were rather instruments of the author's direct address of his reader (see "The Speeches in Acts and Ancient Historiography," in *Studies in the Acts . . .* [note 78 above], 138–185). For this very reason, the interpreter must bear in mind the distinction between the point being made by the speaker to his listeners, according to the situation that is narrated, and the point being made by *Luke to his reader* through the composition of the speech. In Dibelius' happy phrase, this latter point is always "the directional sense of the event" at hand with reference to the *overall process of sacred history* to which Lk-Acts is dedicated (this phrase not well captured by the English translator of *op. cit.*, on pp. 125, 134; cf. pp. 110 and 118 of the original, FRLANT 60⁴ — Göttingen:

Vandenhoeck und Ruprecht, 1961). — ". . . less from the historical situation than from the context of the book as a whole," thus remains a valid principle for interpreting the speeches (see Dibelius, *op. cit.*, 174ff.).

81. For Luke, the name "Israel," like the designation "people" (*laos*), forms a salvation-historical continuum that includes all the followers of Jesus and from which the Jews who reject him are excluded (see H. Conzelmann, *St. Luke*, 145ff., 162ff.; W. Eltester, "Nazarethperikope," 125ff.; G. Lohfink, *Sammlung Israels*, 55, 58, 62). — J. Jervell sponsors the different view that "Israel" never refers to the Church composed of Jews and Gentiles in Lk-Acts, but designates only the repentant portion of the empirical Israel, to whose name the Christian Church does not lay claim (*Luke*. . . , 43, 49, 72 n. 22). — Attempts at nuance in the discussion, usually through distinction of the "empirical" and "eschatological" Israel, do not seem to shed light on the specifically Lucan use of the name (e.g., H. Flender, *St. Luke*, 132ff.; A. George, "Israel . . . ," 522f.). — See the following note.

82. An expression such as "the new Israel" is clearly not helpful toward an understanding of Luke's ecclesiology. If one uses "the true Israel," as G. Lohfink does (*Sammlung Israels*, 55, 60, 74; *e contra*, Conzelmann, Eltester, cited in previous note), he must remember that our historian means to show the Christian Church born out of the womb of the Israel of old, hence not as an outsider laying claim to Israel's historic prerogatives (rightly Lohfink, *op. cit.*, 74).

83. I think that the "wish" of Jewish-Christian ecumenism has been the "father of the thought" in the analysis of Luke's passion narrative offered by Gerard S. Sloyan in *Jesus on Trial* (Philadelphia: Fortress Press, 1975) 89–109. The Lucan account does not reflect an older, more reliable tradition when it records no verdict of death against Jesus as the outcome of the Sanhedrin deliberation (at Lk 22:71). Luke's purpose is to have the people and their leaders together in calling for the execution (Lk 23:4f., 13ff.), in order then to record the separation of people and leaders under the cross (23:35) and the beginnings of remorse among the people (23:48). All this sets the stage for the apostolic summons to repentance in Acts, where the leaders' separation from the people in a hardened rejection of Jesus is clearly implied (Acts 3:17ff.; also 13:27). — On the redactional patterns followed in the instances mentioned, see A. Büchele, *op. cit.* (note 38 above).

84. "During the period of the first apostolic preaching, the true Israel was being assembled from the ranks of the Jewish people! And that Israel which then remained obstinate in rejecting Jesus lost its right to be the true people of God . . . ," according to G. Lohfink's reading of Luke's thought (*Sammlung Israels*, 55; also 43).

85. The status of "forgiven people" will apply no less to later Christian adherents, since all must turn from a background of error and sin. This will be illustrated in the case of the Greek audience of the Areopagus sermon (Acts 17:30f.), where a past of ignorance and idolatry is the foundation of the preacher's typical, concluding call for repentance. The earliest Jewish audiences of the mission preaching thus set the tone for all who would be won over by it. Theirs was the situation of most serious guilt — the perennial guilt of prophet-murder in Israel — yet forgiveness was held out to them, and "those who were to be saved" (Acts 2, 47) accepted it!

86. See Acts 2:38ff.; 26:18; also 5:31; 10:43; Lk 3:3; 24:47.

87. Rightly H. Schürmann, *Lk.* I, 229; E. Haenchen, *art. cit.* (note 62 above), 164; M. Rese, *Christologie des Lukas*, 153; U. Busse, *op. cit.* (n. 62) 31ff. It is surely not enough to talk of a "free rendition" of the LXX (*pace* H./W. Bartsch, *Wachet*, 62), given the very specific addition to the basic text and the principle of its adhesion to the subject-matter thereof.

88. See R. Bultmann, in *TDNT* 1:511. — It is wrong to require that *aphesis tōn hamartiōn* appear in the quotation in order for the precise sense of *forgiveness* to be intended (thus U. Busse, *op. cit.* [note 62 above], 32), for Luke — or his tradition — is respectful of the source and, since it is a question of prophecy, is content to remain properly insinuative of the fulfillment.

89. See Acts 10:43; 20:21; 26:20. The argument of Peter in his temple sermon, in moving from the announcement (Acts 3:19-21) to its scriptural foundation (Acts 3:22-26), is precisely this identification of Jesus as the prophet, like Moses, whom all the prophets had anticipated. See notes 53–55 above.

90. So. N. Brox, *Zeuge*, 43–69; U. Wilckens, *Missionsreden*, 146f., and *Resurrection*, 70–72; Günter Klein, "Lukas 1, 1-4 als theologisches Programm," in G. Braumann, *Lukas-Evangelium*, 187; G. Lohfink, *Himmelfahrt*, 267–270; G. Schneider, *Lukas 22, 54-71*, 204ff.; E. Kränkl, *Jesus*, 167–175; I. H. Marshall, *Luke*, 42–43; C. H. Talbert, *Luke*. . . , 17–32.

91. The distinction between "witness of *facts*" and "witness of a truth or *viewpoint*," such as is advanced in the *"martys"* article by H. Strathmann in *TDNT* 4:480ff., is not appropriate for the Greek word's employment in the New Testament, and least of all in Lk-Acts. Rightly critical of the distinction in New Testament interpretation is O. Michel, "Zeuge . . . ," 19, 27; see also E. Nellessen, *Zeugnis*, 277.

92. Rightly Chr. Burchard, *Zeuge*, 133, 135, who would have done better, in view of his specification along these lines, to drop the depiction "vouchers for the facts" altogether. Similarly, despite his excessive emphasis on factual guarantee as Luke's objective, D. P. Fuller, *Easter Faith*, 224f. Most satisfactory in stressing the prior importance of the Lord's instruction in the equipping of the witnesses is J. Roloff, *Apostolat*, 191. See also V. Stolle, *Zeuge*, 149, 151; H. Flender, *St. Luke*, 159f.; C. M. Martini, "L'apparizione agli Apostoli . . . ," 235f., 241–242; apparently also C. F. Evans, *Resurrection*, 112.

93. Acts 5:32 declares: "And we are witnesses of these *words* (*rhēmatōn*)"; and even acknowledging a broader meaning of *rhēma* than purely linguistic, the content of 5:31, to which this statement directly refers (along with 5:30), includes the heavenly exaltation of Christ and the message of forgiveness, surely not "factual" data of the kind a "witness" can "vouch for"! Moreover, the co-witness of the Holy Spirit, which Peter claims, makes it plain as day that the *message* is the point of reference, and not the facts alone that form *part* of its content.

94. The insight that makes the *adversary-proceeding* between Jesus' spokesmen and a sinful humanity, typified by the accused Israelites, an ingredient of the Lucan "witness" conception has been sponsored in recent discussion by K. Löning, *Saulustradition*, 148ff., and (with respect to Paul and Stephen) V. Stolle, *Zeuge*, 144–147, 153f., 224f. E. Nellessen prefers to speak of a conclusion drawn from the context of the word's use in Acts, rather than an explicit component of the witness-idea (*Zeugnis*, 278); but we think this is a minimizing of the motif which, in view of the association of the *martyr*-vocabulary with the prophet-murder tradition (see notes 96–97 below), falls short of the full tradition-historical and redaction-critical data concerning this motif in Lk-Acts.

95. Paul, in his turn, will embark on a "going to Jerusalem" that will bring on the prison period of his ministry and the constant danger of death (see Acts 19:21 [Lk 9:51!]; Acts 20:22f.; 21:11-13). The "journey" will thus be no less symbolic of Paul's harsh destiny than it had been of the Lord's own. Appropriately enough, it will be only when that journey is over and Paul is Jerusalem's prisoner that the "witness" status will be conferred on him (Acts 22:15).

96. 2 Kg (LXX, 4 Kg) 17:13; 2 Chr (LXX, 2 Paralip) 24:19; Neh 9 (LXX, 2 Esdr 19):26.

97. R. H. Charles, ed., *The Apocrypha and Pseudepigrapha of the Old Testament in English* II (Oxford: Clarendon Press, 1913) 12: "And I will send *witnesses* unto them, that I may *witness* against them, but they will not hear, and will slay the *witnesses* also. . . ." On the text and its familiar prophet-murder schema, see O. H. Steck, *Israel*, 159–162.

98. As against J. Zmijewski (*Eschatologiereden*, 161–169), I do not think this statement expresses the altogether singular idea of a "testimony" of the exalted Christ in favor of the suffering confessors. It is for the gospel, not for the confessors, that "witness" is given in the *status confessionis* (so virtually all the commentators, e.g., E. Klostermann, 201; W. Grundmann, 381). We agree with E. Nellessen (*Zeugnis*, 105, 106) that our redactor meant

to bring out the quality of "witness" (=testimony) in the complete event of a Christian confessor's prosecution by an adversary tribunal.

99. So H. Conzelmann, *St. Luke*, 127f., 213 (with n. 1); H.-W. Bartsch, *Wachet*, 120f.; S. G. Wilson, *Gentiles*, 47–48; J. Dupont, ". . . Luc 24, 47," 131ff.

100. The connection between the status of suffering *confessor* and that of *witness* can be seen in the literary relationship between the statement of the newly converted Saul's future service to Christ, in Acts 9:15f., and Paul's restatement of the same mandate (delivered by Ananias) in Acts 22:15 (cf. also 26:16). Moreover, it is clear that Acts 9:15f. is an editorial enlargement of the prior tradition, not by a pre-Lucan redactor (*pace* K. Löning, *Saulustradition*, 32ff.), but by Luke himself, who expresses the risen Lord's plan for Paul in language deliberately redolent of the Christian *status confessionis* in a hostile world, as programmed in Lk 21:12-19 (see esp. Lk 21:17 as to "bearing the Name"; Chr. Burchard, *Zeuge*, 101; also G. Lohfink, *op. cit.* [note 50 above], 127f. n. 189).

101. E. Käsemann, *Der Ruf der Freiheit* [3] (Tübingen: J. C. B. Mohr, 1968) 167; cf. the English translation by Frank Clarke: *Jesus Means Freedom* (Philadelphia: Fortress, 1969) 125.

102. See R. J. Dillon, *Luke 24*, 279–290. We are suggesting the soteriological category of *martyrium*, in place of that of atonement, as a fruitful one in which to find Luke's positive evaluation of the death of Jesus. This suggestion derives from the analysis of Luke's passion narrative made by M. Dibelius, in *From Tradition to Gospel*, 201f.; also by H. Flender, *St. Luke*, 54; G. Voss, *op. cit.* (note 57 above), 110f., 118ff.; A. George, "Le sens de la mort . . . pour Luc," 207ff.; R. Glöckner, *Verkündigung*, 183ff.

John H. Sieber

THE SPIRIT AS THE "PROMISE OF MY FATHER" IN LUKE 24:49

> And behold, I send the promise of my Father upon you, but stay in the city, until you are clothed with power from on high (Lk 24:49).

The phrase "the promise of my Father" in Lk 24:49 refers to the Holy Spirit; the promise will be fulfilled at Pentecost (Acts 2). The same phrase appears once again in Acts 1:4, and the similar words spoken by Peter in Acts 2:33 constitute a third occurrence in Luke-Acts of this particular way of referring to the Spirit. Since the advent of the Spirit marks for Luke the beginning of the Christian Church, these references to the Spirit as the promise of God are significant for Lucan theology; nevertheless, they have received scant attention from most commentators. In this essay I hope to make a contribution to the study of this phraseology.

It is necessary to begin by reviewing the current status of Lucan studies; for if we are to understand these words about the Spirit, we shall need to do so in the light of the role that the Spirit plays in Lucan theology.[1] Studies in Luke-Acts today are dominated by the field of study called "redaction criticism" (*Redaktionsgeschichte*). This rather new branch of study attempts to inquire into the original author's theology, his intentions or purposes in writing as he did, rather than into such matters as literary sources or the historicity of the accounts. Redaction critics ask questions such as these: "Why did Luke arrange these stories in this order?" "How did he understand the use of the word 'promise' in this phrase?" "How does this thought fit into his theological framework as a whole?" The general result of the application of this type of questioning has been to deepen greatly our appreciation for the theological sensitivity and creativity of the evangelists.[2]

The fundamental work for redaction studies of Luke-Acts is that done by the German theologian Hans Conzelmann.[3] He has analyzed the basic purpose of Luke-Acts as the writing of what he calls "salvation history" (*Heilsgeschichte*). By this term he means that Luke intended for his books to relate the history of God's saving actions.

Conzelmann sees the Lucan schema for this salvation history as having three major periods or epochs. The central period is comprised of the public ministry of Jesus of Nazareth; the telling of its story takes up the major part of the Third Gospel. Jesus' ministry thus marks for Luke the midpoint of history, the central and crucial act of God for the salvation of humanity. The other two periods revolve around this central time. It was preceded by the epoch that Conzelmann calls the period of the Law and the Prophets, a time roughly contemporaneous with what Christians today generally call the Old Testament period. It was succeeded by the era of the Church, a time initiated by Pentecost and continuing on in time indefinitely; the Acts of the Apostles tells the story of its early years and presents Peter and Paul as examples for later Christians to emulate. Thus, as Conzelmann sees it, the period of the Law and Prophets served, in Luke's mind, to prepare for the coming of Jesus, while the Church bears witness to the fact that he has come and calls the world to repentance and the forgiveness of sins. This plan for salvation history can be summed up by the following outline:

1. The period of Israel, which ended with John the Baptizer as the last prophet (Lk 1:5–3:20).
2. The period of Jesus' public ministry (Lk 3:21–23:46)
3. The period of the Church (Acts 2:1–28:31).[4]

Between the ending of the second period (Jesus' ministry) and the beginning of the third (the Church's witness), Conzelmann has posited an intermediate or interim period composed of the resurrection accounts, the post-resurrection teachings of Jesus to his disciples, and Jesus' ascension (Lk 23:50–Acts 1:26). It is only the Lucan account that provides for this special time of instruction, just as Luke alone makes the ascension a separate event from the resurrection.

The major purpose in creating this period of time was to provide an opportunity for the risen Lord to give further teachings to his disciples. It is in the interim period, for example, that Jesus reveals to them the distinctively Christian interpretation of the Old Testament, especially as it related to understanding his death (Lk 24:26-27, 32, 44-45). By far the most important part of this post-resurrection teaching is Jesus' charge to his disciples to preach repentance and the forgiveness of sins in his name to all the world (Lk 24:47; Acts 1:8; see Acts 2:29-42). The wording of this command provides us with Luke's understanding of the mission of the Church, and it is comparable to the passage at the end of the Gospel according to Matthew usually called "the Great Commission" (Mt 28:28ff.). Before it can begin its witness, the Church must await what was promised of old, the coming of the power of God as Spirit (Lk 24:49).

The coming of the Spirit at Pentecost and later in subsequent baptisms is, therefore, essential to Luke's understanding of the work of the Church in the third period of salvation history. Upon closer examination, we discover that the Spirit's work is also important for the other periods as well. During the time of the Law and the Prophets, the Spirit was sent down to specific individuals from time to time; for example, the angel Gabriel announces to Zechariah that his son John "will be filled with the Holy Spirit" (Lk 1:15). A little later Mary is told "The Holy Spirit will come upon you" (Lk 1:35). Elizabeth herself is filled with the Spirit when she meets Mary (Lk 1:41), as is Zechariah later (Lk 1:67). In these passages as well as in the words of John the Baptizer in Lk 3:16, the work of the Spirit during the period of Israel is understood by Luke as that of preparing for the coming of Jesus.

The public ministry of Jesus constitutes "a redemptive epoch of a unique kind, in which the Spirit rests upon one person only, Jesus."[5] At the baptism of Jesus in Lk 3:22, the Spirit descends upon him as an answer to prayer. He enters the wilderness and, "full of the Spirit" (Lk 4:1), meets the temptation at the hands of Satan, and then returns victorious "in the power of the Spirit" (Lk 4:4). The public ministry itself is begun with these words from Scripture: "The Spirit of the Lord is upon me" (Lk 4:18).[6] Luke regards Jesus' full possession of the Spirit as a part of his anointing to the office of Messiah (Lk 4:18; Acts 4:27, 10:38). It is especially significant that the last passage about Jesus and the Spirit (Lk 10:21) occurs in the context of the return of the seventy disciples, where it prefigures the work of the Spirit during the period of the Church.

Besides describing Jesus as the unique bearer of the Spirit, Luke also assigns to him the task of sending the Spirit to his followers after his ascension. The usual New Testament opinion is that God sends the Spirit. John the Baptizer makes the first mention of Jesus as one who will baptize with the Spirit. Although the other synoptic Gospels report the saying (Lk 3:16 par.), Luke makes several small changes in it that explicitly point forward to Pentecost. The most significant of these is the addition of the words "with fire" to John's prophecy; they connect it securely with the Lucan account of the coming of the Spirit with "tongues as of fire" in Acts 2:3. In Lk 24:49 Jesus himself promises to send the Spirit, a promise repeated in Acts 1:4-5.[7] This promise of the Spirit was of particular importance to Luke and his Church, as a comparison of Lk 11:33 and Matthew 7:11 shows, for it is part of Jesus' assurance that the Spirit would aid the Church in times of persecution, an issue that was evidently crucial for the Church in Luke's day (Lk 12:12).[8]

The work of the Church began, according to Luke, with the descent of the Spirit at Pentecost (Acts 2:1ff.).[9] Under the Spirit's guidance, the disciples immediately begin to preach, bearing witness to people assembled from the whole world that God has made salvation possible through repentance and baptism in Jesus' name. The close parallels between this account and that of the start of Jesus' own ministry are signals that Luke regards the Church as continuing Jesus' mission. In full possession of the Spirit after Pentecost, the disciples will carry their message from Jerusalem to Rome, in fulfillment of the command of Jesus (Lk 24:47; Acts 1:18).

Thus, Luke understands the role of the Spirit as a decisive one for all three epochs of salvation history. Through the prophets the Spirit points ahead to Jesus. Jesus himself accomplishes his mission as the unique bearer of the Spirit. In the power of the Spirit the Church is enabled to carry out her mission to the world. It is against this larger picture that Lk 24:49 and the phrase "the promise of my Father" can be better understood.

The phrase "the promise of my Father" refers to the Spirit. Jesus commands his disciples to stay in Jerusalem and to await the fulfillment of this promise before beginning their witness to him. Acts 1:5 explicitly connects the promise to the Spirit, while Acts 2:33 joins it securely to the Pentecost account. The term "promise" is, therefore, for Luke a good word, because it signifies the promises of God, which are always fulfilled.[10] Other examples of its use support Luke's positive use of the word; for example, Abraham is said to be a recipient of the promise (Acts 7:17). Or, the promise refers to Jesus himself (Acts 13:23, 32). In a narrower sense the term "promise" is, for Luke, synonymous with the prophecy of Scripture (the Old Testament).

In Lk 24:49 the word "promise" is, therefore, used for the Spirit, because Luke is thinking about some prophetic promise or promises that he believes have been fulfilled by Pentecost. We must ask now exactly what promise he may have had in mind. The basic and obvious answer is provided by Luke himself in Acts 2:17-21, where he has Peter quote the prophet Joel as an essential part of the first Christian sermon. Since only Luke among the New Testament writers uses Jl 2:28-32 to explain the presence of the Spirit among Christians, it seems clear that it was this Old Testament prophecy that provided him with the necessary means of linking the work of the Spirit in all three periods of salvation history. Though the Apostle Paul knew of ecstatic speech and other gifts of the Spirit as end-time phenomena, he does not appeal to the Joel passage for support from Scripture.[11] To Luke, however, Joel's prophecy provides a major key for understanding the mission of the Church, for from now on it promises that all who confess Jesus' name and are baptized will receive the Spirit.[12] Furthermore, Luke's continuation of the quotation through the section on signs and wonders (Acts 2:19-21) shows that for him the coming of the Spirit marks the beginning of the end-time.

Most commentators on Lk 24:49 conclude their remarks about the promise at this point, if they bother to mention it at all. I would like to suggest that there are two other prophetic promises that Luke may also have had in mind when he calls the Spirit "the promise of my Father." The first of these prophecies has already been mentioned above in the section showing that Luke regarded Jesus himself as the sender of the Spirit. Although the verb "promise" does not itself appear on Jesus' lips in either Lk 24:49 or Acts 1:4, in both passages Jesus himself does promise to send the Spirit upon his followers.[13] Indeed, Acts 1:4 specifically states that it is from Jesus that they heard the promise. How can that be so? First, through the saying of Jesus quoted in the succeeding verse about the baptism by the Holy Spirit. Although this saying is elsewhere attributed to John the Baptizer, it is in Acts 1:5 credited to Jesus.[14] Second, there is in the term "promise" an oblique reference to the post-resurrection teachings of Jesus that included especially a reinterpretation of the Old Testament. That reinterpretation would presumably have included the passage from Joel as one exemplar. Thus, Luke himself may well have considered even his interpretation of Joel's prophecy to have been part of the teaching of the risen Christ. In both cases Jesus himself makes the promise about the sending of the Spirit.

If the argument about Acts 1:5 is valid, we ought to add also the words of John the Baptizer to the reasons for Luke's willingness to use the word "promise" in connection with the coming of the Spirit. John and his work in the Lucan scheme belong to the period of the Law and the Prophets. When John speaks his word about Jesus baptizing with the Holy Spirit in Lk 3:16, he speaks, in Luke's mind, as a representative of the prophets of old.[15] Luke's addition of the word "fire" to the text shows that he himself made this connection. Thus, only in the account of Luke-Acts is the prophecy made by John explicitly fulfilled.

I suggest, therefore, that Luke had three sets of prophecies in mind when he allows Jesus and Peter to refer to the Spirit as "the promise of my Father." He thought first of all of the Joel passage that promised the outpouring of the Spirit on all people in the last days. He believed that this prophecy had been fulfilled at Pentecost down to the last detail. At the same time he connected that Old Testament promise with the prophecy made by the last prophet, John the Baptizer, that Jesus himself would send the Spirit upon his disciples. Finally, he understood both of the above prophecies in the light of his conviction that Jesus himself was the sender of the Spirit and had promised to do so himself. Jesus' promise included both the interpretation of the old prophecies and the program for the mission of the Church, preaching repentance and the forgiveness of sins to the whole world under the guidance of the Spirit.

Before concluding the discussion of the Spirit as promise, it is necessary also to comment briefly on the appearance of the words "my Father" in the phrase. We note first that "Father" is not a preferred name for God in Luke-Acts; rather, Luke normally uses "God" (*theos*), a usage that reflects his Hellenistic training.[16] Nonetheless, in all three passages that refer to the Spirit as "promise," we also find the term "Father" for God. Indeed, it appears that the two terms are closely related in Lucan writings. In all, the word "Father" is used fifteen times in Luke-Acts as a reference to God, almost always in sayings he received from Q, a source in part common to Luke and Matthew. Its occurrence on the lips of the twelve-year-old Jesus is one of the non-Q instances, while its use in the Lord's Prayer is one of those from Q (Lk 2:29 and 11:2 respectively). Of the remaining thirteen uses, six are connected with words about the Spirit: Lk 10:21; 11:13; 24:49; Acts 1:4; 1:7; 2:33. We need to ask whether this concurrence is merely coincidental or has some special meaning.

We must begin with two rather technical observations. First, both the frequent use of "Father" in the Q source and the Christological expansions of that usage by Matthew argue that sayings using "Father" were remembered in traditions that come from Syria and Palestine. Second, the similarity between some of these Q sayings and some of those in the Gospel of John indicates that there may have been some relationship between the group that produced Q and the Johannine community; for example, the possible relationship between Lk 24:49 and several verses from Jn 14–16 has not been carefully studied. Exactly what these relationships might have been are work for future studies.

The origin of the use of "Father" for God in Christian traditions in general is not in doubt, however. It must be traced to Jesus himself, for studies have shown clearly that one of the most distinctive features of Jesus' manner of talking was his use of the word *Abba* for God.[17] Although *Abba* was translated into Latin as *Pater* and much later just as formally as "Father" in English, it was in fact a name used by small children for their fathers and was more akin in fact to the Greek *pappa* or the English "Daddy." It expressed, therefore, a close and intimate relationship, and through it Jesus taught his first followers to have that kind of attitude toward God. Since the Judaism of Jesus' day had increasingly magnified the distance between man and God, it was a striking and even revolutionary teaching, one that his followers remembered and passed along to succeeding generations of believers.

It would appear, then, that the use of the word "Father" in connection with the work of the Spirit was not accidental. It expressed for all early Christians their confidence that God was still active in their lives and ministry. Since for Luke both the existence of the Church and the carrying out of its mission depended upon the work of the Spirit, it was only natural that he express his confidence in the promises of God at these places with the use of the term "Father." For him, both terms — promise and Father — convey his confidence that God was faithful and that he would continue to send the Spirit to the Church of all ages.

NOTES

1. The author of the twin work Luke-Acts will be called Luke for the sake of convenience. Although it is impossible to know his name, the consensus about him is that he was a Hellenistic Jewish Christian who wrote between 80 and 90 A.D.

2. Those readers to whom the work and methodology of redaction criticism is new may wish to consult the article by R. T. Fortna, "Redaction Criticism" in *Interpreter's Dictionary of the Bible*, Supplementary Volume, 729–735.

3. Hans Conzelmann, *The Theology of St. Luke*, trans. Geoffrey Buswell (New York: Harper & Row, 1960). A summary of Conzelmann's position can be found in most of the newer introductions to the New Testament, e.g., Norman Perrin, *The New Testament: An Introduction* (New York: Harcourt, Brace, Jovanovich, 1974), 200–205. A critique of Conzelmann is offered by Eric Franklin, *Christ the Lord* (Philadelphia: Westminster Press, 1975).

4. See Conzelmann, *St. Luke*, 16–17.

5. Conzelmann, *St. Luke*, 184. See also note 4, 180, and 173–184 for his longer discussion of Jesus and the Spirit.

6. Many of the references to Jesus and the Spirit show that Luke understands spirit in terms of power, especially the power to perform miracles and accomplish God's will. See Conzelmann, *St. Luke*, 181–183.

7. See R. J. Dillon and J. A. Fitzmyer, "Acts" in *JBC*, 174–175.

8. See Carroll Stuhlmueller, "Luke," in *JBC*, 117.

9. Conzelmann, *St. Luke*, 213–215. In Luke's understanding, the Spirit cannot be sent until Jesus ascends and is exalted as the Messiah. See Franklin, *Christ the Lord*, 29–34.

10. In non-Jewish circles the word "promise" usually had negative connotations. Promises were made when no results were intended. For the larger discussion of the meaning of the word, see the article by J. Schniewind and G. Friedrich, "epangelia," in *TDNT* 2:576–586.

11. Gal 3:14 and Eph 1:13 may indicate that there was a non-Lucan tradition that spoke of the Spirit in terms of the word "promise."

12. In its own historical setting, the Joel prophecy was probably meant as a comment on the words of Moses in Num 11:24, a wish that all people might become prophets of God. In the Book of Joel the promise itself refers only to Israel; Luke's use of the prophecy extends its range to include also the Gentiles. See also J. A. Thompson, "The Book of Joel," in *The Interpreter's Bible* 6:752–754.

13. The "I send" of the RSV translators, while technically correct, should be understood as a future tense, "I will send" or "I am going to send."

14. Dillon and Fitzmyer, "Luke," 169, say that this attribution illustrates "the tradition's tendency to assimilate the two figures, John and Jesus." My argument is that Luke changed the attribution because of his conviction that Jesus was the sender of the Spirit.

15. After this paper was written, a brief comment on the possibility of connecting Lk 3:16 with the promise was discovered in W. Baird, "The Acts of the Apostles," in *The Interpreter's One-Volume Commentary on the Bible*, ed. Charles Laymon (Nashville: Abingdon, 1971), 730b.

16. Most commentators agree that Luke, prior to his conversion to Christianity, had been either a Hellenistic Jew or a Gentile god-fearer.

17. See the articles on "abba" by G. Kittel in *TDNT* 1:5–6 and by G. Schrenk on "patēr" in 6:984–990.

David Stanley, S.J.

SIGNIFICANCE FOR PAUL
OF JESUS' EARTHLY HISTORY

Query About a Scholarly Consensus

I propose here to question an assumption with regard to Paul's attitude to Jesus' earthly history, that many present-day scholars appear to accept as an incontrovertible axiom, namely, that Paul set little value by the details of the earthly history of Jesus.[1] It is my own conviction, on the contrary, that this fairly prevalent minimizing of the function of Jesus' history in Pauline thought can obfuscate the understanding of Paul's presentation of the Christian life as a continuous advance from sin to salvation. Moreover, if one is to see the theology of Paul in proper perspective, it is imperative to realize that the celebrated thesis of justification by faith is *not* the focal point of Paul's proclamation of the gospel, "the dynamic power of God leading to salvation" (Rom 1:16). That thesis is indeed of supreme value for orthodoxy, but the place of privilege in the theological thought of Paul must be accorded to Christ risen as "the last Adam" (1 Cor 14:45).[2] Finally, to exaggerate the significance of Paul's seeming silence about the details of Jesus' life is to leave unexplained his constant emphasis upon the value of tradition and also his insistence upon "imitation," a theme characteristic of his spirituality. Nor, in fact, does this hypothesis leave room for an adequate explanation of Paul's "mysticism of the apostolate."

Some Preliminary Considerations

The truth that Christianity, like the religion of Israel, is a historical, not a mythical religion is one that Paul fully subscribes to: that God has acted from within history to reveal himself to mankind. He sees human history as reaching its majority with the incarnation of God's only Son, "born of woman, made subject to law" (Gal 4:4), "born of the seed of David according to the flesh" (Rom 1:3). He recognizes the relevance of man's history — Adam to Moses, Moses to Christ, Christ to the termination of history (Rom 5:12-21) — for a proper evaluation of what God has effected in Christ. In Galatians and Romans, Paul sets great store by the reality of God's promise to the first historical person mentioned in the Bible, Abraham. His anguish at his own race's refusal to accept the gospel, his preoccupation to explain the partial blindness of God's people as temporary, not as total rejection, are only comprehensible in the context of Paul's deep respect for the historical.

The mention by Paul of two visits to the apostles in Jerusalem, particularly in an *apologia*, where he is intent upon defending his own apostolic commission as in no sense derivative from any human authorization, surely implies a concern to learn more about the Christian traditions regarding Jesus' life and teaching. The stated purpose of the first visit was "to get to know Cephas," or perhaps better, "to interrogate Cephas" (Gal 1:18). On the second occasion he exposed privately to "the men of repute" his own gospel, "to make sure that the race I had run, and was running, might not be run uselessly" (Gal 2:2). Such concern to question those who had personally followed Jesus during his mortal life surely implies more than a mild interest in the teaching of Jesus as a criterion against which to measure the authenticity of Paul's own preaching.

It is frequently stated, in extenuation of the comparatively rare allusions by Paul to any saying or action by Jesus, that this is the consequence of writing letters, not a Gospel. That these are two distinct forms of literature is undeniable. Paul, it is agreed, wrote real letters to real Christians with real problems, arising from their earnest attempts to live the gospel. He is undoubtedly solicitous to help his readers apply Jesus' teaching to their concrete historical situation.

Yet is it not in fact a relic of the fundamentalist approach to the Gospels to think of them as biographies of Jesus? Surely Mark's purpose in creating the Gospel-form, a type of literature that is unique and without any real parallel outside the New Testament, is much closer to that of Paul than has sometimes been estimated. Redaction criticism as well as Form criticism has sought to alert us to the profound evolution undergone during the pre-Gospel period and through the innovative refashioning on the part of each evangelist, by his rephrasing of Jesus' words and composing narratives of his public ministry and passion. This means, of course, that the words of Jesus attributed to him in any Gospel have been reinterpreted, reformulated, adapted, and lived on, by two or three generations of anonymous Christians (the *Formgeschichtler*). In this way they have become part of that tradition, to which the evangelist, Mark for instance, has in turn, by his editorial realignment, frequently imparted a new sense through his positioning of them in the context of his book (the *Redaktionsgeschichtler*). Thus Norman Perrin shrewdly observes:

> We see, therefore, that the Gospel material represents a flowing together of past, present, and future. It takes the form of stories and sayings from the past because the Jesus who speaks is the Jesus who spoke and because the Jesus to come as Lord/Son of man is the Jesus who came as eschatological prophet. There could have been no Gospel at all without the conviction that Jesus was to be known in the present as risen, and there would have been no Gospel of Mark without the conviction that the risen Lord had a message for the church for which Mark wrote.[3]

Now it is interesting to recall that no Redaction critic considers Mark to have had no interest in the traditions regarding what Jesus said and did. Indeed, that interest constitutes the motivation prompting the evangelist to fashion his own distinctive version of Jesus' actions and sayings, so as to give them a contemporary relevance for the suffering community to which he addressed his Gospel. Willi Marxsen, one of the earliest Redaction critics, draws a parallel in fact between Paul and Mark. Mark, he notes, "proceeds, as does Paul, from the *Kyrios*. But what is unique is that he does not, as Paul, develop his message conceptually, but by visualization. For this purpose he appropriates pieces of the tradition known to him and shapes them anew into *one* proclamation, *one* gospel."[4]

Paul's Concern for the Evangelical Tradition

The point I am attempting to make is that once the viewpoint of the recent techniques in Gospel-criticism be accepted,[5] the too-often repeated assumption that Paul displayed little if any interest in Jesus' earthly career should be subjected to radical revision and stated in more nuanced fashion. A perusal of Paul's letters will disclose the high reverence in which he, as one who never knew Jesus during his public ministry, regards them, and his repeated acknowledgment of his own indebtedness to his predecessors in the Christian faith for "handing on" to him those materials that he "received" and then handed on, via his gospel, to those communities he founded (1 Thess 2:13; 4:1-2; 2 Thess 2:13, 15; Phil 4:9; 1 Cor 11:23; 15:1-2, etc.). It is indeed true that Paul includes but a single narrative from Jesus' life (1 Cor 11:23-25). He does, however, allude to Jesus' teaching explicitly (1 Thess 4:15; 1 Cor 7:10; 9:14; Rom 14:14; Col 2:6-8).[6]

Paul's emphatic refusal to "know Christ according to the flesh" (2 Cor 5:16) must not be taken as unconcern for what the evangelical tradition had preserved of Jesus' words and activities. Indeed, a precious proof of the authority these held for him can be gathered from his habitual practice of calling Jesus' words a command or saying "of the Lord," the risen Christ. He asserts that he "had received from the Lord" the account he gives of Jesus' words and actions at the Last Supper (1 Cor 11:23ff.).

A remark by Paul, often misunderstood by commentators, is relevant here. "The gospel preached by me is not of human origin; nor did I receive it from any human being, nor was I taught it except through a revelation (*apokalypsis*) by Jesus Christ" (Gal 1:11-12). Günther Bornkamm rightly rejects the suggestion that "For the primitive Church's traditions about Jesus, Paul substituted his own vision of Christ," since "In that case . . . he would have been a disruptive 'enthusiastic' crank who, for the sake of his own experience, jeopardized the unity of the church."[7]

What then is the meaning of this lapidary statement? It expressed Paul's consciousness that to "receive through tradition" was to him no natural process of data-gathering, but a profound, personal experience of the action of the risen Christ through his Spirit as dynamic agent of the gospel.

"Become Imitators of Me, As I Am of Christ" (1 Cor 11:1)

The conception of *imitation* is peculiar to Pauline theology, and, except for 3 John 11 and Hebrews 6:12; 13:7b, the verb or the adjective is not used elsewhere in the New Testament. The basic reality underlying the expression is not some kind of external copying in behavior; rather, it is analogous *experience* felt within the person. Thus Paul can say of the Thessalonian community in its endurance of persecution, "You indeed have become imitators, brothers, of the churches of God in Judea" (1 Thess 2:14).

Mostly, however, Paul proposes himself as the concrete model for those communities of which he is founder (2 Thess 3:7, 9; Phil 3:17; 1 Cor 4:16; Gal 4:12). This imitation of himself is in reality oriented to the imitation of "the Lord" (1 Thess 1:6), "of Christ" (1 Cor 11:1). While he does not use the term "imitation," he twice holds up Christ as an example to be followed for Christian conduct (Rom 15:2-3, 7). The case is different in the hymn (Phil 2:6-11) Paul cites, where any human imitation of the Redeemer in his saving work would be impossible. In that instance, it is a question rather of the career followed by Christ forming a *pattern* for authentic Christian existence.

Pauline usage would seem, then, to propose a *mediated* imitation of Christ as a consequence of having accepted with faith Paul's gospel, an experience that created a personal relationship between himself and the churches he "fathered" (1 Cor 4:15) by his apostolic authority. In short, Paul candidly recognizes in himself an authentic representative of the living evangelical tradition. The Apostle's sensitivity to the human need of a model to follow, in addition to being inspired by principles, both for himself and his communities must, in my judgment, be taken to demonstrate his concern for, and interest in, Jesus' earthly history.[8]

Pauline Mysticism of the Apostolate

Paul's lack of contact with Jesus during his public ministry and passion appears to have been considered by some of his contemporaries as a serious disadvantage. And indeed Luke, for whom Paul is manifestly the chief protagonist in Acts, felt that he did not rank with "the twelve apostles," because he did not fulfill one essential condition for candidacy announced by Peter on the occasion of the election of Matthias: "He must be one of those who have shared our company the whole time the Lord Jesus lived among us, from John's baptism until the day he was taken up [to heaven] from our midst" (Acts 1:21-22).

There are however certain passages in Paul's letters in which he expresses what is often called his "mysticism of the apostolate," and these testify to a profoundly personal, indeed mystical experience of certain features of Jesus' earthly history.[9] Here it is possible to give only a sampling. "Yet we carry this treasure in what is no stronger than earthenware jars — which shows that such transcendent power is God's and does not come from myself. . . . Continually I carry about in my person the dying of Jesus, in order that Jesus' life may be manifested in my mortal flesh" (2 Cor 4:7-11). As a result of his sufferings in prison, Paul writes to his beloved Philippians: "Now as always I shall speak out boldly, so that Christ will be glorified in my person whether in life or through death. For me living is Christ, while to die is an asset" (Phil 1:20b-21). And to the refractory element in Corinth he declares: "Then you will have the proof you seek of the Christ who speaks through me. He is far from weak with you: on the contrary, he makes his power felt among you. True, he was crucified out of weakness, but he lives by the power of God; and I who share his weakness [now] shall by God's power live with him in your service" (2 Cor 13:3-4).

Here once again we have Paul's personal testimony to his familiarity with Jesus' earthly career and to its paramount importance in his eyes, as a vital criterion for assessing and discerning the quality of his own following of Christ through the trials and triumphs of his apostolic ministry.

Paul's Realistic Approach to the Mystery of the Incarnation

The most striking evidence for the seriousness, as well as the reverence, with which Paul regarded Jesus' earthly history is to be sought in the utter realism with which he accepted the mystery of the coming of God's Son to share the lot of fallen humanity. This truth, revealed from the beginning of his glorified existence by the risen Jesus to his disciples, has in subsequent centuries tended to be repeatedly obscured by misguided piety. It was, of course, denied very early in Christian history by the Docetists, adherents of a heresy alluded to by the author of the First Letter of John (4:1-3). The two greatest theologians among the writers of the New Testament, Paul and the author of the Fourth Gospel, wrestled with the problems involved in expressing the orthodox faith in the divine Personhood of Jesus without prejudice to his complete humanness.

It may be helpful here to take cognizance of the parallels in the presentation of this mystery between these two inspired writers. To speak of the incarnation is, for Paul as for John, an inadequate statement of the reality. In Paul's view, account must be taken of the Father's initiative in "handing Christ over to death for our sins" and "raising him for our justifying" (Rom 4:25). To John, with his conviction that "the Spirit is the life-giver: the flesh is useless" (Jn 6:63a), to state "The Word became flesh" (Jn 1:14a) is to assert a paradox that can only be solved at Jesus' death when "he handed over the Spirit" (Jn 19:30b).

In the second place, each of these thinkers draws upon the typology exhibited in the story of Abraham's sacrifice, or, as the rabbis termed it more accurately, "the binding of Isaac" (Gen 22:1-14), as a meaningful medium for presenting the mystery of salvation. To depict God, our loving Father, as "having handed over [to death] his own Son for the sake of us all" (Rom 8:32), or even to state "God so loved the world as to give [up to death] his only Son" (Jn 3:16) is to risk making a caricature of this unique Father-Son relationship. We must first review Paul's approach to these difficulties, and then contrast it with the explanation in the Fourth Gospel.

Paul begins by insisting upon the full reality of the Son's acceptance to be a member of the sinful family of the first Adam, whose disobedience had made mankind "hostile to God" (Rom 1:30), so that all human beings "were constituted sinners" (Rom 5:19). While Paul is well aware that Jesus was no sinner, yet by his becoming man the Son of God was somehow most truly, if indeed mysteriously, alienated from the Father. "Him who knew no sin God made into Sin, so that we, in him, might become God's Justice" (2 Cor 5:21).

Despite his use of abstractions ("Sin," "Justice"), Paul does not flinch from admitting the realistic consequences of the incarnation. "Christ bought us freedom from the curse of the Law by being made a curse on our behalf. As Scripture has it, 'Cursed is every man who has been hung on a gibbet.' And this, that Abraham's blessing might be extended to the pagans through union with Christ Jesus, and that we might receive the promised Spirit through faith" (Gal 3:13-14). Paul avoids pronouncing Jesus to be accursed, yet he dramatically depicts his oneness with the entire cursed humanity. "What the Law could never do, because it had been rendered impotent through the flesh, God achieved by sending his own Son in the likeness of sinful flesh to deal with Sin; and he condemned Sin in the flesh, in order that the just demands of the Law might be fulfilled in us, who live our lives, not on the level of the flesh, but with the help of the Spirit" (Rom 8:3-4). The personification, Sin, must not be allowed to obscure the bleak admission that the divine condemnation of Sin occurred first in the flesh of Jesus.

Thoughtful reflection on these texts will disclose why Paul faces up so courageously to the awful implications of the truth revealed for faith by the incarnation. For this supreme proof of the Father's love for his rebellious children cannot be plumbed except by realizing its grim consequences for a Father whose holiness cannot brook any trace of sin. Only if the Son's membership in the family of the first Adam be seen as genuine, is it possible to perceive the meaningfulness and the love manifested by his Father's initiative in his death — and resurrection from death. For these two actions are, for Paul, but two aspects of a single saving event, by which Jesus is revealed as the first redeemed man. God's liberation of him from the thrall of the consequences of "being made subject to the Law" (Gal 4:4) in Adam, by compassing Jesus' death becomes comprehensible as the first step in his transformation into "life-giving Spirit" as "the last Adam" (1 Cor 15:45), the new progenitor of the "new creation" (2 Cor 5:17a). This breath-taking portrayal of the work of man's redemption is possible only because Paul took a realistic look at the incarnation. Morna D. Hooker's astute assessment of the grandeur of the Pauline conception deserves mention here: "It is notable that the great majority of references to suffering and death in Paul speak of them in terms of our life 'in Christ,' and not 'in Adam.' This is very strange . . . yet because Christ is fully one with man in all his experiences, these can now be understood in terms of life in Christ."[10]

Paul attests abundantly to his attaining that goal, which made him think of his entire apostolic career as a marathon race, "the supereminent advantage of the knowledge of Christ Jesus my Lord" (Phil 3:8-14). This avowal by Paul himself cannot be lost sight of in any adequate appreciation of his interest in Jesus' earthly history. The Apostle can only attempt to articulate his personal relationship to the risen Jesus by declaring, "With regard to my present historical existence, I live my life by faith in the Son of God, who loved me and handed himself over [to death] for my sake. I will not make void the gracious gift of God!" (Gal 2:20-21). Gratitude to his risen Lord can never allow Paul to forget "the graciousness of our Lord Jesus Christ: how for our sake he beggared himself being rich, that you through his destitution might be enriched" (2 Cor 8:9). If Paul believes that Christ risen "now lives by the power of God," he is not unmindful also that "he was crucified out of weakness" (2 Cor 13:4).

The Paradox of Jesus' Earthly History: The Fourth Gospel

Long familiarity with the statement "The Word became flesh" from reciting the *Angelus* has perhaps obscured for us the startlingly paradoxical nature of this Johannine formulation, with the result that we are apt to miss its significance for its author. John has in fact intended his reader to see this as the fundamental motif presiding over the entire structuring of his book.

From the first verse of the ode, which he prefixed to his Gospel as a prologue, John asserts the divinity of the Word, later to be identified as "Jesus Christ" (Jn 1:17). As the Word, he is the perfect expression of the Father, and his divine existence already in eternity stands in marked contrast with that "becoming" that characterizes all that is created (Jn 1:3). Hence his announcement that "the Word *became flesh*" is calculated to evoke a double surprise. "Flesh" for this Gospel-writer connotes man's creatureliness and impotence in face of the divine power: "The Spirit is the life-giver: the flesh is useless" (Jn 6:63a). How, then, can the divine Word, by assuming such creaturely weakness, reveal a new, divine presence to history in the person of Jesus Christ (Jn 1:18)?

Secondly, how does John dare to claim that the Word, "through whom all things came to be" (Jn 1:3), himself *"became"*? Indeed, after voicing such a paradox, our author immediately subjoins what is taken to be an affirmation of Christian faith by the apostolic community, "We have beheld his glory" (Jn 1:14b). "Glory" for John, as for the Old Testament writers, denotes God's self-revelation in *power*.

To indicate how the fourth evangelist resolves the riddle posed by his mention of the incarnation (and thus to see what attitude he takes towards Jesus' earthly history), it may be helpful to collate a series of texts from the body of this Gospel. The context of the remark already quoted, "the flesh is useless" (Jn 6:62a), is provided by the Johannine version of the words of Eucharistic institution: "The bread I will give — it is my flesh for the life of the world" (Jn 6:51b). How can "useless flesh" give "life"? A clue to this conundrum is found in the announcement of Jesus at the feast of Sukkōth: "If anyone thirst, he must come to me; and he must drink — I mean, the man with faith in me! As Scripture says, 'From his heart will flow rivers of living water'" (Jn 7:37-38). The gloss on these words by the evangelist is to be noted: "He said this concerning the Spirit, which those who found faith in him were destined to receive. But the Spirit was not yet given, since Jesus was not yet glorified" (v. 39).

Where does John perceive the glorification of Jesus to be realized? It is at the very moment of Jesus' death on the cross, when he is finally "lifted up" (Jn 3:14) as "Son of Man." For only then "will you know that I AM" (Jn 8:28), only then "will I draw all men to myself" (Jn 12:32). It is no small part of John's innovative genius that he has seen the passion and death of Jesus as his "glory," his ultimate and effective moment of self-revelation, which enables him to reveal the "God no human being has ever seen" (Jn 1:18). This creative insight has presided over the entire Johannine presentation of Jesus' death, so markedly different from the picture given by Mark or Matthew.

Our evangelist first has Jesus declare that God has brought his work of self-revelation through the human life of Jesus of Nazareth to a triumphant conclusion: "It has been brought to perfect fulfillment" (Jn 19:30a). The use of the passive indicates God himself as the agent of this revelation. How is this divine plan realized? John gives an immediate answer: "And bowing his head, he *handed over the Spirit*" (Jn 19:30b). By so depicting (proleptically) the gift of the *risen* Lord, John has finally resolved the problem he raised in the prologue, and has thereby also given his attestation to his own highly distinctive experience of Jesus' earthly history. He tells his reader in effect: This divine Word has, through the glorification of his "flesh" (which is otherwise "useless") at death, made that "flesh" the bearer of the life-giving Spirit of God. And he has *ipso facto* disclosed to the eyes of faith his own self-identity as "the only Son" (Jn 3:16). The fourth evangelist, like Paul, has intuited the values present in Jesus' earthly history, but he has articulated his insight with creative originality.

NOTES

1. Rudolf Bultmann, *Theologie des Neuen Testaments* (Tübingen: J. C. B. Mohr, 1948) 1:185, categorically asserts of Paul: "In der Tat zeigen seine Briefe *kaum Spuren des Einflusses der palästinischen Tradition* von der Geschichte und Verkündigung Jesu." Hans Conzelmann, *An Outline of the Theology of the New Testament*, trans. John Bowden (New York and Evanston: Harper & Row, 1969) 161, echoes this view: "Paul's origin in the Hellenistic community makes it clear why he ignores the historical activity of Jesus (for example, he says nothing of the miracles of Jesus and takes only a few of Jesus' sayings from the synoptic material)." Günther Bornkamm, *Paul*, trans. D. M. G. Stalker (New York and Evanston: Harper & Row, 1969) 110, states of the Pauline letters: "The Jesus of history is apparently dismissed. Paul himself never met him." See a summary of similar views in Werner Georg Kümmel, "Jesus und Paulus," *NTS* 10 (1963–64). The nuanced opinion proffered by D. E. H. Whiteley, *The Theology of St. Paul* (Oxford: Basil Blackwell, 1970) 100, comes nearer my own: "St. Paul displays no interest of a 'biographical' nature in the earthly life of Jesus considered as past history; he is concerned with the acts and teaching of Our Lord only so far as they are relevant to the present and future."

2. J. A. Fitzmyer, *Pauline Theology, A Brief Sketch* (Englewood Cliffs, N.J.: Prentice-Hall, 1967) 51, observes of the thesis of the Christian's justification, "It is not the key to

Pauline theology, nor does it sum up the Christian experience for the Apostle — A. Schweitzer has referred to it as 'a subsidiary crater.'" D. E. H. Whiteley, *op. cit.*, 160, warns: "We shall do well to remember Davies' warning that in some contexts justification is merely one metaphor among many others employed by St. Paul to describe his deliverance through Christ, and that we are not justified in petrifying a metaphor into a dogma."

3. Norman Perrin, *What Is Redaction Criticism?* (Philadelphia: Fortress, 1969) 78.

4. Willi Marxsen, *Mark the Evangelist* (Nashville and New York: Abingdon, 1969) 215.

5. That the Catholic Church has accepted with approval the methodologies of Form and Redaction criticism, by a decree of one of her official organs, the Pontifical Biblical Commission, is clear from the *Instructio de historica Evangeliorum veritate*. See *CBQ* 26 (1964) 305–312.

6. In addition there are a number of perceptible allusions to the parables of Jesus in the letters: see "Pauline Allusions to the Sayings of Jesus," *CBQ* 23 (1961) 26–39.

7. Günther Bornkamm, *op. cit.*, 20.

8. See "'Become imitators of Me': The Pauline conception of Apostolic Tradition," *Analecta Biblica* 11 (1959) 291–309.

9. In addition to the texts cited, see 1 Thess 2:15; 1 Cor 4:9-13; 2 Cor 6:3-10; 11:23-29; Gal 2:20; Col 1:24.

10. See M. D. Hooker, "Interchange in Christ," *Journal of Theological Studies*, n.s. 22 (1971) 348–361.

J. Massyngberde Ford

PAUL THE TEACHER OF ISRAEL, PROPHET, AND REBELLIOUS ELDER

Paul's dramatic conversion from Judaism and Pharisaism, his passionate devotion to the Christians, even to making innovative exceptions with regard to the law for the Gentiles, for example in circumcision and the dietary laws, together with the continual opposition of Palestinian and Diaspora Jewry to his teaching — all give one the impression that he was regarded as an apostate by his people and, perhaps, that the Gentile Christians had "adopted" him.[1] Is this, however, an accurate picture as seen from either the Pauline Epistles or Acts, differing, in some cases radically, as they do?

Acts cannot be discounted. Eckert, for one, points out that Paul's pre-Christian life is confirmed in Acts (Acts 23:6 and 26:5; see Phil 3:5; Acts 7:58; 8:3; 9:1f., 13f., 21; 22:4f., 19; 26:4-11).[2] One can only draw indirect conclusions from the statements of the Apostle, but Acts does seem to be a good background. Acts 22:3-5 and 26:4-11 do not so much explain his persecution as confirm that his Gentile mission was not contrary to his Jewish observance. The Lucan Paul remains an observant Jew after his conversion. Eckart does not think that the so-called apostolic decree could have originated with the Council reported in Acts 15[3] and that there was not a unified theology in the Jerusalem church.[4]

It is the purpose of this essay (1) to extend Jervell's thesis,[5] namely, that Paul was recognized as a teacher in Israel or of Israel; (2) to suggest that Paul was still considered as a genuine member of his people by his people; (3) that he thought, taught and practiced as a Jew, even to the extent of performing supererogatory works,[6] but that his fellow Jews regarded him as a rebellious elder or prophet who should be judged by the Sanhedrin, and they attempted to mete out the appropriate treatment. Finally, Paul, unlike Jesus, cleverly outwitted his opponents by using his Roman citizenship to go to Rome; a rebellious elder could not be tried except in Jerusalem (see below, p. 301).

I begin with Jervell's thesis. He has put forward persuasive arguments to prove that Paul was regarded as "the teacher of Israel." He examines the later speeches in Acts and finds that they are apologetic rather than missionary in nature: *apologeisthai* and *apologia* occur in 22:1; 24:10; 25:16; 26:1, 24. Jervell comments that Luke devotes as much space to Paul's trial as he does to his missionary work. Biographical material is introduced into the speeches in Acts 22:1-21; 23:1ff.; 24:10-21; 26:1-23. The main characters in the drama are Paul, Felix, and Festus; the latter appear to be pro-Jew and against Paul and his Jewish (or Jewish Christian) accusers. Jervell demonstrates that Paul had been responsible for the conversion of many Jews (Acts 21:20) as well as Gentiles (one may add that Acts refers to the conversion of many priests even before the conversion of Paul[7]).

Dibelius, however, avers that a third complex of material about Paul begins earlier, namely, at 21:15, so that the unit 21:15–26:32 comprises Paul's reception in Jerusalem, his imprisonment, the hearings, and the appeal to Caesar.[8] In fact, according to Dibelius, Luke recounts five hearings of Paul, all of which delay the decision of his case.

1) In 22:30–23:10, the captain commands the Sanhedrin to be present, and all Paul says is that he is a Pharisee and son (or disciple) of a Pharisee and that he is called to account for his hope in the resurrection of the dead. As Schubert observes, in cycle 3 (22:30–28:22) the most striking point is the "I" style.[9]

2) In 24:1-13, Paul is before Felix again. It is a defense before the Sanhedrin. Paul denies causing rebellion in the Temple or synagogues or elsewhere in the city. He is a pious Jew and advocates the double resurrection (that is, of the just and the unjust); he speaks about being surprised during a purificatory act in the Temple.

3) In 24:24-25, Paul is before Felix and Drusilla, and speaks of justice, temperance, and judgment.

4) In 25:6-12, Paul defends himself before a deputation from Jerusalem; he denies any offense against the Law, the Temple, or the emperor and appeals to Caesar.

5) In 26:1-32, Festus and Herod Agrippa II are present, and Paul states that he sees the promise made to the Jewish ancestors fulfilled. He asserts that his call comes from the same God as the Jews honor; his message teaches that the Messiah, like Moses and the prophets, must suffer, but this will be followed by his resurrection.

Dibelius discerns Luke's motive, namely, that he wishes Paul to say something in each defense that could be used as a model for all Christians undergoing similar experiences.[10] Finally, in Acts 27–29 there are nineteen verses about Paul that portray him as a man who is farsighted, associated with heavenly powers, and fearless.[11] When he does not die after the snake bite, the pagans think that he is a god.

Yet there is sufficient reason to emphasize in this particular block of material (22:30–28:31) that Acts 21:15-21 is very important. Walter Schmithals discusses whether this pericope is a historical account.[12] Dibelius thinks that Luke has sources for the missionary activity and the journey, but Schille takes the opposite point of view.[13] Schmithals suggests that the form is a missionaretology (the story of a virtuous missionary), although he confesses that we cannot discern the sources of Luke in detail. Acts 21:15-21 shows Paul's friends' fear of the *Jews* rather than of the Jewish Christians.[14] Luke's object is to portray Paul as *the* example of Jewish Christianity in obedience to the Law (see 23:1ff.; 24:14ff.; 26:4ff.).

The historical narratives, which suppose a disagreeable separation between Jews and Jewish Christians, are changed in Acts 21:19-26 in favor of a narrative that makes the Jewish Christians champions of the Pharisees. The narrative about the Nazirites is plausible and fits in with the collection for the Jerusalem poor,[15] as does the circumcision of Timothy, occurring apparently immediately after the Apostolic Council.[16] Timothy is circumcised because of the hostility of the Jews; Paul did not want unnecessary objection to Christianity.[17] All three events — the vow, the collection, and the circumcision — show a solidarity with Jerusalem Jewry. Christianity is a variety of Judaism. Thus, if one examines Acts 21:15-21, it forms an emphatic introduction to the portrayal of Paul as an orthodox Jew, even if, as Haenchen suggests, Luke has implicitly placed Paul's vow at Cenchreae in a different historical setting.[18]

Cox sees the text of 22:30–23:11 as an independent unit.[19] In verse 9 both Codex Bezae and Greek manuscript 017 read "lest we fight against God."[20] Here one may have a conscious modeling on Gamaliel's speech in Acts 5:34-39. Luke is aligning Paul with Gamaliel. Paul, like the early Christians, is tried for breaking away from Judaism, but his defense is the same, namely, that he preached only the doctrine contained in the Law and the prophets.[21]

This pericope shows that Paul asserts that there is no doctrinal breach between orthodox Judaism and his own doctrine. He preaches only "the hope of the Jews." This speech does not have the form common to speeches in Acts — it has no appeal for attention, no kerygma, no proof from Scripture. The essential "proclamation of salvation" is found nowhere. What we do have here is a type of structure that best answers to the designation "controversy." Cox finds in Acts four types of controversy: (a) against official Judaism; (b) against Jewish Christians; (c) against non-believers, and (d) against Gentiles. Acts 22:30–23:11 "is a controversy against official Judaism, and one of a group of three, all bound together by one context." Our present speech cannot be understood outside its larger context, which is chapters 22–26.

Acts 22–26 form a unit at the end of Acts. ". . . it takes the form of three statements of position made by Paul before different groups of people, but always bearing on the point that Christianity is the 'hope of the Jews,'" the one true Judaism. The three stages of the one controversy are 22:1-12; 23:1-10; 26:2-23. In chapter 22 Paul speaks to the crowd (first controversy); in chapter 23 he defends himself before the tribune (second controversy) and then is taken to Caesarea. The third and final controversy is before Agrippa. These controversies have a common structure: an address; a statement of Jewish orthodoxy; a statement of Christian faith (as the logical development of Judaism); the reaction of the audience.[22]

Paul's conclusion is that he is an orthodox Jew and it is only by accepting Christ that he remains true to the Law and the prophets. The controversial question of the resurrection forms a chain that runs throughout the disputes.[23]

Acts 22:30–23:11 is, indeed, the central point of the three disputes. According to Dibelius, Acts 22 in the Temple is "one of the four discourses which underline the four major turning points in Acts." With it the tempo changes, as we have remarked, and there are no more free missionary journeys, but Paul is more or less under house arrest. Although the form of the speeches is the same, it is obvious that Paul's beliefs become more explicit. In 24:14 is found the kernel of the statement, namely, that faith in the resurrection is in complete conformity with orthodox Judaism. Paul and the followers of the Way are the true sons and daughters of Abraham. The expectation of Israel was the coming of the messianic age (see Rom 4:11 and Gal 3).

The idea of resurrection, although a late belief, was born in the heart of Judaism. Martyrdom made them think of future life, when they would "drink of life under God's covenant" (2 Macc 7). The *Book of Jubilees* believes that the bones of the righteous will arise and the spirits of the just will have great joy.[24] At Qumran the *Rule of the Community* speaks of eternal blessing and joy, crowns of glory and eternal life (1 QS 4:7-8), and although there is no explicit reference to the resurrection of the body, the Qumran covenanters would be unlikely to adopt the Greek belief in the immortality of the soul alone. The *Damascus Document* refers to the righteous living for "thousands of generations" (7:6). Cox concludes: "Therefore even if the phrase 'hope and resurrection' has no immediate connotation in the text of Acts 23, in Pharisaic theology which was the point of issue it certainly raised the idea of the 'Messianic age.'"[25] Further, the Pharisees were the teachers of the lay people and the missionaries, especially in the first centuries B.C.E. and C.E., and eventually excommunicated those who did not believe in the resurrection.

It is important to realize that in Acts 23 and 24 Paul declares that he is still a Pharisee. According to Jervell, the speeches, discussed above, have three factors and three accusations. The problem has to do with Paul as the teacher of Israel and what he teaches the Jews. He is spoken of as the *protostatēs*, a leader of the Nazarenes (Acts 24:5). The Jewish charges are apostasy from Moses (Acts 21:28 and 28:17) but, as we have seen, Paul defends himself ably and he, with the Twelve, is regarded as the new Israel.[26]

In summary, we have the following important criteria regarding the "Jewishness" of Paul in Acts:

1) The Sanhedrin judges that it is its duty to try Paul. Even if the Jewish leaders wish to use the Roman authorities or pretend that Paul's demeanor is political, in reality they realize that they are judging a religious case. Dauvillier points out that the rabbinic judges had given Paul thirty-nine stripes, even though this was illegal, since he was a Roman citizen.[27] Further, with the connivance of the high priest and the elders, more than forty Jews committed themselves under pain of anathema neither to eat or drink until they had killed Paul. The tribune Lysias took the initiative to send Paul to Caesarea. Porcius Festus showed a concern for justice when the high priest and notable Jews wished to condemn Paul without a hearing; he invited the accusers to come to Caesarea. Festus feared the Jews, and instead of pronouncing Paul innocent, he asked him to present himself to the Jews at *Jerusalem* (italics mine), to be judged in his presence. "The point is to suggest to him that he renounce his rights as a Roman citizen — and note that Festus even asked his consent — and also to submit himself to the alleged jurisdiction of the Sanhedrin."[28]

2) Paul makes it clear that he is still a Pharisee and that Christianity is a fulfillment of their hopes. Doeve[29] thinks that there may be a play on the word "Pharisees" when Paul speaks about "being separated" from his mother's womb. But *aphorizō* does not seem to be a translation of *phrsh* in the LXX.[30] There is some ground, though, to suppose that for the Apostle the verb *aphorizein* corresponded to *phrsh* in Hebrew or Aramaic. Paul is zealous.[31] In Philippians he is zealous in the persecution of the Christians, but in Galatians he is zealous with regard to the traditions of the elders. According to Josephus (*Ant.* 13, 297; 18:12), the Pharisees paid great attention to the traditions of the fathers. But Paul's persecution of the Church was the other side of the picture of his devotion to the traditions of the elders. Jesus said that not a jot or a tittle would pass away. Although he criticized hypocritical behavior, he declined to pass judgment on the institutions of the scribes and the Pharisees. Before the Council (Acts 15, and perhaps even until 135 c.e.) the Church was still a Jewish sect. Even the Pharisees had difficult relationships with Herod because of their allegiance to the tradition of the fathers.[32]

Burchard comments on Paul's announcement that he is a Pharisee before the Sanhedrin (Acts 23:6).[33] This seems to be historical, not Lucan redaction (see Phil 3:5). He also points out that Acts 26:9-11 is parallel to Acts 8:3; 9:1f. and 22:4b-5. Paul had agreed to the death sentence for Christians — that is, in Luke's meaning, he has agreed with the Sanhedrin. At the beginning of the speech, he allows Paul to be extolled as a Pharisee. Luke perhaps thought of him as a Pharisaic member of the Sanhedrin, although this cannot be stated unambiguously. For him, Christians were blasphemers,[34] and later the Sanhedrin does to Paul what he did to the Christians. Pre-Lucan tradition about Paul as persecutor is 8:3; 9:1f.; 22:19.[35] In Acts the Pharisees support Paul because of his belief in the resurrection of the dead. So Paul is acquitted by a prominent party of Jews. Acts 26:1-32 shows the climax of Paul's contention, namely, that he is a strict Jew, a Pharisee.

3) Paul denies rebellion against the Temple, the Law, and the synagogue (contrast Stephen and the Epistle to the Hebrews). Hay says that Paul does not repudiate the authority of the pillars either implicitly or explicitly.[36] The past tense *ēsan*, then, points to the status enjoyed by the "pillars" at the conference and implies nothing about their condition before or afterwards.[37] In summary, he says that Paul's emphasis in Gal 2 on *dokeō* and his reference to the proverb about God's impartiality are meant to remind the Galatians to judge by reality, not appearances.[38] But by "appearances" Paul has in mind the Jerusalem leaders themselves, with the status of apostleship that at least some of them possessed at the conference. The reality he would have them judge by is not these leaders' motives or "actual standing in the sight of God" but simply the kerygma.

4) Paul supports voluntary Jewish piety, such as the Nazirite vow, the collection for the Jerusalem saints, and in certain cases, it would seem, circumcision, e.g., Timothy and perhaps Titus. In Acts 21:15-21 one finds "many thousands among the Jews of those who have believed; they are all zealous for the law. . . ." In Acts 21:22-27, Paul helps with the Nazirite vow. In Acts 22:30–23:10, Paul fails to recognize the high priest but states, "I did not know, brethren, that he was the high priest; for it is written, 'You shall not speak evil of a ruler of your people.'" In Act 24:1-13, high priests and elders and a spokesman, Tertullus, come to examine Paul. Paul is accused by the Jews but answers that twelve days ago he was worshipping in Jerusalem and there was no tumult in the Temple, synagogue, or city. He had come to bring alms and offerings to the nation;[39] he was purified in the Temple.

5) As Stanley has ably demonstrated, before Festus and Herod Agrippa II, Paul asserts that the promise to the Jewish ancestors has been fulfilled and that his call is like that of Moses and the prophets.[40] In the third account of Paul's conversion, Festus remarks that Paul is raving, an

expression used of the frenzied ecstasy of the prophets of the Hellenistic mystery cults. Paul corrects him and says that he is not raving but prophesying. Therefore, he takes himself out of the ecstatic type of prophecy (see 2 Cor 12:1-9) and places himself in the more mature prophecy. He is a prophet who is socially, religiously, and politically concerned and who reinterprets Scripture (as he does most ably in the Epistle to the Romans). Paul has already stressed the importance of prophecy to the Corinthians (1 Cor 11–14), but his main thrust here is that belief in the prophets entails belief in his message also, since he is like the prophets. Thus, on the eve of his departure for Rome, Paul openly voices his assurance that he is a prophet, linked with the Old Testament prophets and also with the New Testament apostles, whom some regard also as prophets.

Moreover, with regard to his mission to the Gentiles, interestingly enough, Paul sees this as opening their eyes. So instead of Paul's eyes being opened, he now works to open the eyes of others. He speaks about opening their eyes and turning them from darkness to light, the exact experience he had on the road to Damascus.

Paul sees himself not only as a prophet but also as the Servant of the Lord from Deutero-Isaiah. In Acts 26:16-18 we find the language of the Servant Songs, the Servant who brings light to the Gentiles. Isaiah 42:6ff. speaks of "my servant, my chosen one." "I, the Lord, am God who called you in justice and grasped you by the hand and filled you with strength, [again the experience of Paul on the road to Damascus] who gave you as a covenant to the people, as a light to the Gentiles to open the eyes of the blind, to rescue from bonds those who are prisoners and those who live in darkness" — exactly the reverse of what Paul was doing before his conversion when he was committing Christians to darkness and to prison. In Mt 12:18ff. this text from Isaiah is applied to Christ. But actually it is Paul who fully implements Jesus' mission to the Gentiles. Jesus had the theology of the Gentiles; Paul had the active mission.[41]

A point crucial to our argument is found in Acts 25:6-12. Paul is accused in Caesarea, but neither the Jews who are present nor Festus wants to decide his case there. At this point Paul is asked whether he will go to Jerusalem and "there be tried on these charges before me [Festus]?" Only at Jerusalem could a rebellious elder be convicted (see below). Paul, therefore, plays his trump card, that is, the appeal to Caesar, presumably not to avoid suffering but not to be condemned and therefore able to carry his ministry to the end of the world (Acts 1:8). Paul affirms his innocence vis-à-vis the Jews, but also recognizes that he will die if judged by the Jews. This might set a precedent for other converted prominent Jews. He will not die if he is tried by the Romans, who find no cause for capital punishment. The end of Acts shows him still alive. In Acts 26:31-32, Agrippa confesses to Festus that Paul could have been freed under Roman law. It is arresting that neither the Palestinian nor Asian Jews follow him to Rome, and the Roman Jews do not try him. It can be presumed or conjectured, therefore, that this action would be futile, for, to repeat, a rebellious elder could not be tried outside of Jerusalem. Why did the Jews not persecute other Christians in the same way as they did Paul? Probably because these Christians were uneducated in Jewish law, that is, they were not rebellious elders.

The final speech naturally leads to a discussion of Gal 1–2. Here one must admit that Paul appears more a prophet than an elder, but his prophetic calling does include preaching and teaching and the interpretation of Scripture (see Acts 26:27; 28:24-28 and Paul expounding the Scripture in the various synagogues). One might compare also the Teacher of Righteousness at Qumran, who also possessed the prophetical power of interpretation of Scripture. The Jews might not accept people as prophets, for many, although not all, believed that prophecy had ceased with Malachi.

Paul's Prophetic Assertion in Gal 1:11–2:20

Bornkamm discusses Paul's concept of spiritual freedom.[42] He believes that the metaphor comes from the release of slaves, prisoners, or war captives. The Galatian freedom was threatened from two sides, *nomos* and *sarx*. But there was not an intentional fall from Christianity. He comments that nomism and anomism are two brothers from one root.[43] Gal 5:14 is in strict harmony with Mt 7:12; Mk 12:29ff., etc.[44] The freedom of a believer is bound up with love of one's neighbor. Mere keepers of the law are vicious and biting. Paul developed the idea of personal freedom rather than that of political freedom fostered by Stoics.[45] Christian freedom is under Christ. It is under this concept of freedom that Paul can play in his role as prophet and teacher, but it was equally true that the rebellious elder or false prophet was placed under bondage by the Jews precisely because they could receive no new revelation.[46]

1) In contrast to 1 Cor 15:1-7, Paul says that he did not receive this gospel through human hands.[47] In Acts 22:17-21 one learns about Paul's vision in the Temple. As Langevin asserts, Gal 1:11 is important, for it shows profound certainty on Paul's part that his calling is from God[48] (one has the same circumstances with regard to prophets in the Old Testament). Paul does not receive his gospel by way of apostolic kerygma or catechesis, but God revealed his Son to him.[49] One becomes a prophet when the Spirit of Yahweh comes on him (see Hos 9:7; Num 11:29; Jl 3:1).[50] Or it is the word of God which constitutes the prophet, for example, in Ex 4:16, where Aaron will be Moses' mouth and prophet

(Ex 7:1). One may also compare Am 7:14-15; Is 6 and 8:11; Jer 20:7-9 and their compulsion to become prophets.[51] The citation from Jeremiah is significant for Paul (see Phil 3:12, where he is seized by Jesus). Thus Gal 1:15-17 recalls the day of Paul's investiture in terms that evoke the memory of two great figures in the Old Testament: Jeremiah and the Servant of Yahweh.[52] Gal 1:15-16 is consonant with Jer 1:4-10 and Is 49:1-6; note the words "call," "from the womb," and "nations," which are common to these texts. Paul is inspired by Is 49:1-6 to describe his personal vocation. He compares his own mission to that of the Servant of Yahweh, who also works for the Gentiles. Salvation of the Gentiles will be requisite for the conversion of Israel (see Dt 32:31 and Rom 10:12 and 11:11, 14).[53] Deutero-Isaiah makes a parallelism between justice and mercy (Is 45:8) and salvation (*soteria*, Is 46:13, and *soterion*, Is 51:6, 8; see also Jer 1:5b and Gal 1:15-16). Jeremiah emphasizes the divine initiative when he describes his calling. Whether Paul speaks about his life before or after his conversion, he sees in it God's initiative (Gal 1:11-12 and 2:2).[54] There is a parallel also between Jer 1:5b, 10 and Gal 1:16a. Paul is "set apart" (*aphorisas*) and Jeremiah (1:5) is "sanctified" (*hēgiaka*). The verbs have a similar sense. "Sanctify" is a religious idea; *aphorizein* means "to separate".[55]

2) Paul's gospel came through the revelation of God. Denis traces the development of the meaning of "apocalypse."[56] It is not in the prophetic milieu of Deutero-Isaiah.[57] It is employed with reference to anticipated eschatology. Primitive uses can be examined. In Lk 17:30 it is identified with parousia. In 2 Thess 1:7 and 1 Cor 1:7, it is the wrath of God which will be revealed. In 2 Thess it is a revelation of the parousia of the man of lawlessness. In these cases there is nothing intellectual about the word "apocalypse," but it is a revelation of the judgment of God. Rom 1:16-17 is useful for Gal 1:18, for it is used in relationship to the activity of the Apostle.[58] The gospel is the salutary action that Paul must preach especially to the Gentiles. It is still difficult to attribute an intellectual value to "apocalypse" here. Denis compares Gal 1:12, 16 with Rom 1:17.[59] Paul's apostolic activity is a prolongation of the apocalypse of Jesus which converted him. This vision of which he speaks in 1 Cor 15:8 is represented as an apocalypse of Jesus, and Paul uses the expression which he employs several times in Thessalonians, Romans and Corinthians.[60] This time it is a question of immediate and actual contact with the glorified Savior, an anticipation of eschatology. One might speak of a particular parousia, accomplished for the Apostle and destined, as for the gathering of the elect at the general parousia, to introduce him into the divine sphere. Thus Paul is a witness to the risen Christ.

In 1 Cor 2 there is an accumulation of intellectual terms, so that we cannot reduce apocalypse to a pure event in which God makes himself present.[61] Evolution and intellectualization of the theme occur in, for example, Ephesians (see Rom 1:15, etc.).[62] The mystery that has been hidden for a long time is revealed (Eph 3:3).[63] Now it is made manifest by prophetic writings.[64] Thus "apocalypse" expands from parousia of Christ in eschatological glory, purifying fire, etc., to a more intellectual concept. One is also able to distinguish in the apocalypse of Jesus Christ of which Paul speaks in Gal 1:16 in illumination of his intellect, destined to make him understand who the Son is whom God reveals.[65] The apocalypse of Gal 1:16 is that of a person, a real event like the parousia of the Lord, according to 1 Cor 1:7 and 1 Thess 1:7. It also constitutes a call for him with a special grace to be an apostle with a mission similar to that of the Servant of Yahweh (see Gal 1:15).

Denis refers to Gal 1:15-17 as a solemn statement, with terms from the Old Testament; they are very rhythmic and are constructed mainly of the three verses: the first part, the protasis of the period (vv. 15-16), and climax in mission to Gentiles.[66] *Eudokein* appears eleven times in Paul.[67] Sometimes it is used in no special sense, but there is one instance in Col 1:19, and our Galatian text provides good parallels. *Eudokia* occurs six times in the epistles, sometimes of people, sometimes of God (Phil 2:13; Eph 1:5, 9).[68] Outside Paul the verb is used ten times in the whole New Testament. The only place where the infinitive follows (as in Galatians) is Lk 12:32: "It has pleased God to give you the kingdom." The noun occurs three times outside Paul: in Lk 2:14 and in the song of jubilation in Mt 11:26 and Lk 10:21.[69] *Apokalyptein* is not paralleled in Isaiah but is in Mt 11:26 and Lk 10:21.[70] Isaiah 49:1 has: ". . . called from the womb and called me by my name," and Paul has: " . . . called from the womb and called me by his grace."[71] "To separate" (*aphorizein*) can be used in LXX in an adverse sense (excommunicate), but also in a positive sense, i.e., consecration of country, people, offerings, Israel (Lev 20:26; Num 8:11),[72] of the first-born in Ex 13:12, and in the Alexandrian text of 29:26, etc. In Judaism one finds separation or consecration for a function (Dt 4:12, 15; 34:10; Num 12:8; Ex 33:11; Am 7; Is 6:5-7 Jer 1:5; Is 49:1).[73] But Paul adds the "apocalypse," and this is found in Dan 1:17; 1 *Enoch* 64:5 and 62:7; *As. Mos.* 1:14.[74] One can say that a particular choice applied to prophets but also to apocalyptics. One may compare Paul to Deutero-Isaiah; Samson (Jg 16:17); Jeremiah (Jer 1:4-5); as well as the Servant of Yahweh (Is 49).[75]

3) The idea of "flesh and blood" can be paralleled in Mt 16:17. Dupont speaks about the investiture of the Apostles Peter and Paul resting on a revelation of Jesus Christ that was given to them by the Father and has nothing to do with flesh and blood.[76] Redaction of the Gospel is later than Galatians. Paul would have a source used in the Gospel or an oral tradition like the logion incorporated in Matthew.

On the other hand, we might say that Matthew has reported concerning Peter in terms in which Paul spoke about his vocation.[77] This second hypothesis has been propounded by A-M. Denis and supported by P. F. Refoule. Denis thought that the redaction of Mt 16:17 had been influenced by Gal 1:16; perhaps Galatians depended on a hymn reported in Mt 11:25-27. Here Jesus thanks the Father for revealing himself to little ones, that is, the twelve who were beneficiaries of a revelation.[78] This revelation showed the good pleasure of God, which finds an echo in the verb *eudokesen* in Gal 1:15. The metaphor of building in Mt 16:18a is unique to the Gospel but is frequent in Paul. Only here in Mt 16 and 18 does the word "church" appear in the sense of a hierarchy, but it is habitual with Paul and is found in Gal 1:13. One could argue for the late redaction of Matthew.[79] Gerhardsson thinks that the points of contact between Gal 1:16 and Mt 16:17 make sense if one takes into account the intention of Paul in Gal 1–2.[80] Paul is obliged to defend his apostolate; he shows that his mission is of equal value to Peter's.

4) In Gal 1:17 Paul says that he did not go to Jerusalem to those who were apostles before him: he is not denying a visit to Jerusalem, but it was a visit for the purpose of seeing the apostles.

5) After three years, Paul states, he visited Cephas, but none of the other apostles save James. Trudinger remarks that Bligh does not think that James counted as an apostle.[81] "Thus construed, Paul's meaning in Gal 1:19 is, other *than* the apostles I saw none except James, the Lord's brother." Many scholars link Gal 1:19 with Acts 9:26-27, for this would fit this translation, since it shows Paul meeting with the "apostles" and not just with Peter. Foerster, however, thinks that the *dokountes* in Gal 2:2, 6, 9 are connected with James, Cephas, and John, but Paul conveys an ironic, indifferent or depreciating tone.[82] Paul is not critizing James (or the three pillars)[83] but the early Jewish-Christian community in Jerusalem, perhaps the Pharisees or scribes. Perhaps the opponents from Galatia came there.

6) The visit after fourteen years with Barnabas and Titus was *in answer to a revelation*. They laid before them the Gospel of the Gentiles, lest they should be running in vain. This seems to be a private consultation, not the Council. Titus (Gal 2:3) was not compelled to be circumcised. J. N. Sanders, however, thinks that Gal 2:3-5 really means that Paul had Titus circumcised and that the omission of "not" in verse 5 by Codex Bezae and its Latin version, with the support of many Latin Fathers, is the correct reading, and it is probably safe to assume that the interpolation of "not" was due to Marcion, as Tertullian believed.[84]

7) In Gal 2:7 Paul compares his mission to the Gentiles with Peter's to the Jews, but I would think that too little attention has been paid to Acts 10–11:18. While it is true that Gal 1–2 may be linked with Mt 16 and also with the Song of Jubilation, Paul may be emphasizing that just as Peter literally had an apocalypse or revelation (the vision of the sheet

containing animals, Acts 10) so Paul, too, received his calling directly from God. Neither Peter nor Paul consulted the other apostles, although both gave accounts of their work subsequently.

8) Sanders remarks that it is commonly held that Paul wrote Galatians between the quarrel with Peter and the Council.[85] If Galatians is approximately the same time as the Corinthian epistles, then Gal 2:10 (the collection for the poor) fits 1 Cor 12:1. Sanders thinks that Luke was mistaken in saying that Paul was present at the Council. Luke gives speeches by Peter and James and says that they listened to Paul and Barnabas, but he does not record a speech of Paul's "because Paul was not there to make one."[86] Peter appears to have been satisfied with the Council because the Gentiles would not be an inferior caste in the Church. "He had in fact fought Paul's battle for him, and done more for the Gentiles within the Church than Paul himself."[87]

9) Paul gives a definite statement about the position on the law, but does not condemn Peter for his Jewishness as long as he recognized the Gentile freedom.

10) In conclusion, one might agree with Jack T. Sanders that Paul does not give biographical statements simply for information but to prove that his gospel came through a revelation of Jesus Christ.[88] With regard to the parallelism and contrast in Gal 1:11f. and 1 Cor 15:1, 3, "there is hardly any way out of the conclusion that Paul is found here in what seems to be an absolute contradiction." According to 1 Cor 15, he received the gospel from men, but Gal 1:11f. affirms precisely the contrary. In Galatians, Paul is writing in anger over the coming of the Jewish Christians to preach another gospel. The situation is very similar to that which led him to write 2 Cor 10–13 (see 2 Cor 11:31). In both cases Paul is trying to convey a theological position.

Gal 1–2 show Paul accepting a "new" revelation, namely, mission to the Gentiles. He expresses this in Old Testament prophetic terms and equates his revelation to that of Peter (Mt 16 and Acts 10–11:18). His opponents are not James, the brother of the Lord, or Peter, James, and John, but the people from the Jerusalem community. He made several journeys to Jerusalem, two of which concerned his mission, one privately and one publicly. Galatians and Acts are compatible, although Galatians is historic rather than historical.[89]

The Rebellious Elder and False Prophet

While supporting Jervell and other authors, namely, that in Acts Paul is portrayed as the teacher of Israel, I should like to suggest that from the point of view of the Jews, Paul was considered not as a schismatic but as a rebellious elder and/or false prophet. The rabbinic material on rebellious elders is meager, but the following points are pertinent to our inquiry.

The rabbinic material on rebellious elders is scripturally based on Dt 17, and traditional teaching is found in the Mishnah and Talmud, the tractate on *Sanhedrin. Sanh.* 84b includes a rebellious elder among those who are executed by strangulation (others are the striker of a parent, a kidnapper, a false prophet, and one who testifies falsely). *Sanh.* 86b identifies the rebellious elder as one who defies a ruling of the *beth din* (or the Sanhedrin).

There were three tribunals, all in Jerusalem, at which the trial was held, and the rebellious elder stated, "Thus I have expounded and thus have my colleagues expounded, thus have I taught and thus have my colleagues taught." The rebellious elder was judged only if his offense was intentional and also, according to Rabbi Judah, "for a matter of which the fundamental principle is Biblical, whilst its interpretation is by the Scribes" (*Sanh.* 87a and cf. 88b). The elder was supposed to base his teaching on tradition, *not upon his own judgment (Sanh.* 88a).

The offender was not executed by his local *beth din* nor later by the one at Javneh, but was taken to the great *beth din* in Jerusalem and kept there for the next festival so that the people would fear and not act presumptuously, although Rabbi Judah said that the judgment should not be delayed. At the time of his execution, messages and proclamation were not sent to all places. On the Temple Mount alone can a rebellious elder be judged (*Sanh.* 14b). The execution was to be strangulation (based upon Dt 17:12-13). The ruling about a rebellious elder did not apply to an ordinary person but to a regularly ordained rabbi, judge, or elder over forty years of age or one of the twenty-three jurists constituting the minor Sanhedrin of a city or town. This may be why Peter and John and Stephen were not treated as rebellious elders.

Similarly, a false prophet among the Jews was one who delivered his message in the name of another god, and the community was committed to pass the death sentence on him (Dt 13:2ff.; see 18:20-22). In rabbinic law, however, a prophet is false if he professes to receive a revelation not found in Moses:

> . . . R. Hiyya b. Abba — said [The double form of] *manzapak* was declared by the Watchmen [prophets]. (But, is that reasonable: surely it is written, *These are the commandments*, [teaching] that a prophet may henceforth [i.e., after Moses] make no innovation! — Rather they were in existence, but it was not known which were [to be used] medially and which finally, and the Watchman came and fixed [the mode of their employment]). But still, *'these are the commandments'* [teaches] that a prophet may henceforth make no innovations? — Rather they had forgotten them, and they [the Watchmen] reinstituted them. (*Shab.* 104a).
>
> Another explanation: FOR THIS COMMANDMENT. . . IT IS NOT IN HEAVEN (xxx, 11f.). Moses said to Israel: "Do not say: 'Another Moses will arise and bring us another Torah from heaven'; I therefore warn you, IT IS NOT IN HEAVEN, that is to say, no part of it has remained in heaven." *Dt R* 8:6).

Paul in Acts

In view of the authority received from the Sanhedrin and the high priests to persecute the Christians, it might be conjectured that Paul was an elder or judge.

One notices that when Paul and Barnabas go to attend the Jerusalem Council (1) James, the Christian Jews *par excellence*, and elders are present; they are mentioned in 15:2, 4, 6, 22, 23 and 16:4. Presumably they are Jewish elders but are probably converts to Christianity and keeping their status, as would the priests who were obedient to the Word (Acts 6:7); there is no cleavage between Church and synagogue; (2) the questions under discussion are circumcision and the Noachic laws, both of which are firmly established in Scripture, not in "the traditions of men" (Mk 7:8); (3) the Council is in Jerusalem, where all matters concerning dissident teaching must be judged.

In Acts 16:19ff. it is pagans, not Jews, who attack Paul and Silas. Further, in Acts 17 Paul is accused of a political offense, naming another king, not Caesar. It is in Acts 18 that the Jews themselves revile Paul (v. 12) and, making a united effort, accuse him of persuading men to worship God contrary to the law (v. 13), an accusation that could be made against a rebellious elder or prophet. But the Jews do not arrange a trial for Paul, and his disciples withdraw to the hall of Tyrannus. In Acts 20:3, the Jews in Greece make a plot against Paul, but again there is no mention of trying him. It is in Acts 20:17ff. that Paul predicts to the Ephesian elders — probably, again, Christian Jews — that he will be imprisoned in Jerusalem, and in Acts 21:4 the disciples tell him not to go to Jerusalem, and Agabus (v. 11) foretells what will happen to him in the Holy City. They must have a foreboding that he will be treated as a rebellious elder or prophet. It is almost as if Paul is not in danger of trial and the death penalty as long as he stays away from Jerusalem.

When Paul arrived in the City, James and, again, *all the elders* are present (Acts 21:18) and they warn Paul about the Jews who think that he is "teaching contrary to Moses," a matter sufficient for the trial of a rebellious elder. James and the elders advocate that he help the four men with the Nazirite vows so that all may know that Paul is an observant Jew (v. 24). In Acts 21:27ff., however, Jews from Asia (it is significant that they travel so far and to Jerusalem) protest against Paul, saying that he speaks against the "people, the law and this place"; they attempt to kill him (v. 31), and the mob cries "Away with him" (v. 39). Paul answers by declaring his Jewishness.

Acts 22 comprises the second account of Paul's conversion on the road to Damascus. Paul emphasizes his Jewishness and that of Ananias, and relates that it was in the *Temple* that the "God of our fathers" commissioned him to go to the Gentiles.[90] In verse 30 Paul is set before the chief priests and the council (most versions give "council" for the Greek *synedrion*). J. M. Gilmore states: "They must have argued that the Sanhedrin was the proper court to decide whether Paul's religion was heretical or not. It is consistent with this assumption that Paul regarded a remand to Jerusalem as equivalent to being handed over to the Jews — he well knew what the verdict would be."[91]

In Acts 23:12 there is another plot to kill Paul; he is to be tried before the Sanhedrin (v. 28). In his defense in Acts 24, Paul steadfastly affirms that he believes "everything laid down by the Law or written by the prophets," and again in Acts 26, "nothing but what the prophets and Moses said would come to pass" (see Lk 24). In Acts 25:3 the Jews ask for Paul to be sent to Jerusalem, but Paul appeals to Caesar (v. 12), even though he has done no political wrong. It would seem incorrect to interpret this to serve as a way to evangelize in Rome; it is the only way Paul can save himself from being condemned by the Jews in Jerusalem and thus killed.

The Jews do not consent to come to Paul. When Paul does arrive in Rome, he tries to persuade the Jews by arguing from the Law of Moses and from the prophets. The Jews confess that they have no information against Paul, perhaps because it was useless for the Jerusalem Jews to send the accusations to Rome, where, according to their laws, he could not be tried. Further, the trial and the end of the narrative in Acts do not lead to Caesar and the Romans at all, but to the Jews in Rome, whom Paul has already prepared by sending the Epistle to the Romans, the manifesto of his belief that Christianity is the outcome of Judaism. In Paul's two meetings with the Roman Jews, he wants to give them an account of his relationship to Israel and to the Law in connection with the trial (28:20; see vv. 17-19). In Acts 26:23 Paul states specifically that Christ is said to fulfill what is said by the Law and the prophets. He has never spoken so explicitly before.

Thus, in his own eyes and in the sight of his fellow Christians, Paul remains a true Jew, a Christian Jew rather than a Jewish Christian. To the Jews he is a rebellious elder and/or false prophet, and is in no way to be classed with sectarian Judaism, such as the Hellenists (e.g., Stephen, who *did* speak against the Law, the people and the Temple), the Qumran covenanters, or the Samaritans. Seen in this light, too, the portrayal of Paul in Acts is consonant with what we see of him as a theologian in the Pauline corpus, especially Galatians and Romans. In Romans, his passion for his countrymen is abundantly clear (Rom 9). While placing no burden upon the pagans, Paul observes his Jewish heritage to the best of his ability.

NOTES

1. For a fairly comprehensive discussion of Paul's situation see A. Mattill, "Luke as a Historian in Criticism since 1840," Pt. 2, University Microfilms International, Ann Arbor, Mich., 1978, Appendix C, 395–403.

2. Jim Eckert, "Paulus und Jerusalemer Authoritäten nach Galaterbrief und der Apostelgeschichte," in *Schriftauslegung*, ed. Josef Ernst (1972) 283–304.

3. *Ibid.*, 299.

4. *Ibid.*, 303.

5. Jacob Jervell, *Luke and the People of God* (Minneapolis: Augsburg Publishing House, 1972) 153–183.

6. See Mattill, Appendix G, 421–425.

7. Acts 6:7.

8. M. Dibelius, *Studies in the Acts of the Apostles*, (London: S.C.M. Press, 1973) 211–214.

9. Paul Schubert, "The Final Cycle of Speeches in the Book of Acts," *JBL* 87 (1968) 3.

10. Dibelius, 213.

11. *Ibid.*, 214.

12. Walter Schmithals, *Paulus und Jacobus* (Gottingen: Vandenhoeck & Ruprecht, 1963) 70–80.

13. Cited by Schmithals, 71.

14. Schmithals, 74–75.

15. *Ibid.*, 75.

16. *Ibid.*, 78.

17. *Ibid.*, 79.

18. *Ibid.*, 80.

19. D. Cox, "Paul before the Sanhedrin: Acts 22:30–23:11," *SBFLA* 21 (1971) 54–75.

20. *Ibid.*, 55.

21. *Ibid.*

22. *Ibid.*, 58–59.

23. *Ibid.*, 61; "in all conscience" is found only in Acts, both times in this controversy.

24. *Ibid.*, 70.

25. *Ibid.*, 71.

26. Jervell, 174.

27. Jean Dauvillier, "A propos de la venue de saint Paul à Rome," *Bulletin de littérature ecclesiastique* 61 (1960) 51.

28. *Ibid.*, 6–8.

29. J. W. Doeve, "Paulus der Pharisäer und Galater 1:13-15," *Nov. Test.* 6, no. 2/3 (1963) 170.

30. *Ibid.*, 176.

31. *Ibid.*, 177.

32. *Ibid.*, 178–80.

33. Christoph Burchard, *Der Driezehnte Zeuge* (Göttingen: Vandenhoeck & Ruprecht, 1970) 39.

34. *Ibid.*, 46–47.

35. *Ibid.*, 48.

36. David M. Hay, "Paul's Indifference to Authority," *JBL* 83, no. 1 (1969) 36–37.

37. *Ibid.*, 37–38.

38. *Ibid.*, 42.

39. These could hardly be brought by an apostate.

40. David Stanley, "Why Three Accounts?" *CBQ* 15 (1953) 315–338.

41. See J. Jeremias, *Jesus' Promise to the Nations*. (Naperville, Ill.: Alec R. Allenson, 1958).

42. Gunther Bornkamm, "Die Christliche Freiheit Redigtmeditation über Ga. 5:13-15," in *Das Ende des Gesetze* (Munich: Kaiser 1961) 1:133–138.

43. *Ibid.*, 135.

44. *Ibid.*

45. *Ibid.*, 136.

46. *Deut. R.* 8:6 and *Shabb.* 104a.

47. It is possible that the gospel about which he speaks here is not the basic Christian kerygma but precisely the preaching of the Good News to the *Gentiles*.

48. Paul-Émile Langevin, "Saint Paul, prophète des Gentils," *Laval théologique et philosophique* 26, no. 1 (1970) 3–16.

49. *Ibid.*, 5.

50. *Ibid.*, 6.

51. *Ibid.*, 7.

52. *Ibid.*, 7–8.

53. *Ibid.*, 14.

54. *Ibid.*, 11.

55. *Ibid.*, 12.

56. A-M. Denis, O.P. "L' investiture de la function apostolique par 'Apocalypse' Étude thematique de Gal. 1:16," *Revue biblique* 64, no. 3 (1957) 335–361.

57. *Ibid.*, 335.

58. *Ibid.*, 338.

59. *Ibid.*, 339.

60. *Ibid.*, 340.

61. *Ibid.*, 345.

62. *Ibid.*, 352–353.

63. *Ibid.*, 355.

64. *Ibid.*, 357.

65. *Ibid.*, 361.

66. A-M. Denis, "L' Élection et la vocation de Paul, faveurs célestes, Étude Thématique de Gal. 1, 15," *Revue Thomiste* 57 (1957) 405–428.

67. *Ibid.*, 409.

68. *Ibid.*, 410.

69. *Ibid.*, 411.

70. *Ibid.*, 413.

71. *Ibid.*, 415.

72. *Ibid.*, 417.

73. *Ibid.*, 418.

74. *Ibid.*, 419.

75. *Ibid.*, 421.

76. Jacques Dupont, "La Revelation du Fils de Dieu en faveur de Pierre (Matt 16:17) et de Paul (Gal. 1:16)," *Recherches de Science Religieuses* 52, no. 3 (1964) 411–420.

77. *Ibid.*, 412.

78. *Ibid.*, 413.

79. *Ibid.*, 419.

80. *Ibid.*, 420.

81. L. Paul Trudinger, "Eteron de ton apostolon ouk eidon, ei me Jakobon, A note on Galatians 1:19" *Nov. Test.* 17, no. 3 (1975) 200–202.

82. Werner Foerster, "Die *dokountes* in Gal. 2," *ZNW* 36 (1938) 286–292.

83. J. N. Sanders, "Peter and Paul in Acts," *NTS* 2, no. 2 (1955) 133–143, remarks that in Gal. 2:9 most manuscripts read James, Cephas, and John, but Codex Bezae, Greek manuscript 011, and some Old Latin texts supported by Marcion, Tertullian, and the Vulgate read Peter, James, and John. In this case James may not be the

Lord's brother but the son of Zebedee. Before the persecution that caused the Church to spread out, James, the Lord's brother, did not have a commanding position in the church of Jerusalem; zeal for the Law made him acceptable to the non-Christian Jews for a time.

84. *Ibid.*, 139.

85. *Ibid.*, 140.

86. *Ibid.*, 142.

87. *Ibid.*

88. Jack T. Sanders, "Paul's 'Autobiographical' Statements in Gal. 1–2" *JBL* 85, no. 3 (1966) 335–343.

89. *Ibid.*, 342.

90. See David Stanley, *op. cit.*

91. J. M. Gilchrist, "On What Charge Was Paul Brought to Rome?" *ET* 78 (1967) 265.

John Koenig

VISION, SELF-OFFERING,

AND TRANSFORMATION FOR MINISTRY

(ROM 12:1-8)

In the last chapter of his Gospel, Luke records a missionary word of Jesus by which the risen Lord foretells that his disciples will preach repentance and forgiveness of sins in his name to all nations. The Holy Spirit will descend from on high to empower this preaching and, as Luke's Pentecost story shows, will also come to those who accept the offer of repentance (Lk 24:47-49; Acts 2:1-38). Paul does not have much to say about repentance as such in his letters (Rom 2:4; 2 Cor 7:9f.; 12:21 are the only references). He prefers to describe the initiation of Christian life in terms of release from bondage to superhuman powers (Gal 1:4; 4:3-9; 5:1; Rom 6:5-7, 18-23; 7:1-6, etc.). On the other hand, the Apostle knows about a repentance-like movement *within* Christian life which he sometimes refers to as "transformation." God's mercy stimulates this movement, and new manifestations of the Holy Spirit result from it. But it is also a real human act, a worshipful self-offering to God which may be part of what Paul means when he urges his Philippian readers to "work out your own salvation. . ." (Phil 2:12).

A Working Translation of Rom 12:1-8

> 1 Therefore I am calling upon you, brothers and sisters, through the awesome mercies of God, once again to make a bodily offering of yourselves, a living sacrifice which is holy and well-pleasing to God. This physical act is your true spiritual worship. 2 And as you make your offerings, don't let yourselves be conformed to this evil age, but instead submit again and again to transformation by the renewing of your perceptive

This article was originally presented as a paper for a study of the Division of Theological Studies, Lutheran Council in the U.S.A.

selves so that you may continue to learn by experience what the will of God is, namely, good and well-pleasing and perfect. 3 For through the special grace bestowed upon me I am addressing every one of you as individuals. And I say: Don't think arrogantly, beyond the limits assigned you, but think in such a way that level-headed wisdom results. Let each one do this according to the measure of faith which God has apportioned to him. 4 Here is what I mean. Just as we have many organs and limbs in a physical body, and these parts do not all have the same function, 5 just so we many believers make up one body in Christ, and individually we work together as one another's bodily parts. 6 In so doing, we have charismatic gifts which differ according to the particular grace bestowed on us. If someone is granted the gift of prophecy, that gift should be used in right relationship to our common faith. 7 If someone else receives a call to minister, let it be truly exercised in ministry. If another can instruct, let that one be devoted to teaching. 8 If a person is known as one who exhorts in the Spirit, then we expect a commitment to this activity. Let the one empowered for sharing wealth give liberally; the one whose gift is to be a protector of the weak, let him work at it zealously. And finally, the believer who is able to do acts of mercy should perform them cheerfully.

The Visionary Context of Rom 12:1-8

Close by the entrance to New York's World Trade Center is a large elevator that whisks visitors from street level to the 107th floor observation deck. Next to the elevator is a prophetic sign that reads: "It's hard to be down when you're so far up." Unlike so many billboards, this one makes good on its promise, for as you step from the elevator onto the enclosed observation deck, with its massive plate-glass panels extending from the ceiling to a point *below* floor level, your knees begin to quiver. Before you, and literally at your feet, lie all five boroughs of the city, the full range of New York Harbor, and the New Jersey coast from Fort Lee to Perth Amboy. Out east in Queens you can see planes landing and taking off at Kennedy Airport, hundreds of feet beneath you. If your heart can take it, you may travel by escalator to the 110th floor, the very roof of the building. Here you walk out onto a flat open promenade — if it is not closed to visitors because of high winds. Up there under the open sky one is consumed by a vulnerability mixed with lightheaded joy. Only the worst sort of despondency can prevent a feeling of tremendous awe. "It's hard to be down when you're so far up."

Something like this exhilaration is going on as Paul moves from the eleventh to the twelfth chapter of Romans. In 11:33 the Apostle breaks into an almost ecstatic hymn of praise to God:

> O the depth of the riches and wisdom and knowledge of God! How unsearchable are his judgments and how inscrutable his ways! "For who has known the mind of the Lord, or who has been his counselor?" "Or

who has given a gift to him that he might be repaid?" For from him and through him and to him are all things. To him be glory for ever. Amen (11:33-36).

These are the intoxicating words that introduce us to the exhortations of Rom 12:1ff. Why does Paul praise God so loftily at this point? The most probable explanation is that he has just concluded an emotionally trying discourse on the perplexing relationship between Israel and the Church (chs. 9–11). His resolution of this perplexity, which he calls a "mystery" (11:25), is that "a hardening has come upon part of Israel, until the full number of the Gentiles come in [to faith], and so all Israel will be saved. . ." (11:25f.). Struggling through his thoughts on the fate of his brother and sister Jews, Paul discovers anew the inexorable mercy of God. And it astounds him.

> Just as you [Gentiles] were once disobedient to God but now have received *mercy* because of their [Jewish] disobedience, so they have now been disobedient in order that by the *mercy* shown to you, they also may receive *mercy*. For God has consigned all men to disobedience, that he may have *mercy* upon all (11:30-32; italics added).

Here Paul breaks into his hymn (11:33-36). We must consider it unlikely that the Apostle has simply forgotten about this paean when he moves, with apparent abruptness, to a call for obedience on the part of the Romans. To be sure, the exhortation beginning at 12:1 harks back to Paul's description of the Spirit-led life in chapters 5–8. He presupposes that his readers have understood something about spiritual gifts even before he writes (see 1:11-12). Indeed, the Apostle reminds the Romans of such gifts in 11:29, where he notes that "the gifts (*charismata*) and the call of God [granted to Israel] are irrevocable."

Thus Paul lays the groundwork for 12:1 on several levels. When he calls upon his readers "by the mercies of God," he means not only the new mercy poured out upon Christians through the Spirit (5:5), but also those ancient mercies still at work in Israel by virtue of the divine faithfulness. God's expansive will for all creation, plus the personalized charisms he bestows on all Christians, fly through Paul's mind as he composes his appeal in 12:1. Rom 9–11 represents no detour from his purpose. On the contrary, it is the Apostle's exposition of God's grandeur at the end of chapter 11 that effectively triggers his ethical reflections in chapters 12–15. The "therefore" of 12:1 refers primarily to the verses that immediately precede it and only secondarily to chapters 5–8. I want to make this point as forcefully as I can because the contemporary interpreters of Romans I have consulted most frequently[1] give no attention to the "visionary" quality of the experience Paul wants to share with his readers by means of 11:13-36. Yet it is this awe before God (11:20) that Paul presumes upon as the common experiential ground between him and the Roman congregation. It is this, he thinks, that will facilitate their assent to his hortatory statements in 12:1-8.

The Form and Flow of Paul's Thought

Rom 12:1-8 is a discrete literary unit. It begins with an appeal "by the mercies of God" (v. 1) and ends with a directive to those members of the congregation who are called to do acts of mercy (v. 8). In 12:1-8 Paul employs wide-ranging terms like body, transformation, the will of God, grace, and faith to move his readers toward a proper view and use of their charismatic gifts (vv. 6-8). He closes by encouraging the Romans to commit themselves anew to the particular *charismata* with which they have been blessed. The gifts mentioned in verses 6-8 are prominent ones that lead to diverse forms of ministry. However, they can in no way be interpreted as an exhaustive list, since Paul elsewhere enumerates many others not mentioned here (see 1 Cor 7:7; 12-14; 2 Cor 1:8-11).

Verses 9-21 of Rom 12 stand apart from our passage in that they encourage special acts not linked to particular *charismata*. We may call these activities "charismatic" insofar as they flow from and return to the Spirit (see esp. v. 11). But in verses 9-21 the gifts themselves do not become objects of attention. Paul's statements here are almost wholly imperative. Of course, 12:1-8 also contains numerous imperatives, and in this sense it can be properly classified as an exhortation, a form of address common in the Hellenistic world. But the imperatives employed in verses 1-8 are far from conventional. Behind them all stands Paul's conviction that because of God's new creation in Christ, with its special graces meted out to apostles and congregation alike, his written appeal will actually *empower* the Romans to accomplish what is required. So much for the literary form of our passage.

But we must also pay attention to the flow of Paul's thought within this form, for studying Rom 12:1-8 is like plunging into a stream. Refreshment comes by enjoying the swirling force of the water. In this regard, a most striking phenomenon is the interplay among various sets of apparent opposites. Paul begins by asking the Romans to present themselves as a physical, bodily offering. This, however, he immediately labels a "spiritual worship." Then, in verses 4 and 5 he comes back again to the body, but this time it is the corporate body "in Christ." Yet, the corporate interaction of believers makes no sense apart from an affirmation of every individual's place in the plan of God. Transformation awakens a sense of personhood distinct from that of the group; right thinking must be done by "every one of you" with the measure of faith that God has meted out to each (v. 3). The *charismata* serve first of all to individuate believers, to distinguish them from others (vv. 6-8). But this differentiation serves the sole purpose of mutual ministry. Thus, at the end, Paul returns again to corporate talk.

Still another pair of opposites surfaces when the physical bodies of believers are set into a paradoxical relationship with human minds. By offering their bodies, the Romans will open themselves to a renewal of their minds so that they may cease thinking haughtily and instead reflect "with sober judgment." This thinking, however, is no intellectual exercise, but rather a contemplation of charismatic selfhood that leads inevitably to practical service. And of course all this "mind" talk of Paul's will cause the Romans to recall 11:34: "Who has known the mind of the Lord?" The conventional answer, of course, would be "no one." But Paul thinks differently. He holds that believers have the "mind of Christ" (1 Cor 2:16), the Spirit (Rom 8:5-6). And so, wonder of wonders, they can, by God's grace, see into the divine purpose — albeit "in a mirror dimly" (1 Cor 2:6-16; 13:12). This seeing has actually happened to Paul (Rom 11), and it is probably what he wants to stimulate in his readers when he urges them to "be transformed by the renewing of your minds, so that you may prove what is the will of God, what is the good and acceptable and perfect" (12:2).

Although we could probably continue to spell out pairs of opposites in 12:1-8 (e.g., gift-task, large-small, conscious-unconscious, rational-superrational, etc.), the point has been made that Paul's pairings are opposites in motion. They flow, they dance; and so, in the plan of God they are not really opposites after all.

Verse-by-Verse Observations

Verse 1. Parakalō is one of Paul's favorite words and means "exhort" or "call upon," as in Rom 15:30; 16:17. It carries strong imperative force. But for Paul the word does far more than command. Elsewhere in the corpus of his letters, it can also mean "beseech" (2 Cor 5:20), "comfort" (2 Cor 1:6-7), or "encourage" (1 Thess 5:14; 1 Cor 14:31). In light of the firm connection between 12:1 and the exhilarating display of God's mercy in chapter 11, it seems wise to stress the empowering dimension of the word here. Paul not only directs; he also encourages, just as the charismatically gifted exhorter of 12:8 does.[2] In fact, it is fair to assume that even as he begins this section, Paul already thinks about the special apostolic grace given to him (v. 3), namely, his prophetic authority for building up the Church (1 Cor 14:3-4, 31; 2 Cor 13:10). What the Apostle demands, he also helps to evoke "through the awesome mercies of God."

The phrase "through the . . . mercies of God" is unusual in Greek because Paul uses a genitive case with the preposition. One would expect the preposition *dia* to govern an accusative case here, so as to produce the meaning "because of." Yet the most literal translation of our text is "through" rather than "by" (RSV); and here as in so many other places the literal meaning proves best. Paul exhorts *through* the mercies of God; that is, he gets "wound up" in them. Thus the mercies themselves exhort (Schlier, 354). The context in which our verse appeals suggests that we should disagree with Ernst Käsemann when he calls these mercies "the entire salvation history as divine self-revelation" rather than "individual demonstrations of mercy" (Käsemann, 314). In fact, Rom 11 describes an extremely specific (and to Paul's mind, astounding) manifestation of God's mercy. It is a new angle on a particular aspect of God's saving plan: the place of the Jews.

The Greek verb for "make an offering," *parastēsai*, occurs in the aorist tense. This does not indicate a one-time event now past, but rather, as Schlier puts it, an act that is done "always anew" (Schlier, 355). In a parallel passage Paul tells the Romans: "Do not yield (*parastēsate*) your [bodily] members to sin as instruments of wickedness but yield (*parastēsate*) yourselves to God as men who have been brought from death to life . . ." (Rom 6:13; see also vv. 16 and 19). The verb *parastēsai* seems to have occurred regularly in pagan circles as a technical term for the offering of sacrifices (Schlier, 355).

Käsemann is right in stressing the materialistic side of "bodies" in verse 1. To translate the word as "selves" (NEB) is to dilute it. For Paul, our physical bodies are the dwelling place for the Spirit (Rom 8:9-11; 1 Cor 6:19) and Christ (2 Cor 4:7-12). They are the instruments through which we work to serve our neighbor and please the Lord (2 Cor 5:9-10). Paul's emphasis on physicality in verse 1 means that the phrase "spiritual worship" is ironic. Recent research indicates that in first-century circles the word we have translated "spiritual" (*logikē*) would have designated something other than strict empirical logic. The Stoic philosophers used it to describe the harmonious relationship between humans and the world through the divine spirit common to both. For the Stoics, even rationality was ultimately spiritual (Käsemann, 316). Paul writes: "This physical act is *your* spiritual worship" (italics added). Almost certainly, he is polemicizing here against other types of spiritual worship known to the Romans that he regards as not sufficiently physical, not sufficiently linked to practical, everyday service in the Church (Schlier, 358). These may be forms of *Christian* worship that Paul judges to be "escapist."

We can agree with Käsemann that in both 12:1 and 2 a Christian baptismal liturgy based an Old Testament sacrificial imagery informs Paul's words (Käsemann, 315). The tight knot between Rom 6:1-11 (baptism as death with Christ) and 6:12-19 (sanctification through bodily offering) already makes this probable. However, the closest linguistic parallel would be 1 Pet 2:2, 4-5:

Like newborn babes, long for the pure spiritual (*logikon*) milk, that by it you may grow up to salvation. . . . Come to him . . . and like living stones be yourselves built into a spiritual house, to be a holy priesthood, to offer spiritual sacrifices acceptable to God through Jesus Christ.

Käsemann wishes to move from this evidence to the conclusion that Paul is mounting a heavy attack on cultic worship — indeed, that he is substituting everyday service in the world for what tradition has called holy times and spaces (Käsemann, 316–317).[3] I do not find this substitutionary idea in the text. If Paul is calling for a *conscious* offering of bodies, and subsequently for a *conscious* submission to "transformation by the renewing of . . . perceptive selves," then he must be distinguishing between some times and spaces in which believers are performing these desired activities and others in which they are not. Thus the Apostle retains the notion of "holy" life-segments. Whether these events happen in worldly works of love or in ceremonial acts of congregational worship (or some combination of the two) is a separable question.

Verse 2. The two main verbs in this verse are present tense imperatives: *syschēmatizesthe* ("be conformed") and *metamorphousthe* ("submit to transformation"). In Greek, the present imperative indicates continued or repeated action. The simple *kai* ("and") that connects verse 1 with verse 2 suggests that Paul sees the resistance to conformation and the submission to transformation as features of the bodily offering (Schlier, 358). Avoiding conformation to this present evil age (see Gal 1:4; 2 Cor 4:4) means living in awareness of the danger that one may be seduced into the death throes of those principalities and powers that still battle against the reign of Christ (Rom 8:35-38; 1 Cor 10:6-13; 15:20-28). "The form of this world is passing away," and those who fail to maintain a critical distance from it will pass away with it (1 Cor 7:25-31).

But what does *metamorphousthe* mean? Is it simply a positive way of talking about our efforts to remain "un-conformed"? In light of contemporary history-of-religious research, this interpretation seems insufficient. For inhabitants of the ancient world, metamorphosis, as applied to humans, almost always denoted a fundamental change in one's being. Käsemann, recognizing this and wishing to minimize any privatistic or mystical overtones attaching to the word, suggests that for Paul metamorphosis refers to a repeated transfer of the believer from the old aeon, where he is constantly tempted to dwell, back again into the new (Käsemann, 317). This thesis makes sense, particularly if we are right in seeing baptismal images behind Rom 12:1-2.

The apostle amplifies what he means by transformation through the clause "by the renewing of your perceptive selves so that you may continue to learn by experience. . . ." Käsemann and Schlier, both students of Bultmann, are quick to interpret this renewal of mind as a strengthening of one's ability to make critical (existential) decisions

(Käsemann, 318; Schlier, 361). Schlier moves somewhat beyond this view when he notes that *nous* ("mind" or "perceptive self") should probably be understood not just as a decision-making agent but also more broadly as the whole "inner man" who is being renewed every day (2 Cor 4:16).[4] This view is certainly correct and receives added support from the fact that *nous* and "inner man" appear to be used synonymously in Rom 7:21-25.[5] But who is this "inner man"? He or she is probably the human spirit in communion with the Holy Spirit. "When we cry, 'Abba! Father!' it is the Spirit himself bearing witness with our spirit that we are the children of God" (Rom 8:15f.). The *nous* or human spirit or inmost self is our capacity for a trusting, childlike relationship with God. This the Spirit nurtures in us again and again through vision-like revelations of the future. Paul refers to this inner "seeing" in at least three passages outside Romans:

> But we impart a secret and hidden wisdom of God, which God decreed before the ages for our glorification. None of the rulers of this age understood this; for if they had, they would not have crucified the Lord of glory. But as it is written, "What no eye has seen, nor ear heard, nor the heart of man conceived, what God has prepared for those who love him," God has revealed to us through the Spirit. For the Spirit searches everything, even the depths of God. For what person knows a man's thoughts except the spirit of the man which is in him? So also no one comprehends the thoughts of God except the Spirit of God. Now we have received not the spirit of the world, but the Spirit which is from God, that we might understand the gifts bestowed on us by God (1 Cor 2:7-12).
>
> And we all, with unveiled face, beholding the glory of the Lord are being transformed (*metamorphoumetha*) according to his image from one degree of glory to another; for this comes from the Lord who is the Spirit (2 Cor 3:18, my translation).
>
> So we do not lose heart. Though our outer nature is wasting away, our inner nature (literally: "inner man") is being renewed every day. For this slight momentary affliction is preparing for us an eternal weight of glory beyond all comparison, because we look not to the things that are seen but to the things that are unseen; for the things that are seen are transient, but the things that are unseen are eternal (2 Cor 4:16-18).

The constitutive elements of these texts dovetail surprisingly well with those of Rom 12:1-8, though not every element appears in every text. Common to all of them, however, is language about the believer's perception of God's glory as an eschatological gift. While the Greek word for glory (*doxa*) does not occur in Rom 12:1-8, it is present in the verse immediately preceding 12:1 as an attribute of God. Moreover, in 8:18, 21, and 30, as well as 9:23, it shows up in exactly the eschatological sense we have just been examining. Paul is very much aware of God's merciful glory as he urges the Romans on to transformation by the renewing of their perceptive selves. He wants them to "see" what he has just described in 11:25-36. In our passage the word I have translated "learn by experience" (*dokimazein*) has a definite "visionary" coloring. It refers first of all to perceiving the overwhelming, inspiring will of God for all. Then, but only consequently, it also means "make a personal decision for God's will" or "try it out in practice." What most modern interpreters seem to have missed in this passage is the towering sense of wonder that Paul is trying to express for himself and engender in the Romans.

But we need to say still more about this transformation-renewal. For one thing, it may well be accompanied by pain. In 2 Cor 4:16f., Paul notes that the process involves a wasting away of the outer nature. This he experiences as an "affliction" that is preparing him for future glory. According to Phil 3:10, which I understand as yet another description of transformation, Paul hopes that he may further know Christ "and the power of his resurrection and may share his sufferings, becoming like him in his death." As far as Rom 12:1ff. is concerned, the pain of transformation might reside in a sudden discovery that one is not so important as one has thought within the plan of God (v. 3; see also 11:17-25).

As we noted above, the present imperatives "don't be conformed" and "submit . . . to transformation" can denote either continued or repeated activity. But which is it? Insofar as resistance to this age and submission to transformation are conscious, willed activities, Paul must be thinking of *repeated* events. Indeed, his directives in 12:1ff. make no sense if the processes he recommends are automatic. The phrase "renewal of perceptive selves" therefore suggests specific, identifiable alterations in one's state or condition.

On the other hand, when we read in 2 Cor 4:16f. that the renewal of the inner man takes place "every day," we must wonder whether this rejuvenation is not relatively constant and unconscious as well. Moreover, since Paul describes transformation as a work of the Spirit (2 Cor 3:18), we must reckon with the possibility that there is far more to it than meets the everyday eye and will of the believer. After all, the Spirit prays for us when we do not know how to pray (Rom 8:26f.). To the degree that transformation *becomes* conscious, it seems to mean a new discovery that God's will is in fact "good and well-pleasing and perfect." Whether conscious or unconscious, the whole process has more to do with grace received than grace put to work.

Verse 3. But now grace does come into play, both as apostolic authority and as motivating power for ministry. Or rather, Paul names as grace what he has been using all along in his authoritative letter to the Romans, that is, the particular charism that he has received at the time of his calling to be an apostle (Rom 15:15ff.; 1 Cor 3:10; 15:10). The phrase "through the special grace given to me" prepares Paul's readers for the discussion of *charismata* to follow. It assures them that the discussion itself will be a charismatic message from the Apostle (Schlier, 365). As a charismatic, the Apostle is able to speak not only to large groups of people but also to the hearts of individuals, to "every one of you."

The substance of Paul's message is contained in a word-play around the verb *phronein*, "to think." (Even exhortations can be fun!) Each Roman is bidden not to think arrogantly or haughtily (*hyperphronein*), but to think so that sober and practical wisdom (*sōphronein*) results. Käsemann helps us here by pointing out that in verse 3 Paul takes a significant turn from baptismal-eschatological language to terminology that was common parlance among the diverse popular philosophies of the Hellenistic era. *Sōphrosynē* was one of the four cardinal virtues explicated by Aristotle in his *Nichomachean Ethics* (1117b, 13); but it was also used in Hellenistic Jewish circles (Käsemann, 320). Among its definitions one finds "reasonableness," "mental soundness," "good judgment," and "self control."[6]

Käsemann suggests that Paul employs these almost pedestrian variants of the common word for "think" to counteract enthusiasts in the Roman congregation who are overly proud of their charismatic gifts or jealous of the gifts given to others (Käsemann, 320). This hypothesis is quite plausible and finds a parallel in 2 Cor 5:13, where Paul writes, "For if we are beside ourselves, it is for God [or before God]; if we are in our right mind (*sōphronoumen*), it is for you" (cited by Schlier, 367). Here Paul appears to be both affirming his authority as an ecstatic and insisting that such ecstasy needs to be set aside (though not forgotten) for the everyday tasks of ministry. This is very close to the train of thought we encounter in Rom 12:1-3. With verses 1-2 Paul has almost encouraged ecstasy. He wants the Romans to feel uplifted and inspired by the magnificence of God's mercy. But this is an ecstasy of the "big picture" that produces astonishment rather than pride. "Do not become proud (*mē hypsēla phronei*), but stand in awe" (Rom 11:20). Properly "seen," God's mercy can never lead to selfish escapism from the everyday material world. When rightly appropriated by individuals, it creates humility before both God and neighbor. With his talent for paradox, Paul announces that the true ecstasy of transformation brings forth sobriety and commitment to earthy tasks. This is the case because transformation means not only contemplating glory (2 Cor 3:18) but also sharing in the suffering and death of Christ (Rom 8:17; 2 Cor 4:10; Phil 3:10).

But there is another perspective on Paul's *phronein* language that bears mentioning. It is not just the lingo of popular philosophy, not in the letter to the Romans. In Rom 8 Paul has already described what he calls the *phronēma tou pneumatos*, the "mind-set of the Spirit":

> For those who live according to the flesh set their minds on the things of the flesh, but those who live according to the Spirit set their minds

(*phronousin*) on the things of the Spirit. To set the mind on the flesh is death, but to set the mind on the Spirit (*to phronēma tou pneumatos*) is life and peace (Rom 8:5-6).

Further on in the same chapter, Paul adds this promise:

> Likewise the Spirit helps us in our weakness; for we do not know how to pray as we ought, but the Spirit himself intercedes for us with sighs too deep for words. And he who searches the hearts of men knows what is the mind of the Spirit (*phronēma tou pneumatos*) because the Spirit intercedes for the saints according to the will of God (Rom 8:26-27).

In other words, when the Romans read 12:3 they will remember that for Paul right thinking involves communion with the Holy Spirit. It is the Spirit's plan that through their bodily offering they will be inspired to see panoramically and think soberly so that practical wisdom results. But even when they feel perplexed about God's will for them (8:26), the Spirit will intercede on their behalf. Thus the *phronēma* words in Rom 12:3 carry a heavy and mysterious freight. They are not as rationalistic as they appear to be on first reading.

What shall we make of the expression *metron pisteōs*, translated "measure of faith" by the RSV? Cranfield concludes that *metron* stands for "measure" in the sense of "yardstick" and that *pisteōs* means "the faith by which one believes" (Cranfield, 26). On this hypothesis, Paul refers to the believing of each reader insofar as this functions to produce a proper self-image. But Cranfield can find no other Pauline text in which the believer's faith is seen to work this way. His interpretation lends greater power to the believer's subjectivity than Paul would allow (Rom 8:26; 2 Cor 1:9; 4:8). When the Apostle speaks elsewhere of a *metron* (2 Cor 10:13) or *kanōn* (2 Cor 10:13-16; Gal 6:16), he means something more objective than the trust commitment of the individual. Käsemann is closer to the truth when he suggests that *metron pisteōs* could just as well be read *metron pneumatos*, "portion of the Spirit" (Käsemann, 323). This view squares with what we have learned so far about the Spirit's implied presence in this passage. Thus interpreted, the phrase in question becomes a circumlocution for "charismatic gift." "To each is given the manifestation of the Spirit for the common good" (1 Cor 12:7). There is an element of human response involved in the *metron* because one has to receive it and think in accordance with it. But here the sacramental element reigns. God metes out the *charismata* as he wills (1 Cor 12:11).

Verses 4-5. We need not say much about these verses, since they present us with a compressed version of Paul's earlier reflections on the Body of Christ in 1 Cor 12. It is true that in our text the Apostle writes of "one body in Christ" as opposed to the one "body of Christ" (1 Cor 12:27), but this difference is of little significance. The Greek conjunction *gar* in verse 4 (translated "for" in the RSV) indicates that what follows should be seen either as a consequence or a fuller exposition of verse 3. My translation, "Here is what I mean," reflects the second possibility. The expression *kath heis* is an idiomatic one that is best rendered "individually." It parallels the "every one of you" in verse 3.

Verses 4-5 do move beyond the thought of verse 3 by insisting that whatever goes on inside believing individuals must ultimately happen for the sake of the community. The gifts that distinguish one Christian from another find their true home in the body of the Church. In that setting their practitioners experience vitality through mutual giving and receiving (see Rom 1:11-12). In the community, gifted individuals with their minds renewed by the Spirit become giving saints. Their believing identities do not come to maturity until they discover their proper ministry in the body.

Verse 6. "We have charismatic gifts (*charismata*)." Paul is not imparting new information to the Romans with this declarative statement. Even when he mentions *charismata* for the first time in the letter (1:11f.), he does not feel the need to explain what they are. He presumes that the Romans already know. *Charismata* are part of the common experience of the early Church. "Each one has his own special gift (*charisma*) from God, one of one kind and one of another" (1 Cor 7:7). This does not need to be argued in the Roman congregation. What does need exposition is the proper connection between *charisma*, individual, and congregation. To this purpose Paul devotes himself in verses 6-8.

The clause "which differ according to the particular grace bestowed on us" parallels the beginning of verse 3 almost exactly. The Apostle has his special grace, and so does each reader. These differ according to God's will (1 Cor 7:7; 12:4-11), but always in such a way that, rightly understood, they complement one another (1 Cor 12:18-26). The RSV wording ". . . let us use them" is a paraphrase that does not appear as such in the Greek text. But it fits perfectly well with the flow of thought, since Paul's intent is clearly to help his readers make new commitments to the gifts that are already theirs. The Apostle reflects on his calling to be a teacher of charismatics in 1 Cor 2:12f.:

> Now we have received not the spirit of the world, but the Spirit which is from God, that we might understand the gifts bestowed on us by God. Which gifts we also speak about, not with words taught from human wisdom but with those taught from the Spirit, as we interpret spiritual gifts to spiritual people (1 Cor 2:12-13; v. 13 is my translation).

In Rom 12:6-8 Paul is exercising exactly this role.[7]

The first gift he names is prophecy. This also enjoys pre-eminence in 1 Cor 14, where it is the only *charisma* that all Christians are urged to seek (14:1-5, 31). The Apostle does not write to the Romans about the *office* of prophet. There are such people, and they rank next to apostles in importance; but as the Greek text of 1 Cor 12:28f. shows, Paul does not consider any office to be in and of itself a *charisma*. In our passage, prophecy (*propheteia*) means that authoritative proclamation of God's will for the present that may issue from any believer at any time but that emerges regularly in congregational worship (1 Cor 14). We should probably not think of this phenomenon as ecstatic in the strict sense, for believers could practice it in an orderly fashion and even withhold it at will (1 Cor 14:29-33). But neither was prophecy a prepared message, carefully researched. Instead, a believer felt led or constrained by the Spirit to speak in words that he had not consciously rehearsed ahead of time (1 Cor 14:29-30). Prophecy is perhaps the most comprehensive of the *charismata*, since it spills over into the gifts of teaching and comforting (1 Cor 14:31).

Paul does not think that he needs to encourage the activity of prophecy itself at Rome (contrast 1 Thess 5:19f.; 1 Cor 14:1). Instead, he wishes to emphasize that this *charisma* must be practiced according to the check and balance of what he calls the "analogy of faith" (*analogia tēs pisteōs*). Cranfield understands this phrase to mean that those prophesying are to measure their messages by their own beliefs as they know them (Cranfield, 30–31). But this interpretation, like his view of *metron pisteōs*, overestimates the power of an individual's subjectivity in Paul's thought (see v. 3 above). We should probably see in the *analogia* a reference to liturgical and catechetical confessions (especially baptismal formulations) that were widely known in the Church and could legitimately be called "the faith" as a body of things to be believed (Käsemann, 329). Schlier agrees, pointing to such confessional material in Paul as Rom 1:3f.; 4:25; 8:34; and 1 Cor 15:3ff. (Schlier, 369–370). The meaning of prophesying "in right relationship to our common faith" would be that all new messages must be judged by prophets and hearers alike in the light of their consistency with what is already known about God's will in Christ.

But perhaps we need to supplement this view. In Rom 1:11f., Paul states:

> I long to see you, that I may impart to you some spiritual gift (*charisma pneumatikon*) to strengthen you, that is, that we may be mutually encouraged by each other's faith, both yours and mine.

Here "faith" is belief being shared. One could almost translate it "personal testimony." It is not so much a doctrinal statement that requires assent as a story about God's mercy which calls that mercy into action among the hearers. Thus words about one's faith can both produce and limit the practice of *charismata* such as prophecy. This sort of inter-subjectivity probably lies behind Paul's notion of *analogia* in 12:6.

Verses 7-8. These verses list (without definition) six charismatic gifts and encourage those so gifted to devote themselves to the activities that follow from their empowerings. We must assume that Paul does not bother to describe these gifts because he assumes a familiarity with them on the part of the Romans. What needs emphasis in Rome is the message that one ought to bloom where one is planted. Transformation brings a new consciousness of where one fits in the mercies of God. Perhaps we can say that transformation clarifies or even mediates each person's *charisma.* But along with this new giftedness comes a sense of humility and responsibility. Not every believer can practice every *charisma;* each must do the task toward which his gift leads. Noteworthy is the fact that none of these *charismata* seems particularly glamorous or spectacular by current standards. Healing and glossolalia are not mentioned.

Ministry (*diakonia*) is the most general gift. This word could apply to apostolic ministry as a whole (2 Cor 4:1; Rom 11:13) or to particular phases of it (Rom 15:31; 2 Cor 8:4; 9:1, 12-13). But in our passage Paul must also be thinking of those diverse tasks that turn up at all levels of the Church's life (1 Cor 12:5). One example might be the service of hospitality extended to believers by the household of Stephanas (1 Cor 16:15). In Paul's time the office of deacon (Rom 16:1; Phil 1:1) was probably related to the activity called *diakonia* in the same way as the office of prophet related to *propheteia.* That is to say, the activity extended beyond the office. The same would be true of teaching. Here the teacher (*didaskōn*) designates anyone charismatically skilled at instructing, particularly (we may guess) in connection with catechesis for baptism (Gal 6:6).

We must speculate a great deal about the nature of the four *charismata* listed in verse 8. The fact that we must do so highlights the distance between our view of ministry today and Paul's, where all members of the congregation experienced divine calls to rather specific tasks. The *parakalōn* is one who exhorts or encourages, either through prophecy in worship (1 Cor 14:31) or through authoritative discourse, as in Rom 12:1-8 itself. Schlier sees the *parakalōn* as a pastor of souls (*Seelsorger*) or preacher, the latter judgment being based on 1 Thess 2:1-3, where Paul writes:

> For you yourselves know, brethren, that our visit to you was not in vain; but though we had already suffered . . . , we had courage in our God to declare to you the gospel of God in the face of great opposition. For our appeal (*paraklēsis*) does not spring from error or uncleanness . . . (cited by Schlier, 371).

The *metadidous,* or "sharer," may be one who apportions his inheritance or income to the needy (Eph 4:28). It is also possible that he is the one responsible for managing the corporate treasury of the church. If so, we might want to take a hard look at the job descriptions of financial officers in our contemporary churches, who usually see themselves as guardians of the budget, not givers. The *proïstamenos* may be an organizer (Käsemann cites 1 Thess 5:12 as a parallel; see p. 330); but Schlier's observation that Paul focuses on caring ministries in verse 8 leads us rather in the direction of Rom 16:2, where Phoebe the deacon is described as a "helper of many" (*prostatis pollōn*). Literally, the verb means to "be a protector or supporter" of someone in need. Finally, the *eleōn* is one who does acts of mercy such as nursing, visiting prisoners, and burying the dead (Tb 1:3; 4:7; Prov 22:8-9 are cited by Schlier, 372, and Käsemann, 330).

Conclusions and Horizons

One of the most striking features of Rom 12:1-8 is the quasi-mystical experience it presupposes. Paul actually expects that his readers will come to "see" the wideness of God's mercy in a concrete way that is distinguishable from their former perceptions. The word "transformation" was not lightly used in the ancient world.

Paul's intention is that the Romans will be moved by his disclosure of God's mercies to offer themselves bodily. Since this exhortation is presented to the congregation as a whole, the Apostle probably has a corporate self-offering in mind, perhaps during a worship service at which his epistle will be read.

Once the Romans have offered themselves as a group, however, each one of them will undergo some renewal of mind, some new apprehension of God's will specific to the situation of every individual. For some, this will prove to be a humbling experience. The "big picture" will show them how small they really are.

At the same time, however, each Roman will also sense his or her giftedness in a new way. This could mean the discovery of a new *charisma* or the recovery of an old one and a rededication to it. Through this renewal, all believers will move from proper thinking about their uniquely tailored places in God's plan to practical wisdom about their tasks in the congregation. New power for mutual ministry will follow.

Throughout this process, the Spirit is at work: leading, helping, interceding, and bestowing *charismata*. And this observation prompts an additional thought about transformation. It cannot be simply a willed and conscious act. In Rom 12:2 that side of it receives stress inasmuch as Paul urges his readers to submit to it at definite moments. He calls believers to become aware of transformation and affirm it whenever possible. But transformation itself proceeds at many levels, some of which we do not know consciously. By the Spirit's gracious power our "inner man" finds itself renewed every day (2 Cor 4:16). Submitting to transformation means returning again and again to this energy of God even now at work in us (Phil 2:12f.). It means calling the Spirit to mind, tasting God's mercies anew, and giving ourselves up to them. Although Paul does not speak much of repentance, Rom 12:1-3 articulates the substance of it as well as any New Testament passage I know.

How can the vision, self-offering, and transformation for ministry expounded in Rom 12:1-8 actually occur in the life of a contemporary Christian congregation?

We have already noted that Paul builds upon baptismal imagery in our passage. This fact suggests that the event of baptism (or its remembrance) could be an occasion for transformation. Not only the candidates themselves but also members of the congregation would be offering themselves up to the Lord. Here a liturgical act might function as a channel for the Spirit.

But so could a moral challenge. In 2 Cor 8 Paul urges his readers to imitate their neighbor congregation in Macedonia, where Christians have responded to the needs of poor believers in Jerusalem as follows:

> . . . they gave according to their means, as I can testify, and beyond their means, of their own free will, begging us earnestly for the favor of taking part in the relief of the saints — and this, not as we expected, but first they gave themselves to the Lord and to us by the will of God (2 Cor 8:3-5).

Here we glimpse roughly the same congruence of events described in Rom 12:1-8. In this case, the self-offering gets set in motion by the needs of others. But it is no less worshipful than at baptism. Upon hearing about Jerusalem's poverty, the Macedonians first offered themselves to the Lord. This, apparently, enabled them to "see" more clearly both their task and the resources for it. From worship flowed abundant giving, more than Paul expected, since the Macedonians themselves were quite poor (2 Cor 8:1-2).

Finally, it seems that vision, self-offering, and transformation for ministry might occur in that most regular and characteristic of the Church's public acts, the Eucharist. The Eucharistic liturgy itself helps to initiate vision by the proclamation of God's word in singing, prayer, Scripture reading, and preaching. The natural response to this disclosure of God's mercies is our approach to the Lord's table to offer ourselves anew. But there at the altar we also receive. With the sacramental bread and wine comes further vision, that is, a keener perception of our charismatic gifts and tasks within the congregation. Paul may be alluding to this new clarity when he cautions the Corinthians that "anyone who eats and drinks [the Eucharist] without discerning the body eats and drinks judgment upon himself" (1 Cor 11:29). The presumption behind Paul's stern words is that gathering for the Lord's Supper ordinarily leads believers to a heightened sense of interaction with their brothers and sisters in the Body of Christ. The charismatic quality of this interaction is spelled out in detail a few verses later when Paul launches into a description of spiritual gifts within the community (chs. 12–14). As far as 1 Corinthians is concerned, Eucharist and *charismata* belong together in the Apostle's mind. It seems probable that the same relationship holds in Rom 12, even though it is not explicitly stated.

Vision, self-offering, and transformation for ministry comprise a dynamic trio in the Pauline experience of Christian life. If we are right to find them operative within baptism, the Eucharist, and situations of special need, then the contemporary Church might learn a great deal more about its ongoing salvation (Phil 2:12f.) by identifying them and articulating them publicly. Perhaps we can even create more liturgical space for believers to talk to one another about their transformations in periods of worship (Eph 5:18-20).

NOTES

1. C. E. B. Cranfield, *A Commentary on Romans 12–13* (Edinburgh: Oliver and Boyd, 1965); Ernst Käsemann, *An die Römer; Handbuch zum Neuen Testament*, 3rd ed. (Tübingen: J. C. B. Mohr, 1973); Heinrich Schlier, *Der Römerbrief*, Herders Theologischer Kommentar zum Neuen Testament (Freiburg: Herder, 1977). Henceforth, I shall cite these works in the body of the article with the author's name and page number.

2. Here I agree with Schlier, 352, against Käsemann, 314.

3. See also his essay "Worship in Everyday Life: A Note on Romans 12," in *New Testament Questions of Today*, trans. W. J. Montague (Philadelphia: Fortress, 1969) 190–192.

4. Within the "genuine" letters of Paul (I exclude Colossians and Ephesians), the stem *anakain-* ("renew") occurs only in Rom 12:2 and 2 Cor 4:16.

5. Unlike many contemporary interpreters, I take Paul to be describing a quality of Christian experience throughout Rom 7. Note the close connection between 7:24 and 8:10-13.

6. F. W. Gingrich, *Shorter Lexicon of the Greek New Testament* (Chicago: Chicago University Press, 1965) 213.

7. For a more extensive treatment of this apostolic function, see my article "From Mystery to Ministry: Paul as Interpreter of Charismatic Gifts," *Union Seminary Quarterly Review* 33 (1978) 167–174.

Peter F. Ellis

SALVATION THROUGH THE WISDOM

OF THE CROSS (1 COR 1:10–4:21)

The centrality of the cross in Pauline theology and in 1 Cor 1:10–2:5 has long been recognized. What has not been recognized with equal clarity has been the reason for Paul's emphasis on the wisdom of the cross in 1 Cor 1:10–2:5 and the integral relationship of 1:10–2:5 with what follows in 2:6–4:21.

What we hope to demonstrate is that Paul has adopted a subtle theological and psychological line of argumentation that runs all the way through 1:10–4:21. He has probably done this in order to spare the feelings of the troublesome teachers at Corinth and their enthusiastic hangers-on. The format of the argumentation, as will be shown, is a powerful argument for the unity and integrity of the whole section.

The argumentation is presented in chiastic form, that is, Paul begins with a general treatment of his problem, which lies in the Corinthian teachers' failure to understand the cross as wisdom (section A: 1:10–2:5); moves on to what appears to be a digression — a discussion of mature versus immature Christians (section B: 2:6-16); and then concludes by returning to the themes of 1:10–2:5 (section A) and by giving practical solutions and advice concerning teachers, the cross, and true wisdom (section C: 3:1–4:21).

Paul uses the same chiastic presentation in chapter 7, chapters 8–10, and chapters 12–14. It should be noted that in each of the three sections of chapters 1–4, Paul's words about wisdom are always in the center, as can be seen in the following division of the text:

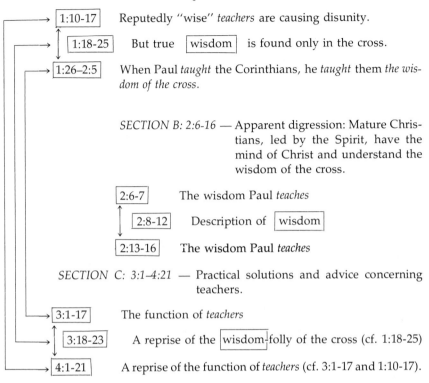

SECTION A: 1:10–2:5 — The problem: teachers, the cross, and wisdom.

1:10-17   Reputedly "wise" *teachers* are causing disunity.

1:18-25   But true   wisdom   is found only in the cross.

1:26–2:5   When Paul *taught* the Corinthians, he *taught* them *the wisdom of the cross.*

SECTION B: 2:6-16 — Apparent digression: Mature Christians, led by the Spirit, have the mind of Christ and understand the wisdom of the cross.

2:6-7   The wisdom Paul *teaches*

2:8-12   Description of   wisdom

2:13-16   The wisdom Paul *teaches*

SECTION C: 3:1–4:21 — Practical solutions and advice concerning teachers.

3:1-17   The function of *teachers*

3:18-23   A reprise of the wisdom-folly of the cross (cf. 1:18-25)

4:1-21   A reprise of the function of *teachers* (cf. 3:1-17 and 1:10-17).

Section A: 1:10–2:5: The problem: teachers, the cross, and wisdom.

In the three parts that make up section A, Paul deals successively with the immediate problem in the community — the division of the community into factions following one or the other prestigious teacher (1:10-17); the only source of true wisdom — the cross (1:18-25); and finally, the wisdom Paul himself preached when he first came to Corinth — the wisdom of the cross.

What is left unsaid about the unnamed prestigious teachers mentioned in part one (1:10-17) is said implicitly in part three (1:26–2:5) where Paul insists that what teachers should concentrate on is the cross. If the teachers in Corinth concentrated on the preaching of the cross as Paul himself did, there would be no factions in the community!

1) 1:10-17: Reputedly "wise" teachers are causing disunity in the Body of Christ.

The problem is broached in 1:12. Some boast that they follow Paul; some, Apollos; and some, Cephas. The meaning of 1:12d, "I belong to

325

Christ," is unclear. It possibly refers to a group which claimed a mystic relationship to Christ himself and excluded all others. Or it may be Paul's tart response to the factionalism fostered by following the theological "teaching" of one or the other prestigious teacher instead of concentrating on Christ himself and the cross. In chapters 3–4, on the other end of Paul's chiastic discussion of teachers, it is clear that the error of the Corinthians lies in their boasting about and claiming allegiance to certain teachers: e.g., 3:21, "Let there be no boasting about men"; and 4:6, ". . . so that none of you will grow self-important by reason of his association with one person rather than another."

Paul's question "Has Christ then been divided into parts?" (1:13) is best understood in the light of Paul's teaching that the community is "the body of Christ" (see 3:16-17; 6:15; 12:12-31). Different factions imply different parts of the body of Christ as if it had been divided up.

The questions about Paul being crucified for them and their being baptized in Paul's name are similar. Everything flows from the fact that it was Christ who was crucified for them according to the wise plan of the Father, and that it is into his body they were baptized when they became Christians (see Rom 6:3ff.). Christ is central. Paul will deal with his own function and the function of teachers in general in chapters 3–4.

The point of Paul's remarks about baptism (1:13c-17) is not to demean the importance of baptism but to emphasize the relationship of baptism to the cross. By baptism they have become one with Christ and his body the Church. Who baptizes is of no consequence. Perhaps Paul is attacking here a view of baptism imported into Christianity from the pagan mystery religions — the view that baptism creates a special relationship between the baptizer and the baptized. Against this Paul insists that baptism is into Christ and into him crucified. Only the cross gives meaning to baptism, not the one who baptizes.

2) 1:18-25: But true wisdom is found only in the cross.

In 1:18-25 Paul goes to the heart of the problem in Corinth by contrasting the true wisdom, the wisdom of the cross, with the false wisdom, the human wisdom of the philosophers, or perhaps the so-called saving "knowledge" or "wisdom" of the gnostics.[1] Since the cross represents the self-sacrifice of Christ in obedience to the will of the Father, it follows that those who understand wisdom as obedience to the will of the Father will no longer put their confidence in knowledge as such, even the highest theological knowledge.

Paul deals with wisdom in three key passages: 1:18-25; 2:6-15; 3:18-23. None is easy to understand, but a consideration of Paul's opponents, a comparison with a similar situation at Philippi, and some idea of what wisdom meant to Paul will go a long way clarifying all the wisdom texts.

The probable reason for Paul's forthright emphasis on the cross as wisdom is because his opponents at Corinth in one way or another have been indulging in a gross over-intellectualizing of the faith. They could be philosophical-minded Greek Christians who were scorning the crucifixion as rationally foolish (1:22) and the resurrection of the corpse or body as simply unworthy of belief (15:1-34). Or they could be incipient gnostics who were claiming to have been already saved either through their knowledge alone of Christ or through the rite of baptism as a rite that conferred upon them "saving knowledge." Finally, they could be believers in an exaltation theology who were claiming they already shared with Christ his triumph and all that went with it. Whatever they held and taught, it did not correspond to the real wisdom of the cross and to the emptying of self that it called for.

In another but different situation of disunity at Philippi (cf. Phil 2:2, 12 with 1 Cor 1:10-12), Paul reproached the Philippians and urged that they be of one mind with Christ in their abandonment of self-interest (see Phil 2:6-11). In Philippians 2:7-9, Paul understands the mind of Christ to be such that

> he emptied himself
> and took the form of a slave,
> being born in the likeness of men.

> He was known to be of human estate,
> and it was thus that he humbled himself,
> obediently accepting even death,
> death on a cross!

In both Phil 2:6-11 and in 1 Cor 1–4, where Paul talks about wisdom and the cross, he is not so much talking about the crucifixion as an example to be imitated as about a "state of mind." The mind of Christ is to do fully the will of the Father, even if it means going to the cross. This is wisdom. It is a moral, not an intellectual, disposition.

More important even than a consideration of Paul's opponents and a comparison with the situation at Philippi is an understanding of what wisdom meant to Paul as a Jew.

In the wisdom tradition of the Old Testament, to which Paul as a Jew was heir, wisdom was not primarily a matter of knowledge. It was the art of living successfully and happily, and neither of these could be achieved unless a man did the will of God. As the wisdom writers put it: "The beginning of wisdom is fear of the Lord." By fear of the Lord, they meant obedience to the will of God.[2] Thus the obedient man is the wise man, and vice versa.

In Paul's mind, although he does not bother to say it in 1 Cor 1–4, the cross is wisdom because by accepting the cross, Christ did the will of the Father perfectly. The cross is the wise plan of the Father, because the Father planned that man should be saved through the obedience unto death of his Son rather than through any purely human endeavor, however intellectually brilliant or impressive.

The meaning of 1:21, "Since in God's wisdom the world did not come to know him through wisdom . . . ," is best understood in the light of Rom 1:18ff. where Paul indicts the philosophers, because even though they have the rational capacity to recognize the existence of God from the evidence of creation, they nevertheless refuse to accept in their blind, moral unwillingness what their reason through creation tells them about God.

Paul speaks of four different kinds of wisdom: 1) The wisdom of the philosophers (1:21) which is human-centered, leaves God out of consideration, and is therefore bad. 2) Rhetorical wisdom (1:17; 2:4-5), or the art of persuading by clever speech, which is frequently used against the truth and in defense of error, and is frequently therefore also bad. 3) Wisdom which is capable of discerning from the evidence of creation the existence and goodness of God which is good. 4) That wisdom which is God's overall plan for our salvation through the sending of the Son to the cross (1:21-25; 2:6-16), which is the highest wisdom. Here, of course, in 1:18-25 the contrast is between the first and the fourth kinds of wisdom.

Whether Paul's opponents are philosophical-minded Greek Christians, gnostic Christians, or exaltation theology Christians, Paul's answer to all his opponents is the same: the cross represents God's wisdom and power, and the power of the gospel to save is precisely in the preaching of the crucified Christ.

Substantially, Paul does nothing more than state the central motif of Phil 2:6-11 — that the "mind" of Christ was to be obedient to the will of the Father even unto the death of the cross — and call this death a manifestation of the wisdom of God. He does not explain how it is wisdom or even what is particularly wise about it. He simply takes for granted that the wise among the Christians who have the spirit and mind of Christ will be able to understand this wisdom of the cross. It will not be until Rom 1–8 that Paul will attempt to explain how the passion, death, and resurrection of Jesus constitute the wise plan of the Father.

Paul's argument is an argument which presupposes the Old Testament understanding of wisdom as fear of the Lord, that is, obedience to the will of God. It also presupposes faith. Since even his opponents have faith, however misguided their ideas about the faith, he is able to appeal to them. Against opponents without faith and without an understanding of the Old Testament concept of wisdom as fear of the Lord, his whole argumentation about the cross being God's wisdom would have made little sense.[3]

3) 1:26–2:5: When Paul taught the Corinthians, he taught them "the wisdom of the cross."

Paul's argument is not flattering but it is persuasive. He points out what the Corinthians themselves can testify to from their own experience, namely, that those in Corinth who received and understood the message of the cross in the beginning were, in general, the poor and the unlettered, not the intellectuals. They must admit, therefore, that their acceptance of the gospel did not depend upon their intellectual abilities to grasp it but upon the inherent power of the preached message of the cross (1:26-29). If they want to boast then, it is evident they cannot boast about anything they themselves have accomplished but only about what God has done for them in bringing them to accept the wisdom, justice, sanctification, and redemption given to them through the cross of Christ (1:30-31).

In 2:1-5, Paul continues to argue from the Corinthians' own experience. They must remember that when Paul first taught them he did not sway them to accept the faith by means of powerfully persuasive language or what they understand as rhetorical wisdom (2:1-3 and see 1:17). He quite simply preached the humanly foolish message of the cross. On the basis of this message of the cross and the "convincing power of the spirit," they believed, thanks not to rhetorical wisdom but to the power of God (2:4-5).

Section B: 2:6-16: Apparent digression: Mature Christians, "led by the Spirit, have the mind of Christ and understand the 'wisdom of the cross.'" [4]

Even though Paul talks about a wisdom for the mature (2:6-7), he is not giving a superior or even hidden teaching that he has not previously taught. Instead, he is indirectly accusing the Corinthians of being immature.

Mature Christians understand the wisdom of the cross because they have the spirit and the mind of Christ. Since the Corinthians cannot seem to grasp the importance of the cross, they cannot really be mature. They are acting like children (see 3:1ff.) who are incapable of adult nourishment. [5] As Conzelmann says, "The division between believers of a lower and higher order arises from the fact that the addressees do not conform to the true status conferred on them (3:1ff.)." [6] To the degree that the Corinthians do not grasp the importance of the cross as wisdom, they are incapable of understanding Paul's message (2:6-7).

When Paul speaks about the cosmic effects of the crucifixion in verses 8-9, he is not speaking about a new wisdom but about a new dimension of the wisdom of the cross. If the "rulers of this age" had known the mystery of the cross — that through the crucifixion they would be defeated — they would not, for obvious reasons, have crucified Jesus (2:8). This remark proves that the wisdom Paul preaches for the mature is not a superior or hidden teaching but the same wisdom of the cross he spoke about in 1:10–2:5. In 2:10-12, Paul expresses the same idea in a different way: those who understand the wisdom of the cross are the spiritually mature because they have been instructed by the Spirit of God who alone knows the wisdom of God and communicates it to believers. The spiritually mature are those who have the mind of Christ as expressed in Phil 2:6-11 (v. 16).

In verses 14-15, Paul again expresses the difference between true Christians who understand the wisdom of the cross and immature Christians who do not — implicitly repeating what he had said in verse 6 about the distinction between the mature and the immature. If the Corinthians are not led by the Spirit, then they do not understand the mystery of the cross and vice versa (cf. vv. 14-15 with 1:18-19).

The teaching and the mystery it entails is esoteric only to the degree that it is understood by those taught by the Spirit and not understood by the rulers of this age (vv. 6 and 8) and by those like to them.[7]

Section C: 3:1–4:21: Practical solutions and advice concerning teachers.

1) 3:1-17: The office and work of Christian teachers.

In 2:6-16, Paul has almost reduced the Corinthians to the status of non-Christians. Now he mitigates his language and quite simply says they have been acting like children. They have shown they are only children in Christ by their manner of concentrating on certain prestigious teachers rather than on the cross and the self-sacrifice it calls for and thereby causing factions in the community. Paul will have to show them, therefore, the relative unimportance of teachers, whether it be himself or Apollos or any other teacher (3:1-4).

The relationship between the community and its teachers is described in pictorial language: verses 5-9, planting and growing of crops; verses 10-15, the functions of builders in relation to the building and the building materials; verses 16-17, a warning to trouble-makers to beware of destroying the community which is God's temple.

It should be observed that the theme of this section — the "building" of the Corinthian community — which is the temple (building) of the Holy Spirit, is central to the whole letter (see 3:9, 16; 6:19; 8:1; 10:23; 12:12-28; 13; 14:3-5, 12, 17, 26).

This section deals with the foundation of the building (Christ), the laborers, and the kind of work the laborers do in the advancement of the building project. In 8:1, Paul deals with the dynamic of building in his words: "Knowledge inflates, love builds." In chapter 13, the great paean to love, Paul extolls and describes this building dynamic. The section on the gifts and the Body of Christ in chapters 12 and 14 is still another attempt on Paul's part to deal with his theme of building up the community.

The apostles, the prophets, and especially the teachers are the builders of the community. Their work is important, but it is always and only a means to an end which is the building up of the community as the Body of Christ and the Temple of the Holy Spirit. All is therefore for the community. As Paul says in 3:22-23:

> All things are yours,
> Whether it be Paul, or Apollos, or Cephas,
> Or the world, or life, or death, or the present,
> or the future:
> All these are yours, and you are Christ's and
> Christ is God's.

In 3:5-9, Paul cuts down to size the divisive teachers in Corinth by reminding them that nothing they do amounts to anything if God does not do the really effective work in the background. Paul uses himself and Apollos as examples. They will receive a reward in relation to their labors, but they are only co-workers. God is the real builder. And the community is the building — the temple of God (vv. 7-9).

In 3:10-15, Paul pursues the building metaphor and the theme of the laborers and the quality of their work. Jesus Christ is the foundation of the building (3:11). Paul is the one who laid this foundation in Corinth (3:10 and see 4:15). The teachers in Corinth are now building on this foundation laid by Paul (3:10, 12) and the quality of their work — "gold, silver, precious stones, wood, hay, or straw" (v. 12) will only be known on judgment day (vv. 13-15).

The implication of the warning in 3:16-17 is that however poorly some builders (teachers) build, their fate will be nothing compared to the dire fate in store for builders (teachers) who not only do not build but by their teaching destroy the building (community).

2) 3:18-23: A reprise of the wisdom-folly of the cross theme.

Following his warning in 3:16-17, Paul repeats the gist of his teaching about the wisdom of the Cross, first expounded in 1:18-25. It is a second warning and is directed like the warning in 3:16-17 to the divisive teachers in the community. But it is also directed to the groups in the community who have fostered the forming of divisive factions by boasting about their favorite teachers. Paul warns them: "Let there be no boasting about men" (3:21), and reminds them that the teachers are their servants: "All things are yours, whether it be Paul, or Apollos, or Cephas . . ." (3:22).

3) 4:1-21: A reprise of the function of teachers.

Chapter 4 wraps up in much more specific language almost everything Paul has said in chapters 1–3. Specifically, Paul underlines the function of teachers. They are servants and administrators of the mysteries of God, nothing more (4:1). There is an implicit warning here to the teachers to be aware of their status as servants and not to mistakenly consider themselves something more, as they, or at least their followers, seem to think.

The community is then advised to evaluate their teachers for what they are — servants — and judge them on the basis of how faithful they are to the work that service entails, and not on the basis of eloquence or anything else (4:2).

What the Corinthians think of Paul is unimportant. Paul leaves the judgment to God (4:3-5). Paul seems here to be defending himself against certain accusations by the Corinthians. But what their accusations are is not clear, unless it be that he is not as eloquent in a rhetorical sense as their favorite teachers. Paul's lack of eloquence is implicitly admitted in 2:1-5 and 4:19-20.

The contrast Paul draws between the exaltation theology of the Corinthians (4:6-8) and the crucifixion theology of the apostles as followers in the way of the cross of Jesus (4:9-13) provides a psychological portrait of Paul's opponents at Corinth and a preview of Paul's argumentation for the charism of true apostleship in 2 Corinthians. It provides as well a fitting inclusion-conclusion to the whole of chapters 1–4. The crucifixion theology Paul and the other apostles live is the lived wisdom Paul preached when he first came to Corinth (1:26–2:5).

NOTES

1. It should be noted that 1:18-25 is chiastically balanced with 3:18-23. The reader who compares the two will find them mutually complimentary and enlightening.

2. See G. von Rad, *Wisdom in Israel*, 65–70, and especially his comments on p. 67: "The thesis that all human knowledge comes back to the question about commitment to God is a statement of penetrating perspicacity . . . It contains in a nutshell the whole Israelite theory of knowledge."

3. But see L. Gilkey, *Naming the Whirlwind*, 380ff.

4. Explaining the difficulties in this section would require more space than the limited scope of this paper allows. The major commentaries, especially H. Conzelmann's *1 Corinthians*, should be consulted. It is possible, however, to give the general argumentation.

5. Whether they are mature or immature, there is still only one wisdom — the wisdom of the cross! If and when they do become mature, they will recognize the wisdom of the cross as true wisdom and as solid food. What is more, they will not feel that they have to look elsewhere, e.g., to philosophy or some human system of thought, for the true wisdom. They will see that the cross, and the cross alone, is the true and only wisdom.

6. See *1 Corinthians*, 59.

7. B. A. Pearson, *The Pneumatikos and Psychikos Terminology in 1 Corinthians*.

Ivan Havener, O.S.B.

A CURSE FOR SALVATION —

1 CORINTHIANS 5:1–5

There is a general tendency in our time to idealize primitive Christianity, but this often involves a certain selectivity that ignores or even denies some aspects of primitive Christianity as revealed in the New Testament that do not appeal to our modern sensitivities. In chapter five of 1 Corinthians, we find a situation described that helps to underscore how foreign to and/or undesirable for our own ecclesiastical life-style and manner of thinking practices in primitive Christianity could be. In brief, we have in this chapter a case of ecclesiastical discipline that is apparently carried out in a completely undemocratic, highly authoritarian manner by the Apostle Paul. It involves a ritual curse for the physical destruction of the guilty Christian for the purpose of his salvation on the Day of the Lord.

In the following, an attempt is made to describe more precisely the situation Paul is addressing, as well as to clarify the process and rationale for his actions. First, however, a fairly literal translation, incorporating my exegetical decisions, is presented here:

v. 1 Briefly stated,[1] sexual immorality among you is being heard about, indeed, such immorality which is not (heard of) among the Gentiles — that someone is keeping the wife of his father.

v. 2 And are you arrogant and not rather sorrowful, so that he who has done this deed might be removed from your midst?[2]

v. 3 For I, being absent in the body but present in the spirit, have already, as one present, passed judgment on the one who has done such as this:

v. 4 When you and my spirit are assembled together under the invocation of our Lord Jesus,

vv. 4–5 (I have decided) to hand such a one over to Satan by the power of our Lord Jesus for the destruction of his flesh, so that his spirit may be saved on the Day of the Lord.

The general sense of the text is that a member of the Corinthian congregation is involved in an extended, incestuous relationship with his stepmother, akin to marriage.[3] Paul is shocked that the congregation has not acted to remove this person from its midst, a situation giving rise to scandal, because this immoral conduct is also looked down upon by the Gentiles, who are themselves noted for their sexual immorality.[4] The impression is given that the congregation may even be proud of this conduct rather than sorrowful, since "all things are lawful" according to its understanding of Christian freedom (1 Cor 6:12; 10:23). Paul's reaction contrasts with that of the congregation, for even in his physical absence he has already passed judgment on the wayward brother. But Paul is not satisfied with this; the congregation must still act. Therefore, he speaks of a ritual action in an assembly of the congregation where he is present in "spirit." The assembly only carries out, however, what Paul's decision already is, namely, to hand the offender over to Satan for the destruction of his physical body, so that his spirit may be saved on the Day of the Lord.

This understanding of the text conflicts rather sharply at three key points with an interpretation recently offered by Jerome Murphy-O'Connor.[5]

The first problem area has to do with the question of what the first of two prepositional phrases in verse 4, *en tō onomati tou kyriou hēmōn Iēsou* ("in the name of our Lord Jesus"), modifies. Murphy-O'Connor suggests that it modifies the participle immediately preceding it, *katergasamenon* ("the one who has done this"), so that we read as follows, "For I . . . have already passed judgment on the one who has done such as this in the name of our Lord Jesus." Grammatically this proposal is more logical than connecting the prepositional phrase with the verb *kekrika* ("I have passed judgment. . . . in the name of our Lord Jesus"), as is frequently suggested by commentators.[6] As far as the content of the interpretation of Murphy-O'Connor is concerned, there is also no difficulty, because verse 2 indicates that the congregation is not particularly upset with this situation and may consider this incestuous relationship an expression of the Christian freedom of their brother. If the congregation could think in this way (Some members, it will be remembered, did not even break with their idolatrous past — 1 Cor 10:14ff.), certainly it is not impossible nor even improbable that this man should think that he was acting "in the name of our Lord Jesus." Murphy-O'Connor's surprise that this possibility has not been taken seriously is well justified.

Having said this, however, I have serious reservations about the correctness of Murphy-O'Connor's interpretation and find that he has not dealt adequately with another possibility which, in my view, has more to say for itself. The evidence that Murphy-O'Connor offers, namely, that Paul elsewhere uses the prepositional phrase *en tō onomati tou kyriou* ("in the name of the Lord") following the verb it modifies, is somewhat misleading. In fact, only 1 Cor 6:11 among the certainly genuine letters of Paul uses the verbal form before this prepositional phrase,[7] and Murphy-O'Connor has overlooked the fact that in the Christ-hymn of Phil 2 (v. 10), Paul quotes a similar expression that uses the inverse order: *en tō onomati Iēsou pan gonu kampsē* ("at the name of Jesus every knee should bow").[8] It is this latter, liturgical context that may well shed light on the usage in 1 Cor 5:4.

In 1 Cor 5:4, Paul is making a solemn pronouncement with regard to a liturgical assembly, emphasizing the role of the Lord Jesus in the proceedings. Therefore, in my opinion, he begins with the invocation of the Lord Jesus.[9] In this case, the order of the Greek clause has the prepositional phrase placed before the verbal form that it modifies: *en tō onomati tou kyriou hēmōn Iēsou synachthentōn* ("under the invocation of our Lord Jesus when you and my spirit are assembled together . . ."). The specific mention of the invocation is not to be lightly dismissed, as though it were a needless repetition of what every congregational assembly does, as Murphy-O'Connor suggests,[10] because in ritual curses the name of the Lord is, in fact, solemnly called upon. Moreover, we have a clear example of such a curse in this same letter — 1 Cor 16:22: "If anyone does not love the Lord, let him be cursed. Maranatha!" Here the Lord (= *Mar*) is specifically invoked.[11] If this analysis is correct, the sense of 1 Cor 5:4 is this: "When you and my spirit are assembled together under the invocation of our Lord Jesus . . ."

This brings us to the second key difficulty of our passage, in which the second prepositional phrase of verse 4 presents a problem similar to that of the first prepositional phrase: what does it modify? There are two generally accepted possibilities; the phrase *syn tē dynamei tou kyriou hēmōn Iēsou* ("by the power of our Lord Jesus") modifies either *synachthentōn* ("gathered together") in verse 4 or the infinitive *paradounai* ("to hand over") in verse 5.

Murphy-O'Connor agrees, correctly in my opinion, with Robertson and Plummer that it is unlikely that both prepositional phrases in verse 4 are meant to modify one and the same verbal form, that is, either *synachthentōn* ("gathered together") or *paradounai* ("to hand over").[12] Because Murphy-O'Connor takes the first prepositional phrase with the verbal form preceding it ("the one who has done such as this in the name of our Lord"), he likewise takes the second phrase with the verbal form preceding it ("When you are assembled, I being with you in spirit, and empowered by our Lord Jesus . . .").[13] We have objected, however, to the first decision of Murphy-O'Connor, suggesting, instead, that the first prepositional phrase more likely belongs to *synachthentōn* ("gathered together"). If we then follow our proposed understanding of the text, the second prepositional phrase is structurally parallel to the first and must be taken to modify the infinitive *paradounai* ("to hand over"): [14]

en tō onomati tou kyriou hēmōn Iēsou	prepositional phrase
synachthentōn. . . .	verbal form
syn tē dynamei tou kyriou hēmōn Iēsou	prepositional phrase
paradounai. . . .	verbal form

The advantage of this suggestion is that the rhetorical parallelism is found within the same line of thought; the sense is connected:

> When you and my spirit are assembled together
> under the invocation of our Lord Jesus,
> (I have decided) to hand over
> by the power of our Lord Jesus . . .

The sole objection which Murphy-O'Connor has raised against taking the second prepositional phrase with *paradounai* ("to hand over") is that "One would expect power to be predicated of the agent rather than the action, since it is power which gives the capacity for action." [15] Yet if the action is, in fact, carried out by the power of the Lord Jesus, we have concomitant action by the agent through whom the Lord Jesus acts, but the emphasis rightly lies on the action of the Lord who has been invoked — not on the human agent. We find a similar situation in the Gospel of Mark in the pericope of the unknown exorcist (Mk 9:38): *eidomen tina en tō onomati sou ekballonta daimonia* ("we saw someone casting out demons in your name" — Note the word order of the Greek, as well: prepositional phrase followed by verbal form.) The emphasis in this Marcan passage is on the action of casting out, that is, how it is done, rather than on the person doing it.

A third problem concerns the identification of the verb which commands the infinitive *paradounai* ("to hand over") in verse 5. Once again there are basically two possibilities. Either the commanding verb is to be supplied, since it is simply understood, or the verb *kekrika* ("I have passed judgment on / have decided") from verse 3 has the infinitive clause as a second object.

The former position is favored by Murphy-O'Connor, who supplies the idea of "one must" or "it is necessary" and incorporates this into his own translation through a passive expression: ". . . such a person should be handed over." [16] His decision is based primarily on the observation that Paul's discontent with the congregation for not having yet acted on its own with regard to this matter presupposes that the normal functioning of the congregation includes this kind of disciplinary action; see v. 3; 5:12; 2 Cor 2:6 and the similar situation in Mt 18:15-17. This presents Murphy-O'Connor with the difficulty, then, of explaining why Paul found it necessary to emphasize his actual presence in the congregational assembly. He suggests that Paul wanted to encourage the members of the congregation to meet their responsibility. [17]

But the latter view is to be preferred: there is no need to supply a verb since the *kekrika* ("I have decided") of verse 3 is still in full force, and this makes better sense in terms of Paul's argumentation. He is underscoring *his* decision here — not because the congregation could not and should not take the same action on its own — but rather, because it has failed to do so in a singularly scandalous situation; therefore, Paul feels it necessary to exercise his apostolic authority completely, leaving nothing to chance in this specific situation. He is very definitely not sharing in a collegial exercise in the sense of one among equals, even as he just emphasized his authoritative, fatherly role in the verses immediately preceding our pericope:

> I do not write this to make you ashamed, but to admonish you as my beloved children. For though you have countless guides in Christ, you do not have many fathers. For I became your father in Christ Jesus through the gospel. I urge you, then, be imitators of me. Therefore I sent to you Timothy, my beloved and faithful child in the Lord, to remind you of my ways in Christ, as I teach them everywhere in every church (1 Cor 4:14-17).

Paul is taking the initiative and emphasizes his spiritual presence as one who is really present (twice in verse 3), as one who has already made up his mind, and as one whom his children should imitate. Therefore, the congregation now merely ratifies what Paul has decided [18] — not in the sense that it could not have done this itself but in light of the fact that it did not do so. Here Paul remains very much the spiritual father of his congregation, an authoritarian figure as fathers in his culture often were.[19]

One final matter needs clarification: what exactly is meant to happen to the one who is the recipient of this ritual curse? According to the text, Paul has decided "to hand such a one over to Satan by the power of our Lord Jesus for the destruction of his flesh, so that his spirit may be saved on the Day of the Lord," but there are some aspects of this disciplinary action which need explanation.

Most discussion of this passage focuses upon the meaning of the phrase *eis olethron tēs sarkos* ("for the destruction of his flesh"); it is basically a question whether this refers to the handing over of the offender to the realm of Satan with the possibility of future repentance and readmission to the Christian community or to his physical death. As we shall see when we look at this phrase more closely, the latter position is to be preferred.

The term *olethros* ("destruction") appears only in three other New Testament passages, always in the sense of final ruin and perdition within an eschatological setting; see 1 Thess 5:3; 2 Thess 1:9; 1 Tim 6:9. In these passages the physical bodies of those destroyed are certainly included, and this destruction does not admit any notion of repentance. Those who take the term in a non-physical, "religious" sense in 1 Cor

5:5, as J. Cambier does,[20] do so on the basis of analogy with such words as *thanatos* ("death") which can be understood in a physical sense and in a religious sense. Still another viewpoint is that the term is not to be understood in the sense of "death," rather, in a sense which includes the deterioration or weakening of the physical body, thus leaving open the possibility for the future repentance of the sinner.[21] The normal meaning of *olethros* remains a "destruction" which includes the physical body.

Crucial to our understanding of this punishment is the meaning of *sarx* ("flesh") and its contrast with *pneuma* ("spirit"). We note, first of all, that the contrast here is between *sarx* ("flesh") and *pneuma* ("spirit"), not between *sōma* ("body") and *pneuma* ("spirit") as in verse 3.[22] "Body" in verse 3 obviously refers to the physical body and "spirit" to that which is, at least, not physical. Is Paul using "flesh" in verse 5 in the sense of "physical body" and therefore in much the same way as he uses "body" in verse 3, or is he using "flesh" in the sense of the man's "moral corruptness"? If we look at Paul's use of the term *sarx* ("flesh") in 1 Corinthians without reading into our context his use of the term elsewhere, especially from Romans and Galatians, then the evidence provides us with some very helpful hints.

Sarx ("flesh") clearly means or, at least, includes "body" in a substantial, physical, or metaphorical sense in 1 Cor 6:16; 7:28; 15:39 (four times), 50.[23] Different, however, are the two remaining passages, 1 Cor 10:18 and 1:26, which use the same Greek expression, *kata sarka* (lit. "according to the flesh"), without a verb. In these two verses the "flesh" is related to the earthly, human sphere. Therefore, "Israel according to the flesh" (10:18) is the earthly nation whose members belong to it by natural descent, and "the wise according to the flesh" (1:26) are those on earth who are wise according to human categories.[24] The "flesh" of 10:18 and 1:26 is morally neutral, neither good nor bad, and does not fit the context of 1 Cor 5:5 which would require a negative moral evaluation of "flesh," if that term were to be understood in a "religious" sense. But the other passages using "flesh" in 1 Corinthians always have a notion of "body" associated with them, whether or not one can speak of a "religious" sense.

This, in turn, suggests that whatever moral, ethical overtones *sarx* ("flesh") may have in 1 Cor 5:5, if indeed there are any at all, it is not likely that these moral aspects can be separated out from a "substantial" understanding of the term in such a way that the physical body is excluded altogether. This supposition is strengthened by the use of the term in two passages, already mentioned, which are significantly similar to our passage: in 1 Cor 6:16-17 Paul uses *sōma* ("body") and *sarx* ("flesh") synonymously, contrasting them with *pneuma* ("spirit"): "Do you not know that he who joins himself to a prostitute becomes one body (*sōma*) with her? For, as it is written, 'The two shall become one flesh (*sarx*).' But he who is united to the Lord becomes one spirit (*pneuma*) with him." Likewise, in 1 Cor 15, we find an implied parallelism between verse 44: "It is sown a physical body, it is raised a spiritual body. If there is a physical body, there is also a spiritual body," and verse 50: "I tell you this, brethren: flesh and blood cannot inherit the kingdom of God, nor does the perishable inherit the imperishable." In these verses we find the *soma psychikon* ("physical body") contrasted with the *sōma pneumatikon* ("spiritual body"), even as *sarx kai haima* ("flesh and blood") = "what is perishable" [25] is contrasted with "what is imperishable" = ("spirit" ?).

These last named verses are especially important for our understanding of 1 Cor 5:5, for in them we see that Paul's concept of the resurrection body does not include resuscitated, physical flesh. [26] Paul can therefore speak of "spirit" apart from the physical body, and it is this spirit = "spiritual body" which will be saved on the Day of the Lord. Yet this does not make Paul's manner of thought necessarily Greek or Gnostic, as though the evil body would be separated from the soul. For Paul, the physical body is not evil in itself, and the punishment which he describes should not be construed as the destruction of the intrinsically evil physical body. Paul's emphasis lies instead on the destruction of the physical body as a punishment for a particularly scandalous sin, [27] and this needs to be understood in light of the fact, that for the Jews long life was considered a special blessing of God; see Ex 20:12; Ps 128:5-6. Paul removes this blessing of life on earth by means of this punishment *syn tē dynamei tou kyriou hēmōn Iēsou* ("by the power of our Lord Jesus"). Nor is this the only place where such a punishment is spoken of in 1 Corinthians; see also 11:29–30, where physical illness and death are judgments of the Lord, resulting from a faulty discernment of the "body" in the eucharistic assembly. This punishment is understood as a present chastisement, so that those who have committed the fault may not be condemned along with the world (verse 32) at the final judgment. [28]

Viewed from this perspective, the handing over to Satan [29] in 1 Cor 5:5 becomes understandable, for Satan does what he does best — namely, he destroys what is normally considered a blessing of God by cutting short the earthly life of the offender. It certainly would make no sense to hand the man over to Satan for the destruction of his "evilness." Why should Satan help the fellow to repent? That would put Satan in the embarrassing position of dividing his own kingdom, a point which the Marcan Jesus thought to be patently ridiculous; see Mk 3:23–27 parr. Furthermore, here as in 1 Cor 11:29–32 there is no mention of repentance, even as we saw no concept of repentance associated with the word *olethros* ("destruction") elsewhere in the New Testament.

Finally, there is one more textual observation which, if it does not significantly strengthen our position, at least, does not detract from it. That concerns the infinitive *paradounai* ("to hand over"), which is almost universally ignored by the commentators. Paul uses this word frequently in the sense of deliverance to physical death or to the passion of Jesus which ends in physical death; see 1 Cor 11:23; 13:3; Gal 2:20; Rom 4:25; 8:32. The implication in these passages is that the death sentence is carried out by others who are hostile; certainly suicide is not indicated in 1 Cor 13:3 or Rom 8:32. This is an important observation, distinguishing these passages from 2 Cor 4:11, where deliverance to death[30] is understood not in a physical sense but in a religious sense, and where the implied agent of the death, if there is any at all, is not a hostile being.

In the light of these arguments, it seems more likely that this ritual curse requires the physical death of the sinner rather than a milder physical punishment and/or a temporary handing over to the Satanic realm of evil, in the hope that he would eventually see his folly, would repent and then be readmitted to the congregation. In fact, there is no mention of repentance whatsoever in this passage, and indeed there is no need for repentance, because the capital punishment required by Paul leads ultimately to the sinner's salvation.[31] We have here, in effect, a curse for salvation.

The death penalty assumes, of course, an expulsion from the community; see 1 Cor. 5:2, 7, 13, but this is hardly an excommunication in the sense of the ecclesiastical discipline alluded to in 2 Cor 2:5–11, which is only partially similar to 1 Cor 5:1ff. There is no direct parallel between the passages, because in 2 Cor 2:5–11 both the offense (a personal affront to Paul's character or authority?) and the punishment (an excommunication without death penalty?) are of a different nature.[32] In 1 Cor 5:5 Paul describes the sinful situation much more precisely than in 2 Cor 2:5ff. because of its particularly scandalous nature, a sin repugnant not only to Jews and Christians but also to Gentiles. This heightened sinfulness calls for a harsher punishment upon the offender, and in view of a similar penalty for an equally specific situation in 1 Cor 11:29–32, it cannot be said that such a penalty is foreign to Paul's manner of thinking and practice. It is, rather, foreign to *our* manner of thinking and practice. Therefore, what Wilhelm Bousset[33] said with regard to 1 Cor 11:29 holds true for 1 Cor 5:1–5, "Wir stehen wieder vor einer uns fremd gewordenen Welt."

NOTES

1. The Greek word *holos* never appears elsewhere at the beginning of a sentence where it refers to succeeding action, as it does here. The sense is "briefly stated" or "in short," anticipating information to follow; see Anton Fridrichsen, "Exegetisches zum Neuen Testament," *Symbolae Osloenses*, 13 (1934) 43–44.

2. The sadness of the community should result in its taking action against the guilty one by removing him from its midst. There is no notion, however, of the mere bereavement itself effecting this removal; so J. Cambier, "La chair et l'esprit en I Cor. V.5," *NTS* 15 (1969) 222.

3. See especially the *religionsgeschichtliche* materials gathered by Ernst von Dobschütz, *Christian Life in the Primitive Church*, ed. W. D. Morrison and tr. George Bremner (London: Williams & Norgate; New York: G. P. Putnam's Sons, 1904) 44–45, 387–389.

4. C. F. Georg Heinrici, *Der erste Sendschreiben des Apostel Paulus an die Korinthier* (Berlin: Verlag von Wilhelm Hertz, 1880) 159, noted correctly that it was not only the sin that demanded censure but, above all, the position that the congregation took with regard to that situation.

5. Jerome Murphy-O'Connor, "I Corinthians, V, 3-5," *Revue Biblique* 84 (1977) 239–245.

6. For example, this has been done in the most recent major commentary in English by William F. Orr and James Arthur Walther, *I Corinthians*, in *The Anchor Bible* 32 (Garden City, N.Y.: Doubleday & Company, Inc., 1976) 184; this seems to place, however, an almost impossible burden on the reader to know that the prepositional phrase is supposedly dangling.

7. Murphy-O'Connor, *op. cit.* 240, cites also 2 Thess 3:6 and Col 3:17. Apart from the question whether these are genuine writings of Paul, the verb of the apodosis where the prepositional phrase occurs in Col 3:17 is only implied and cannot be used as evidence to support his argument.

8. The prepositional phrase *en tō onomati* ("in the name") is followed by a verb nine times in the New Testament, as compared to thirty-one times for the opposite (fourteen of which are found in the Johannine writings); only 1 Cor 5:4 is unclear.

9. Although Hans Bietenhard, art. "Onoma," *TDNT* 5:271, acknowledges that the most general meaning of *en (tō) onomati* in the New Testament is "with invocation of," Rudolf Bultmann is probably correct in this instance in going a step further to suggest that the name is actually called out as part of the curse; see Rudolf Bultmann, *Theology of the New Testament* 1, tr. Kendrick Grobel (New York: Charles Scribner's Sons, 1951) 126–127 and Wilhelm Heitmüller *"Im Namen Jesu." Eine sprach- u. religionsgeschichtliche Untersuchung zum Neuen Testament, speziell zur altchristlichen Taufe* in FRLANT Bd. 1, Heft 2 (Göttingen: Vandenhoeck & Ruprecht, 1903), 74.

10. Murphy-O'Connor, *op. cit.*, 240.

11. See a similar formulation in *Didache* 10, 6. The invocation as an intrinsic part of the curse indicates that Erik Peterson may have been correct when he suggested that the Maranatha of 1 Cor 16:22 was used apotropaicly; see Erik Peterson, *Heis Theos: Epigraphische, formgeschichtliche und religionsgeschichtliche Untersuchungen*, in *Forschungen zur Religion und Literatur des Alten und Neuen Testaments*, N.F. 24 (Göttingen: Vandenhoeck & Ruprecht, 1926) 130–131. Even though Günther Bornkamm disagrees with Peterson's view, he admits that "In any case, the Maranatha appeals to the heavenly judge and lends threatening emphasis to the Anathema"; so Günther Bornkamm, "The Anathema in the Early Christian Lord's Supper Liturgy," *Early Christian Experience*, tr. Paul L. Hammer (New York and Evanston: Harper & Row, Publishers, 1969) 171. Peterson's argument is preferable.

12. Murphy-O'Connor, *op. cit.*, 239; cf. Archibald Robertson and Alfred Plummer, *A Critical and Exegetical Commentary on the First Epistle of St. Paul to the Corinthians*, in *The International Critical Commentary* (New York: Charles Scribner's Sons, 1911) 98.

13. Murphy-O' Connor, *op. cit.*, 245, 240.

14. See Heinrici, *op cit.*, 162 n. 1.

15. Murphy-O'Connor, *op. cit.*, 240.

16. *Ibid.*, 242, 245.

17. *Ibid.*, 243–244.

18. So also Hans Conzelmann, *1 Corinthians*, in *Hermeneia*, ed. George W. MacRae and tr. James W. Leitch (Philadelphia: Fortress Press, 1975) 97.

19. Although his translation reflects the position I am arguing against, Otto Kuss has captured well what the role of Paul is, "Da sie (die Korinther) es nicht getan haben, muss der Apostel eingreifen; er ist ja auch für die Korinther letzte Instanz. Mit apostolischer Vollmacht entscheidet er feierlich und endgültig. . . . Die Gemeinde handelt als Ganzes unter Führung ihres Gründers und obersten Leiters Paulus"; see Otto Kuss, *Die Briefe an die Römer, Korinther und Galater*, in *Regensburger Neues Testament* 6 (Regensburg: Verlag Friedrich Pustet, 1940), 138.

20. Cambier, *op. cit.*, 230–231.

21. So Earl Edwards, "Fratellanza e separazione," *Ricerche Bibliche e Religiose* (Milano), 8, n. 3 (1973) 45–49.

22. Anthony C. Thiselton, "The Meaning of *SARX* in I Corinthians 5.5: A Fresh Approach in the Light of Logical and Semantic Factors," *Scottish Journal of Theology*, 26/2 (1973) 215, considers this to be a significant distinction and sees no connection between 1 Cor 5:3 and v. 5.

23. Eduard Schweizer, art. "Sarx," TDNT 7: 125–126, 129, includes all of these passages as well as 1 Cor 5:5 under the heading "*sarx* = body," except 1 Cor 15:50, which he discusses separately but says nonetheless, "Having to deal here with adversaries who think wholly in substantial categories, Paul in this v(erse) links *sarx kai haima* ("flesh and blood") with the thought of substance."

24. *Ibid.*, 127.

25. Schweizer agrees with this equation; see *ibid.*, 128–129.

26. So Reginald H. Fuller, *The Formation of the Resurrection Narratives* (New York: The Macmillan Company; London: Collier-Macmillan Ltd., 1971) 18–19.

27. See Hans Bietenhard, "Kennt das Neue Testament die Vorstellung vom Fegefeuer?" *Theologische Zeitschrift*, 3 (1947) 103.

28. See especially Wilhelm Bousset, "Der erste Brief an die Korinther," in *Die Schriften des Neuen Testaments neu überstezt und für die Gegenwart erklärt*, 2, 3rd ed. (Göttingen: Vandenhoeck & Ruprecht, 1917) 133; Kuss, *op. cit.*, 167, and more recently Kenneth Hein, *Eucharist and Excommunication. A Study in Early Christian Doctrine and Discipline*, in *European University Papers*, Theology Series 23, vol. 19, 2nd ed. (Bern: Herbert Lang; Frankfurt/M.: Peter Lang, 1975) 101.

29. It seems strange to find that Satan is the agent of the Lord Jesus for carrying out a punishment which culminates in salvation. Satan is usually thought of as God's enemy, but occasionally he can be the agent of God-given pain or punishment; see 2 Cor 12:7; 1 Tim 1:20. This apparent inconsistency in thought with regard to Satan is found also in Jewish writings close to and contemporary with the New Testament period. See Timothy C. G. Thornton, "Satan — God's Agent for Punishing," *The Expository Times*, 83 (1972) 151–152.

30. In Rom 1:24, 26, 28 there is deliverance over to various sins or sinful states, in Rom 6:17 to a standard of teaching, and in the remainder of passages where the term appears in the genuine letters of Paul reference is made to traditions which are handed on.

31. Edwards, *op. cit.*, 45, dismisses the notion of a physical death in one sentence,

because it presents the problem of how one comes to salvation on the Day of the Lord. This decision assumes *a priori* that there is only one way to come to salvation on the Day of the Lord.

32. Hein, *op. cit.*, 111–112 and also Erich Fascher, "Zu Tertullians Auslegung von 1 Kor. 5:1-5 (de pudicitia c. 13-16)," *Theologische Literaturzeitung*, 99 (1974) cols. 9-12.

33. Bousset, *op. cit.*, 133; tr., "Again we stand before a world which has become foreign to us."

Jerome D. Quinn

THE HOLY SPIRIT IN THE PASTORAL EPISTLES

In the eighties of the first Christian century, a small volume of Pauline correspondence appeared. In it there were three compositions in epistolary form, arranged with a letter to Titus preceding two letters to Timothy. All explicitly professed to come from the Pauline apostolate, and the final one from Paul's last days in Rome, a couple of decades previous. The correspondence certainly aimed at insuring the continuation of the *Pauline* apostolate and the *Pauline* teaching. There appear to be materials in the little volume that had originated in the previous generation and even in the Pauline mission. Concepts and terms in this correspondence regularly coincide with those in the letters that surely were dispatched by the historical Paul. Yet Titus, First and Second Timothy (the Pastoral Epistles as they have been dubbed in recent centuries — hereafter PE) make no explicit citation of, or appeals to, those Pauline documents of the first Christian generation. In this and in other respects the approach of PE to Paul resembles that of the author of Luke-Acts.[1]

Considerations such as these have dictated that studies of PE — historical, sociological, theological — be made in their own right. Comparison and contrast with other documents, Pauline or Lucan, is inevitable as the data peculiar to PE are gathered for analysis and evaluation. Yet PE make their own contribution to the teaching upon which they reflect. Their teaching on the Holy Spirit is paradigmatic in that regard.[2]

The Letter to Titus and the Spirit

There are two references to the Holy Spirit in Titus, one explicit, well known, often used, in 3:4-8; the other, implicit, seldom adverted to, and disconcerting, in 1:11-14. Precisely because the teaching of PE is regularly expected to be trite and that on the Spirit to be, above all, quite domesticated, it may be just as well to begin a study of the Spirit in PE where this correspondence began it, that is, in the setting of Christian congregations in the towns of Crete, where the teaching of the local

345

Pauline leadership is portrayed as pitted in a deadly struggle against a movement manned by native Cretan converts from Judaism.

> These men have to be muzzled, for they are the kind who teach things that they ought not and overturn entire households, to their own financial gain, shame to say. A countryman of theirs, *a prophet of their very own*, said:
>> "Liars ever, men of Crete,
>> Nasty brutes, that live to eat."
> This is a truthful testimony and good reason to refute them sharply, so that they recover their health in faith instead of hanging on Jewish myths and commandments of men who are abandoning the truth (Tit 1:11-14).[3]

It may be a coincidence that the only other New Testament references to Crete are in Acts (27:7, 12-13, 21), which also has Cretan Jews and proselytes (2:10-11) witness the Pentecost manifestation of the Spirit. The Jewish population of the island, already implied in 1 Macc 15:23, was by the first Christian century more notable. From their number Josephus took a wife. As late as the fifth century they were still open to the fatal allurements of a prophetic figure who claimed to be Moses redivivus.[4]

The passage cited from Titus excoriates converts from Cretan Jewish circles. To what extent the literary scenario of blistering vituperation and total rejection corresponds to a historical crisis in the latter part of the first Christian century remains problematic. The unmitigated bitterness of a Gal 5:12 has not made the historical reality of Paul's opponents at that juncture any less credible. Similarly, the fierce rhetoric of this passage in Titus may well envision actual opponents, conceived of as past persuading but not beyond range of verbal annihilation. That annihilation took the form of a dactylic hexameter quoted from a Greek poet whom the author of this letter thought was a Cretan, probably Epimenides.[5] He had crystallized with savage sharpness and unforgettable clarity a judgment on the Cretan character that became a commonplace of the Hellenistic world. With those who are "always liars" any argument is pointless. The text cited bolts together a pair of pliers that grips and crushes the opponents. On the one hand, the Hellenistic world at large since Pindar had regarded a poet as a prophet, a spokesman for people in general as well as for the infallible god, a man whose words were meant to be memorable, to shape the judgment and activity of the public.[6] On the other hand, Paul himself is made the guarantor of the accuracy of the pagan poet-prophet's censure of his countrymen. "This is truthful testimony." The apostolic word legitimates the prophetic word; he stands behind the popular estimate, in this instance, of the poet as prophet. There is no wiggling out of the grip of these pliers.

To begin one's teaching on the Spirit with the introduction of the figure of a prophet is not surprising. In the Old Testament tradition, the

Spirit of Yahweh was understood to initiate and vitalize the prophetic vocation.[7] Even a pagan, Balaam, touched by that Spirit, could only pronounce a blessing on Yahweh's wandering refugees (Num 22–24), though that blessing apparently did not salvage his later reputation (see Jude 11; 2 Pet 2:15; Rev 2:14). But in PE, previous to any citation of the Old Testament, a pagan prophet is quoted without demur, in an oracle that brings not a blessing but a condemnation upon those who claim Israel's credentials. The critical moment in the verification of the old pagan prophecy comes when the apostle to the pagans recognizes its truth. With that, two witnesses have testified and the Jewish Christian troublemakers stand convicted by the Torah that they invoke (see 1 Tim 5:19).

The relationship between prophet and apostle can be further illustrated from the Corinthian congregation, where, already in the fifties of the first century, the Apostle had the last, critical word about the prophetic interventions (see 1 Cor 14:37-38). The innovation in PE is the readiness to accept a pagan's judgment on the vicious acts (see 1 Tim 1:10) of his countrymen, whether they be Jew or Gentile, as in fact a prophetic judgment. If there are Christian, even Jewish Christian, liars, there are pagans who have revealed the truth about them, and "the truth whoever says it comes from the Holy Spirit."[8]

In Tit 3:4-8a, the Holy Spirit figures explicitly in the first of the five great *pistoi logoi*, "authentic statements of the faith," transmitted by PE.

> But then the humane munificence of our savior, God, shone out and he saved us, no thanks to any upright deeds that we performed ourselves but because of his own mercy, when we were reborn and renewed through a washing and by the Holy Spirit that he poured out lavishly on us, through Jesus Christ, our savior. His was the grace that made us upright, so that we could become heirs with a hope of life eternal. That is the Christian message meant to be believed.

As the closing sentence indicates, the realities that have just been articulated are to be received by faith. The *logos*, the message cited, is moreover the confession of a believing community, as the sevenfold repetition of the first person plural implies. The explicit mention of "a washing," of being "reborn," of an outpouring of the Spirit, of a change of heart suggests that the text cited here stood in some relation to the liturgical celebration of baptism in a Greek-speaking church. Perhaps that congregation already used for the sacrament a Trinitarian formula that can be glimpsed in the references to "our savior, God" (=the Father), "Jesus Christ, our savior," and "the Holy Spirit." The community that framed this *logos* had evidently undergone some influence from the Pauline teaching; yet the Pauline expressions alternate, without a hint of embarrassment, with other formulations.

Obviously the author of PE accepted this *logos* as authoritative and Pauline. Still, it is no quotation from a Pauline letter but emanates from a credal summary that in turn goes back to the celebration of baptism by a church that had in its turn learned something from Paul. Some have proposed that behind the credal statement transmitted here one can detect a very archaic baptismal hymn, sung in the celebration of that sacrament by the Roman church. Paul would have been alluding to, and commenting on, such a hymn in Rom 8:14-25 (cf. 1:4; Gal 3:23 and the use of "renewal" in Rom 12:2). The composition might still be more or less extant in 1 Pet 1:3-5.[9] In any event, the old hymn was deliberately reworked into the credal confession of a Church that had been considerably influenced by the Pauline apostolate.

The author of PE had no qualms about quoting such a sacramental, ecclesial, and Pauline *logos* in the "Pauline" epistolary that he was writing for a new generation to whom (he was convinced) Paul had also been sent. There would be no difficulty about his proposing the Pauline materials in this "message." But what authenticated the obviously non-Pauline elements? Simply the sacramental practice and the authority of the congregation that had worked up the *logos*? Much more probably the author of PE understood the old hymnic materials as revelation given by the Spirit through the prophetic order to the church.

To have said that in the ancient world poets were prophets is to imply that those prophets composed and sang oracles in poetic form. The choirs of Levites who sang the psalms and canticles of Israel in the post-exilic temple services were firmly linked by the Chronicler with the old prophetic order (see 1 Chr 25:1-8; 2 Chr 7:6 with 29:25-30; 35:15, 25).[10] Their singing of their compositions aimed beyond imparting knowledge and individualist gnosis; the prophetic hymn was targeted for liturgy, that is, for a worshipping community that was expected to respond at a level deeper and more intense than the purely intellectual.[11] Such prophetic hymns rapidly took their place alongside the Torah as authoritative Scripture in Israel.[12] Similarly, the prophetic hymns of the first Christian generation offered a base in revelation for later exhortation and teaching.[13] In this *logos* of Titus, the old hymn agreed with what Paul had taught. Prophet and apostle authenticated each other; sacramental celebration with prophetic hymns and apostolic teaching came as gifts from the same Spirit (see Rom 1:11-12; 12:6-8; 1 Cor 14:15, 26-33; Eph 5:18-19; Col 3:16). The *pistos logos* of Tit 3:4-7 preserved and transmitted both.

The description of the Holy Spirit transmitted in Tit 3:5-6 is no stereotype in comparison with other first-century formulations, though some aspects have their precedents. Thus the Trinitarian reference here to God-Spirit-Jesus Christ surfaces also in 1 Tim 3:15–4:1; 1 Cor 12:4-6, and 2 Cor 13:14, not to mention Mt 28:19. Yet the names themselves and their order vary in each of these loci.

As one looks more closely at the explicit terminology for the Spirit in PE, notable variations surface. Only here in Tit 3:5 and below in 2 Tim 1:14 is the Spirit described as "holy" (anarthrous *pneuma hagion*).[14] In 1 Tim 3:16 *en pneumati* is quite unqualified; in 2 Tim 1:7 the anarthrous *pneuma* is modified by a series of nouns in the genitive (cf. 1 Tim 4:1, *pneumasin planois*). *Tode pneuma* occurs in 1 Tim 4:1 where, for the only time in PE, the Spirit is subject of a sentence with a verb of speaking (*legei*). The closing blessing of 2 Tim 4:22 adds to *to pneuma* the possessive second person singular, *sou* (cf. 2 Tim 1:7).

To describe the Spirit as holy is evidently not yet for the author of PE a reflex formula. In fact, the Greek term, *hagios* ("holy") had not previously occurred in Titus, and apart from its one later use of the Spirit, the only other adjectival use of this word is the reference in 2 Tim 1:9 to the God "who saved us and called us for a holy life (*klēsei hagiai*)." The one other use of the term in PE is nominal — 1 Tim 5:10, where *hagiōn* ("the saints") refers to living Christian travelers. For PE, because the Spirit is "holy," those called to the Christian life are holy. As one returns to the initial appearance of "the Holy Spirit" in Tit 3:5, it seems far from arbitrary that the Spirit is described as holy precisely in conjunction with the baptismal "washing" that gave birth to a family that would inherit life eternal. That family (note again the first person plural) looks back upon a once-for-all, tangible event in which the "savior God . . . saved" them through the one whose name meant "savior."[15]

"A washing" (*loutron*) that gave rebirth and renewal "by the Holy Spirit" was the means of this rescue. The washing here certainly refers to the sacramental baptism of Christians, but the Greek term used here occurs elsewhere in the New Testament[16] only as Eph 5:26 speaks of Christ's sacrificial love for the Church "that he might sanctify (*hagiasēi*) her, having cleansed her by the washing (*tōi loutrōi*) of water with the word (*en rhēmati*)." The adjectival genitive "of water" in Ephesians becomes in Titus the adjectival "of rebirth and renewal." Where the author of Ephesians had emphasized the visible and audible components of the *loutron*, PE underline its effects, unseen and unheard, strictly proper to the Holy Spirit.

The baptismal washing is the Father's instrument (*dia loutrou*)[17] for transmitting a complex reality that pertains uniquely to the Spirit. The quasi-hendiadys of "rebirth and renewal" is as densely packed a description of that reality as can be found in the New Testament. The visibility of the "washing" forestalls understanding the phrase of a purely interior, subjective, and unseen process. The invisibility and interiority of the Spirit to whom "rebirth and renewal" belong prevents their being understood in a completely external, objective, and visible fashion. The Spirit who can and does create a new heart within the individual also causes change in the human world, that whole web of visible relationships by which persons are bound to one another.

The ancient Greek texts, profane and religious, Jewish and Christian, that refer to rebirth (*paliggenesia*) have been collected and reviewed adequately. [18] There is no denying that the Hellenistic world would have found the Christian use of this term intelligible; it had been bandied about in educated and religious circles. In this instance as elsewhere, the language of PE and of this *logos* shows "an approximation to the phraseology of the world around, a lessening of the feeling of isolation, and an increase in intelligibility to the ordinary contemporary man, had he happened on these books." [19]

The Christian penchant for the parabolic language of a new birth to describe their origin can be verified in traditions as diverse as Jas 1:18; 1 Pet 1:3; and Jn 3:3-8 (where the Spirit and water are also explicitly linked with the process). For that very reason it is surprising to find that the one other New Testament use of *paliggenesia* is in a saying of Jesus about the Twelve as participating in his own final judgment of Israel (Mt 19:28; cf. Lk 22:28-30; Q?). [20] What was the link between being born again and the day of final judgment that made *paliggenesia* exactly the term for compressing into one Greek word what an expansive Semitic phrase described as "When the Son of Man shall sit on his throne of glory . . ."? For the answer to this question one must appeal to the Jewish principle for probing the mysteries of the end time. *The Epistle of Barnabas* (6.13) formulated it thus: "The Lord says, 'See, I make the last things as the first (*ta eschata hōs ta prōta*).' " In other words, the end of this world was foreshadowed in its beginnings. The Apocalypse was the mirror image of Genesis. Jesus could appeal to this principle to set aside Moses on divorce (Mt 19:4-8 = Mk 10:3-9). The Qumran sectaries could cite it for their elucubrations on the sacred calendar. [21] In this way the *genesis* of history in God's creation finds its consummation in a *paliggenesia*; the birth of creation reaches its perfection in a rebirth that Christians identified with the risen Jesus' glorious *parousia* in judgment.

Paliggenesia was precisely the term to articulate the hope of Christians for their vindication in the final resurrection and judgment that their Lord was ushering in. That hope was a new patch on the old apocalyptic garment popular on the Palestinian scene among the Qumran sectaries and the Zealot guerillas. Their fervor climaxed in the suicidal frenzy of the great revolt that was to usher in a cosmic victory of God over all those who oppressed his people. Among Jewish Christians, who breathed such an atmosphere, it is no accident that the term "rebirth" moved from the wide screen of Jesus' cosmic intervention on a vast, public, and drastic scale to the sacramental order. There apocalyptic enthusiasm could be depoliticized. There the new creation of man began as God changed his heart, not as men changed their government.

In Titus, the inseparable complement to rebirth is renewal, *anakainōsis*. Each term qualifies the other, but where *paliggenesia* had a secular and religious (Jewish as well as pagan) history previous to its appearance in Christian documents, the same cannot be said for *anakainōsis*. It has yet to be documented in pre-Christian Greek and first appears in Christian sources. The earliest use is in Rom 12:2, where the second great section of the epistle opens its paraenesis with Paul's urging those believers, "Do not be conformed to this age (*aiōni*) but be transformed by the renewal of mind (*tēi anakainōsei tou noos*) that you may prove what is the will of God, what is good and acceptable and perfect." The noun seems to be a Pauline neologism that is closely related to his usage (alone in the New Testament and the apostolic Fathers) of the cognate *anakainoun* (2 Cor 4:16; Col 3:10),[22] which emphatically refers to the inner, unseen part of the human person. The unusual term appears to have caught the ear of the Roman church, and whoever fashioned the *pistos logos* of Titus put an unmistakably Pauline stamp and interpretation on the *paliggenesia* by joining it to *anakainōsis*. The former term was susceptible to being explained in the visible, external, cosmic sense of an apocalyptic *manqué*. The Pauline *anakainosis*, with its emphatically internal sense, gave the definitive touch to understanding the rebirth effected by the Holy Spirit, a rebirth of the human mentality, of the inner person, that was to issue in a new, holy way of life. The imagery of birth emphasizes the break with the past and the entrance into a new existence. The "renewal" suggests that the Spirit has renovated the heart of a man which has thus become set on "what is good and acceptable and perfect."

The *pistos logos* goes on to describe the Holy Spirit, in Tit 3:6, as one that the Savior God "poured out lavishly on us, through Jesus Christ, our savior." The description of the coming of the Spirit in terms of a once-for-all "pouring out" (the Greek, *execheen*, is aorist) upon the faithful deliberately suggests that visible baptismal washing (see *Didache* 7:3) in which the sacramental waters had flowed over the believer. Of no less importance was the fact that this was precisely the terminology used by the LXX translation of the prophets to describe the way in which Yahweh's spirit would pour out over Israel, in Zech 12:10[23] and LXX Jl 3:1-2.

The downpour of a rainstorm, bringing life and growth to a desert,[24] is the image that Joel exploits when he transmits Yahweh's oracle: "And it shall come to pass afterward, that *I will pour out my spirit* on all flesh; your sons and your daughters shall prophesy, your old men shall dream dreams and your young men shall see visions. Even upon the menservants and maidservants in those days, *I will pour out my spirit*" (cf. Jl 2:23-24 with Is 32:14-15; 44:3-5). For Acts 2:17-18, the apostolic interpretation of the Pentecost events opened with this very prophecy and closed with a repetition of the crucial verb to describe the exalted Christ who, "having received from the Father the promise of the Holy Spirit, . . . has poured out (*execheen*) this which you see and hear" (2:33). Significantly, in the later narrative about the pagan Cornelius, a cognate form of this verb occurs to describe how the six Jewish Christians who had accompanied Peter "were amazed because the gift (*hē dōrea*) of the Holy Spirit had been poured out (*ekkechytai*) even on the Gentiles" (Acts 10:45; see Rom 5:5). Thus the Old Testament prophetic text is alluded to at just those points where the Spirit comes upon, first Israel, then "upon all flesh."[25] The work of the Spirit, like the work of Jesus, must be "according to the Scriptures."

The *pistos logos* has enhanced the verb *execheen* with the adverb *plousiōs*, "lavishly," which is, in PE, used in a good sense (1 Tim 6:17-18). Here in Titus the Spirit's munificence to men is, like the Spirit, radically unseen and internal (see Col 3:16 and 2 Pet 1:11, the only other New Testament occurrences of *plousiōs*). The lavish outpouring "on us" (*eph' hēmas*) is not to be taken in a monopolistic sense. The use of the first person plural for the community of believers happily combines both the personal, internal experience professed together as well as the universal purpose of that common profession of faith, for the community seeks and hopes to share the lavish blessings poured out "on us" with all human beings (see Tit 2:11-14). When this letter of "Paul" to "Titus" takes up the first person plural of the *pistos logos*, the reader would be meant to understand the phrase of the Spirit poured out on Paul the Jew, and Titus the Gentile, who, like the whole congregation of believers, are to take the lead in sharing the Spirit's gifts with all people.

The act of the savior Father that has poured out the regenerating renewal of the Spirit upon his people has taken place not simply "through (*dia*) a washing" but also "through (*dia*) Jesus Christ our savior." In Titus the only uses of *dia* are in this *pistos logos*. In fact, for all the many uses of this particle in 1–2 Timothy, the PE do not employ this phrase again, though it is rather frequent in the rest of the Pauline correspondence.[26] Again the language of the *pistos logos* has at this point the Pauline cachet, while the following phrase, "our savior," is peculiar to PE, where its formulaic character suggests a liturgical usage.[27]

The goal and purpose of the divine saving intervention described in this *logos* are prefaced by a phrase that takes up the Pauline cause and language from the Apostle's historic confrontation with his Jewish Christian colleagues on the relation of works (of the Law) to justification. "His [God's] was the grace that made us upright" [literally, "made upright (*dikaiōthentes*) by the former's grace"] uses the verb *dikaioun* as Paul used it at every turn in Galatians and Romans.[28] This verb, in another sense, will be linked with the Spirit once more in PE in the hymnic fragment of 1 Tim 3:16 to be analyzed below. In this *pistos logos* the verb stands as a credal commitment to the Pauline side in the controversy about God's righteousness and human works, functioning in a way that the Nicean *homoousios* does in identifying the Athanasian party in the Arian controversies of the fourth century.

Paul himself was the only one who could adequately summarize his own theology of justification. Still, the attempts of the second Christian generation to do so, whether in the Lucan corpus [29] or in this *pistos logos* or in *First Clement*,[30] witness to the determination of that generation to continue the Pauline apostolate (not just the Pauline teaching, important as that was) to churches that had forgotten or had ignored or were embarrassed by the works and words of the slave (see Tit 1:1) who had not been above his Master, in life or in death. For PE, the Church and its ministry are to be visibly, recognizably upright and to pursue holiness (Tit 1:8; 2:12; 1 Tim 6:11; 2 Tim 2:22) without any compromise of the Pauline gospel on the utter gratuity of the holiness enlivened by the Spirit and by the grace of the savior God (see 2 Tim 1:8-11). In the previous generation Paul had thus taught and had directed churches from which he was bodily absent. He had done so through his coworkers and emissaries as well as in writing. PE set out to continue the Pauline apostolate in a new generation from which Paul was physically absent but a time in which he could still direct and teach through those who had inherited his ministry as well as through a new "correspondence."

The Letters to Timothy on the Spirit

It is at the center of this volume of PE and of First Timothy itself that 1 Tim 3:14–4:5 returns explicitly to the Spirit, in a passage that forms a "piece in pause" or an interlude between the Pauline exhortations that precede and follow. A reference to prophecy in 1 Tim 1:18 will be treated with 4:14 below; at this point it suffices to note the parentheses of prophecy that frame this interlude and its teaching on the Father, "the living God," the Son "who was revealed in human flesh," and the Spirit whose oracle is quoted in 4:1.

The piece opens with an abrupt return to the first person singular (last read in 1 Tim 1:3, 18) and an apology for this written exhortation in lieu of Paul's own presence, his apostolic parousia, in R. Funk's happy phrase.[31] After defining "God's house," that is, his temple, as "the church of the living God,"[32] the author describes "the truth" ensconced there, in a vision of "the mystery of godliness," undeniable and overwhelming.

> . . . He who was revealed in human flesh,
> was made victorious in the Spirit:

> He who was seen by God's messengers,
> was heralded to the pagans:
> He who was received in faith, in the world,
> was taken up in glory (1 Tim 3:16).

The text is a gem from the treasury of first-century Christian liturgy with many facets to its surface and fires within it. In genre, it is a hymn, quite conceivably with an Aramaic prototype whose rhythm can still be heard behind the two Greek accents of each line and whose end rhyme has become the six-times-repeated Greek aorist passive ending.[33] The lines quoted are a torso, the precise features of whose head are quite lost, though the initial masculine pronoun must have referred to Jesus under one or more Christological titles, and the opening formula may be hypothesized from the way in which this genre of composition opens in the hymns and prayers of contemporary Judaism.[34] One might submit:

> Confess the Lord,
> Christ Jesus,
> God's Son. . . .[35]

The extant lines that follow illustrate M. Hengel's observation that scientific theological prose was not the instrument the first Christians employed to articulate the mystery of Jesus. That task was primarily reserved for the language of the worship of Jesus; and in the liturgical assembly it was done particularly in the "hymns inspired by the Spirit," with their "bold Christological sketches" of the paradox of the humiliation and exaltation of the Christ. The worshippers heard what they believed in their hearts sung out in prophetic praises, and they responded to it.[36] This text of First Timothy as a whole glorifies Christ in the mission of the apostles,[37] specifically the mission to the pagans. One can only surmise whether it was originally one of those enthusiastic, ecclesial acclamations in Judea, occasioned by the conversion and apostolate of Paul, praises that the Apostle himself adduced in Gal 1:22-24: "And they glorified God because of me (*en emoi*)." Such prophetic hymns were regarded on a level with the Scriptures of Israel as revealing and authenticating what God and his Christ were accomplishing.[38]

In this study, the reference to the Spirit in the second stich must be discussed in terms of the first, its antithetic parallel. The rare Greek verb *phaneroun* behind "who was revealed" and the unusual sense of the verb *dikaioun*, here translated as "was made victorious," already signal the poetic density of the fragment,[39] just as the passives betray the Semitic circumlocution for the divine name. It is God himself who has revealed and vindicated Christ Jesus, his Son. The traditional apocalyptic schema, which turns on "hidden/revealed," is here used paradoxically.[40] This revelation (cf. Tit 1:3 with 2 Tim 1:9-10) took place "in human flesh" (*en sarki*); the vindication occurred "in the Spirit" (*en pneumati*). The Greek preposition *en* may refer to the order or sphere of an activity; it may, with a deliberate poetic ambivalence, reflect the Semitic *b* which has also an instrumental meaning. Thus God's Son was to be seen in the human order, in that which was by nature mortal and fragile, the flesh; it is, ironically, by means of that perishable complex that the imperishable God has appeared (see 1 Tim 6:14-16). The mystery of the earthly life and the scandalous death of Jesus is the concrete referent of this language.[41]

In antithetic parallelism with the first stich, the second acclaims Jesus as "made victorious in the Spirit" (*edikaiōthē en pneumati*). If the previous "in human flesh" indeed designated the whole mortal existence of Jesus as the sphere in which, and the means by which, God had finally revealed "the mystery of the faith" (1 Tim 3:9, cf. with 16), his own Son,[42] then *en pneumati* designates the sphere of rebirth and renewal (Tit 3:5), the order of eternal life in contrast to that of mortal life, which in a special sense lies in the Spirit's gift and power.

Can this work of the Spirit be further specified? Hebraic categories do not demand that the spirit be taken as in conflict with the flesh.[43] The verb, *dikaioun*, moreover, occurs here in a sense that is marginally Greek and by no means Pauline either.[44] It is rather Jewish "translation Greek" for the Hebrew root *ṣdq*, which means not only "to justify" but also "to redress, to vindicate, to deliver, to save, to make victorious." Thus the Son, whom God revealed in the ineluctable mortality of the flesh, he also rescued and vindicated *en pneumati*. That victory and vindication might be taken of the powerful acts in the Spirit that accompanied the earthly ministry of Jesus (see Lk 4:18; Acts 10:38), acts for which he bestowed the same Spirit on his followers after his resurrection (Lk 24:49; Acts 2:33; 10:44, 47). Yet the primary reference of the text seems to be to the victory of Jesus' own resurrection, which not only complemented that scandalous revelation "in human flesh" but also preceded his appearance to, and commissioning of, the apostolic messengers, events that prompt the next lines of this hymn.

But in what sense does the resurrection victory belong to the Spirit? The entry, even bodily, into a new order, into eternal life in contrast to the mortal one that had ended on the cross, is appropriately attributed to the Spirit of rebirth and renewal (Tit 3:5; see 1 Pet 3:18). This hymnic terminology may lie behind such Pauline formulations as, "If the Spirit of him who raised Jesus from the dead dwells in you, he who raised Christ Jesus from the dead will give life to your mortal bodies also through (*dia*)[45] his Spirit which dwells in you" (Rom 8:11; see 1:3-4). On the other hand, when Paul is himself reflecting on the role of the Spirit, he does not exploit this link with the resurrection. The author of PE accordingly distinguishes nicely here between the writing of his "Paul" in 3:14 and the hymn cited in 3:16.

The emphasis on the Spirit's powerful acts among believers, in their prophecies, revelations, healings, tongues, blessings, and prayers,[46] appears explicitly in the second part of this interlude in First Timothy. Here, after the citation of the archaic prophetic hymn to Christ, the author introduces a Christian prophetic oracle:

> Here is the Spirit (*tode pneuma*) expressly declaring (*rhētos legei*) that in latter times some people, who pay heed to specious spirits (*pneumasin planois*) and demonic doctrines (*didaskaliais daimoniōn*), will apostatize from the faith . . . (1 Tim 4:1).

In the following verses (2-5), which the author of PE laminated grammatically into the oracle of 4:1, the more generic prophetic saying has been applied to specific teachings on the use of food and sex. The author of PE scores such "demonic doctrines" as incompatible with the teaching of Scripture (specifically Gen 1) and that *sensus fidelium* which expresses itself in grateful prayer for all of God's creatures. The forbidding of marriage and enjoining dietary taboos do not proceed from "God's Spirit" that had been brought upon the very origin of creation (see LXX Gen 1:2). The Scripture, itself all "God-enspirited" (2 Tim 3:16), actually reveals that sexual procreation as well as human nourishment from all the fruits of the earth belonged to God's will for mankind and were "very good" (cf. LXX Gen 1:26-31 with 1 Tim 4:3-4). To this "word of God" (1 Tim 4:5) the response of believers had been prayers of thanksgiving for his gifts of family and food (1 Tim 4:4-5). Such sanctifying prayer (cf. *hagiazetai* and 2 Tim 2:21) also proceeds from the Holy (cf. *Hagion*) Spirit who dwells within believers (see 2 Tim 1:3-14).

The very Spirit who has given the word of God and enkindled the response of believers to that word is the Spirit "expressly declaring" the oracle of 1 Tim 4:1. Only here in PE, as noted previously, is the Spirit the subject of a sentence, and his personal role clearly emerges at this point when speech is attributed to him with an introductory formula that materially recalls the LXX introduction to Yahweh's prophetic oracles. The Spirit can replace the LORD as the person in whose name the Christian prophet speaks.[47] Here is the Spirit,[48] who spoke through the sacred letters that transmit the perennially pertinent words of the prophets (cf. 1 Tim 5:18 with 2 Tim 3:15-16), now speaking through the Christian prophets (see 1 Cor 12:10), through their hymns and the written collections of their sayings (for *rhētos*[49] here implies the verifiable citation of a document). As what Paul says comes through PE (see *legein* in 1 Tim 2:7; 2 Tim 2:7), so what the Spirit says comes through the collections of the Christian prophetic oracles.

The language of the oracle itself is no more stereotyped than that of its introduction. The Greek phrase here translated as "in latter times" is not documented otherwise in biblical Greek or the apostolic Fathers. It is, however, a variant on the biblical expressions for the consummation of human history, whose hot apocalyptic connotations are somewhat cooled in this verbal recycling. The plural emphasizes the diverse times and brief seasons of that one age, which includes not only the astounding spread of the faith in the Son of God but also wide resistance to it. If the preceding prophetic hymn was sung by an exultant young Church, filling with an unexpected hundredfold harvest of converts, it was balanced, perhaps even in its original setting, by another prophetic intervention warning of the day when this happy situation would go sour. The high tide of converts to the faith is immediately (at least for the author of PE) compared and contrasted with a later ebbing into apostasy. The God who had brought about the former had also warned of the latter. The most primitive Christian eschatological outlook is here, as also in the preceding hymn, simply presumed. The prophet and his hearers are convinced that they are living in the last age that had begun with Jesus' resurrection and that was going to be consummated with the general resurrection. PE cite the old oracle in conjunction with the hymn to remind a new generation of Christians that they had prophecies from their fathers that the last age would in fact have bad days as well as good, losses as well as gains. The very Spirit who gave the victory to Jesus had predicted the setbacks among his followers.[50]

The nucleus of the oracle, whose sophisticated literary character has already appeared in the introductory phrases, is articulated with a staccato of alliteration in *p*, *t*, and finally *d* sounds that suggest a certain vehemence and intensity, even when partially reproduced in translation.[51] The last age will not be all sweetness and light. "Some people" (a discreet way of saying "many")[52] are going to abandon the faith. Their apostasy is "an eschatological phenomenon,"[53] which belongs to the dark side of the last age. This precise terminology for apostasy is not characteristic of PE or of the rest of the Paulines. In fact, "the apostasy" of 2 Thess 2:3 (cf. 9-12) may be an allusion to the language of just such an oracle as that cited here in 1 Tim 4:1. In any event, this oracle envisions an abandonment of the faith, that is, of the ecclesial confession of Jesus (cf. Gal 1:23).

For the Jew, apostasy was consummated in the abandonment of the practices that identified one as a member of the Jewish community (see 1–4 Macc *passim*; Acts 21:21); for PE, though they recognize the former (Tit 1:16; 1 Tim 5:8), emphasis falls on the denial of right belief and the acceptance of a variant teaching about the gospel (e.g., 1 Tim 1:3-7; 6:3-5). The ultimate moment of apostasy in which a believer utterly disowns his Lord, under the threat of persecution, figures explicitly in the *pistos logos* cited by 2 Tim 2:11-13 (cf. 2 Tim 3:10-13). It was in those crucial moments of persecution that the Lucan tradition emphasized that the Holy Spirit would teach a believer what he ought to say (Lk

12:11-12; see parallels and Acts 5:32). Once that vein had been tapped, the power of the Spirit could be perceived welling up behind every right confession of the faith in words.

Conversely, apostasy could be seen as beginning with a different articulation of that faith, in words that could not be reconciled with those that the Spirit had taught. Consequently, those who made such a heterodox confession must have ultimately another spirit as their teacher; or as the archaic oracle cited by PE puts it, they "pay heed (*prosechontes*) to specious spirits and demonic doctrines." The verb *prosechein* here (as in Tit 1:14; 1 Tim 1:4) almost means "addicted," as to alcoholic spirits (1 Tim 3:8). As there is only one Holy Spirit, one apostle, one teacher, one teaching recognized by PE,[54] so behind apostasy stand multiple teachers, demonic spirits from whom proliferate varied teachings about Jesus (see 2 Cor 11:13-14). The Spirit brands such spirits as "specious" (*planois*), pretending to be true (see 2 Cor 6:8), authoritative, and credible while really false, unauthorized, and incredible.

The Jewish background for this oracle may be seen in the Qumran doctrine on "the two spirits of truth and perversity" (1QS 3.18-19) that vie for and are even within the human heart. In the Damascus Document (CD 12.2-3), Belial's company of spirits controls the opinions of those who differ from the views of the sectaries. A sort of metastasis from these spirits occurs, which results in corresponding "spirits" in human beings.[55] The hymnist of 1QH 1.21-23 can call himself "a spirit of straying"[56] and "void of understanding" for having once held the incorrect teachings of the Jerusalem priesthood on the liturgical calendar.[57]

The oracle of 1 Tim 4:1 balances and parallels the Semitic "specious spirits" with the rather more Greek phrase "demonic doctrines" (*didaskaliais daimoniōn*). In contrast to the one, authentic Pauline doctrine about the meaning of the letter of the Scriptures of Israel, there stand interpretations as multifarious as the pseudo-divine demons who spawn them. The PE do not otherwise use the term *daimonion*, which in fact occurs only once elsewhere in the Pauline corpus, in 1 Cor 10:20-21. There the link between pagan worship and the worship of "demons" has spun off of the language of LXX Dt 32:17 (see Bar 4:7, 35; LXX Ps 105:37, etc.), which in turn practically made *daimonion* into a technical term in Hellenistic Jewish literature for the deities of paganism, contemptuously branded as spirits hostile and injurious to man.[58] The original form of the oracle here in PE must have had its own language influenced by that Jewish Greek tradition. The author of PE surely understood his written exposition of the Pauline teaching as opposed to such "demonic doctrines" as are listed in 4:2-5. The implication is that to abandon Paul's gospel was to relapse into the paganism from which that gospel had rescued believers. To what teachings this prophecy in its original setting referred can only be surmised. The language, however, is of a piece with the Jewish polemical assault on idolatry and the polytheistic cults of paganism as "the beginning and cause and end of every evil" (Wis 14:27), a basic thrust to which the author of PE is faithful.

In PE there is a massive emphasis on the Spirit in relation to one person, Timothy. At 1 Tim 1:18-19, the apostolic commands that the author has Paul write, conclude thus:

> This is the charge I am setting out before you, Timothy, my child, a charge that *accords with the prophecies that led to you in the first place (kata tas proagousas epi se prophēteias)*. They were given to help you put up a good fight, keeping your faith and a clear conscience.

Another block of exhortations and commands follow the piece in pause analyzed above. Again one reads of Paul saying to Timothy:

> Until I arrive, concentrate on your public reading [of the Scriptures of Israel], on your preaching, on your instruction (*tēi didaskaliai*). Neglect not that gracious gift within you (*tou en soi charismatos*), the one given you under prophetic direction (*dia prophēteias*) with an imposition of the hands of the presbytery (*meta epitheseōs tōn cheirōn tou presbyteriou*). (1 Tim 4:13-14)

The same emphasis continues into the second letter to Timothy, where the great opening thanksgiving prayer (2 Tim 1:3-14) has:

> So I, with good reason, remind you, Timothy, to rekindle that gracious gift of God (*to charisma tou theou*) which is within you through the imposition of my hands (*dia tēs epitheseōs tōn cheirōn mou*); for God gave us not a dastard spirit (*pneuma deilias*) but one of dynamic strength (*dynameōs*) and of charity (*agapēs*) and of discretion (*sōphronismou*). (2 Tim 1:6-7)

Then after reviewing the gospel deposited with Paul for his apostolate, the prayer issues, almost imperceptibly, into exhortation:

> With that faith and charity which are yours in Christ Jesus, hold unto the prototype of the wholesome words that you heard from me. Keep that excellent deposit (*tēn kalēn parathēkēn*), Timothy, through the Holy Spirit who dwells in us (*dia pneumatos hagiou tou enoikountos en hēmin*). (2 Tim 1:13-14)

In the light of all these texts, the final blessing of this letter, "The Lord be with your spirit, Timothy" (2 Tim 4:22), is no trite formula.

The concentration of all these data around the figure of Timothy alone may illustrate a penchant of PE for focusing on one figure and quite ignoring others as the author seeks to ensure the unity of believers against the inroads of the heterodox. If such is the case, the relation of Paul through Titus to the presbyter-bishops for the cities of one area (Tit 1:5-9) may serve a rather different function from the much more detailed description in the passages just cited, of the relation of Paul and others to Timothy, not to mention the relation of Timothy to presbyters (1 Tim

5:17-25) as well as to "trustworthy Christian men, the kind who will be competent to teach others" (2 Tim 2:2). The full analysis of these paradigms must be reserved for a later work. For the present study it will suffice to observe that the data that pertain to the Spirit explicitly surface in the descriptions of the way in which Timothy came to share in the Pauline apostolate.

The PE do not place the Spirit at Timothy's disposal; at every turn they emphasize that he is at the Spirit's disposal. The repeated mention of prophecy as the context for Timothy's initiation into an apostolic ministry continues to use a category that has appeared, in one fashion or another, at every stage of this analysis of the way in which PE regard the Spirit. The "historical Paul" had no qualms about defining the apostolic task that he and Silvanus and Timothy had performed in Corinth in the early fifties as a "ministry of the Spirit" (cf. 2 Cor 1:19 with 3:4-8). Moreover, if he had to rank the many *charismata* of the one Spirit, then the very first of the Spirit's palpable effects is apostles, "second, prophets; third, teachers" (1 Cor 12:28; cf. 12:4).[59] The PE see the teaching ministry of their "Timothy" emerging out of the historical choice of the apostle and the intervention of the Spirit in prophecy. The man whom Paul had designated for the apostolate by the imposition of his two hands had also been the Spirit's choice, revealed by prophetic oracles, which led a body of presbyters to impose their hands on him.

How did PE conceive of this intervention by the Spirit? Probably in the way that Acts conceived of it, particularly Acts 13:1-3. There the prophets and teachers of the church in Antioch, including Barnabas and Saul, assembled for liturgical worship and fasting, heard a prophetic oracle from the Holy Spirit, saying, "Set apart for me Barnabas and Saul for the work (*eis to ergon*) to which I have called them." A fast, along with public prayer (*proseuxamenoi*), then issues in imposing hands on and dispatching the two.[60]

Similarly, here in PE, a public gathering is envisioned for a liturgy of the Word.[61] The body of presbyters presides. Among them a variety of individual roles exist already (see 1 Tim 5:17). Portions of the Old Testament Scriptures are read out to the assembly by one of its leaders; those with prophetic and teaching endowments then preach and instruct.[62] In the course of the preaching (which would quite naturally include prayer), one or more of the prophets, in the name of the Spirit, designated Timothy for an imposition of hands that would endow him with God's gift for concentrating "on your public reading [of the Scriptures of Israel], on your preaching, on your instruction." It is possible that 1 Tim 6:11-16 is the summary of just such an ordination charge and prophetic sermon (cf. 1 Tim 1:18 with 6:12; 2 Tim 2:3-4; 4:5, 7), from its opening address to the man of God (an Old Testament designation for a prophet) to its final doxology.[63] In any case, the presbyteral imposition of hands has been a phenomenon accompanying[64] a divinely bestowed charism for continuing[65] leadership in Christian assemblies for liturgical worship.

The PE emphatically link that gift with the imposition of Paul's own hands (2 Tim 1:6), which, like the baptismal washing of Tit 3:5, is understood instrumentally, of God's thus taking this man for the apostolic work (cf. 2 Tim 4:5 with 2:6, 15; 3:17; and 1 Tim 4:10).[66] The gift, like a flame, can die down and flare up; and it is not by chance that it is in a context of prayer that Paul reminds his colleague "to rekindle that gracious gift." The charism was for leading the prayer of the Church; it is fed by the continuing prayer of the Apostle and the one with whom he shared his task. For that leadership the first requisites are the harvest of the Spirit, and thus in 2 Tim 1:7 the effects of the charism (that is, of the work of the Spirit) are themselves described in terms of antithetical spirits (see 1 Tim 4:1). The Spirit produces a spirit in a person (2 Tim 4:22).[67] The Spirit of God does not evoke a spirit of personal cowardice," a dastard spirit," to use an English phrase that suggests the effect of the term *deilias*, unique here in the New Testament. Sharing a ministry like Paul's demands courage from God. To lead men in prayer, the Pauline collaborator must have not just "the appearance of godliness" but "its dynamic" (2 Tim 3:5), which works wonders beyond human strength.[68]

With a polysyndetic series of *and*'s the author ensures that the wonders of which he speaks will not be understood apart from charity, probably charity toward neighbor, as in 1 Cor 13:1-3. This spirit of charity is, in its turn, as much the effect of the Holy Spirit (see Gal 5:22) as the preceding dynamic power and the following "discretion" (*sōphronismou*), a completely unbiblical term, unattested in the apostolic Fathers and quite startling in its context here. Again, the Spirit shatters stereotypes. The term, which began to appear as a popular philosophical buzz-word in the Hellenistic Greek of the first century B.C., meant both having self-control and the actual conveying of it to others (cf. *logos* with *logismos*). In Paul and his co-worker, that ability to practice and teach a virtue, on which the Hellenistic world set the highest premium, was simply part of the wonderful work of the Spirit, ordered toward a fearless preaching and instruction about the Scriptures that were read out in public Christian worship.

As the Spirit through his "gracious gift" had designated Timothy for the liturgical reading of "the sacred Letters" that he had known "from tenderest years" from the Jewish side of his family (2 Tim 3:14-15; cf. 1:5 with Acts 16:1), it is important to note that for PE:

> All the Scripture [is] inspired by God (*theopneustos*) and effective —
>> for instruction (*pros didaskalian*);
>> for censuring;

for straightening persons out;
for giving training in upright conduct,
so that the man of God may be "compleat," i.e., completely equipped for
every good work (2 Tim 3:16-17).

The same Spirit who through prophetic words and apostolic action gave his charism to Timothy for his ministry, also made the written texts of Israel's sacred letters another means by which God would address his people. The Spirit is no more imprisoned by the letter of the Scripture than by the baptismal washing or by the imposition of hands. God freely acts through the hands of people, whether writing or pouring the baptismal waters or imposing them in prayer. The Spirit is no more imprisoned in the apostolic minister than in "the prophet . . . a man borne along by the spirit" (LXX Hos 9:7 — *pneumatophoros*; cf. Num 24:2-4 of the pagan Balaam, as well as 2 Pet 1:21). As Paul was the Lord's prisoner, not Nero's, and the Word of God cannot be manacled at all (2 Tim 1:8; 2:9), the Scriptures, and the prophetic-apostolic minister who proclaims them, belong to the Spirit (but not vice versa). Tit 1:12 has shown that for this author even a pagan poet could be moved by the Spirit in prophecy. Thus 2 Tim 3:16 emphasizes that *all* Scripture (as contrasted with *some* other writing) has been produced by God's Spirit.[69] From that origin derives its effectiveness "for every good work" (*pros pan ergon agathon*) of the man who has received a prophetic ministry, who is "the man of God." In the four-member list of ministerial activities for which Scripture is effective, the "instruction" that heads the list takes one back to 1 Tim 4:13 and that *ordo servandus* for the liturgy of the Word that opened with the public reading of the OT and concluded with "the instruction."

One finishing touch remains in PE for their portrait of the ministry of the Spirit that is shared by Paul and Timothy. That occurs in 2 Tim 1:13-14, the concluding exhortation of the thanksgiving prayer cited above. There Timothy is the one who has heard (not read) the paradigmatic Pauline words, heard them in Christian faith and love. The prayer had opened (1:5) with Paul's thanksgiving for the faith which dwelt (*enōikēsen*) in Timothy and his Jewish mother and his grandmother. The same verb recurs as the prayer closes, to describe the Holy Spirit "who dwells in us" — that is, in Paul and Timothy. This verb is, in the New Testament, exclusively Pauline. It describes people as the temple of God (see 2 Cor 6:16, citing a non-LXX Greek Lev 26:11-12), of the Spirit (Rom 8:11), of "the word (*logos*) of Christ" (Col 3:16).[70]

Here PE develop further that figure of Christians as themselves a temple for the God in whom they believe and whom they worship. The temple in the ancient world was a veritable bank, an inviolate place in which people deposited their treasures for safekeeping by the deity who dwelt there and the priests who served him (see 1 Macc 6:2; 2 Macc

1:13-16). The temple in Jerusalem was no exception (see 1 Macc 1:21-23; 2 Macc 3:6, 9-23). Already in 1 Cor 9:13 it is taken for granted that the privileges and duties of the Jerusalem priests in their temple can be compared with, and serve as warrants for, what the apostolic workmen do in the service of the living God's temple, the Church (see 1 Tim 3:15). For PE, the Apostle and the one with whom he has shared his apostolate have received the gospel as a "deposit" (*parathēkēn*; see 2 Tim 1:12 and 1 Tim 6:20), a precious and attractive (*kalēn*) treasure to be guarded under Christ (cf. *phylaxai . . . phylaxon*, 2 Tim 1:12, 14). Apostolic ministers, whether they give or receive, whether a Paul or a Timothy, are also being watched over and sustained by the Spirit as they guard the treasure that has been deposited with them for safekeeping and for entrusting (*parathou*) to other believers, "the kind that will also be competent to teach others" (2 Tim 2:2).

Thus the Spirit who speaks through the prophets, Jewish and Christian, through written compositions from the past and through living persons in the present age, also guards and protects the transmission of the gospel treasure. That transmission is no simply material transfer of records from one safety deposit box to another. For that, a divine intervention would be otiose. What is at stake is a living and authoritative continuity in teaching and interpreting the Word of God (see Tit 2:5, 7-8, 10).[71] That word has not been manacled; it did not die with Paul, its paradigmatic teacher in PE. The Spirit had given it life and power in the Apostle. The same Spirit who dwelt in Paul also dwelt in the Timothy who had shared the Pauline apostolate, who had heard the Pauline teaching, who had received the imposition of Paul's hands.

The same Spirit who had once designated Timothy for this apostolic work will now put him on guard against the opponents of the gospel, Paul's gospel and his (see 2 Tim 4:15). The link of Timothy with the Spirit continues to the very last words of PE. The final prayer of the apostle is that the Lord, the Risen Jesus whom they both serve, stay with and protect that spirit in Timothy that has been the gift of the Holy Spirit (2 Tim 4:22).

Summary

The Holy Spirit, in the teaching of PE, stands at the origin of creation and its renewal in the work of Christ Jesus. The author of this correspondence has traced out the lines of force that run between the Spirit and the visible "orders" in the human world, from the created order itself (see 1 Tim 4:1-5), through the whole order of Christian moral conduct (cf. Tit 2:1-15 with 3:5-6), to the various orders in the Christian community — apostolic, prophetic, sacramental (see Tit 3:5; 1 Tim 1:18; 4:14, etc.). There is, accordingly, no abhorrence of human society, of human institutions, of human art and virtue in PE. There is rather a completely disarming openness to them that still manages to remain independently critical (see 1 Tim 6:1-10, 17-19).

The author of PE has some of the superb confidence of Paul himself (see 1 Cor 7:40) that he can tell the difference between the works of the Holy Spirit and those of unholy ones. The conviction that Paul had shared his authority, his teaching, his apostolic mission serves to warrant this confidence. The apostolic task in PE complements the prophetic work. Moreover, the same Spirit who gave apostle and prophet to the people of God has also given the Scriptures and other literature for the formation and the direction of all (cf. Tit 2:11-15 with 2 Tim 3:14-17 and 1 Tim 4:1; 5:18). The roles of prophet and apostle converge in the assemblies of the Christians for communal worship. There the Spirit ultimately stands behind the hymnic and other confessional compositions that have grown out of Christian liturgies of the Word and of sacrament, in which the Pauline and prophetic teaching continue.[72] The Spirit and his dynamic are inseparable from the external, tangible expressions of teaching and of godliness (cf. 2 Tim 1:6-7, 13-14 with 3:5). The privileged paradigms of the Spirit's power are, for PE, Christian believers who have placed their personal lives, internal and external, mental and bodily, in the service of the Father and the Son and the Holy Spirit.

NOTES

1. For a detailed exposition of the points submitted here, see "The Last Volume of Luke: The Relation of Luke-Acts to the Pastoral Epistles," in *Perspectives on Luke-Acts*, C. H. Talbert, ed. (Danville, Va.: ABPR, 1978) 62–75; and "Paul's Last Captivity," in the forthcoming volume from the Sixth International Congress on Biblical Studies held at Oxford in April 1978.

2. For a synopsis of some results of this method, see "On the Terminology for Faith, Truth, Teaching, and the Spirit in the Pastoral Epistles" in the sixth volume of the U.S. Lutheran-Catholic Dialogue, to be published in 1979 by Augsburg Press. A fuller exposition is reserved for my commentary on PE in volume 35 of the Doubleday Anchor Bible (in preparation).

3. The translation of PE here and later is the author's and is based on that prepared for the Anchor Bible.

4. Socrates, *Hist. Eccl.* 7:38 (*NPNF* 2:174–175); see R. Meyer, *TDNT* 6:827.

5. R. Renehan, "Classical Greek Quotations in the New Testament," *The Heritage of the Early Church: Essays in honor of. . . . G. V. Florovsky*, D. Neiman and M. Schatkin, eds. (Rome: Pont. Institutum Studiorum Orientalium, 1973) 17–45, esp. 34–37.

6. H. Krämer, *TDNT* 6:783–784, 788, 792–793; cf. "the God who is without deceit (*ho apseudes theos*)" of Tit 1:2 with the classical Greek loci cited by Krämer on p. 789.

7. F. Baumgärtel, *TDNT* 6:362–363; E. Sjöberg, *ibid.*, 381–386.

8. *"Verum a quocumque dicatur, est a Spiritu sancto"* — Thomas Aquinas, *In Titum* 1, *lectio* 3, *ad fin.* On Philo's reluctance to recognize prophecy among even proselytes to Judaism, see H. A. Wolfson, *Philo* (Cambridge, Mass.: Harvard Univ. Press, 1948) 2:51–52, 401 n. 25.

9. M.-E. Boismard, *Quatre Hymnes Baptismale dans . . . 1 Petr.* (Paris: Cerf, 1961) 15–56.

10. For linguistic data and historical problems, see W. F. Albright, *Archaeology and the Religion of Israel* (Baltimore: Johns Hopkins Press, 1953) 126–128, and R. de Vaux, *Ancient Israel*, 2nd ed. (London: Darton, Longman, Todd, 1965) 384–386. Historical connections between the choirs whom the Chronicler called prophets and the prophetic guilds of pre-exilic Israel are debated. It suffices for the point at issue here that the generation to which the Chronicler addressed his work found it quite credible that temple choirs would succeed bands of prophets.

11. See G. Friedrich, *TDNT* 6:854; G. Delling, *TDNT* 8:498; and E. Lohse, *Colossians and Philemon* (Philadelphia: Fortress Press, 1971) 150–152.

12. G. Delling, *TDNT* 8:496 n. 51 for Philo; *ibid.*, 499, on Luke's use of Psalms as authoritative; *ibid.*, 500–502; E. Cothénet, *DBS* 8:1310–1311.

13. See p. 354 on 1 Tim 3:16; also M. Hengel, *Son of God* (Philadelphia: Fortress Press, 1976) 76, with his citations of R. Deichgräber and the New Testament texts. G. Delling, *TDNT* 8:498 n. 69, cites Eusebius, *Hist. Eccl.* 5.28.5 with its quotation of an anonymous writer of *ca.* 200 A.D., who said, "For who does not know . . . all the psalms or songs *(psalmoi/ōidai)* written from the beginning by faithful brethren, which celebrate the Word of God, even Christ, and speak of him as God?" See Clement of Alexandria, *Exhortation to the Greeks* 1:4P. *ad fin.* and 5P., citing Tit 3:3-5, in his comparison of "the new song" of the Christians with the old tunes and songs of paganism. J. Behm, *TDNT* 1:722, suggests that glossolalia as well as prophecy used singing.

14. See BDF #257.2; 474.1 on the article with *pneuma hagion.*

15. See the Greek: *tou sōtēros . . . theou . . esōsen . . . dia Iēsou . . . tou sōtēros.*

16. A. Oepke, *TDNT* 4:302–307. 1 Cor 6:11 uses terms cognate to those here in Titus. The apostolic Fathers do not use the noun, *loutron*, at all, though Justin employs it often of baptism. The verb occurs in *1 Clem.* 8.4 and Hermas, *Vis.* 1.1.2. The links of this documentation with the Roman congregation may be significant. The popularity of the baths in imperial Rome *(TDNT* 4:296) and the strikingly *communal* character of this convenience may help explain the usage here.

17. The Western text, with its reading of *dia pneumatos hagiou* (D* G it Ambst), brought the "causality" of the Spirit into exact parallel with the instrumentality of the washing, *dia loutrou*, and of Jesus, *dia Iēsou Christou.* Much more instructive for the sense of *dia* here is 1 Tim 4:14, *dia prophētias*; 2 Tim 1:6, *dia tēs epitheseōs tōn chierōn mou*; and 2 Tim 1:14, *parathēkēn phylaxon dia pneumatos hagiou*, all discussed later.

18. F. Büchsel, *TDNT* 1:686–689; M. Dibelius and H. Conzelmann, *The Pastoral Epistles* (Philadelphia: Fortress Press, 1972) 148–150.

19. A. D. Nock, *Essays on Religion and the Ancient World* (Cambridge, Mass.: Harvard Univ. Press, 1972) 1:342–343 and see 101 n. 224.

20. For a discussion of this text see my study, "Ministry in the NT," *Biblical Studies in Contemporary Thought* (ed. M. Ward; Somerville, Mass.: Greeno-Hadden, 1975) 135–136.

21. 1QH 12.4-11, esp. 7-8; cf. *1 Clem.* 9.4, with its appeal to the Noah story of "a rebirth of the world."

22. See E. Lohse, as cited in note 11 above. The noun appears again in a Christian document of Roman provenance, Hermas, *Vis.* 3.8.9, who writes of "the renewal of your spirits *(pneumatōn).*" See the use of *anakainizein* in Heb 6:6 and Hermas, *Sim.* 8.6.3; 9.14.3. For later Christian usage, also of invisible, internal renewal, see *LPGL*, 105.

23. For Jn 19:37, this passage is one of the pair cited to show that Jesus' death indeed

fulfills the Scriptures. See LXX Ezek 39:29, of the time "when I pour out my heart upon the house of Israel, says the Lord Yahweh." LXX Sir 1:9; 18:11 use this verb of God's pouring out his wisdom and his mercy.

24. J. Behm, *TDNT* 2:468–469.

25. Cf. *1 Clem.* 2.2; 46.6 and Barnabas 1.3 for later use of this terminology in connection with the Spirit.

26. In the Lucan volumes, it is found only in Acts 10:36, where it may emanate from the source being redacted at this point.

27. The only other uses in the Paulines of the noun *sōtēr* are in Phil 3:20; Eph 5:23, which may also derive from a Roman imprisonment and reflect the usage of Roman Christians.

28. This verb, which occurs twenty-three times in Galatians and Romans, appears again in the undisputed letters of Paul only in 1 Cor 4:4; 6:11.

29. See Acts 13:38-39.

30. *1 Clem.* 32.3-4.

31. R. Funk, *Language, Hermeneutic, and Word of God* (New York: Harper & Row, 1966) 274; see 267.

32. For an exegesis of these phrases and especially "pillar and pedestal for the truth," see the essay cited in note 2 above.

33. See *BDF* #488.3 on this highly stylized homoioteleuton. For an Aramaic retroversion, see J. F. Strange, *A Critical and Exegetical Study of 1 Tim 3:16* (Ann Arbor, Mich.: University Microfilms, 1970) 59.

34. On the textual variants of the initial *OC*, see B. M. Metzger, *A Textual Commentary on the Greek New Testament* (New York: United Bible Societies, 1971) 641. For the genre, see J. M. Robinson, "Die Hodajot-Formel in Gebet und Hymnus des Frühchristentums," *Apophoreta*, ed. W. Eltester (Berlin: A. Töpelmann, 1964), 194–235, of which a preliminary English form appears in his "The Historicality of Biblical Language," *The Old Testament and Christian Faith*, ed. B. W. Anderson (New York: Harper & Row, 1963) 130–150.

35. (*Ex-*) *homologeisthe Kyrion/Christon Iēsoun/theou huion.* The PE never call Jesus "Son"; Titus does not even use the term "Lord," found in every other New Testament document. *Diognetus* 11.3-5 refers to "the Son"in a context reminiscent of 1 Tim 3:16. On such hymns to Christ, see W. Bousset, *Kyrios Christos*, trans. John E. Steely (Nashville: Abingdon, 1970) 303–305.

36. See Rom 10:10-13 as well as M. Hengel, cited in note 13, and W. Bousset in note 35.

37. The generic term for "messengers," *aggeloi*, was applied not only to spirits sent from God but also to men (e.g., those sent by the Baptist, Lk 7:24), including those who were called apostles (see, e.g., Gal 1:8; 4:14; 2 Cor 11:13-14, and the title *euaggelistēs*, 2 Tim 4:5). In this instance the poetic language of the hymn has preserved the archaic poetic terminology of the Jerusalem prophet who varied and enhanced the kerygmatic, "He was seen . . . then by all the apostles (*ōphthē . . . eita tois apostolois pasin*)" (1 Cor. 15:7).

38. Note that Acts 11:18 and 21:20 have key members of the Jerusalem church "glorify God" because of the conversion of pagans by Peter and Paul, and see note 13 above.

39. On the rare *phaneroun*, see R. Bultmann, *TDNT* 9:3–4; for *dikaioun*, see note 44 below.

40. With E. Lohse, cited in note 11, pp. 73–75, and *contra* R. Bultmann, *TDNT* 9:4–5; E. Schweizer, *TDNT* 6:416–417.

41. *Contra* E. Schweizer, "Two New Testament Creeds Compared," *Current Issues in New Testament Interpretation*, ed. W. Klassen (London: SCM, 1962) 169.

42. See *Barnabas* 5.6, 10-11; *Diognetus* 11.2-5, as well as the ninth Oxyrhynchus saying of Jesus = *Gos. Thom.*, Saying #28 (86:21-22), discussed by J. Fitzmyer, *Essays on the Semitic Background of the New Testament* (London: Chapman, 1971) 392–396.

43. For Qumran, the flesh is the whole sinful man as the arena in which two opposing spirits battle (see 1 Tim 4:1). See R. Meyer, *TDNT* 7:114; D. Hill, *Greek Words and Hebrew Meanings* (Cambridge: University Press, 1967) 234–235 note 4, 239.

44. *LSJ, s.v.*; C. H. Dodd, *The Bible and the Greeks* (London: Hodder, 1935) 47–53; M. Dibelius, as cited in note 18 above, p. 62; J. Jeremias, *The Central Message of the New Testament* (New York: Scribner's, 1965) 51–55; J. Zeisler, *The Meaning of Righteousness in Paul* (Cambridge: University Press, 1972) 154–155.

45. On the doubtful reading of *dia* with the genitive (="through"), see B. Metzger, cited in note 34 above, p. 517. E. Schweizer opts for the accusative in *TDNT* 6:422, note 591, but his argument is reversed if, in fact, there is here in Rom 8:11 an allusion to this archaic hymn with its instrumental *en pneumati*.

46. E.g., 1 Cor 12:3, 8 [*dia*], 13; 14:16, *s.v.* l.; Eph 6:18; see Lk 1:17; 2:27; 3:16; 10:21, *s.v.* l.

47. Cf. e.g., LXX Jer 2:2, 31 and Rev 2:1, 8, 12, 18 with Acts 21:11, *tade legei to pneuma to hagion*; G. Friedrich, *TDNT* 6:849.

48. This sense presumes that the initial *tode* is in fact one Greek term, the demonstrative pronoun, ushering the Spirit on stage to speak (see *1 Clem.* 63.2; *LSJ, s.v.*, 1197; *BDF* #289 on the literary character of the term).

49. This adverb is elsewhere unattested in biblical Greek or the apostolic fathers. Cf. Philo, *Leg. all.* 1.60 and the usage in the fragments of Philodemus of Gadara, an Epicurean philosopher of Palestinian origin who taught in Rome (S. Sudhaus, ed., *Philodemi Volumina Rhetorica* [Leipzig: Teubner, 1892] 1:25, 105). Polybius, 3.23.5, would also suggest that the term was familiar in Rome. For papyri of the Christian era, see J. Moulton and G. Milligan, *Vocabulary of the Greek Testament* (Grand Rapids, Mich.: Eerdmans, 1972) *s.v.*, p. 564. J. O'Callaghan has proposed that this text of 1 Tim 3:16–4:3 (or its source?) lies behind 7Q4.1, 2 which would be read *rhē*]*tōn* (see his *Los Papiros Griegos de la Cueva 7 de Qumrân* [Madrid: BAC, 1974], 34–44).

50. See note 46 above.

51. The effect, in Greek, was perhaps to convey contempt, as in *Oedipus Rex*, 371 (to a prophet!).

52. Cf. Tit 1:10 with 1 Tim 1:3, 6, 19.

53. H. Schlier, *TDNT* 1:513; see S. Brown, *Apostasy and Perseverance in the Theology of Luke* (Rome: Pontifical Biblical Institute, 1969).

54. See the essay cited in note 2 above.

55. 1QS 3.14; see A. Dupont-Sommer *The Essene Writings from Qumran* (Cleveland: World, 1962) 77 note 5, and below on 2 Tim 1:7; 4:22.

56. *Rwḥ htwʻh*; cf. *rwḥwt pšʻ* in 1Q36.2.5 (D. Barthélemy et al., *Discoveries in the Judaean Desert*, 5 vols. [New York: Oxford Univ. Press, 1955–1968] 1:138); 1 Jn 4:6; 2 Thess 2:11; the *v.* 1, *pneumasin planēs* in 1 Tim 4:1.

57. 1QH 2.13-15; 4.11-26, etc., thus use the terminology for "straying."

58. See W. Foerster, *TDNT* 2:9–10, 12; H. Conzelmann, *1 Corinthians* (Philadelphia: Fortress, 1975) 172–174.

59. See H. Conzelmann, cited in note 58, pp. 207–208; 214–215, as well as *TDNT* 9:403: "*charisma* is linked with *charis* on one side and *pneuma* on the other . . . ."

60. See the study cited in note 20 above, pp. 144, 153–154. Some have argued that Menaen and Saul alone are "teachers" here (see *TDNT* 6:849, note 426). Acts 14:23 suggests a setting similar to the one in 13:1-3 for the later appointment of presbyters by Paul and Barnabas.

61. E. Cothénet (*DBS* 8:1314) takes *dia prophēteias* instrumentally, in the singular, with "prophecy" used generically for the whole service of the word and prayer enclosing the imposition of hands.

62. This explanation takes 1 Tim 4:13 as an *ordo servandus* and understands *tēi parak-*

lēsei, tēi didaskaliai of those who were prophets (see 1 Cor 14:3) and teachers (*didaskaloi*; see Rom 12:7) in the worship assembly. Some of the teachers were certainly also presbyters (1 Tim 5:17); the same may be true of the prophets.

63. The germinal study has been that of E. Käsemann, "Das Formular einer neuestestamentlichen Ordinationparänese," *Neutestamentliche Studien für R. Bultmann*, ed. W. Eltester (Berlin: A. Töpelmann, 1954) 261–268. See also E. Dekkers, "*Prophēteia-praefatio*," *Mélanges . . . Chr. Mohrmann*, ed. L. J. Engels et al. (Utrecht-Antwerp: Spectrum, 1963) 190–195, with the critique of N. Brox, "*Prophēteia* im ersten Timotheusbrief," *BZ* 20 (1976) 229–232.

64. For *meta* in 1 Tim 4:14, see *BAG s.v.*, 511, #2; this generic, anarthrous imposition of hands contrasts with *dia tēs epitheseōs* of 2 Tim 1:6, where the following *tōn cheirōn mou* makes the *dia* emphatically instrumental (*pace* M. Dibelius, as cited in note 18 above, p. 98).

65. On the durative force of the present imperative here, see J. H. Moulton, *A Grammar of New Testament Greek* (Edinburgh: Clark, 1908³) 1:125.

66. The *erg-* and *kop-* terminology recurs in describing the tasks of bishop and presbyters (1 Tim 3:1; 5:17-18); see note 64 above.

67. See note 55 above.

68. This passage and 2 Tim 3:8 are oblique references by PE to the signs and wonders that accompanied the Pauline apostolate (note *hēmin* and cf. Rom 15:18-19; 2 Cor 12:12; 1 Cor 2:4). The reluctant advertence of PE to this aspect of Paul's mission is quite in character with the historical Paul. Not only the Lucan tradition (see Acts 8:10, 13) but 2 Tim 3:8 also is quite aware of the ambiguities of the miraculous. In 2 Tim 1:8, *dynamis* is God's power given to Paul's co-worker to bear suffering.

69. Contrast E. Schweizer, *TDNT* 6:454.

70. In contrast, sin (*hē hamartia*) dwells as an unclean spirit in the sanctuary where God's Spirit ought to be (Rom 7:17).

71. See the essay cited in note 2 above.

72. The tissue of terminological and conceptual links between PE and documents, all Roman but as diverse as Paul's Letter to the Romans, *First Clement*, and the *Shepherd* of Hermas, makes it likely that the worship and life of the Roman church in the latter part of the first century was the setting from which the author of PE drew the materials for his program for a Pauline renewal of the churches of the second Christian generation.